THE 5TH LITTLE GIRL

THE 5TH LITTLE GIRL

SOUL SURVIVOR OF THE 16TH STREET BAPTIST CHURCH BOMBING
(THE SARAH COLLINS RUDOLPH STORY)

BY:
TRACY SNIPE
(IN CONVERSATION WITH SARAH COLLINS RUDOLPH)

AFRICA WORLD PRESS
TRENTON | LONDON | CAPE TOWN | NAIROBI | ADDIS ABABA | ASMARA | IBADAN | NEW DELHI

AFRICA WORLD PRESS
541 West Ingham Avenue | Suite B
Trenton, New Jersey 08638

Front Cover: Sarah Collins Rudolph standing in front of 16th Street Church by Frank Couch
Book and cover design: Lemlem Tadesse

Library of Congress Cataloging-in-Publication Data

Names: Snipe, Tracy David, author. | Collins Rudolph, Sarah J. (Sarah Jean), 1950-
Title: The 5th little girl : soul survivor of the 16th Street Baptist Church bombing (the Sarah Collins Rudolph story) / by: Tracy Snipe (in conversation with Sarah Collins Rudolph).
Other titles: Fifth little girl
Description: Trenton : Africa World Press, [2021] | Includes bibliographical references and index. | Summary: "Once described by the Reverend Dr. Martin Luther King Jr. as "one of the most tragic and vicious crimes ever perpetrated against humanity," the bombing of the 16th Street Baptist Church in Alabama, instantly killed Addie Mae Collins, Carol Denise McNair, Carole Rosamond Robinson, and Cynthia Dionne Morris Wesley on September 15, 1963. This egregious act of domestic terrorism reverberated worldwide. It also sparked the passage of landmark civil rights legislation and a notable artistic response, signified by the jazz musician John Coltrane's elegiac composition, "Alabama." Orchestrated by white supremacists, the blast left twelve-year-old Sarah Collins temporarily blind. For decades, she slipped into anonymity. In this intimate first-hand account, Sarah imparts her views on topics such as the 50th year commemoration, restitution, and racial terrorism. This story also delves into the bond between Sarah and her mother, Mrs. Alice Collins. In the backdrop of a national reckoning and global protests, underscored by the deadly violence at Mother Emanuel in Charleston, SC, and tragedies in Charlottesville, VA, and Pittsburgh, PA, Sarah's unflinching testimony about the '63 Birmingham church bombing is illuminating"-- Provided by publisher.
Identifiers: LCCN 2020050929 | ISBN 9781569025406 (hardback) | ISBN 9781569025413 (paperback)
Subjects: LCSH: Collins Rudolph, Sarah J. (Sarah Jean), 1950- | Collins Rudolph, Sarah J. (Sarah Jean), 1950---Family. | 16th Street Baptist Church Bombing, Birmingham, Ala., 1963. | African Americans--Alabama--Birmingham--Biography. | African Americans--Civil rights--Alabama--Birmingham--History--20th century. | Civil rights movements--Alabama--Birmingham--History--20th century. | Birmingham (Ala.)--Biography. | Birmingham (Ala.)--Race relations--History--20th century. | Collins family.
Classification: LCC F334.B653 C657 2021 | DDC 323.1196/0730761781--dc23
LC record available at https://lccn.loc.gov/2020050929

Dedication

This book is dedicated to the parents of the six children slain in Birmingham, Alabama on Sunday, September 15, 1963 whose parental example of fortitude and tenacity in the face of adversity forever ensures that Alice Collins, Oscar Lee Collins, Sr., Christopher McNair, Charlie Morris, Estelle Merchant, Alpha Bliss Robertson, Alvin Robertson, Johnny Robinson Sr., Martha Marie Robinson, Lorene Ware, James Ware Sr., Claude Augustus Wesley, Gertrude Wesley and Maxine McNair (who yet lives on) are gone but never forgotten.

Table of Contents

Table of Figures

Acknowledgements

Firstly, we give honor to God for life: As Sarah often remarks, "He is the reason I'm here today." We would also like to acknowledge and thank family members too for their presence in our lives, and for their heartfelt prayers and moral support throughout the course of this book project. They include George Carlson Rudolph, Flora Hardy, Junie C. Williams, Janie C. Simpkins, Addie Bea Collins, Roy Collins, Oscar Collins Jr, and one of the newest family members, Zion JaPrince George Rudolph. We also acknowledge and thank family members Gladys Birch, Doretha Estrict, Juanita Harley, Carl Snipe, Joseph Snipe, Robert Estrict, Josephine Johnson, Mattie Bailey, Johnny Eva Estrict, Jacqueline Snipe, "Cousin Mary" Glover, Karter 'Baby T' Goff, Aiden Omari Washington, Mary Ashely Goss, Natara Snipe and Carlen Gadsden-Jenkins too. Researching and writing this story has been a worthwhile endeavor, grounded by dreams, some rooted in childhood. I read voraciously as a youth. Family ties shaped this normal routine. For example, I remember 'borrowing' and combing through books on my sister Gladys' trusty bookshelf, not to mention my daily routine of reading the newspaper, duplicating the practice of my dad, Lukie Snipe.

During this extensive project, help came in many forms, ranging from invaluable technical assistance to collaborating on programming and reading sections of this manuscript, or simply offering words of encouragement. Thus, I would like to thank colleagues and friends like Roberta Boyd, Donna Schlagheck, Marlese Durr, Susan Carrafiello, La Fleur Small, Yemi Mahoney, Jeanene Robinson-Kyles, Anita Miller, Darryl Dunson, Losell Prince, Raphael Small, Joanne Mawasha, Jennifer E. Subban, Helene Anghmn, Wakiuru Wamwara, Carrie Daily, Mama

Nozipo Glenn, Carla Pettiford, Michael Behrens, Shirley Harris, and writer Chuck Harter. Further, I would like to thank Alana Ema Hall, Hazel Rountree, Pam Green, Sylvia (Fe-Fe) Brown, Regina Dixon, Mary Besley, writer Naaseh S. Henderson, and Jeffrey D. Littlejohn, Tabitha Jefferson Slaughter, Ora Jefferson, Bridgette Weatherspoon, Carlene McKenzie, Tanisha Russell and Nycia Lattimore. Additionally, we wish to thank Shenise L. Dukes, Corleone Deone Lewis Jr., Branden Kelly, Ashley Parker, Evie Robb, Tashana Legette, Matthew, Beverly Guillen, Nicole Greathouse, Kimberly Jackson, Jamie Larson, Kenneth Cardlin, Nicolle Lilly, Stacy Lambright, Terry McClendon, Denise Roby, Stephanie Straup, Ashley Curry, Amy Hardin, Jennifer Andrade, Miranda Emanoff, Faye Kyles Johnson, Tamarus Stokes, Beth Anderson, Orla Sahithi Reddy and Algernon Penn. Finally, we would like to thank Julie W. Carter, legal scholar Maureen Anderson, Alison Stein, Caroline Cease, Ishan K. Bhabha, Barnett Wright, Ken Jordan, Julie W. Carter, Karen Strider-Iiames, Kimberly Barrett, David Hopkins and Miriam Barnard of *Democracy Now*. I would also like to thank Brian Wachter for the accuracy of the transcripts and Sylvia Morgan who implored me to 'take my time' telling this important story 'from the inside out' for the sake of history.

Special thanks to: Ran Raider, John White, Circuit Judge Laura Petro, T.K. Thorne, Rebekkah Mulholland, Chad Lovins, Frank Crouch and Chris L. Snyder, Sarah Dillon, Lynette Jones, Jeff Hughes, Delbert DuBois, Shirley Word Jordan, Zakia Haughton, Blondelle Gadsden and writer-poet Furaha Henry-Jones.

We would also like to deeply thank the following staff members of Africa World Press/Red Sea Press (Kidani Oqubagebreal, Dot, and Sinit) as well as Dr. Girma Demke for his wisdom and expertise. The publisher and editor, Kassahun Chekole guided the process with a steady hand. He listened patiently, making numerous helpful suggestions, especially at the key, pivotal stages of the editorial process. His judicious advice has been invaluable throughout this writing journey.

Sarah and I would also like to acknowledge Addie, Carole, Cynthia, and Denise better known as the "Four Little Girls." Poised and beautiful, even during your short stay on earth, may you live in our hearts eternally and find rest in a home where you indeed will *never grow old.*

Finally to Sarah, the "Fifth Little Girl" turned woman, none of this would have been possible without your invaluable input at each stage of the intricate process of writing the story. You still inspire me to this very day. And, I thank you! We thank you for sharing such a profound and timeless story and a rhema word at this moment in time. Watching your transformation, seeing you take flight has been especially rewarding, as you share the backstory about one of the momentous events of history and in the American Civil Rights Movement.

And when he opened the fifth seal, I saw under the altar the souls of them that were slain for the word of God, and for the testimony which they held (Revelations 6:9, KJV).

Foreword

Throughout life, we tend to talk about those we have lost to murder. However, seldom does the conversation focus on the injured and survivors of an attack. But think about this: survivors have a story too.

One person I know with a compelling story of survival is Sarah Collins Rudolph. On September 15, 1963, Sarah stood with her three friends and older sister in the basement women's lounge of Sixteenth Street Baptist Church, as they prepared for a Sunday morning program. They would never make this program. A bomb detonated at 10:22 a.m., killing Addie Mae Collins, Denise McNair, Carole Robertson, and Cynthia Morris Wesley. The life Sarah Collins Rudolph knew was forever changed.

Her big sister Addie Mae was gone, as were her friends. It seemed as if Sarah's future was gone too. The blast left her temporarily blinded, later making Sarah the wearer of a prosthetic eye. The memories ate away at her, robbing her of restful nights and peaceful days. Yet, she moved on.

She moved on from the hate that planted the bomb that day. She moved on from being left out of history books that chronicled the movement. She moved on from the pain that scarred her childhood.

Despite the outcome of that misfortunate set of factors, Sarah was left as a messenger – a woman who lived through one of the evilest acts ever perpetrated on our soil. However, her part of that story, a story that reshaped race relations in the country, often went unheard.

Growing up in Birmingham, I always heard about the 1963 church bombing that killed four little girls. Those lessons came every Black History Month. I was in elementary school. I remember hearing how these young girls lost their lives simply because of the color of their skin. It was not until I got older that I learned about Sarah. The press and local official mentioned her name even more frequently during the anniversary of the "Birmingham church blast." Nevertheless, the story always went back to the "four little girls."

The omission hurt her. Honestly, once I learned about it and met the survivor, Sarah, it hurt me too.

In August 2017, when I was running for mayor of Birmingham, I met Sarah. I had just pulled up in East Thomas Park. I got out of the car, and I started greeting people. During all the handshakes and hugs, I was face to face with Sarah and her husband, George C. Rudolph.

I sat down next to her and let the moment sink in. Here I was, sitting with a piece of our precious history, a civil rights legacy. Out of all the evil from that bombing, a young girl survived.

Unfortunately, not enough Americans know her story. But we owe it to the four girls lost in that blast to learn more about Sarah.

She is fleetingly mentioned in *4 Little Girls*, film director Spike Lee's Oscar-nominated documentary film. Fittingly, her name also appears on a memorial in Kelly Ingram Park that honors her friends and her sister. National media interviewed Sarah Rudolph in 2001 and 2002, after juries convicted the last two former Klansmen accused in the 1963 church bombing. By the way, she was a witness for the prosecution in both of those trials. Her testimony was heartbreaking. She revealed that the last thing she said when the bombing occurred was, "Addie, Addie, Addie!" as she called out for her sister. Still, how much do we really know about Sarah? How did that tragic day alter her life? How was she able to rebound from the pain of losing childhood friends and a sister too, and how has that experience motivated her to become one of the civil rights movement's most unsung heroes?

I hope you will find your answers in *The 5th Little Girl.* In it, Sarah peels back the painful layers of more than 50 years to dive deep into what the blast did to her, as well as the Collins' family and the nation.

I have often wondered why such an act of evil could be committed in a church, the most sacred of grounds. Well, I have come to learn that God works in mysterious ways. An act of domestic terrorism meant to instill fear instead helped to bolster her faith. It was that dark day more than 50 years ago when Sarah learned to walk in that faith – a journey that has made her much more than a survivor.

Sarah is a beacon. She is a living, breathing miracle. She embodies the real struggle of the civil rights movement – pain, tribulation, steadfast determination and most importantly, victory.

People talk about the roles that the Reverend Martin Luther King Jr. and the Reverend Fred Shuttlesworth played in Birmingham's civil rights movement, but it has taken time to catch up to knowing about Sarah Collins Rudolph. Now is the time to change that. It is my hope that you will become so absorbed in her story that you will want to learn more about civil rights history, the history of our city, and your history.

Mayor Randall L. Woodfin
City of Birmingham

Prologue: Body and Soul

> The wolf also shall dwell with the lamb, and the leopard lie down with the kid, and the calf and the young lion and the fatling together; and a little child shall lead them. (Isaiah 11:6, KJV)

> The war, the battle for birth came.... It was not just for the ability to shop in a store or go to a school. The battle was for the soul of Birmingham! But it was more than just the soul of Birmingham at stake. It was the soul of America. And it was more than just black folk at stake. It was the poor white man.... The immigrant. All of us.[1]

From the Little Rock Nine to Ruby Bridges to the Freedom Riders and youthful protesters involved in the Children's Crusade in Birmingham, Alabama and decades later in Parkland, Florida, young people have often stood on the front lines, redefining modern history. Such memories and profound experiences may buoy them in life, as was the case for 12-year old Sarah J. Collins. A child foot soldier of the Civil Rights Movement, she marched in Birmingham, Alabama along with her mother Mrs. Alice Collins, a tireless grassroots activist. Mrs. Collins participated in boycotts and attended mass meetings at the Sixteenth Street Baptist Church in Birmingham, a city once referred to as "the Bastille of segregation."[2] Like pioneering scholar-activist Anna Julia Haywood Cooper, who was and still remains a powerful voice for black woman universally, she stressed the intrinsic worth of womanhood, Christian principles, and the value of organized social protest to her daughters as a means of combating racial bigotry and glaring injustices in the Jim Crow South. Unfortunately, her daughter Addie Mae Collins perished in a deadly bombing that left a trail of destruction emanating from the women's lounge of the 16th Street Baptist Church on September 15, 1963: The blast claimed the lives of "four little girls," while a fifth girl, Sarah, emerged as the "sole survivor" in one of the most egregious civil rights crimes in 1963, or perhaps ever recorded. The bombing altered her life during a turning point of the burgeoning civil rights struggles.

Almost from the onset of that tumultuous year, Governor George Wallace's defense of segregation in his inaugural address would focus national attention on Alabama. Months later, Rev. Dr. Martin Luther King penned the *Letter from Birmingham City Jail* in response to an op-ed written by "moderate" local clergymen. King, who surreptitiously wrote this seminal essay while confined in jail declared, "I'm in Birmingham because injustice is here."[3] He pointedly illuminated how the inherent moral contradictions of racial segregation and unjust laws in America affected the mindset of little girls and boys, reshaping their *little mental* skies and overall image of their positioning in society. Within weeks of King's release on May 2, 1963, local enforcers of law and order sprayed protestors with high-pressured water hoses, beat marchers with batons, set police dogs on them, and arrested kids in Birmingham — some as young as six: Mass media transmitted such disturbing images, globally.[4]

On June 11, 1963, Wallace made his now infamous "schoolhouse door stance" at the University of Alabama.[5] Later that same evening, President John F. Kennedy delivered a major televised, national address – "The Report to the American People on Civil Rights." Hours later, virulent segregationist Byron De La Beckwith assassinated Medgar Evers in the victim's driveway in Jackson, Mississippi — within earshot of Medgar's wife Myrlie and their children. The murder of the tireless, bold field secretary of Mississippi's branch of the National Association for the Advancement of Colored People (NAACP) went unpunished for decades, until a jury convicted Beckwith in 1994. His trial spurred the opening of other prominent civil rights cases in the Deep South. Myrlie Evers-Williams, who once served as chair of the NAACP Board of Directors, later explained, "Authorities in Mississippi, Alabama and 4 other states have made 24 arrests, leading to 21 convictions. To have that be the catalyst for these other cases is a fulfilling experience." [6]

Figure 1. Governor George Wallace blocks entry to the University of Alabama (1963). Courtesy Library of Congress. Photography credits: Warren K. Leffler

The centennial of the Emancipation Proclamation would usher in a beacon of hope, signified by the March on Washington for Jobs and Freedom, held on August 28, 1963. Decades earlier, President Franklin Roosevelt enacted Executive Order 8802 to dissuade plans for a march proposed by A. Phillip Randolph who supported the integration of the U.S. Armed Forces. Randolph gained prominence as the leader of the Brotherhood of Sleeping Car Porters. In 1948, President Harry Truman desegregated the U.S. military with Executive Order 9981. Along with Bayard Rustin, Randolph later co-organized the March on Washington where Rev. Dr. Martin Luther King, Jr. delivered his iconic "I Have a Dream" speech. Invited singers included Marian Anderson and Mahalia Jackson who belted out Clara Ward's "How I Got Over," a song also later credited to William Brewster. Jackson implored King to "tell them about the dream." At King's request, she sang "I've Been Buked, And I've Been Scorned." The only two women invited to speak on the main stage were Myrlie Evers and Gloria Richardson who led the Cambridge Movement; Richardson's microphone was taken away, seconds into her speech.[7] Daisy Bates who led Arkansas' chapter of the NAACP stepped to the podium due to Myrlie's untimely delay. Bates shared brief remarks.

Figure 2. Civil Rights March on Washington, D.C. A wide-angle shot, showing the Reflecting Pool and the Washington Monument. U.S. National Archives

The Lincoln Memorial Program incorporated a tribute to "Negro Women Fighters for Freedom," honoring Bates, Evers, Richardson, Diane Nash Bevel, and Mrs. Herbert Lee.[8] Keynote speakers included John Lewis, James Farmer, Whitney Young Jr., and Roy Wilkins. Some 250,000 people witnessed King's iconic speech, delivered as he stood in the shadow of President Abraham Lincoln. Skeptical of the impending march, President Kennedy later congratulated King; within months, the capital would serve as his final resting place: On November 22, 1963, Lee Harvey Oswald assassinated the president in Dallas, Texas. In the interim, a bomb planted by Klansmen at the 16th Street Baptist Church in Birmingham, Al. detonated on September 15, 1963, killing Carole Rosamond Robertson Addie Mae Collins, Cynthia Dionne Morris Wesley, Denise Carol McNair, and injuring Sarah Collins. Two boys, Virgil Ware and Johnny Robinson Jr. lost their lives that day, too.

Birmingham was like a killing field that "Bloody Sunday," with her sons and daughters unknowingly on the frontlines in a war-like zone. The bombing unnerved Americans for years to come. On the fortieth anniversary year of the deaths of the four little girls, one writer recalled:

> 'The blast, so fierce it blew the white dresses and patent-leather shoes of their seared bodies while crushing their heads with masonry chunks, would become the boom that finally would catapult the Civil Rights Movement into the hearts and minds of Americans everywhere.[9]

Occurring eighteen days after the March on Washington, the blast transformed King's dream of agape or universal love into an 'American nightmare.' Malcolm X, former spokesperson for the Nation of Islam, criticized the march and its major leaders. On December 10, 1963, he also decried the death of the four little girls in his frequently cited speech, "Message to the Grassroots." [10] His sentiments reflected the more militant views reflected in the Civil Rights and Black Power Movements. Meanwhile, in the aftermath of the blast, family members of the four victims had to deal with the grief and the inordinate length of time — thirty-nine years to be exact — it took to ensure that justice would not be denied.

Under J. Edgar Hoover's dictate and intense public scrutiny, the Federal Bureau of Investigation (F.B.I.) almost immediately began an inquiry. In October of 1963 authorities convicted trucker Robert E. Chambliss ("Dynamite Bob") of possessing and transporting dynamite powder. By 1965 the bureau had compiled extensive evidence against Chambliss, Bobby Frank Cherry, Thomas E. Blanton Jr. and Herman Frank Cash; however, Hoover, "ensconced in his fiefdom and believing himself unanswerable to no one, killed the inquiry" in 1968.[11] The FBI director believed that the likelihood for a conviction was remote.

Within roughly twenty-five years, Chambliss, Blanton, and Cherry stood trial for the bombing. They were members of the Cahaba Boys, a violent offshoot or splinter group of the Ku Klux Klan. In 1977, an Alabama jury, comprised of nine whites and three blacks, convicted Chambliss of first-degree murder in the death of Denise C. McNair. In 2001, eight white and four black jurors would convict Blanton. After several supervised medical delays, an interracial jury, made up of nine whites and three blacks, pronounced Cherry guilty in 2002. Juries in state trials convicted Blanton and Cherry of four counts of first-degree murder in the deaths of the four youths. All three men received life sentences. Chambliss, Cherry, and much later Blanton, died in prison. In 1994, Herman Frank Cash, another suspect, died before authorities formally charged him, while Troy Ingram, a fifth suspect, died in 1971. Notably, Sarah courageously testified at all three trials, beginning in '77.

The press would dub the lone survivor of the children found in the restroom as the "fifth little girl." Sarah had survived the carnage in the women's lounge that claimed the lives of her peers. Pictures in part uncovered the sheer devastation; within days of the blast, photographer Frank Dandridge took a snapshot of the severely injured 'fifth child,' as she lay in a hospital bed with patches covering her eyes — an image that reshaped the collective consciousness of the nation. On September 27, 1963, *Life Magazine* published this famous picture, alongside the speech that attorney Charles Morgan once delivered. Kofi Natamubu observed "photographs of the bombings aftermath-- including the iconic image of the blinded Sarah Jean Collins ... shocked the nation and helped give an emotional push for passage of the Civil Rights Act of 1964."[12] On a pure visceral level, this picture epitomized the brutality of racial violence. Liz Ronk later wrote that it "captured, in one riveting frame, the bilious, lethal aggression that lay behind so much of the anti-integrationist rhetoric of the Deep South."[13] Despite this searing image, discussions about Sarah's fate faded from public discourse. Though far from invisible, she *fell outside of history* or chronicles about the civil rights movement, instead becoming a mere historical footnote.

In this account, Sarah meticulously explains what the five little girls were doing, just prior to an unthinkable act of domestic terrorism that shocked people worldwide. As a child, she could not fathom the extent to which this church bombing would influence collective memories of the movement in the U.S. and abroad. Demonstrators marched in the hundreds and thousands in cities and communities throughout the U.S., including New York, San Francisco and Washington, D.C.[14]The Anti-Defamation League of B'nai B'rith and the American Jewish Committee condemned the bombing. Dick Gregory, Carol Brice, Ruby Dee, Ossie Davis, Odetta and other artists took part in vigils and civil rights demonstrations. The list of celebrities who supported civil rights causes or provided financial backing included Josephine Baker, Harry Belafonte, Sidney Poitier, Lena Horne, Jackie Robinson, Eartha Kitt, Diane Carroll, Marlon Brandon, Sammy Davis Jr., the Staple Singers, Aretha Franklin, Ray Charles, James Brown and Maya Angelou.[15]James Baldwin, Margaret Walker, Gwendolyn Brooks, Chester Himes, June Jordan and Lorraine Hansberry addressed civil rights or engaged in projects promoting civil rights struggles, while Richard Wright's books like *12 Million Black Voices* "helped lay the ground for the civil rights movement of the 1950s and 1960s."[16] In 1964, Baldwin would dedicate *Blues for Mister Charlie: A Play* "to the memory of Medgar Evars (sic), and his widow and children, and to the memory of the dead children of Birmingham."[17] Baldwin later wrote about the Atlanta Child Murders.[18]

Notwithstanding, the 1963 bombing tarnished the reputation of the city of Birmingham and harmed America's globally, calling into question the role of agencies like the FBI. The bombing led to demonstrations in front of the U.S. Embassy in Kampala, Uganda by supporters of the Uganda People's Congress and critical media coverage in the Soviet Union by *Izvestia*, a Moscow-based newspaper which decried the deadly blast as an overt racist act.[19] John Kakonge, leader of the Ugandan congress, circulated a petition that described the incident as an "abominable ghastly murder," while the Vatican's *L'Osservatore Romano* referred to the four victims as martyrs and pronounced the bombing as an act of hatred enacted by the "fanatical followers of segregation."[20] While studying in Paris, France, Angela Davis would read about the blast in the *Herald Tribune*: The title for another news story abroad was "Racist terror reigns in Alabama."[21]

In this atmosphere, J. Edgar Hoover and the F.B.I. also had their share of defenders. Andrew Tully wrote, "There is enough ugly talk abroad without the petulant wail of Negro leaders that the FBI is not doing the job in the battle for civil rights."[22] He continued, Hoover's record is unequaled by any "public servant. And even if he were not the man of rectitude he is, he happens to work for an Attorney General named Bobby Kennedy…"[23] But who would speak for bereft families of the four victims? Roy Wilkins, former executive secretary of the National Association for the Advancement NAACP, forewarned President Kennedy that absent a swift response from Washington, Blacks would "employ such methods as our desperation may dictate..."[24] In time Sarah would find her own voice, speaking her truth.

This intimate memoir about the bombing transports readers to the inner sanctum of the 16th Street Church on Youth Sunday. The lesson that day was titled "The Love that Forgives."[25] Living in the Southland and being the victim of a white supremacist terror attack made this a hard lesson for Sarah to grasp. Instead, she later learned about daunting topics such as martyrdom and living in "America's Johannesburg."[26]

Decades after the blast, Addie Mae's tombstone would describe her as a "civil rights martyr." In effect, all four girls were martyrs, as King proclaimed. Other youthful martyrs would include George Stinney Jr., Emmett Till, Michael Schwerner, James Chaney, Andrew Goodman, Jimmie Lee Jackson, Samuel Hammond, Henry Smith, Delano Middleton, James Byrd Jr., Mulugeta Seraw, Michael Donald, Johnny Robinson Jr. and Virgil Ware.[27] Worlds apart, this list also includes Anne Frank, one of the thousands of Jewish children murdered in concentration camps like at Dachau and in Auschwitz-Birkenau. Three sisters -- Patricia Mirabal, Minerva Mirabal and Maria Teresa Mirabal -- fell victim to an authoritarian regime in the Dominican Republic. Born in 1963, Hector Pieterson died protesting apartheid in South Africa.

Alongside his second wife Winnie Madikizela-Mandela, international statesman Nelson Mandela who once led the African National Congress (ANC) championed anti-apartheid struggles, which reached a turning point with the 1960 Sharpeville Massacre. Yet who could forget Sam Nzinga's picture of Pieterson, a casualty of the Soweto Uprising that began on June 16, 1976? As Mbuyisa Makhubo carried Pieterson's limp body, Antoinette Sithole, the victim's sister, sobbed nearby in utter dismay.[28] There would be other political martyrs. South African youth revered Black Consciousness Movement (BCM) leader Steve Biko. Decades after his murder, Bishop Desmond Tutu steered the nation to restoration with the Truth and Reconciliation Commission.[29]

"Conscientization" is a concept that youth marching in cities today and towns yesteryear intuitively grasped. Writers involved in the Black Arts Movement (BAM) such as Larry Neal, Sonia Sanchez, Nikki Giovanni, Ntozake Shange, Audre Lorde, Ishmael Reed, Don Lee, and Keorapetse 'Willie' Kgositile tackled such issues, too[30] Conscientization expands beyond geography.

In Europe, Africa, Asia, the Americas and Caribbean, scores of youths died defying tyranny. On the other hand, the death of 13-year-old Virgil Ware in Birmingham was the byproduct of a bet exchanged between two Eagle Scouts (Larry Joe Sims and Michael Lee Farley). On a dare from Farley, Sims fired multiple shots, mortally wounding Virgil on the Docena-Sandusky Road that infamous "Birmingham Sunday." Death came by way of an innocent pastime, riding on the handlebar of a bicycle that his older brother James pedaled. Thus, Virgil's name was added to the five children slain in Birmingham, Al. that bleak Sunday.[31]

Figure 3. Nelson Mandela Portrait Sketch Vector Clipart. https://www.goodfreephotos.com

Nevertheless, the idea of martyrdom never occurred to Sarah as she blissfully walked to church on Youth Sunday with two of her sisters, unknowingly marching into history. The children would not get to sing hymns or anthems. Instead, a hateful attack struck a dissonant note. In response, artists composed 'songs of sorrow' and social protest such as Richard Farina's "Birmingham Sunday." This song is a poignant tribute to Addie, Denise, Cynthia, and Carole. Farina recorded this tune, as did his sister-in-law Joan Baez. Its refrain – *and the choirs kept singing of freedom* – comes across as a clarion call for liberty. In Birmingham and cities like Selma youth were marching for freedom."[32] In South Africa, Miriam Makeba sang about life, struggle, and freedom in songs such as "Soweto Blues." At President Nelson Mandela's request, the previously banned artist returned home, within years after Mandela took office; Mama Africa also sang about injustice in *Sarafina*, the film version of a play about a child protagonist that originally premiered on Broadway.[33]

'Songs of freedom' document historic change and political struggle, as do first-hand narratives that underscore storytelling like *The 5th Little Girl.* From survival to obscurity to emerging icon, Sarah C. Rudolph's storied life evokes a blues song – jazzy and yet somber in interludes – and a stirring gospel tune. Herein, they serve as a literary soundtrack of sorts for her youth and adulthood; songs, album titles and liner notes and poems linked with virtuoso jazz saxophonist John Coltrane frame the narrative in the form of vignettes. The epilogue titled "Traneing In" underscores the socio-political context of this pointed thematic choice.

Dealin'

At the mere age of twelve, Sarah found herself figuratively thrust into the "eye of the storm." It began as a quiet storm, breathing life into civil protests that would later arise in Birmingham, Alabama with the strategic incorporation of children into "Project C" (for Confrontation) during the spring of 1963. At the height of the Birmingham Campaign, both high school and elementary students marched, even during school hours. Some literally climbed out of classroom windows to participate. Moreover, with the selective buying-campaign, student leaders, faculty and staff affiliated with Miles College, Daniel Payne College, Booker T. Washington Business College and Birmingham-Southern College made their collective voices heard, too. Modeled on the Montgomery Bus Boycott, they sought to force shop owners in Birmingham, Ala. to integrate stores and hire blacks in key jobs.[34]

Occurring almost a decade after the historic Brown decision in 1954 and seven years after Browder v Gayle (1956), which outlawed segregation on buses, the beginning of classes in September of 1963 would test a federally mandated court order to desegregate schools in the city of Birmingham, a bastion of the Deep South.[35] In terms of school desegregation, protesters would wage similar battles in Boston and other cities such as Detroit and Los Angeles during the 1950s and 1960s, and into the 1970s.[36] However, diehard segregationists planted a bomb at the Sixteenth Street Baptist Church to halt such efforts and to stem the tide of the civil rights movement. The "dastardly bombing" shattered the daily existence of bombing survivor Sarah Jean Collins.

The church bombing forced Sarah Jean to grapple with a complex array of issues that the cultivated persona of 'Emma Jean' struggles to decode in Haki R. Madubuti's revealing poem, "Maturity." Coping with the death of Addie, coupled with the permanent loss of vision in her right eye following the terror attack, shattered long-cherished dreams that Sarah nurtured as a child growing up in America.[37] The bombing and the resulting trauma that accompanied it hastened her maturation.

The College of Liberal Arts at

Wright State University

Presents

Four Women from Birmingham:

Remembering the Little Girls Killed in the 1963 Birmingham Church Bombing

DATE: Thursday, March 11, 2004

TIME: 5:15 p.m. - 7:00 p.m.

LOCATION: Medical Science Auditorium

Figure 4. Four Women from Birmingham program. Courtesy of WSU.

It would take years for Sarah to discuss the bombing at length. The blast left visible scars on her body, invisible scars within her soul. As a coping mechanism, she went underground or silent, not speaking about "that." But everything would change after her spiritual epiphany. When Sarah and I first began to communicate during the fall of 2003, she was on the road to healing. After several telephone conversations, we met on March 11, 2004. With the support of Mary Ellen Mazey, dean of the College of Liberal Arts (COLA) of the College of Liberal Arts (COLA), I invited Sarah to speak on a panel at Wright State University (WSU) in Dayton, Ohio. Dr. Roberta Boyd (Assistant dean in COLA), Dr. Stuart McDowell and I served as coordinators. Moderated by WDTN anchor Marsha Bonhart, our program had many distinguishing features, largely thanks to the novel contributions of Dr. Boyd.[38] Under my guidance, a group of WSU students was later invited to perform at the 16th Street Church in Birmingham in a memorial program where Congressman John R. Lewis delivered the keynote address on September 15, 2004.

In February of 2015, Sarah participated in another program that I spearheaded at WSU, "Daughters Rising from the Dust: Children of the Civil Rights Movement, Speak Out!" This panel formed the core of the three-day Phoenix Project, which included a film series and a forum on police brutality or police-related violence in the black community.[39] In the interim, Sarah entrusted me with the task of penning her life story, a creative collaboration that has proven to be very meaningful.

There are people in Birmingham, and throughout America, who are still unaware of Sarah C. Rudolph's vital link to "The Movement." This unawareness is indicative of a key missing chapter of American civil rights history. Change waits. For example, the International Civil Rights Center and Museum in Greensboro, N.C. displays a graphic, full-scale *Life* magazine picture of a gravely wounded Sarah in a gallery entitled "The Wall of Shame." This exhibition also includes the infamous picture of the then fourteen-year-old Chicago teen, Emmett Louis Till, whose violent death sparked the modern-day civil rights movement. Closer to home, tour guides at 16th Street Baptist Church point Sarah out as one of the victims critically injured in the blast, when visitors ask questions about her, before and while touring the church. Further, the city of Birmingham recognized Sarah at several events during the 50th year commemoration of the 1963 Birmingham church bombing. The administration of former mayor, William Bell, officially presented Sarah with the opportunity to lecture in 2013 (See appendix). Within a year, designer and artist Jan Jader installed a bench at the Birmingham-Shuttlesworth International Airport, honoring Sarah Collins Rudolph, among other local heroes. Other artists have also recognized Rudolph.

Birmingham artist Steve R. Skipper of Anointed Home Arts, Inc. wrote a moving tribute to Sarah. Several of his paintings such as 'DNA Engrained,' masterfully document the civil rights movement. This work shows individuals linked with the city of Selma, the Montgomery to Selma marches and Bloody Sunday like legislators John Lewis and Terri Sewell, Coretta Scott King, Amelia Boynton Robinson, and Oprah Winfrey (by virtue of her role as Anne Lee Cooper in Ava DuVernay's film, *Selma*). The Birmingham Civil Rights Institute also permanently exhibits "DNA Engrained" (Skipper's painting pertaining to the year of 1963) and his artwork "Through Many Dangers." In relation to the city of Birmingham's 50th year commemoration of the blast, Skipper wrote "Unforgettable," a moving tribute that designates the "fifth little girl" as a living martyr. Skipper framed his touching acknowledgment with a picture of George Carlson Rudolph, standing next to his wife, bombing survivor Collins Rudolph:

> 'I now dedicated the project in honor of Mrs. Sarah Collins Rudolph, our living Rosa Parks, and our Lazarus whom Christ has pulled back from the sting of death to be a living testimony of his powerful strength and the undying perseverance of the Movement.'[40]

On September 10, 2013, Congress would posthumously bestow the "four little girls," with the Congressional Gold Medal. In January of that year, former U.S Attorney Doug Jones indicated that he intended to urge legislator Terri Sewell (D-Alabama) to nominate Sarah Collins Rudolph.[41] During the actual ceremony, dignitaries presented a bronze replica of the medal to family members. Sarah described the award as symbolic but attended the ceremony to honor her peers whose deaths spurred the passage of the 1964 Civil Rights Act. The bombing also factored in the passage of the Voting Rights Act of 1965; notably, the Immigration and Naturalization Act of 1965 also went into effect in the interim. Legislators recognized the four girls as heroines of one of the most influential social movements of the twentieth century. But should the "fifth little girl" have received this award, too? Should martyrdom be the price to pay for national recognition or even acknowledgment?

The hand of destiny chose Sarah to pass on the story about the 16th Street Church bombing, one in a "terror campaign." Multiple sources record that from the late 1940s to September of 1963 there were fifty unsolved blasts in the Smithfield subdivision or Dynamite Hill alone. This flirtation with danger seemed destined to end tragically, as it did.

Separated from her peers inside the restroom, Sarah never lost her footing during the blast. Losing her vision was traumatic but imagine the bloodshed her soul would have witnessed. The cruel ironies of life! Nevertheless, years later she still carries fragments of glass in her body.

I Want to Talk About You

Legal scholar Randall L. Kennedy adroitly points out that in spite of the input "of Rosa Parks, Septima Clark, Ella Baker, Dorothy Height, Fannie Lou Hamer and countless others to civil rights struggles, no woman was allowed to give any of the major addresses at the March on

Washington."[42]Often obscured, black women were the glue that held the civil rights movement together, well before the 1950s. For example, consider the pioneering efforts of Ida B. Wells. At the risk of her life, the "Princess of the Press" brought the travesty of lynching into the national limelight, as did writer William Monroe Trotter.[43] Endeavoring to bring change, women like South Carolinians Mary McLeod Bethune and Modjeska Simkins, Victoria Gray of the Mississippi Freedom Democratic Party (MFDP) and Marian Wright Edelman who founded of the Children's Defense Fund, were indeed the very backbone of the Black Freedom Movement. This list of trailblazers could encompass Coretta King, Dr. Betty Shabazz, Jo Ann Robinson, Georgia Teresa Gilmore, Beaulah M. Donald and Shirley Chisolm. The stories of four unsung schoolgirls — Claudette Colvin, Mary Louise Smith, Lynda Blackmon Lowery and Sarah Collins Rudolph — *shaped the nation* too.

Claudette Colvin's protest preceded the historic Montgomery Bus Boycott, ignited by Park's steadfast "rebellion" on December 1, 1955.[44]

In *Claudette Colvin: Twice Toward Justice*, the civil rights icon observes:

> 'When I look back now, I think Rosa Parks was the right person to represent the movement at the time. She was a good and a strong person, accepted by more people than were ready to accept me. But I made a personal statement, too...Mine was the first cry for justice, and a loud one. I made it so that our own adult leaders couldn't just be nice anymore. Back then, as a teenager, I kept thinking, Why don't the adults around here just say something?'[45]

On March 2, 1955, local authorities arrested the high school student after she refused to relinquish her seat on a segregated city bus in Montgomery, Alabama. A year later, Colvin would become one of the four plaintiffs in the landmark court case, Browder v. Gayle (1956); the U.S. Supreme Court would uphold a lower court decision, which determined or ruled that bus segregation in the state of Alabama was unconstitutional.[46]Almost nine months after Claudette Colvin's act of defiance in Montgomery, Rosa Parks would catapult to national fame after her refusal to give up her seat. Parks was extensively involved in civil rights activities prior to her public stance. Despite the challenges and setbacks that she faced after her heroic stance in Montgomery, Alabama, Parks branched out her community activities in Detroit, Mi.

Figure 5. Portrait of Sarah Collins Rudolph by Jermaine Jones. Photo, courtesy of George C. Rudolph

In *The Rebellious Life of Mrs. Rosa Parks*, Jeanne Theoharis opines, "Parks was keenly interested in building a movement to strengthen black voting and economic power nationally…and build black cultural institutions"; according to Theoharis, Parks regarded Malcolm X as her "personal hero."[47] Headed by Patti LaBelle, the group LaBelle briefly reunited in 2005 to pay tribute to Parks with the song "Dear Rosa." [48]

While a single act of defiance, supplemented by a life of resistance would propel Rosa Parks to national acclaim, a lethal bombing forever connects Sarah Rudolph with a tortured history. "History remembers this act because it was violent and an act of terrorism which," claimed the lives of four little girls according to Ey Wade: "History fails us by never mentioning the lone survivor," who was "basically forgotten in history."[49] During the fall of 2005, John Archibald of *The Birmingham News* would further add, "It's not just the icons such as Parks who need tribute" but the overlooked like Rudolph who "if not for the grace of God, would have died as the 'fifth little girl.'"[50]

Who writes history? What factors determine who gets included in historical accounts? To what extent does Collins-Rudolph's omission, pertaining to accounts about civil rights struggles, reflect biases related to the intersection of gender, class, race, and colorism too?[51]

The fifth little girl's place in history is not a given in a world where insuring recognition, and at times justice for young black people, is a forgone conclusion. It has taken years to receive any formal apologies for the MOVE bombing. Recall Tomasa, Delicia, Phil, Nett and Tree — five African-American children who died in the deadly blast decades ago in Philadelphia, Pennsylvania; the Scottsboro Boys and decades later the Central Park Five would languish in prison for years; and the destiny of dozens of black boys at the Dozier Reformatory School in Georgia is fully coming to light.[52] Rarely do brown-skin girls occupy the spotlight in real life dramas, as was the case momentarily with #Bring Our Girls Back, the international campaign to rescue hundreds of Chibok schoolgirls. But equally as meaningful, some schoolgirls like Rudolph later emerge to speak their truth or narrate their own stories.[53]

Over the years, Sarah has read different accounts about the church bombing. She once remarked to me, "It seemed like everybody wanted to get in their two cents."[54] Granted, recounting complex stories is rarely error free, Sarah shares her first-hand testimony about the blast to amend lasting misperceptions and half-truths and to pay homage to her four peers whom Rev. Dr. Martin Luther King Jr. eulogized as sweet princesses "who died within the sacred walls of the church."[55] In reality, a fifth princess, Sarah Collins lived on; Sarah means princess in Hebrew: hence, she is a living princess of the civil rights movement.

I penned this work from Sarah's unique vantage point, writing the story in the first-person, utilizing elements of narrative testimony and creative non-fiction to recapture the immediacy of the lone survivor's recollections about that fateful Sunday, the courtroom trials, and other pivotal episodes throughout her life. Accordingly, this unique research methodology drew heavily from a series of open-ended interviews with Sarah and samples of her selected writings. I rely on contemporaneous hand-written notes too; using the narrative voice and colloquial speech, this format allowed me to incorporate invaluable informal exchanges with Sarah into the memoir, along with excerpts of critical videotaped lectures and interviews. Over the years, Sarah and I have participated in many speaking engagements nationally like at Penn State University

(PSU). I have revisited her televised interview with Patty Satalia at PSU and radio interviews with NPR and Amy Goodman of *Democracy Now*. I have included transcripts from two critical or key interviews in the appendix. Additionally, I refer extensively to portions of a sermon-styled lecture that Collins-Rudolph once presented at the historic First African Methodist Episcopal Church (First A.M.E.) in Seattle, Washington in January of 2012. During this trip to the Pacific Northwest, we lectured in neighboring Federal Way, Washington, too.[56]

In addition to combing through key speeches and personal letters, Sarah provided me with a critical primary resource that I drew directly from, as I refined the central themes of this memoir. I reexamined this work, extracting important, yet lesser-known biographic details.[57] I also presented written follow up questions to Sarah, drawn mainly from her earlier writings and one-on-one interviews. Sarah and I have conversed regularly for well over a decade. Essentially, several chapters of the memoir began as fragments of our "conversations." While conducting research, I interviewed most of Sarah's siblings. Dating back to the 40th year memorial program held at the Sixteenth Street Baptist Church, I have also spoken with various relatives from all the victims' families, including parents (Maxine McNair and the late Christopher McNair). I interviewed attorneys Bill Baxley and Doug Jones, leading trial lawyers for trials related to the infamous church bombing. I also interviewed Samuel Rutledge and Apostle Donald Lewis, among other subjects.

I poured through other primary and secondary sources, including the Bapbomb (the Federal Bureau Investigative files on the Sixteenth Street Baptist Church bombing), photographs, public records, and witness transcripts. Of note, Sarah's oral history is included in the Smithsonian's *Voices of the Civil Rights Project*, often described as "the most extensive archives of personal stories related to civil rights in the world." The Birmingham Civil Rights Institute and Sixteenth Street Baptist Church also highlight quotations accredited to Sarah Rudolph. (See appendix)

Nevertheless, the research would be incomplete without several trips to 'The Library,' or the Rudolph's living room. It houses awards, photographs, historic artifacts and mementoes like a bronze duplicate copy of the Congressional Gold Medal (awarded to the 'four little girls' posthumously) and the *Detroit Walk to Freedom* album. Orchestrated by civil rights leader Rev. C. L. Franklin (father of the 'Queen of Soul') the march in Detroit, Michigan drew about 125,000 participants on June 23,

1963; in opposition to his colleagues, Franklin convened the march to draw national attention to racial discrimination.[58] Decades after the march, Sarah discovered the album among her mom's personal effects.

Our numerous conversations, in combination with the unparalleled access to unique sources, affords me the chance to portray Sarah in all of her humanity and complexity, while integrating aspect of her distinct cadence and style of speech into this memoir. Aspects of her life became intertwined with her political struggles, even later in life. Not too bad for a soft-spoken, fiercely determined Southern black woman with an accent as thick as molasses syrup who good-naturedly describes herself as *just a little country girl.* Make no mistake. Survival tested the fifth girl, validating the Lasswellian notion of politics as the nexus of *who, gets what, when, how.*

A closer analysis of the Sarah Collins Rudolph story lends rationale to restorative justice theory, too. In "The Past on Trial: Birmingham, the Bombing and Restorative Justice," S. Willoughby Anderson observes,

> Restorative justice theory can help to return the focus to all persons involved – victims, offenders, families of each, and the larger community. The movement's theoretical focus places the dignity of individuals at the center of its work. By using restorative justice to craft extrajudicial responses to these long-buried crimes, it may be possible to repair the longstanding harms that go unaddressed by traditional legal practices.[59]

In an in-depth article the *California Law Review* published, Anderson referenced Rudolph's plight in connection to the 2001 and 2002 trials related to the bombing. Anderson notes, "Sarah Collins Rudolph, sister of the murdered Addie Mae Collins, believed that the recent trials would do little to give her personal closure or to bring justice to the victims' families."[60] Moreover, Joseph Bryant of *The Birmingham News* pointedly wrote, "While victims of violence in recent years have some access to victim's relief funds, no such compensation existed for the Collins family in 1963."[61] What should restorative justice look like for Rudolph, and other victims' family members of the deceased? Should it encompass financial restitution or a formal apology from the state? Some proclaim that Rudolph's assertion for monetary restitution has merit, citing Section 1983 of the Civil Rights Act of 1871, and more recently the Rosewood Reparations Act, for example.[62]

Up 'Gainst the Wall

Described as *sacrificial lambs* or blameless, sympathetic victims, the deaths of the four girls led to the path of vital civil rights legislation. Analyzing these events in the context of *post-racial* America reveals challenges in the arenas of civil rights and civil liberties. Has the time has arrived for yet another legislative shift? *Still muddling, not yet through*, the turf we navigate is perilous, especially when it comes to the colossal loss of life of people of color in too often volatile confrontations with law enforcement.

In the distant past, casualties included Eleanor Bumpers, Amadou Diallo and Timothy Thomas. More recently, they include Tamir Rice, Jordan Edwards, Laquan McDonald, Oscar Grant III, Rekia Boyd, Michael Brown, Tanisha Anderson, John Crawford III, Clinton Allen, Ezell Ford, Kajieme Powell, Freddie Gray, Sandra Bland, Philando Castile, Alton Sterling, Keith Lamont Scott, Alfred Olango, Samuel DuBose, Terrence Crutcher, Deborah Danner, Jessie Hernandez, and Sean Bell; other fatalities include Korryn Gaines, Tony Robinson Jr., Paul O'Neal, Walter Scott, Stephon Clark, Antwon Rose II, Botham Jean, "D.J." Henry Jr., Daniel Hambrick, Jemel Roberson, Emantic Fitzgerald Bradford Jr., Jamar Clark, and Eric Garner who repeatedly cried out, *I can't breathe*, before he died.[63] Activists Alicia Garza, Patrice Khan-Cullors and Opal Tometi co-founded #BlackLivesMatter in July of 2013 following the verdict in the shooting death of Trayvon Martin. Expanding globally, this community-centered movement has some parallels yet major differences with the Civil Rights Movement; nevertheless, in countries like Brazil one hears the cry *Vidas negras importam* or *Black lives matter*.[64]

In 2015, Cleveland State University held the Movement for Black Lives forum. As one critic noted, a timely song played during a pause:

> 'In the midst of so many black bodies meeting tragic ends at the hands of the state, the adoption of Kendrick Lamar's "We Gon' Be Alright' as the unofficial anthem of the Black Lives Matter Movement became a brash statement of resistance.'[65]

In 2016, former NFL quarterback Colin Kaepernick immersed the league into this wider debate with the "Take a Knee" stance during the playing of the national anthem in a silent yet powerful protest against police brutality, which is often the focal point of Black Lives Matter advocates. Backlash aside, competitors in many sports joined in protest as did athletes in high school; college basketball players and NBA stars like Kobe Bryant and LeBron James wore 'I Can't Breathe' T-Shirts.[66]

From a historical perspective, Samuel Momodu references Johnny Robinson's police-related shooting death in Birmingham on September 15, 1963 as a precursor to the Black Lives Matter Movement. He notes,

> Johnny Robinson was a sixteen-year-old African-American man who was shot and killed by Birmingham, Alabama police officer Jack Parker on September 15, 1963. Robinson's death occurred on the same day as the Sixteenth Street Baptist Church Bombing in Birmingham that resulted in the deaths of four young girls… Robinson's killing did not get much attention. His death, however, was an early inspiration for the Black Lives Matter Movement….
>
> Parker would later give two different accounts of the shooting. In the first one he claimed that he shot in the air above Robinson's head, and in the second account, he said the shotgun went off accidentally. Other witnesses disputed both accounts, claiming to have heard two gunshots. Two Jefferson County Grand Juries opted not to charged (sic) Officer Parker for Robinson's death.[67]

About six years ago, Sarah Collins Rudolph would participate in a 'staged' funeral in the nation's capital that highlighted black and brown victims of police-related violence. She discussed this perennial problem within the context the killing of four black girls or black bodies and the 'state-sanctioned' violence that demonstrators confronted in the 1960s. Such lethal violence tapped into the soul of a nation confronting racial prejudice. Revolutionary scholar-activist Frantz Fanon once remarked, "Race prejudice obeys a flawless logic. A country that lives, draws its substance from the exploitation of other peoples, make those people inferior."[68] This mindset is still prevalent in many stratums of society but challenged more often now. Yet trial testimony in 2001 reveals that Birmingham police officers disparaged accounts of odd events near the church, reported on by black witnesses in the weeks prior to the blast.[69]

Speaking to multi-racial audiences, Sarah provides witness to a time when bigotry and racial strife defined Birmingham. For instance, the Children's Crusade occurred in this Southern city, inauspiciously when Theophilus Eugene "Bull" Connor officially governed as public safety commissioner. Prior to this crusade, Freedom Riders faced peril, too. On

May 4, 1961, the onset of their trek from Washington, D.C. was peaceful, but Dr. King later "learned of the conspiracy by the Ku Klux Klan, the police and local officials to stop them by brute force" in cities like Birmingham, Al.[70] Vigilantes attacked Freedom Riders in Rock Hill, S.C. and Anniston, Al. To counter such Klan-related activities, in time law enforcement planted informers within such terror networks: FBI informants infiltrated civil rights organizations and groups such as the Nation of Islam and Black Panthers too, though some critics contend that white supremacists deftly lodged themselves in law enforcement.[71]

Sarah addresses being a survivor of terrorism during the 'Jim Crow' era but occasionally delves into issues like gun violence. Birmingham born artist and Ohio resident James Pate has also addressed random gun, especially in black communities through his usage of Klan imagery in *KKK-Kin Killin' Kin.*[72] On January 21, 2013, Hadiya Pendleton, a band member and honor student marched in the Presidential Inauguration Parade. Eight days later, random gun violence claimed the life of the 15-year-old in Chicago, Illinois.[73] Within a month of the teenager's death, Sarah would lecture in Griffith, Indiana, located nearby Chicago.

As a civil rights activist, Sarah often encourages youths to further their education, to vote and cultivate a positive-oriented lifestyle. This emphasis on voting remains critical in an era of increased elements of voter suppression and voter purges in states such as Georgia, Texas, and North Carolina, years beyond the ruling in Shelby v. Holder (2013). While stressing voting, she has also participated in platforms that tackle random guns violence and police misconduct - amplified by social media, cell phone videos and body cams: She occasionally delves into these topics while discussing the 16th Street Church bombing with multiracial, intergenerational audiences, even once sharing her story in prison.

In *The New Jim Crow: Mass Incarceration in the Age of Colorblindness,* (2010) Michelle Alexander reasoned activists must address prisons too:

> 'Far from fading away, it appears that prisons are here to stay. And despite the unprecedented levels of incarceration in the African American community, the civil-rights community is oddly quiet. One in three young African American men are currently under the control of the criminal justice system… yet mass incarceration tends to be categorized as a criminal justice issue as opposed to a racial justice or civil rights issue (or crisis).'[74]

As a *child foot soldier*, Sarah did not face jail but shared her account about battling a hate crime with inmates at the St. Clair Correctional Facility in Springfield, Alabama. Fast forward to the present, as artists and lawmakers readdress the upsurge of Black and Latinx men in jails nationwide documentaries like *13th*, Ava DuVernay's Academy-award nominated work about the prison-industrial complex. Directed by Jennifer Furst and co-produced by Shawn "Jay-Z" Carter, Netflix's *Time: The Kalief Browder Story* explored the outcome of high bail bonds, while HBO aired *Say Her Name: The Life and Death of Sandra Bland.* Chinonye Chukwu would create #IamTyraPatterson, an actual PSA focusing on Tyra Patterson.[75] Chukwu directed the award-winning *Clemency*, starring Alfre Woodard, Aldis Hodge, and Wendell Pierce.[76] Debates aside, prison reforms have emerged. Sponsored by Senators Cory Booker (D-New Jersey) and Mike Lee (R-Utah), the Department of Justice (DOJ) implemented the First Step Act during the Trump Administration.

Having survived a hate crime and an act of domestic terrorism, Sarah empathizes with victims of such attacks abroad in Christchurch, New Zealand, and in Oklahoma City, New York City, Boston, Parkland, and Orlando, as well with survivors at the First Baptist Church in Sutherland Springs, Texas — the site of the worst religious-related mass shooting in the U.S. Children slain at an Amish schoolhouse in Pennsylvania and the deadly assault of six people at a Sikh Temple in Oak Creek, Wisconsin fit into this deadly paradigm, too. Some have also vandalized mosques and defiled cemeteries or other sites such as the Emmett Till Marker in Glendora, Mississippi as well as the Viola Liuzzo Historical Marker in Lowndesboro, Alabama. Then there was the unthinkable at Emanuel.

On June 17, 2015, a white gunman killed nine African Americans at the end of their bible study lesson in the basement of Mother Emanuel in Charleston, South Carolina in an attack described as a blatant hate crime, act of domestic terrorism, and "targeted political assassination." The victims were Pastor Clementa Carlos Pinckney, Cynthia G. Hurd, Rev. Sharonda Coleman-Singleton, Tywanza Sanders, Susie Jackson, Ethel Lance, Rev. Myra Thompson, Rev. DePayne Middleton-Doctor and Rev. Daniel L. Simmons, Sr.[77] Two little girls were among the five survivors. Within days, thousands would later march across the Arthur Ravenel Jr. Bridge in a show of racial unity. Still, the *body* of the black church was attacked, showing "'the increasing terror'" black Americans "'face on a daily basis,'" according to Patricia Lessane.[78] She lamented,

> 'Today Charleston... is in mourning. We are still dealing with last month's shooting of an unarmed black man in a northern suburb, and in the hours since this latest shooting, many of us in the African-American community were left asking: Is there any sanctuary left?'[79]

Mother Emanuel and the 16th Street Church occupy historic roles. Founded in 1873 as the First Colored Baptist Church of Birmingham and renamed the Sixteenth Street Baptist Church, this assembly and Emanuel has hosted leaders like Coretta S. King who later supported the Charleston Hospital Workers Movement, too.[80] Established as the Hampstead Church in 1818, many still invariably link Emanuel with Denmark Vesey. After learning of his planned slave revolt, authorities tried and later hanged Vesey and thirty-four of his co-conspirators at Blake's Landing on July 2, 1822, within days of the aborted revolt that Vesey wanted to carry out on the fourteen day of July — to coincide with Bastille Day.[81] Local officials would burn Emanuel to the ground and later created the South Carolina State Arsenal in order to stamp out future revolts.[82] Intent on starting a race war in the 21th century, the gunman decided on Emanuel, among other sites in the Lowcountry such as Morris Brown A.M.E. Church and the College of Charleston.

Historically, some white supremacists have connected racial purity with violence and religion, yet journalists rarely labeled the Birmingham bombing as "an act of white Christian terrorism," enacted by members of the "strongly Christian Klan": Similarly, fewer stories focused on the Charleston shooter's religious ties.[83] In contrast, media outlets routinely focuses on religion when "Islamic extremists" are suspects in terrorist attacks: with an uptick in random racial attack, often linked with violence attacks, the press more routinely label such attacks as incidents of "white supremacist terrorism" nowadays.

Like many congregations across the nation, the Emanuel African Methodist Episcopal Church memorialized the four children killed in 1963, decades before tragedy struck Mother Emanuel in 2015. Shortly after the racially motivated attack, President Barack Obama remarked,

> This is not the first time that black churches have been attacked. And we know that hatred across races and faiths pose a particular threat to our democracy and our ideals. The good news is I am confident that the outpouring of unity and strength and fellowship and love across Charleston today, from all races, from all faiths from all places of

> worship indicates the degree to which those old vestiges of hatred can be overcome. That, certainly, was Dr. King's hope just over 50 years ago, after four little girls were killed in a black church in Birmingham, Alabama.…[84]

President Barak Obama and First Lady Michelle Obama attended the funeral service of the Rev. Senator Clementa Carlos Pinckney in Charleston. He eulogized Rev. Pinckney as a faithful shepherd, "'slain in his sanctuary with eight wonderful members of his flock, each at different stages in life but bound together by a common commitment to God.'"[85] He continued, "'Blinded by hate,'" the assailant failed to grasp "'the power of God's grace,'" unlike Pinckney and the faithful.[86]

It is confounding that hate crimes on the scale of the bombing and shootings at Mother Emanuel and the Tree of Life continue to reoccur. Still, the investigative response in 2015 contrasted with that of 1963. Despite public pressure, the FBI closed the bombing case in 1968. In 1971, Alabama State Attorney General William Baxley reopened the case and prosecuted Robert Chambliss in 1977. In 1980, a Department of Justice (DOJ) report inferred Hoover foiled other prosecutions.[87] Agents reopened the investigation in 1988 and later in July of 1997, the FBI renewed the inquiry, the day after the premier of *4 Little Girls*.[88]

In contrast with the Birmingham bombing suspects, a vigorous inquiry, amplified by physical and material evidence, resulted in the church shooter's swift arrest. According to reports, the police in Shelby bought the suspect a Burger King meal shortly after his arrest. Still, his relatively quick trial in December of 2016 and death penalty sentencing in a federal court in Charleston, S.C. on January 10, 2017 stand in contrast with the nearly forty year wait for justice in Birmingham.[89] Videotaped footage existed of him both entering and exiting Emanuel, complemented by witness testimony. While Sarah provides a firsthand account of the last few minutes in the lives of her peers, no video exists of anyone placing dynamite beneath the basement steps near the side of their church.[90] Prosecutors convicted Thomas Blanton largely based on the so-called 'kitchen tape,' witness testimony, and detective work.[91] T.K. Thorne's dissects the trials of Blanton and Bobby F. Cherry in the meticulously researched book, *The Last Chance for Justice.*

. . . JOIN THE NATION . . .
IN
A DAY OF
MOURNING
FOR
Our Children Murdered
in Birmingham, Ala.
Sunday, Sept. ~~15~~, 22 1963

At Emanuel A.M.E. Church
SUNDAY, SEPT. 22, 1963
AT 4:00 P.M.

All over the nation SUNDAY, SEPTEMBER 22, 1963 has been proclaimed MEMORIAL DAY for the children who were murdered last Sunday, September 15, 1963, while attending Sunday School at the 16th Street Baptist Church in Birmingham, Ala., U.S.A.

FOR CHARLESTON, SOUTH CAROLINA

Please meet at MORRIS STREET BAPTIST CHURCH at 3:00 P.M. PRAYER at 3:15 P.M.; MARCH to EMANUEL A.M.E. CHURCH for the service.

All ladies will wear black dresses. All gentlemen: dark suits, black ties and black arm bands. All ministers will head their congregations in the silent march. No automobiles will follow this march, please.

The Theme of this MEMORIAL DAY SERVICE is: "TO THE ROCK THAT IS HIGHER THAN I." Psalms 61-2

THE CHARLESTON MOVEMENT YOUTH COUNCIL - NAACP

Figure 6. Emanuel Flyer." Day of Morning" Courtesy of B. Gadsden.

The culprits in Birmingham and the Charleston shooter sought to fuel age-old racial divisions in the United States. The bombers resorted to a campaign of terror in order to uphold segregation, while the mass shooter echoed race-baiting sentiments popularized well over a century earlier in D.W. Griffith's *The Birth of a Nation* (1915).[92] Readers should not confuse this film with the Nate Parker movie *The Birth of the Nation* (2016), which portrays the life of the radical abolitionist and "fiery preacher," Nathaniel 'Nat' Turner.[93] Based on Thomas F. Dixon's *The Clansman* (1905), the second novel in a trilogy, the technically advanced but racially charged Griffith film would exercise a substantial influence on American popular culture. Notably, President Woodrow Wilson screened or showed the controversial movie at the White House. This film would revitalize the Ku Klux Klan (KKK), whose numbers had dwindled. On the opposing front, the National Association for the Advancement of Colored People (NAACP) sought to ban the film. Pioneering black director Oscar Micheaux directed *Within Our Gates* (1920), a critically appraised silent movie, as a rebuttal to *The Birth of the Nation.* Set in the Piedmont of South Carolina in 1915, Griffith's controversial film reignited racial divisions.

A century later, a lone wolf gunman hoped that a massacre in the South Carolina low country would rekindle a national divide, provoking or leading to racial warfare. Though it failed in this regard, the deadly mass shooting at 'Mother' Emanuel inspired some white supremacists and white nationalists to create memes venerating the gunman; the Birmingham bombers had admirers too: Other would be malefactors have attempted to duplicate the deadly mass violence of 2015 in black churches around the country, while some prominent, reformed white nationalists now denounce the shooter and all such acts of violence.[94]

Racial animus consumed the 21-year-old gunman after the shooting death of an unarmed black teenager, Trayvon Martin, in Sanford, Fl. by a neighborhood watch coordinator in 2012 whose closely monitored trial resulted in a verdict of not guilty a year later.[95] A little less than two years later, the mass shooter, a native of Columbia, South Carolina, carried out the attack at the Emanuel African Methodist Episcopal Church. In the wake of the killing, a website (*The Last Rhodesian*) and viral video later surfaced of the gunman brandishing the Confederate flag and apartheid-era South African and Rhodesian flags[96] Within days of the Charleston Massacre, Nikki Haley (former governor of S.C. and U.S. ambassador to the United Nations), weighed in on the matter.[97] On June 24, 2015, the body of the Rev. Senator Clementa Pinckney would lay in state inside the rotunda of the Capitol building; members of the South Carolina House of Representatives "agreed to debate the fate of flag."[98] Within days, 'artist-activist' Bree Newsome of Charlotte, N. C. would scale the flagpole, removing the Confederate flag from the capitol grounds. Newsome instantly became a folk heroine to many.[99]

Prior to this stance, the emotion-laden statements by victims' family members, extending forgiveness at the defendant's audio-recorded bond hearing on June 19, 2015, captured global headlines. As expressed by Alana Simmons, their witness vindicated the notion that "hate won't win." The granddaughter of the Rev. Daniel Simmons, Sr. and former beauty pageant winner launched the #Hate Won't Win Movement. On the other hand, Malcolm Graham, former member of the N.C. Senate and the younger brother of the late Cynthia Hurd, stated unequivocally:

> 'I do not forgive. I don't think you can forgive someone for a hideous act like that two days after it occurred. Forgiveness is a journey, it's just not granted, especially when they never asked for it.' [100]

Extremism violence now shapes views about cities like Charleston; yet, some contend the tragedy there "provides an opportunity for us to have productive conversations, both in our classrooms and with our colleagues, about how… racism relate to our disciplines."[101] Even prior to '63, folk no longer thought of Birmingham as the 'City of Churches.' Carnage at Emanuel hurt the reputation of the 'Holy City' or 'genteel city,' known for its historic synagogues like Congregation Beth Elohim.

Witness testimonies leave impressions, too. Sarah lived to bear witness to a bombing that was *never* supposed to happen during church. At Emanuel, the gunman told Polly Sheppard that he did not intend to end her life. [102] He planned to leave someone behind to tell the world what happened. During the "Rally for Unity," an outdoor event held in Marion Square in remembrance of the Emanuel Nine, Shephard boldly declared, "God saved me."[103] Although smaller in scale than the 20,000 people who once "formed a Bridge to Peace unity chain on the Ravenel Bridge to show solidarity with his victims," this rally still brought people together.[104] The outing featured Joan Baez who famously sang at the March on Washington. In Charleston, S.C., Baez led a diverse audience in freedom songs and sung "The President Sang Amazing Grace." Zoe Mulford, who originally wrote or recorded this song, appeared with her. Baez later spent time with various family members at Mother Emanuel.

Terrorism would strike at the heart of yet another American city the day after an intense mass meeting held at St. Paul's Memorial Church in Charlottesville, Va. On August 12, 2017, a twenty-year Ohio native struck Heather D. Heyer with his minivan, killing her and badly injuring twenty other demonstrators at a protest rally in Charlottesville; Marcus Martin, who risked his own life, heroically pushed his then fiancée, Marissa Blair, from out of harm's way. [105] Sadly, state troopers monitoring the events, H. Jay Cullen and Berke M.M. Bates, would die in a planc crash.[106] In an era increasingly defined by "identity politics," the day before deadly violence erupted on 4th Street, dozens of white nationalists, white supremacists, neo-Nazis and others participated in a tiki torch lit march on the campus of the University of Virginia. On a widely circulated footage, viewers can see and hear marchers chanting slogans like "'Jews will not replace us'" and "'white lives matter.'"[107] The aforementioned protesters staged their rally in Charlottesville, Va., a city once dubbed the "Cradle of the Confederacy," to bring attention to their attempts to preserve a statue of Gen. Robert E. Lee. During the Unite the Right Rally, they would clash with Black Lives Matter advocates, liberal counter protesters and members of Antifa or anti-Fascists. This violent clash dominated national news coverage for days.

After saying, there was blame on "both sides," days later President Donald Trump wrote, "'Racism is evil, and those who cause violence in its name are criminal and thugs, including the KKK, neo-Nazis…and other hate groups."[108] When responding to queries about the violence at an infrastructure news conference on August 15, 2017, he said, "'you look at… both sides. I think there is blame on both sides. I don't have any doubt about, and you don't have any doubt about it either'": At the end of the briefing he stated, "'I believe wages will start to go up. I think that will have a tremendous positive impact on race relations.'"[109]

Scholars, writers and journalists have also addressed racial violence. Angela Davis observed "racial terrorism has shaped the history of this country," a point reiterated by civil rights attorney Bryan Stevenson, founder of the National Museum for Peace and Justice.[110] Still, in an article published by *The Atlantic Weekly*, Angela Nagle detailed how Charlottesville fractured the alt-right "along fault lines that had appeared well before the violence there" and posited that "the rally had been dubbed Unite the Right, but it proved to be the culmination of a vicious period of internecine squabbling."[111]

Founded by Morris Dees in 1971, the Southern Poverty Law Center (SPLC) and the Center for the Study of Hate & Extremism at California State in San Bernardino, led by Brian Levin, both point to the proliferation of hate groups nationally and the surge of racial violence. Observing trends abroad, Dees and Richard Cohen point to what essentially amounts to a form of "transnational white supremacism."[112] Writer Ta-Nehisi Coates notes, "While whiteness endangers the bodies of black people, the larger threat is to white people themselves, the shared country, and even the whole world…"[113] The death of Hoyer, a civil rights activist and paralegal, lays bare his assertion. While appearing on MSNBC's "The Last Word with Lawrence O'Donnell, Mark Thompson (who hosts *Make it Plain* on Sirius XM FM), called Heyer the Viola Liuzzo of this generation.[114]

In the not so distant past, Sarah traveled to Charlottesville, Virginia to give a lecture at an event sponsored by the University of Virginia (Center for Politics). She toured Monticello, as well as the quad. This lecture occurred as scheduled on April 15, 2013, within hours of the deadly Boston Marathon bombing staged by brothers who had become nationalized American citizens.[115] Out of respect for the deceased and injured, as well as an abundance of caution in light of the attack in Boston, the event planners considered cancelling the program honoring black women involved in civil rights struggles primarily in Virginia.

During our conversation within days of the Charlottesville incident, Sarah remarked, "It's getting really bad," and later during a televised interview she elaborated, "I think about how they [the Klan] marched during our time in the '60s and came out with all of this violence…You would think now they wouldn't be doing this."[116] She added, "They're coming with all of this violence. It doesn't make sense at all. It's time for them to just start loving each other and stop all of the violence."[117]

Tragedy often binds people together even from different eras, racial backgrounds and lived experiences. Reconsider the example of Sarah, exhorting people to turn away from hatred – a message that a bereaved mom in Virginia spreads too. Susan Bro shares a similar message that her daughter would have spread globally, had she lived; "'Get your act together. Stop hating. Treat people the way you want to be treated.'"[118]

Dedicated to You

During the summer of 2017, Sarah briefly appeared on the campaign trail along with the former U.S. Attorney Doug Jones, then a candidate in Alabama's Special Senate election. He ran against a controversial Republican opponent, Roy Moore, who twice served as the Chief Justice of the Supreme Court of Alabama. Moore later had to contend with several disturbing allegations in the days, leading up to the election.[119] Jones' slim electoral victory in Alabama on December 12, 2017 stunned observers. The former U.S. Attorney prosecuted Thomas Blanton and Bobby Cherry for the 1963 Birmingham bombing, ending one of the most heart-wrenching examples of domestic terrorism on America soil: Jones had long contended that justice delayed did not translate to justice denied.[120] In the surprising aftermath of the election, one jubilant voter, Michael Nabors, stated, "those four little girls are on their feet tonight at 16th Street Baptist Church, celebrating.'" Nabors further elaborated, "'they're celebrating in spirit."[121] As the fortnight progressed, Sarah exhaled, glued to the television coverage watching the stunning results from an election that instantly made national news, delighted as any fifth little girl could be on this celebratory occasion.

Sarah has not forgotten the lessons that her mom taught her about fighting against racial injustice, and their talks about the still unresolved matter of restitution. *The 5th Little Girl* is essentially a mother-daughter story set during the Jim Crow era. Some readers may think of women like Mamie Till-Mobley and Alice Collins as the longstanding "Mothers of the Movement," a title rightfully bestowed on women like Sybrina Fulton, Gwen Carr, Geneva Reed-Veal and Lezley McSpadden, along with so many others like Congresswoman Lucy McBath (D-Georgia).[122]

With the backing of prominent civil rights groups like the NAACP, Tills-Mobley would come to view her son's brutal death as "the catalyst for a movement," and she courageously stood up for justice for her only child and son, Emmett Till.[123] The Chicago teen brutal lynching-related death stemmed from a brief exchange at Bryant Grocery and Meat Market in the town of Money, Mississippi. Mother Mamie courageously decided to "'let the people'" see her son's body — at once a painful scenario but fateful choice that would fundamentally alter the course of civil rights history. In August of 1955, some 50,000 thousand mourners filed by the glass-enclosed casket of her fourteen-year-old son at the Roberts Temple Church of God in Christ in Chicago, IL.[124] *The Chicago*

Defender and *Jet* magazine published a widely circulated picture of Emmett's grotesquely distorted face, magnifying its impact throughout black America. Till-Mobley later wrote, "I made a commitment to rip the covers off Mississippi USA—revealing to the world the horrible face of race hatred." [125] (The Smithsonian National Museum of African American Museum features the Emmett Till exhibit.)

Historian Crystal Sanders once asked Sarah to try to explain why the public often links the name of Emmett Till with civil rights struggles, whereas the names of the four little girls are still not "ingrained in our memories." In retrospect, such recognition has become increasingly more common place, especially since 2013.[126] For instance, the New Alabama Shakespeare Festival recently presented or staged the play, *Four Little Girls: Birmingham 1963*, featuring public school students who live in Montgomery, Alabama. Playwright Christina Ham wrote the drama to readdress a point that Birminghamiam Angela Davis raised: That for too long the names Addie, Carole, Cynthia, and Denise went unheard.

Some twenty-five years after the blast, *People* Magazine highlighted Sarah and her older sister Junie Collins Williams who identified Addie's body, leading to her later inner struggles and triumphs.[127] Her coming-of-age story, *Saving the Best Wine for Last*, dramatizes the short and long-term effects of trauma on victims' families. (Junie and I are collaborating on her memoir, too.)

The four little girls had a tremendous impact on the course of civil rights struggles but left behind grieving parents and siblings. Mrs. Alice Collins responded to an unspeakable calamity with stoicism, combined with the resolve to fight for justice. Her real-life worldview contrasts noticeably with the persona of the desolate Mother in Dudley Randall's epic poem, 'The Ballad of Birmingham' whose "eyes grew wet and wild," as "she raced through the streets of Birmingham, calling for her child."[128] In perhaps a case of art, imitating life, Maxine McNair cried out for her beloved daughter in the moments after a bomb exploded one Sunday morning at the 16th Street Baptist Church. In retrospect, *her baby* girl Denise should have been safe "singing in the children's choir."

Parents of the bombing victims were nurturing their children up to that bleak morning when lives ended abruptly. Gertrude Wesley gently chided Cynthia, reminding her exuberant daughter to adjust her slip beneath her white dress before she left home early that fateful morning to attend the 16th Street church. According to daughter Shirley Wesley

King, her mom explained "you'll never know how you may come back home," as Cynthia departed *that* Sunday with her dad Claude Wesley.[129]

It would take decades for the families adversely impacted by the '63 church bombing to gain some measure of justice for their children. As an activist, Rudolph persists in an ongoing quest for restitution for the injuries and losses that she also suffered. Against all odds, victims' family members impacted in stark incidents of racial violence and injustice have advocated for social change and legal remedies, too. Sarah Rudolph has bravely traveled this road as a "victim-survivor." On the other hand, watching videos, news coverage, and testifying publicly may lead victims' family members to re-experience second-hand trauma.

More recently, victims' family members thrust into the national spotlight have turned tragedy into activism, including Chris Singleton, Polly Sheppard, Kadiatou Diallo and the late Judy Scott as well as Erica Garner.[130] Scott forgave an ex-police officer but pressed on for justice after the shooting-related death of her son, Walter L. Scott.[131] Polly Sheppard addressed the issue of forgiveness in a town hall hosted by PBS news anchor Gwen Ifill entitled "America After Charleston" that examined structural racism; Rudolph who met Shepperd in Charleston, S.C, roughly a week before the town hall at the Circular Congregational Church, closely followed several of the above-mentioned cases. Within months of the attack at Emanuel, the "fifth little girl" traveled there, along with two of her sisters, to provide moral support and words of comfort to Sheppard and other victims' families of the Emanuel 9.[132]

The incalculable loss of the children personalized the struggle. Still, there is perhaps something in the engaging faces of the 'four little girls' and the story of 'the fifth girl' that has staying power. Described by Alabama journalist Howell Raines as "the signature civil rights crime of the 1960s," the church bombing has left a lasting historical imprint, as did the lynching case of Emmett Till, which the DOJ reopened on July 18, 2018. Organizations like the Emmett Till Legacy Foundation (ETLF), established by family member Debra Watts, are committed to "creating a legacy of hope."[133] Led by Bobby Rush (D-Illinois), the Emmett Till Antilynching Bill is making its way through Congress, as are preliminary discussions about HR 40, spearheaded by Sheila Jackson Lee (D-Texas).[134] More specifically, HR 360 honors the legacy of the youths; the community-based Addie Mae Collins Community Center in New York City and the Carole Robertson Center for Learning in Chicago also honor the legacy of our s*heroes*. Further, Jack and Jill of America Inc. has long celebrated 'Carole Robertson Day,' held by the Birmingham chapter and some two hundred others nationwide.[135]

Still, the bond of sisterhood is unmeasurable. Sisters validate *sistas* in life and in death. Diane Robertson Braddock would name her first-born child and daughter 'Carole,' in memory of her late sister, while Lisa McNair and Kimberly Brock honor the memory of their sister Denise, too.[136] To ensure that their older sister's legacy remains intact, Lisa has served as a strategic advisor to the California-based Sojourn Project.[137] Further, Dr. Shirley Wesley King has participated in several programs, imparting invaluable insights about her adopted parents and Cynthia. The Wesley's raised or informally adopted the precocious little girl and later Shirley, following the death of the sister whom she never got to know firsthand.[138] Hoping to restore her biological sister's actual family roots, Eunice Morris waged a campaign for society to recognize Cynthia last name as Morris.[139] Meanwhile, as Sarah Rudolph's national profile increases, she also honors Addie's legacy as a budding artist and peacemaker. In the second year of the "Stories that Shaped a Nation" program, the event coordinators of the Allentown, Pennsylvania based program posthumously honored Carole, Denise, Cynthia and Addie Mae (as well as Sarah Rudolph and Lisa McNair) as civil rights icons.[140]

Sarah's intimate account about the Sixteenth Street Baptist Church bombing is yet another timely reminder of the real-life consequences of homegrown terrorism and a statement about the lasting impact of post-traumatic stress. She has courageously faced numerous obstacles on the pathway to healing, forgiveness, and redemption. Debra Rubin opines Sarah has become "a national symbol of the civil rights movement in the deep South."[141] A freedom fighter is now emerging from beyond the mere sidelines. History is now rewriting her story, a long-neglected chapter in civil rights struggle. Like a phoenix still rising, this "hidden figure" shines a bright light on a dim period of the nation's history. On the path to becoming the amazing woman and "national treasure" that she is increasingly recognized as today, "The Fifth" imparts a divinely inspired message—a testament that still resonates some fifty-seven plus years later.[142] This remains a story that no one else in the world can tell quite like the *fifth little girl*, given her eyewitness to history on a day that forever altered the course of the national consciousness.

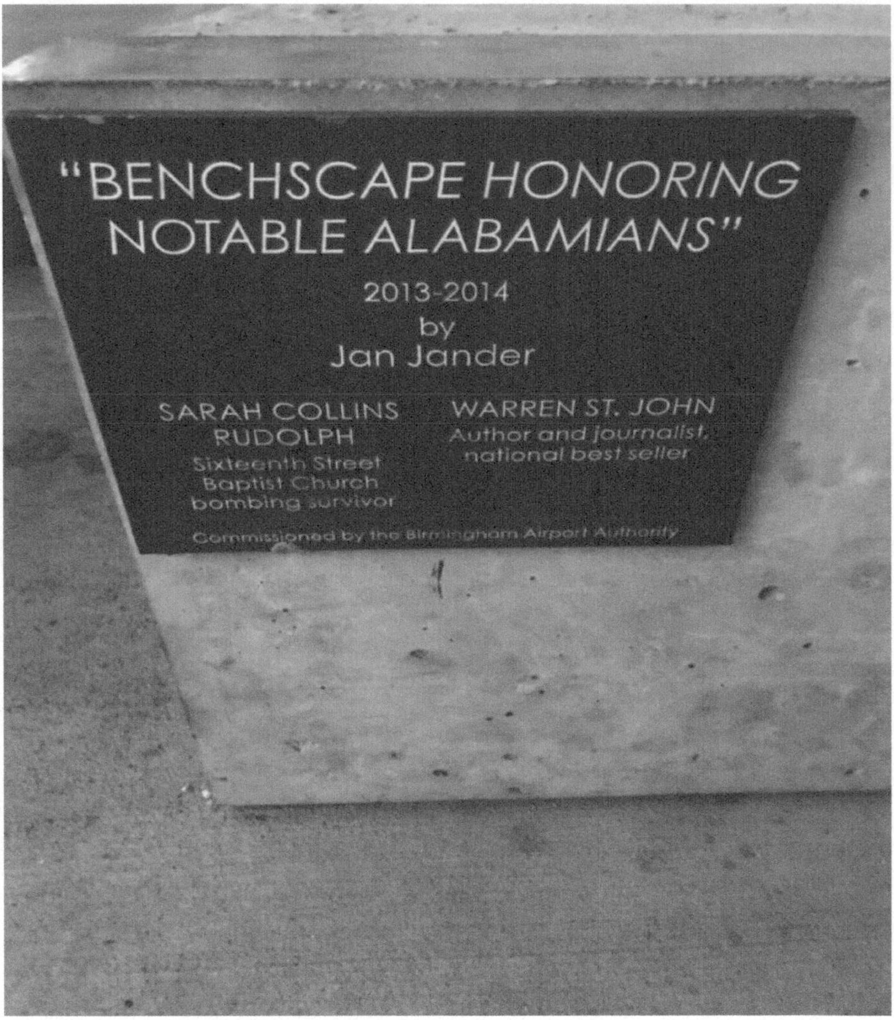

Figure 7. Sarah C. Rudolph Bench at the Birmingham-Shuttlesworth International Airport. Courtesy of George C. Rudolph

---

Notes

1 Remarks rendered by the Rev. Dr. Calvin O. Butts, III (pastor of the Abyssinian Baptist Church in Harlem) at the 40th anniversary commemoration program of the 16th Street Church bombing in Birmingham, Al. on September 15, 2003.

2 Catherine Ellis and Stephen Drury Smith, eds., "Introduction to 'Dick Gregory: Speech at St. John's Baptist Church, 1963'" in *Say It Plain: A Century of Great African American Speeches* (The New Press: London, 2005) 41.

3 Martin Luther King, Jr., "Letter from Birmingham City Jail" in *The Essential Writings and Speeches of MLK Jr.*, ed. James M. Washington (New York: Harper-Collins, 1986), 290.

4 Charlayne Hunter-Gault, *The New Yorker*, May 2, 2013, newyorker.com/news/news-desk-fifty-years-after-the-birmingham-childrens-crusade. (Gault is a civil rights pioneer within her own rights.)

5 Governor Wallace attempted to prevent Vivian J. Malone and James A. Hood from integrating the University of Alabama.

6 A speaker read Evers-Williams' remarks at "The Gathering: Civil Rights Justice Remembered," held at Birmingham-Southern College in early February of 2004. Williams thanked prosecutors, journalists and the staff at Tougaloo College.

7 Robin Young, "Women Were 'Second Class Citizens at '63 March,'" *NPR*, August 28, 2013, WBUR "Here and Now" (NPR) npr.org/transcripts/216550412?storyId=216550412?story=216550412.

8 "March on Washington for Jobs and Freedom August 28, 1963 (Lincoln Memorial Program)," The March on Washington for Jobs and Freedom, https://civilrights.jfklibrary.org/media-assets/the-march-on-washington-for-jobs-and-freedom.html#The-Event-1963—Todays-Program.

9 "Lessons Learned from the Civil Rights Movement," *Baylor Magazine*, September/October 2003. baylor.edu/alumni/magazine/0202/news.php?action +story&story=7585. Ibid.

10 "(1963) Malcolm X: 'Message to the Grassroots,'" *Black Past*, August 16, 2010, www.blackpast.org/1963-malcom-x-meassage-grassroots (1963); "Message to Grassroots: Malcolm X/November 10, 1963, https://teachingamericanhistory.org/ library/document/message-to-grassroots.

11 Colbert I. King, "No Thanks to Hoover," *The Washington Post*, May 5, 2001, washingtonpost.com/archive/opinions/2001/05/05/no-thanks-to-hoover/4dbbadb-c7d7-43d5-aa65-cd3a45c1...; Becky Little, "How Doug Jones Brought KKK Church Bombers to Justice, December 13, 2017, www.history.com>news>how-doug-jones-brought-kkk-church-bomber...; Joe Wilhelm Jr., "Alabama Attorneys Share Lessons of Justice with JBA," *Daily Record*, February 23, 2011, https://www.jaxdailyrecord.com/ article/alabama-attorneys-share-lessons-justice-jba.

12 "Birmingham: An Alabaman's Great Speech Lays the Blame," *LIFE*, Vol. 55, No. 13, September 17, 1963; Kofi Natambu, "The Horrific Birmingham Alabama Church Bombing that Killed Four Black Girls on September 15, 1963 and the Heinous Legacy of Racial Terrorism in the United States, *The Panoptican Review*, September 15, 2013, https:panopticanreview. Blogspot.com/2013/10/the-horrific-birmingham-alabama-bombing.

13 Liz Ronk, "The Girl Who Lived: Portrait of a Birmingham Church Bombing Survivor, 1963," *Time.com* August 6, 2013, https//time.com/3877750/16th-street-baptist-church-bombing-victim-sarah-collins-1963/; Hunter Oatman-Stanford,

"The Struggle in Black and White: Activist Photographers Who Fought for Civil Rights," *Collectorsweekly*, October 7, 2014, https://www.collectorsweekly.com/articles/activists-photographers-who fought-for-civil-rights/.

14 Fred Powledge, "Alabama Bombing Protested Here," *The New York Times*, September 17, 1963; Clarence Hunter, "Pray and Protest: 10, 000 Mourn Alabama Dead," Star, September 23, 1962.

15 Gregory Lewis, "Say It Loud, I'm black and I'm Proud, South Florida Sun-Sentinel, https://www.sun-sentinel.com/news/fl-expm-2008-08-0808070321-story-html.

16 Milton Moskowitz, "The Enduring Importance of Richard Wright," *The Journal of Blacks in Higher Education*, https://www.jbhe.com/features/59_richard wright.htl. ground for the civil rights movement of the 1950s and 1960s.

17 James Baldwin, *Blues for Mister Charlie: A Play*, http link, delawarelibrary.org/portal/Blues-for-Mister-Charlie—a-play-by-James/NrlralUiE.

18 Clarence Page, "Black Anger in Atlanta: James Baldwin Looks at 'Things Not Seen,'" *Chicago Tribune*, October 20, 1985, http://www.chicagotribune.com/news/ct-xprm-1985-10-20-8603f110680-story.html; Audra D.S. Burch, "Who Killed Atlanta's Children?" *The New York Times,* April 30, 2019, https://www.nytimes.com/2019/04/; James Baldwin, *The Evidence of Things Unseeen*

19 Moscow, September 16 (UPI). *The New York Times*, September 17, 1963.

20 "Ugandans Protest Alabama Bombing," *The New York Times*, September 18, 1963; "Vatican Paper Decries Killings in Birmingham," *The New York Times*, September 17, 1963.

21 Alice Kaplan, "Dreaming in French: On Angela Davis," *The Nation*, March 24, 2012, https:/www.thenation.com/article/dreaming-french-angela-davis.

22 Andrew Tully, "FBI Jurisdiction is Limited in Bombings," *Post Herald*, September 25, 1963.

23 Andrew Tully, "FBI Jurisdiction is Limited in Bombings," *Post Herald* (Beckley, W. Va.), September 25, 1963.

24 *"About the Birmingham Bombing," Modern American Poetry*, http://www.engligh.illinois.edu/maps/poets/m_r/randall/birmingham.htm.

25 Barbara Cross said the title for her dad's sermon on September 15, 1963 was "The Rock that Would Not Roll." Rev. John Cross pastored the 16th Street Church. (9/15/04 40th Anniversary Program, 16th Street Church.)

26 Bobby M. Wilson, *America's Johannesburg: Industrialization and Racial Transformation in Birmingham* (Lanham, MD.: Rowman & Littlefield Publishers, Inc.

27 Carrie Johnson, "Johnny's Death: The Untold Tragedy in Birmingham," NPR, September 15, 2010, https://www.npr.org/templates/story.php?story=129856740; Dave Martin, "Virgil Lamar Ware: Person, Pictures and Information – Fold3.com," Associated Press, September 15, 2015, https://www.fold3.com/641423008-virgil-lamar-ware/stories.

28 On June 16, 1976, Pieterson died at the outset of the Soweto Uprising.

29 Thaddeus Mezt, "What Archbishop Tutu's Ubuntu Credo Teaches the World about Justice and Harmony," *The Conversation*, October 4, 2017,

theconversation.com/what-archbishop-tutus-ubuntu-credo-teaches-the-world-about-justice-and-harmony-84730.

30 Hannah Foster, "The Black Arts Movement (1965-1975), Black Past," March 21, 2014, https://www.blackpat.org.>african-american-history>black-arts-movement.

31 Dave Martin, "James Ware Holds a Remembrance of his Brother Virgil, who was Killed when He was 13," September 25, 2015, https://www.fold3.com/page/641423008-virgil-ware/stories. Frank Sikora, *Until Justice Rolls Down: The Birmingham Church Bombing Case* (Tuscaloosa, The University of Alabama Press, 2005), 23. Local authorities in Birmingham Al. brought charges against two teens in Virgil Ware's death; Larry Sims (who fired the fatal bullet) and Michael Farley. Frank Sikora notes, "in January of 1964, Sims was found guilty of man slaughter and given seven months' probation," as was Farley. This incident haunted Sims, a Vietnam vet who wanted Virgil to know that his death help "change society."

32 A novelist and poet too, Richard Farina also wrote the lyrics to "Birmingham Sunday," which he sang; his sister-in-law recorded it on her album *Joan Baez/5.*

33 Numerous South African artists were opposed to apartheid or otherwise directly involved in the anti-apartheid movement including Hugh Masakela, Nadime Gordimer, Dennis Brutus, Andre Brink, Athol Fugard, Zakes Mokae, Ibrahim Abdullah, Mbongeni Ngema and Leleti Khumalo.

34 "Selective Buying Campaign," *Bhamwiki,* https:www.bhamwiki.com/w/Selective_Buying_Campaign; Jesse Chambers, "Miles College Role in Civil Rights Movement has Created a Permanent Legacy," July 7, 2013, https://blog.al.com/spotnews/2013/07/miles_college_role_in_civil_ri.html (Condoleezza Rice discusses the effectiveness of boycotts and the campaign in the chapter titled "1963" in her autobiography *Extraordinary Ordinary People.*)

35 "Browder vs. Gayle: The Women Before Rosa Parks," *Teaching Tolerance*, June 16, 2011. Tolerance.org/magazine/browder-v-gayle-the-women-before-rosa-parks.

36 Matthew Delmont, "The Lasting Legacy of the Busing Crisis," The Atlantic, theatlantic.com/politics/archive/2016/03/the-boston-busing-crisis-was-never-intended-to-work-/474264.

37 Written by Haki R. Madhubuti (nee Don Lee), "Maturity" describes the gut reaction of a girl who has survived a deadly church blast.

38 Dr. Tracy Snipe conceptualized the program. Dr. Jacqueline McMillan favorably compared this event to the appearance of Nobel Peace Prize-winner, Archbishop Desmond Tutu, in Dayton, Oh. Clinical psychologist Dr. LaPearl Winfrey wrote that this program put a "human face on this tragedy," reminding her of why she chose to further her studies. (Email from Dr. Winfrey to Dr. Snipe, March 2004.)

39 In 2015, this event was co-sponsored by WSU's Bolinga Black Cultural Center, which was then led by Dr. Joan Mawasha and Nycia (Bolds) Lattimore.

40 Skipper presented this tribute to Mrs. Sarah C. Rudolph. The Birmingham Civil Rights Institute still displays his painting such as "Through Dangers Seen and Unseen." This institute also includes a quotation attributed to Sarah C. Rudolph.

41 Early in 2013, Attorney Doug Jones stated his intention to recommend Rudolph for this honor in an article published by the *USA Today.* Rep. Terri Sewell (D-Alabama) played a leading role in Congress's effort to honor the four little girls.

42 Randall Kennedy, "The Civil Rights Movement and the Politics of Memory," *The American Prospect Magazine*, May 12, 2015, https://prospect.org/article/civil-rights-movement-and-politics-memory, 84
43 Robert McNamara, "Ida B. Wells: Crusading Journalist Campaigned Against Lynching in America," *ThoughtCo.*, July 31, 2018, https://www.thoughtco.com/ida-b-wells-basics-1773408.
44 Phillip House, *Claudette Colvin: Twice Toward Justice* (New York: Farrar Straus Giroux, 2009) 26. (Authorities arrested Mrs. Rosa Parks on December 1, 1955. For additional references on Claudette Colvin, refer to Rita Dove's poem, "Claudette Colvin Goes to Work," in her *Collected Poems, 1974-2004* (New York: W.W. Norton & Company), 332: In reference to Colvin, Rita Dove writes "…I'm the crazy girl off the bus, the one who wrote in class she was going to be the President."
45 Phillip House, *Claudette Colvin*, 116.
46 Jonathan Gold, 'Browder v. Gayle," *Teaching Tolerance*, Issue 53, Summer 2016.
47 Jeanne Theoharis, "Mrs. Parks and Black Power," rosaparksbiography.org/bio/mrs-parks-and-black-power/.
48 Jeanne Theoharis, *The Rebellious Life of Mrs. Rosa Parks* (Boston: Beacon Press, 2013), 219.
49 Ey Wade, "Voices of Change," *Beads on a String: America's Racially Intertwined Biographical History* (California: Inknbeans Press), 33.
50 John Archibald, "Time to Act as Treasure Fade Away," *The Birmingham News*, November 25, 2012.
51 "The Two Little Boys': Bombing Overshadowed Two Other Killings on that Fateful Day," *The Birmingham News*, September 15, 2013.
52 Michael Coard, "Coard: MOVE 30: Inside the May 1985 Assault on Osage Avenue, May 12, 2015, https://www.phillymag.com/news/2015/05/12/move-30-year-anniversary/; Aamer Madhani and Kevin Johnson, "Police Embrace an Approach of Tolerance and De-Escalation, *USA Today*, May 29, 2016.
53 Hillary Matfess (with further reporting by Christopher Dickey), "Three Years Later, a look at the #BringbackOurGirls Catch-22," Daily Beast, April 14, 2017, https://www.thedailybeast. Com/three-years-later-a-look-at-the-bringbackourgirls-catch-22?ref+scroll; Adaobi Tricia Nwaubani, "The Women Rescued from Boko Haram Who are Returning To Their Captors," *The New Yorker*, December 20, 2018, https://www.newyorker.com/news/dispatch/the-women-rescued-from-boko-haram-who-are-returning-to-their-captors; "Nigerian schoolgirls deserve world's continued attention," *USA Today*, August 6, 2014.
54 Unrecorded telephone call with Sarah C. Rudolph, Wednesday, May 27, 2015.
55 Martin Luther King Jr., "Eulogy for the Martyred Children" in *The Essential Writings and Speeches of Martin Luther King Jr.*, ed. James M. Washington (New York: HarperCollins, 1989), 223.
56 Collins-Rudolph and Snipe served as keynote speakers at an event honoring Dr. King, organized by then city councilmember Roger Freeman.
57 After working on the thematic structure and drafting an outline for this work, I later incorporated and layered it with some of Sarah's writings and speeches, too.

58 R. Riley, usatoday.com/story/news/2013/06/21/Aretha-franklin-detroit-freedom-walk/2447321/.

59 S. Willoughby Anderson, "The Past on Trial: Birmingham, the Bombing, and Restorative Justice," *California Law Review*, April 2008, https://scholarship.law.berkley.edu/californialawreview/vol96/iss2/3, 492.

60 Ibid.

61 Joseph D. Bryant, *The Birmingham News*, "'Fifth Little Girl' Remains Relatively Unknown in Birmingham, Seeks Role and Place as 50th Anniversary Nears (with video)," al.com, Posted November 23, 2012, al.com/spotnews/2012/11/fifth_little_girl_still_relativi.html.

62 Joseph D. Bryant, "Reparations for 1963 Church Bombing Survivor Difficult but Not Impossible," al.com, April 18, 2013, http://blog.al.com/spotnews/2013/04/post_911.html.

63 Of note, civil rights activist Erica Garner-Snipes would die of a heart ailment within years of the highly publicized videotaped death of her father Eric Garner in Staten Island, New York.

64 Stanley Kirshner-Breen, "Comparing Civil Rights Movement to Black Lives Matter," August 3, 2017, https://medium.com/@kbreenconsulting/comparing-civil-rights-movement-to-black-lives; Tatiana Farah and Susie Armitage, "2016 Was the Year Black Lives Matter Went Global," *BuzzFeed News*, December 8, 2016, buzzfeednews.com/article/susiearmitage/2016-was-the-year-black-lives-matter-went-global; Natalie Finn, "How Black Lives Matter Began: Meet the Woman Whose Hashtag Turned into a Global Movement.," *ENews*, June 9, 2020, eonline.com/news/1158910/how-black-lives-matter-began-meet-the-wom en-whose-hashtag-turned-into-a-gl…; Rupa Shenoy, "The Death of a Black Man in Brazil Parallels Eric Garner, Sparking BLM Protests," *The World*, February 25, 2019, pri.org/stories/2019-02-25/death-black-man-brazil-parallels-eric-garner-spakring-blm-protests.

65 Rodney Carmichael, "Why Black Joy and Lil Uzi Vert's Melancholy are all the Rage," *The Record*, NPR, September 1, 2017, https://www.npr.org/sections/therecord/2017/09/01/547264797/why-black-boy-joy-and-lil-...

66 Kofi Yebdah, "A Timeline of Events since Colin Kaepernick's National Anthem Protest," *The Undefeated* (ESPN), September 6, 2016, theundefeated.com/features/a-timeline-of-events-since-kaepernicks-national-anthem-protest/; Micah Peters, "Kobe Bryant and the Lakers Wear 'I Can't Breathe T-Shirts before King's Game," The USA Today, December 9, 2014, https://wusatoday.com/2014/12/kobe-bryant-lakers-i-can't-breathe-shirts-kings; www.espn.com>los-angeles>nba>story>kobe-bryant; Tierney Sneed, "Georgetown Hoyas Join Pro Athletes in 'I Can't Breathe' Protest," *U.S. News*, December 11, 2014, usnews.com/news/articles/2014/12/11/with-i-cant-breathe-shirts-georgetown-hoyas-join-eric-garner-mike-bro....

67 Samuel Momodu, "['Johnny Robinson (1947-1963)']," *Blackpast.org*, November 1, 2017, https://www.blackpast.org/african-american-history/robinson-johnny-1947-1963; Carrie Johnson, "Johnny's Death: The Untold Tragedy in Birmingham,

"NPR, September 15, 2010, https://www.npr.org/templates/story.phy?storyId=129856740. Most accounts indicate that the police officer shot Robinson in the back.

68 Frantz Fanon, "Racism and Culture," in *I am Because We Are: Readings in Black Philosophy*, eds. Fred Lee Hord and Jonathan Scott Lee (Amherst: University of Massachusetts, 1983), 179.

69 In his review of *Bending Toward Justice: The Birmingham Church Bombing that Changed the Course of Civil Rights*, Howell Raines proclaims that Doug Jones' portrayal of the "Klan infiltration of the Birmingham Police Department ('a snake pit') is ruthlessly candid." (Refer to Thomas Lay's testimony, read by D.J. Lay in 2002.)

70 Raymond Arsenault, *Freedom Riders: 1961 and the Struggle for Racial Justice*, (Oxford University Press, London, 2006), Editor's Note. (CORE sponsored the Freedom Rides.)

71 "KKK Series — FBI," www.fbi.gov>history>famous-cases>kkk>series; Ron Stallworth, *Black Klansman: Race, Hate, and the Undercover Investigation of a Lifetime* (Flatiron Books: New York, 2018). Directed by Spike Lee, *BlacKkKlansman* was adapted from Ron Stallworth's autobiography *Black Klansman*); Dennis Harvey, "Film Review: 'The Black Panthers: Vanguard of the Revolution,'" *Variety*, August 18, 2015, variety.com/2015/film/revioews/film-review-the-black-panthers-vanguard-of-the-revolution-1201423939/; (Freedom Archives: COINTELPRO 101 (2011); Alice Speri, "FBI Has Quietly Investigated White Supremacists in Police," *The Intercept*," January 31, 2017, theintercept.com/2017/01/31.the-fbi-has-quietly-inv…'; Kenya Downs, "FBI Warned of White Supremacists in Law Enforcement 10 Years Ago, Has Anything Changed?," PBS, October 21, 2016, www.pbs.org>newshour>nation>fbi-white-supremacists-in-law-enforcement.

72 The Willis Bing Davis Art Studio in Dayton, Ohio opened this display.

73 Karen McVeigh, "Hadiya Pendleton: Murdered Honors Student and Symbol of Chicago Violence," *The Guardian*, January 31, 2013, https://www.theguardian.com/world/2013/jan/31/hadiday-pendleton-inaguration-chicago-shot.

74 Michelle Alexander, *The New Jim Crow: Mass Incarceration in the Age of Colorblindness* (The New Press, London, 2010), 9.

75 Tyra Patterson, "A Conversation with Tyra Patterson: 23 Years of False Incarceration" (lecture, WSU, 2/2/18). Dr. LaFleur Small and Yemi Oluyemi Mahoney convened this forum. (Attorney David Singleton of the Ohio Justice & Policy Center joined his client, Tyra Patterson.) After obtaining parole, the state of Ohio released Patterson from prison on Christmas Day, December 25, 2017. Supported by the Bolinga Center and Women's Center at WSU, Judith Ezekiel and students in "Feminist Activism" and "Women, Gender and Black Freedom Movements," wrote and later published a pamphlet, *Black Women Lives Matter* in 2015, detailing underreported black girls and women slain in police shootings.

76 The film *Clemency* won the prestigious Grand Jury Prize in the dramatic category at the Sundance Film Festival in Salt Lake City, Utah. Chukwu who wrote the screenplay is the first black woman to claim this prestigious honor.

77 Rev. Dr. Norvel Goff, Sr., Dr. Maxine Smith, Willie Glee, Elizabeth Alston and William Dudley Gregorie, *Morning Grace,* ed. Herb Frazier (Charleston, South Carolina: Emanuel African Methodist Episcopal Church, 2016), 27-28.

78 Patricia Lessane, "No Sanctuary in Charleston," (Op-ed) *The New York Times*, June 18, 2015.

79 Lessane, "No Sanctuary."

80 "Coretta Scott King Visits Charleston," http://ldhi.library.cofc.edu/exhibits/show/charleston_hospital-workers_mo/coretta_scott_king_visits_charleston.

81 Carletta Smith, "July 2, 1822: Denmark Vesey and Co-Conspirators Hanged at Blake's Landing," *Black Then*, June 28, 2019, blackthen.com/July-2-1822-denmark-vesey-co-conspirators-hanged-blakes-landing. (See also the documentary, *Denmark Vesey: We've Come this Far by Faith.*); "South Carolina State Arsenal," http://www.cr.nps.gov/nr/travel/charleston/ssa.htm.

82 Ibid.

83 Joela Brown, "The Klan, White Christianity, and the Past and Present: A Response to Kelly J. Barker by Randall J. Stephens," *Race and Religion*, June 26, 2017, https://voices.uchicago.edu/religionculture/2017/06/ 26/the-klan-white-christianity-and-the-past-and-the-present-a-response; "Christian Racism- Bad News about Christianity," *Apartheid and Racism,* www.badnewsaboutchristianity.com/gab_racism.htm; Jaweed Kaleem, "South Carolina Luther Pastor: Dylann Roof was Church Member, His Family Prays for Victims," *Huffpost*, June 19, 2015, https://www.huffpost.com/entry/dylann-roof-religion-church-lutheran_n_7623990.

84 Tanya Somanader, "President Obama Delivers a Statement on the Shooting in South Carolina, The White House (Home.blog), June 18, 2015, https://obamawhitehouse.archives.gov/blog//2015/06/18/latest-president-obama-delivers-statement-shooting-so...shooting-charleston-south-carolina.

85 "Remarks by the President in Eulogy for the Honorable Reverend Clementa Pinckney," The White House (Office of the Press Secretary), June 26, 2015, https://obamawhitehouse.archives.gov/the-press-office/ 2015/06/26/remarks-president-eulogy-honorable-reverend-clementa- pinckney.

86 "Remarks by the President in Eulogy," June 26, 2015.

87 "About the 1963 Birmingham Bombing," Modern American Poetry. (Refer to section labeled Legal Chronology and specific article throughout the entire text.)

88 Rick Bragg, "F.B.I. Reopens Investigation into Landmark Crime of the Civil Rights Era," *The New York* Times, July 11, 1977, https://www.nytimes.com/1997/07/11/us/fbi-reopens-investigation-into-landmark-crime-of-the-civ.

89 Tim Smith, "Is Death for Dylann Roof Justified?" *The Greenville* (S.C.) *News*, January 10, 2017, http://www.usatoday.com/story/news/nation-now/2017/01/10/ dylann-roof-sentencing-reaction/96421044; Tonya Maxwell and Tim Smith, "Federal Jury Sentences Dylann Roof to Death," U.S. A. Today Network, January 10, 2017, https://www.usa today.com/story/news...now/2017/.../dylann-roof-sentencing/96412218; "Charleston Shooting Suispect's Burger King Meal Gets National Attention," *The Charlotte Observer*, June 24, 2015, charlotteobersver.com/news/local/aricle25394389.html.

90 Most sources note that the bombing suspects planted anywhere from ten to twenty sticks of dynamite in the terror attack at the Sixteenth Street Baptist Church.

91 Doug Jones (with Greg Truman), *Bending Toward Justice: The Birmingham Church Bombing that Changed the Course of Civil Rights* (New York: All Points Books, 2019), 140-149.

92 Lou Lumenick, "Why 'Birth of a Nation' is Still the most Racist Movie Ever,' New York Post, February 7, 2015, nypost.com/2015/02/07/why-birth-of-a-nation-is-still-the-most-controversial-movie-ever-made. One rather infamous scene depicts a white actor in black face as a would-be rapist.
Luke O'Bryan, "The Making of an American Nazi," The Atlantic, December 2017, theatlantic.com/magazine/archive/2017/12/the-making-of-an-am...

93 Hitory.com Editors, "Nat Turner," June 7, 2019, history.com/topics/black-history/nat-turner; Tirdad Derakhshani, "Nate Parker's 'the Birth of a Nation' a Powerful Chronicle of American Rebel Nat Turner," The Philadelphia Inquirer, October 6, 2016, inquirer.com/philly/entertainment/movies/20161007_Well_worth-the-hype_Nate_Parker-s_Sundance_sensation_The-Bith_of_a_Nation_is_a_powerful_chronicle_of_American_rebel_Nat_Turner_html. *The Birth of the Nation* signaled the birth of modern filmmaking techniques but fostered the growth of the KKK. In one sequence, the film lampooned black politicians.

94 Jennifer Berry Hawes, "Dylann Roof Pens Jailhouse Letter to Reformed White Supremacist," PostandCourier.com, December 15, 2017, https://postand courier.com/church_shooting/dylann-roof-pens-jailhouse-letter-to-ref; "Dylan Roof Letter to Christian Picciolini, postandcourier. com, December 15, 2017, https://www.postandcourier.com/dylann-roof-letter-to-christian-piccioli ni/pdf _dd05da9c-e.

95 George Zimmerman's lawyers utilized Florida's "Stand Your Ground" defense during his closely monitored trial.

96 "Dylann Roof's White Supremacist Views, Links to Hate Group Revealed After Charleston Massacre," Democracy Now, https://www.democracynow.org/2015/6/22/dylann_roofs_white_supremacist_views_links.

97 Cassie Cope and Andrew Shain, "Gov Haley: 'Time has Come' to Remove Confederate Flag," *The State*, June 22 2015, thestate.com/news/local/article25203127.html; Joseph A. Wulfsohn, "Media Piles on Nikki Haley after Misinterpreted Conference Flag Remarks go Viral, Fox News, December 6, 2019, foxnews.com/media/nikki-haley-confederate-flag.

98 Doug Stanglin, "Pinckney's Body to lie in State Near Site of Controversial Dixie Flag," USA Today, June 24, 2015, usatoday.com/story/news/nation/2015/06/24/Charleston-south-carolina-clementa-pinckney-confederate...; Jamie Self, "Public Pays Respect to Slain Sen. Clementa Pinckney (+ Video)," *The State*, June 4, 2015, https://www.thestate.com/news/state/article2540 3107.html. (I was among the hundreds of people who flocked to the state capitol grounds. (On a sweltering day, a racially diverse crown lined the capital grounds in Columbia for a public viewing. A native son of the S.C., Pinckney's body laid in state in the rotunda.)

99 Charlie Shelton and Frank Stasio, "Meet Bree Newsome, The Woman Who Removed South Carolina's Confederate Flag," wunc/North Carolina Public Radio, March 27, 2017, https://www.wunc.org/post/ meet-bree-newsome-woman-who-removed-south-carolina; Adam Parke, "SC Activist who Tried to Remove Confederate flag in Columbia May Give Items to Smithsonian," *The Post and Courier*, July 2, 2019, postandcourier.com/news/sc-activist-who-tried-to-remove-confederate-flag-in-columbia/article_1a781f. (Newsome's act of defiance would late inspired both political cartoons and criticisms for lawlessness.)

100 Michael Gordon, "Brother of Charleston Shooting Victim Wants Death Penalty for Dylann Roof," The Charlotte Observer, June 16, 2016 (Updated June 17, 2016), charlotteobserver.com/news/local/crime/article84227057.html; Malcolm Graham, "By Big Sister Was Gunned Down in Charleston One Year Ago," *NPR*, June 18, 2016, npr.org/sections/codeswitch/2016/06/18/482499865/my-big-sister-was-gunned-diwb-inc-charletons-one-year...

101 Kimberly Barrett, Sharon Lynette Jones and Tracy Snipe, "Contemporary Reflections of Sons and Daughters of the Ex-Confederacy," *Insight to Diversity*, insightintodiversity.com/up-content/media/issues/october2015.pdf.

102 The shooter did not know that Jennifer Pinckney was in the pastor's study with her daughter; Polly Shepperd, Felecia Sanders and her granddaughter also lived.

103 Polly Shepperd briefly spoke at the third "Emanuel 9 Rally for Unity" at Marion Square in Charleston, South Carolina where Joan Baez was the featured guest.

104 "Dylann Roof's White Supremacist Views, Links to Hate Group Revealed after Charleston Church Massacre," Democracy Now, June 22, 2015, www.democracynow.org.dylann_roofs-white-supremacist-views-links.

105 Brian Witte and Josh Replogle, "Man who Saved Fiancee in Charlottesville: 'Please don't Let Her be Dead,'" the St. Augustine Record, August 16, 2017, https://www.staugustine.com/news/20170816/man-who-saved-fiancee-in-charlottesville-please-dont-let-her-be-dead; Ryan W. Miller, "' 4 Minutes Saved my life': Holocaust Survivor had Bullets Whiz by Outside Tree of Life," *USA Today*, October 29, 2018, https://www.usatoday.com/story/news/nationa/2018/10/29/pittsburgh-judah-samet-survived-holocaust-tree-life-shooting/ 1808116002/.

106 Matthew Haag, "Death of 2 State Troopers Adds Another Layer of Tragedy in Charlottesville," *The New York Times*, August 14, 2017, https://www.nytimes.com/2017/08/14/us/virginia-police-helicopter-crash-html.

107 Paul P. Murphy, "White Nationalists Use Tiki Torches to Light Up Charlottesville March, *CNN*, August 14, 2017, https://wwww.cnn.com /2017/08/12/us/white-nationalists-tiki-torch-march.../index.html.

108 "Statement by President Trump," August 14, 2017, https://www.whitehouse.gov/briefings-statements/statement-president-trump.

109 "Remarks by President Trump on Infrastructure," Infrastructure and Technology, August 15, 2017, https://www.whitehouse.gov/briefings-statements/remarks-president-trump-infrastructure/. (See President Trump's initial remarks on August 12, 2017.)

110 Angela Davis, "'Terrorism is Part of Our History': Angela Davis on '63 Church Bombing, Growing Up in 'Bombingham,'" interview by Amy Goodman, *Democracy Now*, September 17, 2013, https://www.democracynow.org/2013/9/16/ terrorism_is_part_of_our_history; James McWilliams, "Bryan Stevenson on What Well-Meaning White People Need to Know about Race," *Pacific Standard*, Updated February 18, 2019 (Original February 6, 2018), psmag.com/magazine/bryan-stevenson-ps-interview; Corey G. Johnson, "Bryan Stevenson on Charleston and Our Real Problem with Race," The Marshall Project, June 24, 2015, www.themarsahllproject.org.2015/06/24.bryan-stevenson-on-charleston-and-our-real-problem-with-race.

111 Angela Nagle, "The Lost Boys: The Young Men of the Alt-Right Could Define American Politics for a Generation," *The Atlantic*, December 2017Issue, https://www.theatlantic.com/magazine/archive/2017/12/ broth.

112 Heidi Beirich and Susy Buchanan, "2017: The Year in Hate and Extremism," Southern Poverty Law Center, February 11, 2018, https://www,splcenter.org/ fighting-haate/intelligence-report/2018/2017-year-hate-and-extremism; Morris Dees and J. Richard Cohen, "White Supremacists Without Borders," *The New York Times* (Opinion), June 22, 2015, https://www.nytimes.com/2015/06/ 22/opinion/white-supremacists-without-borders.html.

113 Ta-Nehisi Coates, "The First White President: The Foundation of Donald Trump's Presidency is the Negation of Barack Obama's Legacy," *The Atlantic*, October 2017 Issue, https://www.theatlantic. com/magazine/archive/2017/10/ the-first-white-president-ta-nehisi.

114 Viola Liuzzo, a wife and mom from Detroit, responded to Dr. King's call for people to travel down South to help with voter registration after Bloody Sunday.

115 Within days, Tamerion Tsarnaev was killed and Dzhokar Tsarnaev captured.

116 Rick Journey, "1963 Church Bombing Survivor Urges Love after Charlottesville Violence," *WBRC*, August 14, 2017, http://www.wbrc.com/story/36134099/ 1963-church-bombing-survivor-urges-love-after-charlottesville-violence.

117 Ibid.

118 Caroline Simon, "A Year after Charlottesville: 'Stop Hating,' Mother Says," *USA Today*, August 10, 2018.

119 Richard Faussett and Campbell Robertson, "Black Voters in Alabama Pushed Back Against the Past," in *The New York Times*, December 13, 2017, https://www.nytimes.com/2017/12/13/us/doug-jones-alabama-black-voters.html.

120 Joe Wilhelm, "Alabama Attorneys Share Lessons of Justice with JBA," *Jax Daily Record*, February 23, 2011, https://www.jaxdailyrecord.com/ article/Alabama-attorneys-share-lessons-justice-jba.

121 Faussett and Robertson, "Black Voters in Alabama."

122 Lauren Gambino and Lois Bectell, "'Mothers of the Movement' Channel Black Lives Lost into Support for Clinton,'" *The Guardian*, July 26, 2016, guardian.com/us-news/016/ju/26/black-lives-matter-mothers-democratic-convention-hillary-clinton. (Josh Lev, "Michael Brown's Address the U.N.: 'We

Need the World to Know.' Parents Testify at U.N." CNN, https://www.com/2014/11/11/us/ferguson-brown-parents-u-n-/index.html.

123 Tills-Mobely made this remark in the docu-film, *The Untold Story of Emmett Till.*

124 Anthony Brooks, "Reopening the Case of Emmett Till," *On Point* (NPR), July 17, 2018, https:www.wbur.org/onpoint/2018/07/17/Emmett-till-timothy-tyson; Maureen O'Donald, "Alva Dorris Roberts, 'First Lady' of Church Where Emmett Till's Funeral was Held, Dead at 101," Chicago.suntimes, June 6, 2016, https://chicago-suntimes.com/news/ alva-doris-roberts-first-lady-of-church-where-emmett-tills-funeral-was-held-dead-at-101.

125 Mamie Till Mobley and Christopher Benson, *Death of Innocence: The Story of the Hate Crime that Changed America*, (Random House, New York, 2003), xxii.

126 Email to Sarah Collins Rudolph from Crystal R. Sanders, September 19, 2014.

127 Kyle Smith, "The Day the Children Died," *People.com*, August 11, 1977, https://people.com/archive/the-day-the-children-died-vol-48-no-6.

128 Dudley Randall, "Ballad of Birmingham," *Poetry Foundation*, https://www.poetryfoundation.org/poems/46562/ballad-of-birmingham.

129 Shirley Wesley King, "Four Women from Birmingham (lecture, Wright State University or WSU, Dayton, Ohio, March 2004).

130 Lisa Weismann, "Two Emanuel AME Victims' Families Channel Grief Through Sports," June 18, 2016 – Updated July 9, 2016, live5news.com/story/32250732/two-emanuel-ame-victims-families-channel-grief-through-sports/; Vivian Wang, "Erica Garner, Activist and Daughter of Eric Garner, Dies at 27," *The New York Times*, December 30, 2017, ntytimes.com/2017/12/30/nyregion/erica-garner-dead.html; Kadiatou Diallo-Amadou Diallo Foundation, www.amadoudiallo.com>com>who-we-are>kadiaotou-diallo; "America After Charleston," tpt.org/America-after-charleston/video/America-after-charleston-forgiveness-process; Fleming Smith, "'Remarkable' Judy Scott, Mother of Walter Scott, Dies at 76," *The Post and Courier*, January 30, 2020, postandcourier.com/newsw (See also Elizabeth Martin's "Trayvon Martin, Sybrina Fulton and Tracy Martin - Time, January 26, 2017, time.com>ideas>10 questions).

131 Lindsey Bever, "Forgiveness is in My Heart,' a Bereaved Mother told the Officer who Shot Her Son in the Back," *Washingtonpost.com*, December 7, 2017, https://www.washingtonpost.com/news/inspired-life/wp/2017/12/07/forgiveness-is-in-my-heart-a-bereaved-mother-told-the-officer-who-shot-her-son-in-the-back/?utm_terms+.4a45d966efa. A cell phone video recorded by Feidin Santana bolstered claims of police brutality. Mrs. Judy Scott and Anthony Scott addressed WSU students at the New Zion RMUE Church in North Charleston, S.C. They visited Emanuel too. Speakers: Blondelle Gadsden, Willie Glee, Rodney Scott, Bernard Powers and Dr. Millicent Brown.

132 Sarah Pulliam Bailey, "The Charleston Shooting is the Largest Mass Shooting in a House of Worship since 1991," The Washington Post, June 18, 2015, washingtonpost.com/news/acts-of-faith/wp/2015/06/18/the-charleston-shooting-is-the-largest-m…)

133 Emmett Till Legacy Foundation, mightycause.com/organizations/Emmett-Till-Legacy-Foundation. (http://www.emmetttilllegacyfoundation.com)

134 John Conyers, Jr. (D-Michigan) and Sheila Jackson Lee (D-Texas) have backed such proposals; Ta-Nehisi Coates advocates for reparations; undergraduates at at Georgetown broadly support reparations measures and the University of Glascow in Great Britain has set aside funds to study slavery's effect.

135 "Carole Robertson Day," Jack and Jill of America, Inc. Baltimore Chapter," http://jackandjillbaltomd.org/index-php/our-programming/annual-events/11-carole-roberts.

136 Angela Tucker, "Little Girl Gone," *The Atlanta Journal-Constitution*, Updated September 14, 2013, https://www.ajc.com/news/little-girl-gone/rUqn1b11 wBTfRpQua74rnM.

137 "Leadership & Directors," Sojourn to the Past, http://www.sojourn project.org/about--us/leadership-and-directors.

138 Ravitz, "Fifty Years after Birmingham Church Blast"; Shirley Wesley King, "Four Women from Birmingham," (lecture, WSU, Dayton, Ohio, Mach 2004).

139 Eunice Morris's letter dated March 22, 2002.

140 The other honorees were Joan Spencer, Charlayne Hunter-Gault, Diane Nash, Marian W. Edelman, Alice Walker, Toni Morrison, Rita Moreno, and Joan Baez.

141 Debra Rubin, "Survivor Recalls Role in Civil Rights History," January 25, 2016. http:njjewishnews.com/article/29677/survivor-recalls-role-in-civil-rigths movement.

142 S. C. environmental activist Delbert DuBois refers to Sarah C. Rudolph as "The Fifth," while artist James Pate once described her as "a national treasure."

Chapter 1. Acknowledgement

In all thy ways acknowledge him, and he shall direct thy paths. (Proverbs 3:6, KJV)

I have come to tell the story – I have come to testify.[1]

Just as Addie stretched out her arms to tie the sash on Denise's dress, suddenly, I heard a thunderous 'BOOM!' Flying glass, debris and mortar rained down, instantly killing my sister and three friends at the Sixteenth Street Baptist Church in Birmingham, Alabama on Sunday, September 15, 1963. Moments earlier, we were gathered in the ladies' room. I was badly hurt. Initially, the attack left me blind, dazed. It was as if life stood frozen in time at 10:22 a.m. that morning -- a moment I can't forget.

I was only twelve years old when someone bombed our church. According to the people, it sounded like an atomic bomb. Like troops, cut down in the prime of youth, the bombing murdered my older sister Addie (age 14), Carole (age 14), Cynthia (age 14) and Denise (age 11). Usually, when we think of the "four little girls," pictures of troops do not instantly come to mind. The closest any of them ever came to wear a uniform was the outfit Carole sometimes wore as a Scout. From the lovely white dresses that several of the girls wore that Sunday to the kindness they all displayed, my friends symbolized what it means to be "pure in heart." A note in the basement of our church would later describe the vicious racial terror that resulted in the loss of the four lives as an act of white supremacy. Didn't anybody say much about the one survivor; I was the little girl who lived.[2] It took a long time for people to realize that I survived. In fact, some folk still don't know that there was fifth child in the basement restroom at the time of the blast. Years later, journalists, classmates and other people who knew began to refer to me as the 'Fifth Little Girl' or 'Forgotten Girl' and sometimes as 'the Sole Survivor.'[3]

Somebody bombed Arthur Shores' home about a month before a bomb killed the four girls at our church, sending shockwaves across the city, nation, and world. Although Shores was a famous lawyer in Birmingham, the police did not charge anyone. Bombs occurred often in our city, years before I came of age. They intensified when black people began moving into white neighborhoods and on Center Street in larger numbers. There were so many bombs that folk began to call our city 'Bombingham.' Before the Sixteenth Street Baptist Church bombing, people also used to call Birmingham the "Magic City" because of its booming steel industry.

In the distant past, some also called Birmingham the "Holy City" because of its many churches. Our city had several churches that would become active in "The Movement" like Old Sardis Baptist Church, St. Paul United Methodist Church, New Pilgrim Baptist Church, and the historic Bethel Baptist Church. Still, troublemakers attacked men of the cloth like the Reverend Fred Shuttlesworth, pastor of Bethel Baptist Church. Shuttlesworth survived several bombings, and even a beating with brass knuckles at the hands of Bobby Frank Cherry, supposedly.

A fearless leader and a *man of valor* too, Shuttlesworth came within inches of losing his life but none of this stopped him. Years later, in the introduction to *Long Time Coming*, Shuttlesworth would later recall:

> In 1956, a Christmas morning bombing destroyed my parsonage as I lay in bed. No one was ever arrested or prosecuted for that bombing. For a second bombing in 1958, J.B. Stoner was given a 10-year sentence, but 22 years later.[4]

I met Reverend Shuttlesworth when I was a little girl. He was one of the great civil rights leaders that rose in the state of Alabama, or in the nation. The Birmingham Civil Rights Institute fittingly honors him with a statue that graces the front of its building.

Anyway, I never dreamt that terror would also strike at the heart of our house of worship, the famed 16th Street Baptist Church. Bordering Kelly Ingram Park where civil rights demonstrations regularly occurred, our church was like Ground Zero, or the epicenter for all the rallies and demonstrations that gave life to our struggle for racial equality. Reverend King and other movement leaders held mass meetings at the Sixteenth Street Baptist Church because it was large and could seat many people.[5] Folks referred to the 16th Street Church as the "People's Church" too. White supremacists bombed our congregation in their attempt to destroy the energy of the Movement by attacking the body of the church. They didn't succeed, but four lives were lost. After this attack, people began to refer to 'Bomingham' as the "Tragic City" too. Incredibly, it was the twenty-ninth bombing in our city just since 1951, according to some sources.[6] Clearly, we were under siege for years.

Like a wounded soldier on the battlefield, medics quickly whisked me away from the sanctuary that tragic day. Badly hurt, I could not see anything at all after the bombing and would permanently lose sight in one eye. Some recall the smell of dynamite powder after the explosion; I just remember that terrible sound. Sometimes, I still hear that bomb in my sleep. I jumps in my sleep, and I call my sister, 'Addie!'[7] I suppose it is another manifestation of trauma. I still have nightmares too and get anxious when I hear loud noises, like a car backfiring, for instance.

To ease my anxieties, I used to try to think of all the fun I had at the Sixteenth Street Church and the beautiful, stained glass windows dotted throughout the sanctuary. I loved being there with Addie and friends like Denise, Carole, and Cynthia. I am devoting this book to the four little girls and to our veterans, especially soldiers who fought in the Vietnam War and the Korean War or the 'Forgotten War,' and in other conflicts such as the Gulf War. Tens of thousands of men and a much smaller number of women never made it back from the Vietnam War.[8]

Folks may wonder, but why the veterans Sarah? After all, wars tend to be destructive and cause suffering. They often divide or build walls and fences between people. Further, many protested the Vietnam War in particular. Some veterans came back home troubled, sick, and with little acknowledgement. In the more distant past, people even lynched, maimed and blinded some proud black veterans returning home after world wars.[9] Vets like Medgar Evers bravely fought in World War II and later for civil rights at home, even at "'the price of death.'"[10]

Americans really started reaffirming the sacrifices and struggles of veterans, especially after the 9/11 terrorist attack, which shook people up. Like some of our war-weary veterans, I know how it feels to be forgotten, overlooked. I know how people can suffer alone in silence. I have struggled with post-traumatic stress disorder (PTSD) too.[11] Unlike most vets, mine stems from the result of a church bombing. I suffered in silence from PTSD as a little girl, long before I knew all the signs post-traumatic stress.

When I was a child, Birmingham was like a battlefield at times. I was one of hundreds of child foot soldiers who participated in civil rights demonstrations. I marched before and after the deadly bombing. During the spring of 1963, over two thousand children participated in marches initiating from the Sixteenth Street Baptist Church, beginning on D-Day. They lined up and marched from the doors of our church. The police later jailed many of them, and after running out of space in the jails, they confined some kids at the local fairground. The fair is where children should have been enjoying life, eating cotton candy, or riding on the Ferris wheel, not feeling fortunate if they were lucky enough to have toothpaste and a toothbrush.

We soldiered on. My days of organized protests started when I was a student in grade school. Mama allowed my sisters and me (including Addie) to participate in boycotts and to walk the picket lines too in Birmingham.[12] Even as kids, we had a keen sense of what fairness and equality should mean and were willing to stand up for our rights. For example, Denise McNair liked to play with dolls; however, she was socially aware and wanted to march.[13] She and Condoleezza Rice were playmates. Rice became the first black woman to become the National Security Advisor, and later on Secretary of State.[14] Anyway, as a little girl, Denise wanted to be able to dine at the lunch counter at the local Kress.[15]An honor student and clarinetist, Carole attended a meeting on racial healing the very weekend before the bombing.[16] Life also engaged Cynthia. An 'A' student, she regularly attended church and had planned to go to a club meeting later that day. We all had dreams and wanted to exercise our God-given, constitutional rights: our civil or *human rights*. We knew how it felt, living in "bowels of segregation" and we wanted change. Yet we never dreamt of its price.

Why Was I Born?

Who would have thought anyone would bomb a church, murdering four innocent children? As I once shared with a reporter, "'who would think someone could be that cold? Someone who puts a bomb in church has to be working for the devil.'"[17] But looking back, I know that there could have been a fifth body found under the rubble that Sunday…mine. Only a few yards separated me from the other four girls, yet I survived. I have often wondered why. I never experienced "survivor's guilt," but I had moments of despair. Mama told me, "God spared you for a reason, baby."[18] A salt-of-the-earth type of woman, Mama frequently gave stirring testimonials, maybe to lift her spirits and encourage others. Such church services have become a thing of past, but they helped us to get by and sustained us.

Altogether, five of her daughters attended the 16th Street Church that day, but one child never made it back home. The bombing and my sister's murder had a short and long-term effect on the entire family. It silently tore away at us for years. My sisters Addie Bea, Junie, Janie, and I all attended church that day. As I recall, my sister Flora also interacted with Addie that Sunday. Each one of us had a unique relationship with Addie. Most of my sisters would experience hardship or personal trials immediately after the bombing, and even years later.

Some little girls in America such as Marsha Bonhart thought hard about attending church on Sunday mornings, after the bombing while others like Roberta Boyd clearly recall their "hurt, anger and sorrow."[19] As a survivor of a terror attack, I had to overcome my fears and anger too. I have lived with physical, emotional scars, and financial hardship, working hard to earn a living in foundries and later as a housekeeper — all despite my injuries. The bomb physically injured twenty-two folks.[20]

I had questions but did not discuss the bombing for years. No one in my family talked about *it.* We picked up the pieces; tried to move on. The trauma forced me to grow up fast, often alone in the trenches. As a teen and later an adult, I wondered who bombed us. The FBI began an inquiry but neither the state of Alabama nor the federal government really held anyone responsible for years. I still wonder if the state has punished *all* who conspired in this crime. My mind also runs back to Mama and the broken promise to give her restitution or compensation for the murder of Addie and my life-long injuries; like I've said before, Mama "sat there, waited and waited, and she died waiting,'" which still pains me.[21] Still, I carry on with this quest, with her in mind also.

Chronic Blues

Over the years, I've relied on faith to keep me going. I have had a few setbacks along the way. But I worked and prayed even harder. In time, I came to believe God spared me to tell the story of what happened to five girls in a lone Baptist church, for the generations to come. My soul witnessed history. I can't think of anything my friends did to have their lives expire in a bombing.[22] I wish they had the chance to realize their dreams in life, but they had a larger destiny in death: One that allowed other children and grown folk to grasp aspects of the American dream.

I feel badly about losing them in such a horrific way – a bombing is a violent act. I used to cry every time I thought about how they died. I still weep, when I think about anybody having enough hatred inside of their hearts to put a bomb under the stairway in a house of God — a *safe house* — killing four innocent girls.[23] As the 'fifth girl,' I made it out alive. Let me tell you, when you look at me, you're looking at miracle![24] This is my story, but our song.[25] And I believe that people in the United States of America and worldwide need to know the full story, the unvarnished truth about the four girls killed in the bombing.[26]

But it is no bedtime story, no fairy tale. God inspired me to share the story. May this account uplift you, bring you a word of hope or renew your mind to do something good, even in times of uncertainty.

Figure 8. Collins-Rudolph at WSU on March 11, 2004. Courtesy of WSU.

Notes

1 Hannibal Lokumbe, Philadelphia Orchestra Music Alive Composer-in-Residence, wrote and composed *Crucifixion Resurrection: Nine Souls a Traveling* in honor of the Emanuel Nine. The four victims of the Birmingham bombing function as narrators in this imaginative production. The last suite references the plight of bombing survivor Sarah C. Rudolph (as well as Polly Shepherd, Felicia Sanders, and Jennifer Pinckney) and the two young girls who survived the terror attack at the Emanuel African Methodist Episcopal Church in Charleston, S. C. An impressive ensemble premiered *Crucifixion Resurrection* at Mother Bethel African Methodist Episcopal Church in Philadelphia, Pennsylvania on June 17, 2017. Featured artists included Juliette Kang (on violin), Janice Chandler-Eteme (Soprano), Tiffany Goddette (Mezzo-soprano), Rodrick Dixon (Tenor), and with Hannibal Lokumbe, conducting. For further details about this event refer to "Music Alive Composer-in-Residence Hannibal Lokumbe Heads Three Days of Community Events June 15-17, 2017," May 31, 2017, philorch.org/press-room/news/music-alive-composer-residence-hannibal-lokumbe-heads-three-days-co.)

2 Sarah Collins Rudolph, "Conversations from Penn State: Sarah Collins Rudolph" (Episode 709, interview by Patty Satalia, WPSU Penn State, January 2015), https://wpsu.psu.edu/tv/programs/conversations/sarah.

3 In an on-line article, Olivia B. Waxman of *Time* magazine references Rudolph in "16th Street Baptist Church Bombing Survivors Recall a Day that Changed the Fight for Civil Rights: 'I Will Never Stop Crying Thinking About It,'" an on-line article. September 14, 2018, time.com/5394093/16th-street-baptist-church-bombing-anniversary/.

4 Fred L. Shuttlesworth," Introduction and Call to Action," in *Long Time Coming: An Insider's Story of the Birmingham Church Bombing that Rocked the World,* by Elizabeth H. Cobbs/Petric J. Smith (Birmingham, Alabama: Crane Hill Publishers, 1994), 16.

5 Sarah Collins Rudolph, letter to Tracy Snipe, June 12, 2014.

6 Andrew M. Manis, *A Fire You Can't Put Out: The Civil Rights Life of Birmingham's Reverend Fred Shuttlesworth* (Tuscaloosa: The University of Alabama Press, 1999), 403.

7 Jessica Ravitz, "50 Years later, Siblings Remembered"; Tanya Otts, "Long Forgotten."

8 Billy Joel, who wrote the lyrics to "Goodnight Saigon," describes soldiers who fought in Vietnam as "soulmates on Parris Island." Refer to the songs "What's Going On" (co-written by Marvin Gaye, Renaldo 'Obie' Benson and Al Cleveland) and Freda Payne's "Bring the Boys Home" (written by Jann Arden) for other perspectives about the Vietnam War in music. (For additional references and statistics about soldiers killed in this conflict refer to the Vietnam Veterans Memorial, as well as the Vietnam Women's Memorial.")

9 Richard Gergel, *Unexpected Courage: The Blinding of Sgt. Isaac Woodard and the Awakening of President Harry S. Truman and Judge J. Waties Waring* (New York: Sarah Crichton Books, 2019).

10 Rene Evers-Everette, "Daughters Rising from the Dust: Children of the Civil Rights Movement Speak Out" (lecture, Wright State University, Dayton, Ohio, February 18, 2015).

11 The American Psychiatric Association (APA) defines posttraumatic stress disorder as "… a psychiatric disorder than can occur in people who have experienced or witnessed a traumatic event such a natural disaster, a serious accident, a terrorist attack, war/combat, rape or other violent personal assault.

In the past, some have described PTSD as 'shell shock' during World War I and 'combat fatigue' after World War II. However, PTSD does not just happen to combat veterans. PTSD can occur in all people, in people of any ethnicity, nationality or culture, and any age…." Ranna Parekh, M.D., M.P.H., American Psychiatric, Association, January 2017, https://www.psyciatry.org/patients-families/ptsd/wht-is-ptsd.

12 Sarah Collins Rudolph, "Daughters Rising from the Dust," (lecture, Wright State University, Dayton, Ohio, February 18, 2015).

13 Spike Lee, dir., *4 Little Girls*, (New York: HBO Home Video, 2000, DVD).

14 Condoleezza Rice, *Extraordinary, Ordinary People* (New York: Crown Archetype), 98.

15 Lee, "4 Little Girls."

16 John Archibald, "Here's Why Church Bomber's Parole was Important," *al.com*, August 3, 2016, http://www.al.com/opinion/index.ssf/2016/ 08/crowd-protests-bombers-release.html.

17 Kevin Sack, "Survivor of Birmingham Church Bombing Has Few Expectations for Trial," *The New York Times*, April 24, 2001.

18 Sarah Collins Rudolph, "Four Women from Birmingham" (lecture, Wright State University, Dayton, Ohio, March 11, 2004).

19 "Four Women" (lecture, W.S.U., Dayton, Ohio, March of 2004). Dr. Roberta Boyd, Assistant dean in the College of Liberal Arts at W.S.U., hosted the event. Marsha Bonhart, former news anchor for WDTN-TV2, moderated the panel.

20 "To Discuss Racial Situation," AP, *Register*, September 19, 1963.

21 Ibid. Joseph D. Bryant, "'Fifth Little Girl' Remains Relatively Unknown in Birmingham," *Birmingham News*, November 23, 2012, [21] https://www.al.com> spotnews>2012/11>fifth_little_girl_still_relati.html.

22 Sack, "Survivor of Birmingham Church Bombing."

23 Sarah Collins Rudolph, correspondence with Tracy Snipe, June 12, 2014.

24 Sarah Collins Rudolph, "The Message," (Lecture, First African Methodist Episcopal Church, Seattle Washington, June 12, 2012).

25 This line is a variation of the lyrics to the hymn, "Blessed Assurance," written by Fanny Crosby and composed by Phoebe Knapp.

26 Ariel Worthy, "Sarah Collins Rudolph Revisits 16th Street Baptist Church and Recalls the Moment the Bomb Went Off, " *The Birmingham Times*, September 14, 2017, https://www.birminghamtimes.com/2017/09/sarah-collins-rudolph-

revisits-16th-street-baptist-church-and-recalls-the-moment-the-bomb-went-off/; "In New Book, 'Fifth Little Girl,' Describes First Hand Account of Horrific Church Bombing," *Birmingham Times*, September 14, 2017, www.birmingham times.com/2017/09/fifth-little-girl-gives-first-hand-account-of-horrific-bombing.

Chapter 2. My Favorite Things

When I get to be a composer
I'm gonna write me some music about
Daybreak in Alabama — Langston Hughes[1]

When I was a child, I spake as a child, I understood as a child, I thought as a child. 1 Corinthians 13:1(KJV)

I had a relatively happy childhood in Alabama, until life forced me to grow up quickly one cruel September day.

My parents, Alice Jones and Oscar Lee Collins, Sr., joined hands in holy matrimony, enjoying many happy years together before *that* tragic day. Mom and Dad were my role models. My parents helped to mold me into the woman that I am today. Mama was from Marion, Alabama, while my father was born in Dotham, Alabama. After marriage, God blessed them with eight children. In fact, Mama later told us that she had fourteen kids. However, six of them died during infancy or due in part to miscarriages. Aside from Addie Mae, I had four other sisters—Addie Bea, Flora Bea, Junie Mae and Janie Mae as well as two older brothers, Roy Lee Collins and Oscar Lee Collins, Jr. Please don't get Addie Bea (the first-born child and my oldest sister) confused with the younger Addie who was like my best friend.

I was born in Birmingham, Alabama on November 10, 1950. I was the baby of the family, while Addie was the "knee baby." Now you may be wondering why Mama named so many of her girls either "Mae" or "Bea." Well that is a good observation. As I seem to recall, Mama told my inquiring sister, Junie, "MAY BE someday you will all grow up to be somebody?" I must have been the odd girl out because my name was simply Sarah Jean. My nickname was "Sa-Jean." My sisters used to say my name fast. In fact, we all had shortened, hyphenated nicknames.

Growing up, all of my sisters had a special gift or something that made each one of them unique. Addie Bea, the eldest, could sew well. Funny thing is I never saw her sewing on a machine. She would simply cut patterns out and make a dress by hand. She would be so patient, sitting in a room and sewing. She could also make blouses by cutting patterns from newspapers. When she finished, a lovely dress or blouse was often the result. Speaking of beauty, Addie Bea had the most radiant complexion. I thought that she was just gorgeous – that is before life's circumstances overcame her. When I think back on the church bombing, I cannot help but reflect on Addie Bea's life, too. The bombing did not injure her "physically," yet the blast at the 16th Street Baptist Church left her devastated too.

My second oldest sister, Flora, was like the mother figure for us. She had different responsibilities. Sometimes Flora prepared us for church on Sundays. She would press or straighten our hair. She was always ready to give Mama a hand to help us get ready for different events like the circus, Christmas plays and different activities at school.

There were two sets of children. Junie was the oldest of the younger set that included Janie, Addie, and me. Playing the piano was her gift. She learned how to play the piano as a youngster. Junie used to play for the devotion at the 16th Street Baptist Church on Sundays. As the older sister, she often insisted that I fan her, until she drifted off to sleep during those muggy summer nights in Alabama. Eager to please at that stage of life, I agreed. When we were kids, two sisters slept at the head of the bed: the other two at the foot.

"Are you sleeping yet?" I would ask Junie.

"No," she would murmur, as sleep grudgingly snuck up on her. "Keep fanning Sarah." When she finally drifted off to sleep, I could finally get some sleep too.

Janie was about a year younger than Junie. I always thought of Janie as the "pretty sister." She knew how to match her clothes to make herself look great despite our limited wardrobe. Moreover, Janie styled her hair as if she had attended beauty school. She was good at sewing, too.

Always laughing, as a child she kept me in a joyful mood; as adults, we would call each on the telephone and talk for hours at a stretch.

Playing baseball and drawing were some of Addie's favorite activities, while watching Westerns on television like *Gunsmoke* was one of my favorite interests. But that was no automatic deed. I grew up in a home where I battled with my siblings to determine who would get to watch shows like *Oklahoma* and later *The Sound of Music*. Some nights, I lost the battle but won the war; at least *Oklahoma* was a western.

I was closest with my sister Addie. While growing up, we were, like *birds of a feather*, as people say. We were the two youngest kids in the Collins family. I absolutely adored my sister and wanted to be just like her. I wanted to wear glasses because she did. Addie was popular at school and struck up friendships with people easily, however I was shy. Kinda' on the quiet side.

My oldest brother Oscar Lee was the person Mama called on to discipline us, occasionally. When someone got out of line and needed a spanking, she summoned Oscar who was always happy to comply. Oscar had other skills too. He was a good mechanic. The funny thing is he never attended school for this trade. When we were growing up, Mama often called Oscar when someone's car broke down and that person needed help. Sadly, we lost him years ago due to an illness; may his soul rest in peace.

I rarely saw my brother, Roy, since as a young adult he relocated to Buffalo, New York. Later in life, we would often converse on the telephone. While growing up, in Birmingham, sometimes Roy worked with Dad, helping him bus tables, to earn money. Roy was a loveable brother. He doted on Addie. But she looked out for him too. She was the only one of us girls daring enough to open the door for him late at night, even after Momma strictly forbade us. Addie was unflappable, daring at times. Still, Mama could be as tough as nails on us girls, even into adulthood.

As children, we lived in a neighborhood called Smithfield. We never had any trouble or difficulty organizing a baseball team since over twenty-five kids lived in our community. One of our neighbors was a postal worker. Most of the adults in our neighborhood worked in various plants or factories in the city of Birmingham. Some of the women were domestic workers or maids. Mama worked on a variety of jobs. Since our community was close knit, when she was not working on a job outside of the home, at times Mama watched the kids in the neighborhood. If they got out of line, she would physically discipline them and tell their parents after the fact.

We lived in a small-frame, one-story wooden house. Separated by about seven feet, most of the houses in our neighborhood were of a similar design. People in our tightknit community built their homes close together. We could walk on the porch and see clear through the house across the street; folks called them shotgun houses. Our house was near Legion Field Stadium. The street leading to our home at 233 6th Court West was unpaved for years. People would park their cars in our yard just before going to football games. Folks made time for leisure events. On the other hand, work was essential for most adults in our community.

My father used to bus tables at Joy Young's, a restaurant in Birmingham, Alabama that sold Chinese food. This was the only job he had when I was young. My older brothers and sisters do not remember him working anywhere else. Dad worked about two miles away from where we lived. Famous for his work ethic, as a kid, I do not recall him taking a day off. Though he never made a ton of money, he provided for us. Between his steady work and Mama's jobs, we made it by.

Daddy loved all his children; however, he had a special place in his heart for us girls. My sisters and I nearly fell over with laughter when he tried to spank or discipline us. But the outcome was different whenever Mom took up this task. She could be stern with us, an even Dad at times. Mama "ran a tight ship," as the expression goes. Anyway, Daddy used the tiniest switch imaginable. He often came home from work with candy in his pockets. When Dad walked through the door, he often gave us a piece of candy. Later, he would go sit on the porch and smoke his cherished pipe. Don't ask me to remember what brand. I cannot recall. Mama didn't smoke but sat next to him on the porch many evenings, until his habit became unbearable.

As I indicated earlier, Daddy was hardworking and dependable. He worked long days. Busing tables could be physically taxing at times. It left him little time for leisure. His wages were modest. Along with his steady salary, his tips helped to support the household and buy us clothes and shoes. Things were not too expensive. It did not take much to pay for a pair of Buster Brown Shoes. Daddy, or usually Mama, had to measure our feet in advance. Merchants did not allow "Colored" folks to try on shoes in the store, even though folk bought them with their hard-earned wages.

No matter how much money Daddy earned, it was never quite enough, so mother made aprons and potholders for my younger sisters and me to sell — all to help make ends meet. Mama was a talented seamstress. She often made our clothes, too. But anyway, we would go from door to door asking people if they wanted to buy aprons or potholders. We sold the potholders for 35 cents and aprons for 50 cents, but we netted 75 cents for the bibbed aprons.[2] Mama would iron or press these items. I remember how she would take her time and neatly put them into a shoebox. She was so very patient in terms of getting everything ready. It was not easy work, but we tried our best. Addie in particular enjoyed selling the aprons and often looked forward to the task; as I have explained before, we sold a lot of them.[3] Most of all, I just loved being together with Addie and my sisters.

Being the last child came with its share of benefits. Once, I went with Mama to Florida to visit my grandparents. It was one of my favorite trips. I was about five years old when we went to Florida to visit her mother-in-law. I was the only child who accompanied Mama since I had not started school yet. She left Addie Bea in charge of the house while we were gone. Mama fried chicken the night we left to take the train, so we would have a good meal. When we arrived, I met my grandparents for the very first time. They were so nice. Within days, we went shopping, fishing, and even picking oranges. We also attended church with them. I just loved being in Florida.

During this trip, one day I got sick. A big sore grew on my neck. They took me to the local doctor who instructed Mama to give me medicine and keep me at home on bed rest for three days. When the time was up, my neck felt better. I couldn't wait to go outside to play.

My grandparents had their house built on stilts. Since I was so short, I could easily stand under the house. I would walk around, staring at the ground in amazement. There were pennies everywhere. Like pennies from heaven! I would pick them up and excitedly run inside to show Mama and Grandma Eloise and Grandpa Ike what I had found. I oftentimes had my own money to spend when we went to the grocery store because of this hidden treasure.

Figure 9 Eloise Collins, grandmother. Courtesty of Sarah Collins Rudolph

Our time in Florida passed so quickly. Before we left for Alabama, I kissed my grand-parents goodbye, not knowing that would be the last time I would see them. When we got home, everyone was glad to see us, showering us with kisses. A-Bea had the house so warm and cozy. She could get a fire started in the fireplace every bit as good as Mama. We were plum tired after the long train ride and went straight to bed.

After breakfast, my siblings gathered around to inquire about our trip. I was eager to give them all of the juicy details. If only you could have seen their excited faces. Mama finally told them to put on their coats and go to school before it was too late. I was one sad trooper.

I enjoyed rehashing everything. I hated to see my siblings leave, but I knew that I would be going to school soon. Most of my brothers and sisters had attended Bruenetta C. Hill School, which was about seven blocks away from our house. Graymont Elementary was closer by our home but *colored* students couldn't go there until the fall of '63.

But anyway, when Addie was in the first grade, she came home with the following note: "Please have your child prepared to take pictures the next day." Everyone in the first grade had to have a school picture taken. Mama practically stayed up all night cutting out a pattern and sewing. She made Addie the prettiest pink dress. The next morning, she fixed her hair too. She put a bang in the front of her head and two plaits or braids in the back. Addie looked lovely

"How do I look today Sarah," Addie asked me?

"I wish I had a camera to take a picture of you myself," I said. She started laughing. Addie was beautiful on the inside and outwardly.

Mama got the pictures about two weeks later. When I saw Addie's photo all I could do was smile. Addie was pleased. too. Almost at the same time, Mama and I both chimed in "'Addie, you're so pretty.'"

When my siblings returned home from school, they wanted to see Addie's picture too. Everybody wanted a picture, so Mama carefully cut from the picture sheet, giving each one of us the prized possession. Such Kodak, fun-filled moments seem like light years away now.

In September of 1956, my brother Roy enrolled me in school at Brunetta. I could barely contain my excitement. I no longer had to stay at home, while my brothers and sisters went to school without me.

After I started school, Addie and I established a routine. We would eat together. Her class ended before mine, so Addie waited for me at the flagpole. We walked home together, sometimes in the rain. Once it rained so hard that a wool sweater that I wore to school shrank. We laughed about it all the way home. Mama didn't fuss at me. Instead, she told me to take my sweater off and put on a jacket so that Addie and I could go outside to put coal in our shed. We gladly complied.

When administrators closed school for the Christmas break, Mom and Dad made sure we had a wonderful time on Christmas Day. They bought us toys, clothes, and shoes. They bought the girls skates, dolls, Mr. Potato Head and clothespins; the boys often got bb guns or trucks. We got clotheslines too, which were like long shoestrings; we creatively tied them from one bedpost to another to hang out our doll clothes.

We never had a Christmas tree, yet we had some of the loveliest holidays that you can imagine. Mama would put our names on brown paper bags, filling them up with oranges, apples, raisins, nuts, presents, and of course, candy. On Christmas Day, we could barely sit still long enough to eat breakfast. We were so excited and wanted to see what was in our bag. One year, when I looked in mine, I saw some plastic clothespins. There was no clothesline with them.

"What happened to the clothesline?" I asked Mama.

"Santa got them stuck up in the chimney when he came down."

"There is no such a man called Santa Claus," I blurted out.

"Since you're the youngest and you know there is no Santa Claus, I guess won't have to play Santa anymore," Mama promptly said.

I realized that I had talked a little too much. True to form, Mother kept her word and did not buy us any more toys for future Christmas celebrations. Instead, she filled our bags with clothes, shoes, ribbons, and whatnots or supplies we needed for school and church. After that outburst, it is a wonder that Mama did not fill my bag with coal.

Every month Mama ordered a ton of coal and a large chunk of ice to keep the food cold in the icebox. Vendors sold ice for twenty-five cents, while a ton of coal costed about a dollar. They would dump the coal in front of the house. We filled our little red wagon with coal and carried it to the shed in our backyard, as we did the day the mishap occurred with my sweater. It took about an hour to move the coal. It took a little longer that day because the wheel came off the wagon. In the past, Daddy fixed such repairs. He came outside to see if he could repair the stripped-down wheel.

We had unintentionally stripped the wheel by overusing it. Daddy could not repair it, so Mama asked a neighbor if we could borrow their wagon. Neighbors looked out for each other, which saved the day.

When we returned home after our chores, Mama often had hot water on the stove for us to use to bathe with at night. We relied on this method because at times we didn't have running hot water.

On the weekends, we cleaned the house and gathered the wood Dad had chopped up and completed other chores, while getting ready for church. Daddy bought wood from a place called the Wood House. The owners delivered our supply on Saturdays mornings. My parents used the wood to get the fire started, but coal kept the fire burning.

Sundays were like the main event in our household. We would help Mama with the laundry and starched our 'stick-out slips' in preparation; my sisters and I came up with that name because the slips made our dresses stick out when we wore them. We made the starch from flour. Mama got our clothes ready, usually on Saturdays. Sometimes she made matching outfits for the girls. But we often wore Buster Brown shoes, not exactly my favorite choice. Mama often bought our shoes one size larger, so they would last longer. Moving on, the final addition to our outfits was ribbons; they added sizzle, pizazz to any plain Jane outfit. We placed the iron on top of the stove burner to heat them up. We had to be careful. Because if the iron got too hot, the ribbons would burn.

I grew up in the 16th Street Baptist Church. As I recall, our father proposed that we attend this church, although Daddy wasn't a regular. [4] Located in downtown Birmingham, our church had a one of the largest black congregations in the city. Like other congregations, the building had ample space in the basement; churches often served as the center for social gatherings. Doctors, lawyers, and teachers attended our church. In the past it hosted famous leaders such as W.E.B. DuBois, Booker T. Washington, Ralph Bunche, Mary McCloud Bethune, and Paul Robeson. Occasionally, guest speakers still address the assembly.

Figure 10. Sixteenth Street Baptist Church. National Parks Service

Our Mother was a churchgoing, spirit-filled woman. Mass meetings aside, she usually went to went to the 16th Street Baptist Church about twice a month but rarely, if ever, attended Sunday school. I'm not sure if Dad was ever officially a member of the congregation.

Though my parents worked hard for a living, our family was one of the least well-off families in the congregation. Not everyone looked down on us, but we knew that some members did. There were other drawbacks. Whenever something happened, usually one of the Sunday school teachers would blame it on a Collins' kid. We took the fall for everything, seemingly. Whenever problems occurred, one of us usually got blamed. Several of Janie's friends can confirm, some people in the assembly referred to us as "the Collins church rats." I wasn't ashamed of my family's working-class roots. During an interview many years ago with *The New York Times*, I explained, "There were a lot of wealthy kids in that church and they looked down on us because we were poor."[5] Still, Mama sent us there without fail. We had to learn how to take the bitter with the sweet; the 16th Sixteenth Church was *our* home church. In fact, Rev. Fred Stollenwerck baptized me there when I was around ten years old or so.

We had good times there too. I enjoyed Vacation Bible School and the Easter Egg Hunts. I also liked watching Christian movies and going on swimming trips. We all sang in the junior choir. We enjoyed walking together to choir rehearsal on Saturdays. Until I began grade school, church-related activities provided my sisters and me with the outlet to socialize.

Going to church was a part of the norm as a child, but I found other things to do to keep me occupied, too. After we finished work on Saturdays, I would go out and try to find odd jobs. I often made money simply raking leaves. I would earn about a dollar raking leaves for five hours. I would also run errands to the store for the elderly people in our neighborhood. There was a nursing home around the corner from our house. I would go in to ask if anyone needed anything from the store. At times, several different people needed various items from the store. After I returned, they would each give me a dime. One lady even allowed me to bring back supper for her husband who owned a barbershop. Sometimes I also walked around Legion Field after a game in search of soda bottles to earn extra spending change. Usually, the local store gave me three cents for each bottle that I collected.

As I got a little older, sometimes I earned spending money cleaning homes and babysitting. I used to babysit for a white woman who would pick me up on Fridays. Her son had a developmental disability but was no trouble to watch. He usually rested while she was gone. Another lady paid me to watch her daughter, while she went out socializing. No matter how long I stayed, I only got a dollar.

In the Alabama of my youth, the skies weren't *so blue*. Still, within my spirit, I reach back to fond memories of yesteryear for solace, like playing a pickup game of baseball with Addie and friends, and getting ready to attend the 16th Street Church on Sundays. The sounds of music flooded our lives on that sacred day. Oh, such *precious memories*. Still, Mama ran our household with the military efficiency of a decorated, four-star general. She had little choice, getting four girls dressed up, on time. All the attention to detail that went into getting prepared. After getting our hair straightened, somedays my sisters and I added matching ribbons to our hair. Getting my hair press was trying because I was 'tender-headed.'

Traveling down memory lane, I also have flashbacks of hard times. I recall images of the police beating black people with 'billy' sticks; dogs biting folk who withstood the sting of water hoses that must have felt like painful *bee stings*. I've never experienced it, but some say the force from high-pressure water hoses, designed to put out fires, is excruciating. Yet we saw images of young people dancing in spite of the intense physical pain. It made me *feel sad* to see other human beings treating people like this. But neither the police, nor Bull Connor could so easily extinguish this burning fire. They used jails to try to contain it and to demoralize the people. But it only made the *young folks*, *marching with signs*, hold them up higher, determined to bring about the changes artists like Sam Cooke imagined. *I go to the movie* and I can sit anywhere now. In fact, several years ago, I was treated to a private screening in Birmingham, Al.

Yet, institutional racism lives on. Authorities rarely menace people with dogs or 'sikk' them on protestors who have faced armored-vehicles in Ferguson, Mo. and other American cities: No wonder it's led to 'Black rage.' [6] We channeled *rage* into protest. It was still difficult for me not to *feel so bad*, whenever others called us by hateful racial slurs. But we forged ahead.[7] We were standing up not for some, but *all* of our rights. 'Cause we were working on a plan that would lead to real *F-R-E-E-D-O-M.*

Notes

1 Arnold Rampersand and David Russell, eds., *The Collected Poems of Langston Hughes* (New York: Vintage Classic Edition, 1995), 225.

2 Chanda Temple, "Profile of the Victims," *Modern American Poetry*, in "About the 1963 Birmingham Bombing." https://www.english.illinois-edu/maps/poets/m_r/randall/birmingham.htm. (*The Birmingham News*. Online source)

3 Ibid.

4 Letter from Sarah Collins Rudolph to Dr. Tracy Snipe. Not dated (nd).

5 Kevin Sack, "Survivor of Birmingham Church Bombing Has Few Expectations for Trial," *The New York Times*, April 24, 2001.

6 Kory Grow, "Lauryn Hill Dedicates 'Black Rage' Song to Ferguson," rollingstone.com, August 21, 2014, https://www.rollingstone.com/ music/music-news-Lauryn-hill-dedicates-black-rage-song. (Along these lines, many can relate to the contemporary Grammy-award winning singer Lauryn Hill. She addresses freedom and racial equality in "Black Rage," a song Hill dedicated to Ferguson, Missouri.) This song offers Hill's wry interpretation of "My Favorite Things," originally composed by Richard Rodgers; Oscar Hammerstein wrote the lyrics. In 1960, John Coltrane would record his ever-popular cover of "My Favorite Things" along with the 'classic' Coltrane quartet.

Emory University historian Carol Anderson points out that scholars and political pundits have written extensively about the term white rage; Anderson had discussed and written about the "politics" of this term and our national elections, specifically from 2008 to 2016. She has also examined how this term applies to the immigrant community in terms of backlash, "the empowerment of racism," the 'mainstreaming' of white supremacy, and the meaning of racism. Anderson points out the need for dialogue.

For further reference, see NPR host Maria Hinojosa's interview with Carol Anderson, a professor of African American Studies at Emory University. "White Rage: Here to Stay," NPR, November 11, 2016, https://www.npr.org/2016/11/111/501728677/white-rage-here-to-stay.

7 Sarah Collins Rudolph, letter to author, dated April 25, 2014.

Chapter 3. Alabama

"It [Alabama] represents, musically, something that I saw down there translated into music from inside of me." [1]
- John Coltrane

"The whole is a frightening emotional portrait of some place, in these musicians' feelings.' If that 'real' Alabama was the catalyst, more power to it, and may it be this beautiful, even in its destruction." [2]
– LeRoi Jones (Amiri Baraka)

I was glued to my seat on the bus in Montgomery, Alabama. I could feel Sojourner Truth whispering in one ear and Harriet Tubman in the other ear.
— Claudette Colvin

About two blocks from my family's modest, one-level home was an altogether different kind of "world apart," as we lived within throwing distance from a white neighborhood called Graymont. We lived so close by this white community that we could see our distant neighbors running errands. I guess they could also monitor us closely too. During my childhood, Mama worked mostly as a domestic. She also worked part-time in health care as a nurse's assistant. Mother often wore crisp, white uniforms. I thought she looked so impressive, which fueled my early ambition to become a registered nurse. I never worked in the nursing profession. However, I wore white a lot too while cleaning homes later during my life. Sometimes, I stained my colored clothes while doing the laundry. In time, I gradually switched to wearing white clothes at work, almost entirely. White clothes were so much harder to keep clean, yet easier not to ruin. Anyway, Mama cleaned houses for two white women in Graymont. In this line of work, some clients insisted that blacks enter their homes through the back door.

It seemed like the grownups passed this mindset on to kids who grew up in an environment where racism and discrimination was the way things were. Children often acted out in public, as my sisters and I observed regularly when we went to the local grocery on Graymont Avenue. Mama would often send us to Kroger where most whites in the area shopped. Kids would stand behind us in line at the store and say mean things. We did not understand why they called us names like 'Blackie,' 'Black Sambo' or 'Nigger Spook.' No one ever scolded them or gave the children *the look* folks in our community reserved for kids acting out in public or in church, for instance. I wondered why the adults never chastised them; finally, one day it dawned on me why.

When I was a kid, the Kroger in Birmingham didn't employ blacks. My mother and a preacher by the name of Johnny Burrell, along with his wife, Mrs. Beverly Burrell, marched in front of the grocery store in protest. I picketed the store too, along with Addie, Junie and Janie and the Burrell children – Cara, Johnny Jr., and Randolph. Gradually, black folk shopped at this location in fewer numbers and the management closed this store; we couldn't prove it but had an inside family joke that Mama closed Kroger. As kids, we were in awe of her yet never doubted her concern for us. If only all grownups cared so much for children.

No matter where we went, my sisters and I had to be careful in the city. Danger constantly lurked, for little girls like us, as some preyed-on children in the "gallant South." I remember one day when Addie and I ventured out together to sell our aprons and potholders. From out of nowhere, a car packed with white men, probably returning from a game at Legion Field, sped by us. Suddenly, they threw trash out the window at us. We didn't know *what* their intentions were. Frightened to death, we fled for our lives. My feet couldn't carry me away fast enough. If I had wings, I surely would have flown away without looking back either, unlike the mystical Sankofa bird. But I could never leave Addie behind.

This terrifying event left us feeling crushed. We couldn't muster the willpower to go back out that day to sell anything, or even to play. We never permitted fear to dominate our lives; we never told anyone about that episode. However, Addie and I both realized that we weren't safe. As fate later proved, even *sixteen* blocks away from our home.

Manifestation

As I grew older, I started noticing many things that were not right in Alabama like signs that read "Whites only" or "Colored only." While the North and other sections of the country had their share of racial problems, local authorities hung such humiliating signs high above bathroom doors and other places throughout the city of Birmingham. One restaurant in the city served "colored people" at the side window, while waiters served whites on the inside. No matter how cold or rainy it was, restaurant owners served black customers at the side of the window. One of the Jim Crow laws enacted in Alabama stated:

> It shall be unlawful to conduct a restaurant or other place for the serving of food in the city, at which white and colored people are served in the same room, unless such white and colored persons are effectually separated by a solid partition extending from the floor upward to the distance of seven feet or higher, and unless a separate entrance from the street is provided for each compartment.[3]

After a while, the people began to organize rallies and stage mass demonstrations. Congregations like the Sixteenth Street Baptist Church played a major role as a staging ground. Eventually, "Bull" Connor, the Commissioner of Public Safety, stepped into the middle of the fray. Everything reached a boiling point in early May of '63 when firefighters turned high-powered water hoses on adults, teenagers and children, some as young as six. Everything came to a head on the so-called D-Day. Largely inspired by Rev. James L. Bevel, the children marched for two days in a row. Local authorities released vicious dogs on the young people at the very height of the Children's Crusade. The police 'sikked' dogs on peaceful protesters and arrested them, time after time.

Fearless Leaders

Rev. King was concerned about segregation throughout America and he came to Birmingham at the invitation of Reverend Shuttlesworth, founder of the Alabama Christian Movement for Human Rights (ACMHR) to deal with the vexing problem. Hundreds of people would attend mass meetings at local churches throughout the city. Rev. King addressed rallies at the 16th Street Church, a central gathering place. Mama often attended mass meetings there on Wednesday nights. They began right at 7 p.m. The people prayed, sang songs, collected monies, and equally as importantly, they strategized. I could not go too because the organizers held these meetings during school nights. A loyal foot soldier, Mama didn't miss such gatherings. I often feared for her safety at nightfall.[4] During the heyday of civil rights struggles, "Bombingham" could be dangerous to navigate at night and sometimes during the day. But Mama was confident, not easily intimidated by anyone.

Besides Rev. Dr. King, other leading figures like Rev. James Bevel really inspired young people like me. Bevel convinced leaders of the SCLC to involve kids in protests during the historic spring of 1963. He helped plan the "D-Day Campaign," which began on May 2, 1963.

Years ago, I was on a panel with Shirley Wesley King. She recounted this phase of our struggle from her viewpoint as an adult, looking back at her childhood in Birmingham, Alabama:

> I was 13 when the bomb occurred.... Dr. King asked Reverend James Bevel to come to Birmingham because of his work he had done in North Carolina in trying to desegregate lunch counters. And when he came to Birmingham, what he brought was his unique skill in working with young people. They [decided] that children could make a statement and reach the hearts of the people, to have us understand it was wrong...to deny people the rights that they had by virtue of their citizenship.
>
> I was among students who came from many parts of Birmingham, outside of Birmingham: Denson, Alabama; Brighton, Alabama; Fairfield, all around. Because when Dr. King came to Birmingham with Reverend Bevels, Reverend Shuttlesworth, and all the other leaders in the Civil Rights Movement, there was one goal, and that was to help the people to open up and accord to the other people their basic rights. We marched in Birmingham in the streets, not fighting against dogs, but having to contend with dogs set upon up by Bull Connor, the police commissioner. We fought fire hoses... as a group of people just trying to march and raise consciousness. [5]

I didn't march on D-Day, but I had marched and protested in the streets of Birmingham, ever since the earlier days of my childhood, along with my sisters and other kids; so, I can relate to Shirley's remarks, as I marched even beyond '63.

Sometimes adults did not know *all* the specific tactics the youth employed. Bevel had persuaded local radio disc jockeys like Shelly "The

Playboy" Steward and "Tall" Paul White to assist in the cause. The disc jockeys would play songs and use a sort of coded language or speech to throw off the Klan and authorities, while activating the young people. They played motivational songs like "Rock, Rattle and Roll" and "It's Alright," the hit song by the Impressions.[6] I really liked the singer-song writer Curtis Mayfield and some of the other inspirational tunes recorded by the popular singing group such as "People Get Ready" and "Keep On Pushin'" and "Move On Up."

At either rate, I listened to the deejays, too. One show aired on Saturdays, as I seem to recall. Still, I can honestly say that few songs stirred my soul or mirrored our circumstances like Sam Cooke's, "A Change is Gonna Come." The recording industry released the song in 1964, not long after his death. About five years later, James Brown would have similar impact on people too with the song, "Say it Loud — I'm Black and I'm Proud." A few years ago, several playwrights from Philadelphia invited me to the premier of a play about the '63 bombing that featured "A Change is Gonna Come." Child actors interpreted this musical or play about 'The Movement' in their own unique way. It all briefly transported me back in time.

In my opinion, the Sixteenth Street Baptist Church and events like the Birmingham Campaign were all central to this change, not to mention key leaders of the Civil Rights Movement. On April 12, 1963 (Good Friday), the police arrested Rev. King, Rev. Ralph Abernathy, and the Rev. Fred Shuttlesworth, along with numerous local protesters. The Southern Christian Leadership Conference (SCLC) and the Alabama Christian Movement for Human Rights (ACMHR) initiated the march. Jailers placed Rev. King in solitary confinement. Initially, he could not even call his wife Coretta who was in Atlanta, Georgia. In response to eight local clergymen, Dr. King wrote *Letter from Birmingham City Jail* during his stay in jail. In this essay, he addressed our conditions on the ground. The section where he discusses the response of a child to segregation rings so true.

I never personally met Rev. King, but I've always looked up to him. As a child, one day I literally glanced at him, up at the top of the steps of the 16th Street Church from a distance, as he spoke into a bullhorn. I deeply admired Rev. Dr. King. He had an anointed voice and message. He reminded me of Moses, the Egyptian prince who led the led the Israelites from out of captivity and slavery in Egypt to the "Promised

Land" or Canaan in the book of Exodus. While Dr. King led civil the movement, children became a part of the fight for justice, too. The police jailed busloads of youths in Birmingham, as people worldwide watched, amazed. I never skipped classes, but I took part in marches, even before the spring of 1963 and after they bombed our church.

I vividly recall marching with Rev. Fred Shuttlesworth. He amazed me. A complex man and a fearless leader, some folks described him as "the wild man from Birmingham." I compared him to Gideon of the Old Testament. On Saturdays, we collected signs and placards from his office (located on 4th Avenue and 16th Street) and marched peacefully. I was the only child in our family whom Mama took to these marches. Other kids took part too. We took an adult-like approach to protesting. The marches were no time for joking around. We would line up, side-by side in twos, and walk to the County Court House from 16th Street.

We prayed before marching and sang songs like "This Little Light of Mine," "Ain't Gonna Let Nobody Turn Me 'Round" and "We Shall Overcome," the movement's anthem.[7] The lyrics *shine all over the world, I'm gonna let it shine* to the song "This Little Light of Mine" moves me.[8]

Song of the Underground Railroad

Being a child foot solider in 'The Movement' would add to my insights about abolitionists and freedom fighters like Sojourner Truth, Harriet Tubman, John Brown, Frederick Douglass, Gabriel Prosser and Nat Turner: they fought to rid America of slavery in varying degrees, from using moral persuasion to taking up arms. Douglass' faith inspired him. Known for carrying a weapon, Tubman relied on spirituals to share her plans along the Underground Railroad. During our struggle in the '60s, singers also decoded and changed words to match local settings. SNCC Freedom Singers like Rutha Mae Harris, Bettie Mae Fikes, and Charles Neblett still perform together, occasionally.[9] Anyway, as *young folks*, we sang freedom songs like "If I Had a Hammer" to broaden our message and uplift our spirits. In a nod to this past, I once gave a speech at the Madame Walker Legacy Center in Indianapolis, Indiana titled "Journey to Freedom from Racism — Moving Forward While Looking Back; the Story of the 'Fifth Little Girl.'" In terms of "the conductor," to my surprise, the New Brunswick branch of the NAACP would present me with an honor referencing Tubman: Cynthia Erivo was slated to play her in the film *Harriet*; Tubman's image may appear on the $20 bill.[10]

We lived in a black and white world, defined by Jim Crow, which was a mind thing. When my sisters and I sold aprons and potholders, some whites kindly offered us sweets; others treated us with contempt and looked as us like we was viruses, untouchable. This mental warfare began long before our time. Born near the end of slavery, the educator Anna Julia Cooper spent her life advancing civil rights. I'm reminded of her because Dana King, director of the Anna Julia Cooper Education Center for Human Excellence, sponsored my talk at the Salem Baptist Church.[11]During this event and at others, I've remarked on segregation:

> People in the fire department, they put the water hose on the people. Put the dogs on the marchers. The only thing that we wanted... [was] change. We wanted to go in the stores and by our clothes and try our clothes on. They didn't let us try our clothes on...And we couldn't try the shoes on.... We were feeling like we weren't even human beings. We couldn't use the restroom. We couldn't even use the hydrant and get water. They got Black water, White water signs on that. And we wanted all of that changed.[12]

Milestones

As kids, we marched to see our city revise its laws. Our parents wanted to work on better jobs and to send us to school in *our* neighborhoods. We wanted society to recognize our civil rights, our human rights; to treat us like other Americans worthy of *R-E-S-P-E-C-T*.

In time, we landed a blow against segregation. On May 9, 1963, our leaders "reached an agreement with Birmingham business leaders to desegregate lunch counters, drinking fountains, and restrooms and to begin hiring blacks as sales clerks."[13] Officials announced the deal to the delight of many. It all became effective on May 10, 1963. But the resistance began promptly. Time and again, Bull Connors, a cardboard-like villain and his allies or other like-mined folk, struck back. Connors acted out on the behalf of the *good old boy network*. He was a symptom, not at the root of the racial problems in the 'Birminghams' of America.

Round About Midnight

As night fell, not everything was at ease in Birmingham, Al. For example, the Rev. Daniel (A.D.) King's parsonage was bombed on May 10, 1963. He was an unsung hero, too.[14] One of the statues in Kelly Ingram Park depicts the bravery of ministers like him. Anyway, he had a wife and several kids at home at the time of the bombing. Many believed the police was behind the blast.

Before the clock struck midnight, the Gaston Motel, which catered to black people and regularly housed leaders of the movement, was also bombed. A. G. Gaston was a very established black businessman in the state of Alabama. Some believed that the KKK plotted this attack, too. Riots later broke out following these bombings. About twenty-five hundred people were involved in the fierce rioting; dozens got hurt. Tensions were at an all-time high in our city. Some angry black folks burned businesses and fought with the police, too.[15]

This time of unrest unnerved people in Alabama and throughout the South, generally. President John F. Kennedy called on the troops to restore law and order. He considered deploying troops that were located at Fort McClellan near Anniston and at Maxwell Air Force Base in Montgomery, Alabama. The city of Birmingham was simmering during tense days and sleepless nights. The troops did not come to our city because things had calmed, so to speak. However, we could not depend on the "Commissioner of Public Safety" to ensure our *safety*, especially during that intense political period. The city was like a keg of dynamite. Were some officials eager to light the fuse, I wondered.

Bull Connor lost a challenge that went all the way to the Alabama Supreme Court. He had lost the election in a close run-off in April of 1963 but appealed. He was unsuccessful in the mayoral race against another local politician, Albert Boutwell who used to be more in favor of segregation but curbed his hardline views somewhat. The loss of his court challenge and the then recently created mayor-council form of government would force "Bull" out of office in late May of 1963. He stubbornly held on to the end, or the last fight. The court ruling left many folks in our city just thrilled. On the other hand, one of Connor's allies, Governor George Wallace, convinced the former commissioner to seek yet another office, and voters from the state of Alabama would later elect Connor to the state civil commission.

Governor George C. Wallace, a Pharaoh-like leader in my opinion, would continue to fan racial flames, especially during the spring and summer months of '63. Starting at his inauguration on January 8, 1963, Governor Wallace stubbornly declared, 'I say segregation now… segregation tomorrow… segregation forever.'

But Wallace did not stop there. On June 11, 1963, the governor stubbornly "stood in the schoolhouse door" of Foster Auditorium on the campus of the University of Alabama (Tuscaloosa), openly daring then Deputy Attorney General Nicholas Katzenbach. A small group of federal marshals and the Alabama National Guard had accompanied the attorney general. Governor Wallace had to stand down or retreat with the media in tow. He had little choice. Wallace was unable to prevent Vivian Malone and James Hood from gaining entrance to school that day. Later, word got out that Arthur Davis Shores, a well-known black civil rights attorney in Birmingham, was intimately involved in the desegregation court case at the University of Alabama.[16] Agitators bombed Shores' home about a month later on the night of August 20, 1963 in order to get back at him. No one was physically hurt. Still, it seemed like we were fighting against an entire system.

As youth, we were determined not to let nobody "turn us around." We had a stake in the future, an investment in the bigger picture, and we were ready to claim it too. There would be no turning back.

It was a time full of promise, yet danger lurked. Just as we prepared to enroll in school early September of 1963, some white protestors waived Confederate flags, up in arms against the court ruling to desegregate schools.[17] Bear in mind, all of this occurred within about a week of the historic "March on Washington" where Dr. King gave the inspiring "I Have a Dream" speech. His speech left many people throughout America, and around the world, feeling hopeful. Rev. King could see the day when black children and white kids would walk together, holding hands. I lived to see that day. Others dreaded such a time and took drastic measures to kill a dreamer, but his dream lived.

That school term began with a bang in Alabama. Instigators planted yet another bomb at Attorney Arthur Shores' home that exploded on September 4, 1963. One writer noted that the "bombing followed the peaceful registration of two black children in a previously all-white Birmingham elementary school."[18] Graymont Elementary was close by my childhood home. Mr. Shores had led a successful campaign to desegregate public schools in Birmingham, which obviously angered some folks. That bombing injured his wife, Mrs. Theodora Shores. The civil rights attorney was concerned. He had two school age daughters at home, Helen and Barbara. Shores took steps to ensure their safety. However, he was not alone in this regard.

Condoleezza Rice's dad combined forces with some of the other men his neighborhood to protect people in the community. Rice candidly writes in her memoir, *Extraordinary Ordinary People*,

> 'Eventually Daddy and the men of the neighborhood formed a watch. They would take shifts as the head of the two entrances to our streets. There was a formal schedule, and Daddy would move among them to pray with them and keep their spirits up. Occasionally they would fire a gun into the air to scare off intruders, but they never actually shot anyone. Really light-skinned blacks were told to identify themselves loudly upon approach to the neighborhoods so that there wouldn't be any 'accidents.'[19]

Overall, the situation was extremely tense in our city. The Sixteenth Street Baptist Church deployed a safety patrol. Meanwhile, people were furious about the latest bombing and started marching towards Shores' home. His wife, Theodora Shores, got hurt in the bombing. As Frank Sikora accurately recorded:

> 'Blacks reacted in anger, boiling out into Center Street near the Shores' home, in the city's near west side. Police hurried to the scene; shots were fired. A black man was shot and killed as he reportedly ran from a house firing a gun. That night, twenty-one persons were injured, including some officers who were struck by bricks, rocks, and bottles.'[20]

Anyway, President Kennedy indicated that he would send federal troops to the state of Alabama on September 10, 1963 to enforce the Supreme Court's earlier ruling, regarding the desegregation of schools.[21] To recap, one of the schools central to the debate about desegregation, Graymont Elementary, was actually located in my neighborhood.[22] On September 12, 1963, during a climate of fear and uncertainty brewing in our city, Reverend Shuttlesworth sent President Kennedy a dire telegram about this tense situation:

> DEAR SIR: FOR THREE STRAIGHT DAYS NEGRO STUDENTS HAVE BEEN ATTACKED WHILE TRAVELING TO OR FROM WEST END HIGH SCHOOLS BIRMINGHAM ALABAMA. PLEASE TAKE IMMEDIATE

STEPS TO INSURE ADEQUATE ESCORT PROTECTION SO THAT THESE CHILDEN WILL BE SAFE AND THE NATION SPARED ANOTHER POSSIBLE EMBARASSMENT OR TRAGEDY.[23]

In the wake of this toxic, increasingly highly charged atmosphere in Birmingham, Alabama, Momma gently woke us up to get ready for Sunday school on the morning of September 15, 1963.

Notes

1 John Coltrane describes his impressions about the state of Alabama on the liner notes of the album *Live from Birdland* (1964).

2 LeRoi Jones (a.k.a. Amiri Baraka) made this comment about "Alabama" on the liner notes of the album, *Live from Birdland* (1964).

3 "Jim Crow Law in Alabama during the 1930s," jimcrow1930.weebly.com/jim-crow-laws.html. Jim Crow laws in the state of Alabama also pertained to the practice of nursing, buses, railroads, pool and billiard rooms as well as "toilet facilities for males." (At the outset of her speaking engagements, Rudolph often reads Jim Crow laws in Alabama that were on the record books.)

4 Sarah Collins Rudolph, "Daughters Rising from the Dust" (lecture, Wright State University, Dayton, Ohio, February 18, 2015).

5 Dr. Shirley Wesley King, "Four Women," (lecture, WSU, Dayton, Ohio, March 11, 2004). Dr. Shirley W. King is the adopted daughter of Mr. Claude Augustus Wesley and Mrs. Gertrude Wesley. They also "adopted" or raised Cynthia.

6 For further details about radio programming and the Civil Rights Movement, refer to the following: David Marsh, "Shelly Stewart, Radio and the Birmingham Civil Rights Movement," Counterpunch.org, June 12, 2002, https://www.counterpunch.org/2002/06/12/shelly-stewart-radio-and-the-birmingham-civil; Pat Duggins, "Alabama Public Radio—'Civil Rights Radio,'" *Birmingham News/Birmingham Bar Foundation*, April 14, 2017, https://www.apr.org/post/alabama-public-radio-civil-rights-radio; Diane McWhorter, *Carry Me Home: Birmingham, Alabama: The Climatic Battle of the Civil Rights Revolution* (New York: Simon & Shuster, 2001). 359-361, 366-368 and 376.

7 Louise Shropshire wrote "If My Jesus Will," which became the ground basis for the lyrics to "We Shall Overcome," though other singers and folk artists like Pete Seeger, Guy Carawan, Zilphia Horton and Frank Hamilton are generally credited for writing this song. Isaias Gamboa's book *We Shall Overcome: Sacred Song on the Devil's Tongue* tells the lesser-known story about Louise Shropshire.

8 Eric Deggans, "How the Civil Rights Movement Transformed 'This Little Light of Mine,'" *NPR*, December 24, 2018, https://www.npr.

org/2018/12/24/679895682/how-the-civil-rights-movement-tranformed-this-little-light-of-mine. (Singers like Bettie Mae Fikes have provided first-rate covers of this popular freedom song. During the height of the civil rights movement, some singers reworded the lyrics to fit differing local struggles and conditions.)

9 SNCC Freedom Singers participated in a program in Selma, Alabama on activities marking the 50th anniversary of Bloody Sunday. The original members of the group included Rutha Mae Harris, Charles Neblett, Bernice Johnson-Reagan and Cordell Reagan.

10 Maria Fontoura, "Cynthia Erivo is Here to Save the Day," *Rolling Stone*, November 20, 2018, rollingstone.com/movies-features/Cynthia-erivo-widows-harriet-tubman-interview-758223/; Adrienne Lafrance, Juleyka Lantigua-Williams, Shauna Miller, and Gilliam B. White, "What Does it Mean for America to Put Harriet Tubman on the $20 Bill?" *The Atlantic*, April 20, 2016, theatlantic.com/politics/archive/2016/04/harriet-tubman-20-dollar-bill-justice/479199/.

11 Dana King presides over the AJC center and ASALAH. She is also a playwright.

12 Rudolph, interview (with Patty Satalia).

13 Frank Sikora, *Until Justice Rolls Down: The Birmingham Church Bombing Case* (Tuscaloosa, Alabama: The University of Alabama Press, 1991), 7.

14 "Alfred Daniel Williams King," The Martin Luther King, Jr. Research and Education Institute, https://kinginstitute.stanford.edu/encyclo pedia/ king-alfred-daniel-williams; Sheila Poole, "Documentary Focuses on Life – and death- of MLK's brother, A.D.King," *The Atlanta Journal-Constitution*, March 29, 2018, https://www.ajc.com/lifestyles/ documentary-focuses-life-and-death-mlk-brother-king/2IcJ.

15 Frank Sikora, *Until Justice Rolls Down: The Birmingham Church Bombing Case* (Tuscaloosa: University of Alabama Press, 1991), Ibid.

16 Shores represented Vivian Malone and James Hood in their efforts to attend the University of Alabama. In 1956, Autherine Lucy became the first black student accepted to this university. Shores also represented Lucy. In 1955, the previous year, Shores successfully argued on Lucy's behalf before the U.S. Supreme Court. The case was *Lucy vs. Adams*; For a more in-depth discussion of Shores' life refer to Helen Shores Lee & Barbara S. Shores (with Denise Georg), *The Gentle Giant of Dynamite Hill: The Untold Story of Arthur Shores and His Family's Fight for Civil Rights* (Grand Rapids, Michigan: Zondervan, 2012).

17 Frank Sikora, *Until Justice Rolls Down*, 7-8.

18 Eric Pace, "Arthur D. Shores, 92, Lawyer and Advocate for Civil Rights," The New York Times, December 18, 1996, https://www.nytimes.com/...arthur-d-shores-92-lawyer-and-advocate-for-civil-rights-html.

19 Condoleezza Rice, *Extraordinary, Ordinary People*, 93.

20 Sikora, *Until Justice Rolls Down: The Birmingham Church Bombing Case* (Tuscaloosa, Alabama: The University of Alabama Press), 8; Helene Shores Lee & Barbara S. Shores (with Denise George), *The Gentle Giant of Dynamite Hill* (Grand Rapids, Michigan: Zondervan, 2012), 46.

(Lee and Shores give a vivid description of the mob-like atmosphere following the bombing and the death of one of the protesters: "Before the night was over, police ended up shooting 20-year-old John L. Coley in the back of the neck, killing the young black man. Others were stabbed and seriously injured.")

21 Timothy B. Tyson, "About the 1963 Birmingham Bombing," *Modern American Poetry*, https://www.english.illinois.edu/maps/poets/m_r/randall/birmingham.htm. (From the Oxford University Companion to African American Literature, Copyright by Oxford University Press).

22 Jeremy Gray, "Amid Protests, Riots, 5 Black Students Changed Birmingham Schools Forever 50 Years ago this Week," al.com, updated October 15, 2015, https://blog.al.com/spotnews/2013/09/amid_protests_riots_5_black_st.html.

23 On September 12, 1963, Rev. F. L. Shuttlesworth, President of the Alabama Christian Movement Association addressed this urgent telegram to President Kennedy, transmitted from Cincinnati, Ohio. For further reference, refer to "The Bombing of the 16th Street Baptist Church – John F. Kennedy – Civil Rights Movement" File, https://civilrights.jfklibrary.org/media-assetts/the-bombing-of-the-16th-street-baptist-church.

Chapter 4. Moment's Notice

Jesus loves the little children
All the children of the world;
Red, brown, yellow, black and white,
All are precious in His sight,
Jesus loves the little children of the world.[1]

"And it shall come to pass, that whosoever shall call on the name of the Lord shall be saved."
—Acts 2:21 King James Version (KJV)

I remember that day.[2] On that morning, like almost every Sunday, our mother woke us up about 5 o'clock in the morning to fix our hair.[3] She would wash and then straighten our hair. However, on that particular morning my sister Flora did Addie's hair, so we met up with Addie later on down the hill.[4] After we got ready to go to Sunday school, as usual, Junie took the bus because she had to play the piano for the youth devotion service. We all walked about a mile to get to church—Addie, Janie and myself.[5] The 16th Street Baptist Church was about sixteen blocks away from our home. We lived on Second Street, and 16th Street was, you know, a good distance away.[6] By the time we left for Sunday school that morning, we were all in a playful mood, I should add, which is why it took us longer than the typical twenty-five minutes to arrive at church. But I wasn't counting the time.

It was a beautiful day in the beginning. Like high-flying birds, our spirits soared, as we joyfully made our way to church in a futile race with the slumbering sun. While we were walking that morning, we was havin' a good time.[7] We was playin' with Janie's black purse. It had a funny, odd shape, like a football. We were throwin' it like we was playin' football. We were just having a ball and laughing up a storm, running all the way to church.[8] That was the most fun we ever shared on our way to church. My soul was so light, *at ease*. I felt like a sparrow in flight – that is until the shadows later descended. As fate would have it, we were laughin' all the way, not knowing that this was the last time that we would joke or play with our sister Addie.[9]

When we arrived at the 16th Street Baptist Church, it was about ten minutes after ten. I'm not sure about the time because at the age of 12, you really don't pay too much attention to those sorts of things, you know.[10] Anyway, classes were already in session when we arrived that Sunday, much later than normal.

It was kinda on the warm side that morning, so we made tracks to the restroom downstairs to freshen up before class; no one else was inside the lounge when we got there. Janie left shortly. Having arrived late, well after 9:30 a.m., I still remember her parting advice to us.

"Y'all hurry up and go on to class, okay," she instructed us.

Afterwards, Janie headed straight to her class upstairs or in the sanctuary. She was fifteen and attended class with Junie, while Addie and I attended the same Sunday school class in the basement. We knew that classes would be over soon, so we tarried together in the lounge.

I don't recall exactly how long we were in the ladies' lounge. I do remember that no one else was in the lounge when we arrived that morning, or physically entered the restroom until the time Sunday school ended, and our three classmates arrived. Nobody could say anything to Addie or me because we were alone in the restroom. I've heard and read such stories in otherwise solid accounts. Some claim to have been in the restroom too, which is definitely, *not true*. Furthermore, nobody chided Addie and me saying, "You know what happen to hard-headed children who don't listen," as speculated.

We were excited because the 16th Street Church was having Youth Sunday for the first time, and it was going to be such a special day. The adults expected the youth to run the entire service. In other words, we were supposed to take up the collection, give reports, and sing hymns, usher, and lead prayers, too. Normally, Sunday school class began at 9:30 a.m. There was usually a brief pause before church service began at 11 a.m. Service usually ended at around 1:00 p.m.

I was overjoyed just being with my sister, although we arrived late. So many things between my sister Addie and I remained unspoken, as we sat on the couch. For instance, we did not ignore Janie's advice to go to our class on purpose. Our teacher, Ms. Collins, ran a tight ship in Sunday school. Arriving late would have annoyed her. Besides, I did not like how she talked down to and taunted us, nor did my sister.

She watched over us like a hawk, swooping down occasionally to pat us on the back for any good deed, however, she was quick to chide us too. Ms. Collins regularly drew unwanted attention to Addie and me, especially during the dreaded offering time. She knew that our family was one of the poorest in the congregation; still, we rarely gave enough, according to her severe measuring stick. Heaven forbid Addie and I only put four pennies in the collection plate!

"I know your Mama gave each one of you a nickel,"' Ms. Collins would say in a voice, dripping with scorn. '"But you probably went to the store across the street to buy candy with the other penny."

We wouldn't try to defend ourselves or say anything in response. We were, of course, embarrassed. Our parents always emphasized that we had to respect our elders. We did not dream of talkin' back to our teacher in fear that word would get back to Mama, much to our regret.

Deep down inside, I believe that Ms. Collins meant us no harm. However, as kids we felt put down. We would just sit there and take it. What was the use in complainin'? Besides, Ms. Collins already had a made-up mind. Some weekends, Addie and I would scramble just to earn an extra penny or two to put in the plate at offering time, hoping and praying to avoid the finger pointing, public shaming. There were nice people who attended our church too. Not all of the adults in the congregation were so class conscious. At either rate, people should be mindful of how they treat others, and especially how they talk to kids. Words have a lasting effect. Granted we were late, Addie and I shot hooky that day, really to avoid the high drama. Besides, we knew that classes would let out within the next several minutes. We were eagerly looking forward to the main event, the inaugural Youth Sunday.[11]

At one point, I got up and peered outside the tiny window of the lounge door, which stayed closed. Unless they happened to walk by almost exactly at the time of the tragedy, no one else could have seen the four girls or what was happening behind closed doors; otherwise, they would have seen me inside there too, but for a few precious moments.[12]

Within minutes after Sunday school let out, Carole and Cynthia entered the lounge first, followed shortly by Denise. I want to stress that no one changed into white robes. It was nothin' like that. Neither Addie nor I wore a white dress that Sunday. Momma had already made white robes for my sisters and me. She could really sew and passed this gift down to Addie Bea, Junie and Janie. Anyway, Addie and I only wore these robes when we sang with the choir. We left them at church, hanging in the choir room. We usually changed into our choir robes at church but did not get the opportunity to change clothes that Sunday.

I never gave a second thought about what we wore that dreadful day. Two of the four little girls, Cynthia and Carole, were *in white dresses*; Denise wore a lovely dress and sported black patent leather shoes.[13] According to some reports, she wore a purple dress that Sunday.[14] I just recall that her dress had sashes, on both sides. I do not remember the color of Addie's dress, or even my own dress, but in the "sanctified imagination," I see my sister wearing a crimson-red dress, signifying the blood we would shed in the sanctity of the house of worship.

There were about twenty-six children in Sunday school. Aside from the five of us, not another soul physically entered the restroom. None of the four little girls was primping in the mirror, as folk have repeated often. However, everything moved quickly.

I remember that Carole, Denise, and Cynthia immediately went to the restroom stalls; there were three stall or compartments, lined up in row.[15] By the time they returned, Addie had gotten up from the couch, and was standing near the window. I had crossed over to the other side of the compact room to wash my hands at the sink; in hindsight, it was the ceremonious washing of hands, for all of us.

Denise walked out first, followed by Cynthia, and seconds later, Carole. Before the girls had the chance to freshen up, Denise walked over to Addie who, as I said earlier, was now standing up by this time.

"Addie, would you tie my sash?" Denise asked.

Since the sink was facing the other way, I turned my head a tad bit, slightly to the right. I stood somewhat sideways, peering over my right shoulder, still washing my hands. By this point, the four girls were standing across from me near the window. They stood in front of the couch like soldiers at attention, real close together. Denise was in front of Cynthia and Carole, with her back turned towards Addie. We all watched intently but none of us actually got to see her tie the sash.

About the time Addie stretched out her hands to tie Denise's sash, I heard a deafening sound, almost like a freight train -- 'Rrrmmm!' Nearly frightened to death, I instinctively shouted out, 'Jesus!' Seconds later, I cried out for Addie, three times.

My sister didn't answer. Dazed and confused, I stumbled around blindly. I never fell down. God kept me on my feet, as I reached out my arms in vain for any sign of life.

I was only in the restroom for several moments, but it felt like an eternity. Debris and shards of glass from glass window, positioned just above the couch, had blown into my eyes, face, hair and chest. I was covered in dust and bleeding, too. In my mind, being young, I thought that my friends had run outside of the lounge over to the larger central room where we normally held devotion, leaving me all alone. After all, they were standing nearby moments ago. In the twinkling of an eye, I couldn't even feel their presence.

Moments later, I heard someone holler,' "Somebody bombed the Sixteenth Street Baptist Church!"

That's when I realized what had happened. Since the glass or debris was stuck in my eyes, I couldn't see anything. The explosion itself was ear shattering, but I heard that voice so clearly. I declare, I'm surprised the blast did not destroy my hearing too that Sunday.

All alone now, I was standing there in the restroom, just standing there bleeding.[16] Within seconds of the bombing, a man picked me up in his strong arms and carried me out the deep crater or hole that the blast created.[17]

I later discovered his name, Mr. Samuel Rutledge. He was a deacon at the 16th Street Baptist Church. I didn't know him at the time, but this brave soul leapt inside the church basement from the sidewalk, risking his own life. The bomb had destroyed the stairs outside leading to the basement. He heard the explosion, as he sat in Sunday school upstairs and quickly made his way outside. Mr. Rutledge later testified that he slid down the plaster in the frantic moments after the bombing.[18] His young son was attending Sunday that particular morning.[19]

"Where's Addie and the other girls?" I asked him.

"I don't see anyone else," he said.

Moments later an ambulance arrived on the scene and whisked me away.

Time raced by. I later learned that Rev. John Cross, pastor of the Sixteenth Street Baptist Church, tried to calm the people down during the confusion and hysteria. Looking at the damage and drawing on the Sunday school lesson about forgiveness, nevertheless, he deduced that "we should be forgiving, as Christ was forgiving, as He hung from the cross and said, 'Father forgive them, because they know what they do.'" [20]Speaking into a bullhorn, he shared this desperate message in his effort to try to calm everyone down. Meanwhile, unable to locate Addie and me in all the chaos and encouraged to leave, Junie and Janie later made their way home that morning.

Aside from Addie, three of my other sisters attended the 16th Street Church that Sunday. Actually, Junie was in the ladies' lounge but had left before we arrived later that morning. She departed because one of the elders, Ms. Mable Shorter, had chastised her for skipping class in the past. She provides her account in the upcoming memoir, *Saving the Best Wine for Last: Remembrances of the Sixteenth Street Baptist Church Bombing.*

Anyway, an ambulance rushed me to the hospital, washed in blood but alive. During that time, University Hospital did not normally treat or cater to black patients but made exceptions that day. At the hospital, I laid out on a cot, waiting for the eye doctor to come; looked like I laid there over an hour, just waitin'.[21] Before long, Janie came to check on me.

"Where Addie?" I immediately asked her.

"Addie's back is hurtin,' Janie said. "She's coming to see you soon."

As I lay there, I overheard Janie whispering to someone, perhaps a nurse, "'one of my sisters got killed in the bombing.'"

Janie didn't realize that I overheard her, and I didn't let on either.[22] I continued to lay quietly, in shock really. I swallowed back my tears in silence. I wasn't mad at my sister for telling me that Addie had injured her back. Cause Addie and I, we was real close, and Janie didn't want to alarm me any further.[23] She must have already faced the fact of what occurred, as she grieved the loss of a sister she loved dearly, too. About a year or two older, Janie was instinctively protective of Addie and me.

When the doctor finally arrived to check my eyes, I didn't mention the fact to Janie that I knew that Addie had gotten killed.[24] As I laid on that cold, sterile cot, all I could do was hurt inside. I couldn't grasp why anyone had to kill Addie, of all people, not knowing about the fate of my three friends, too.

After the bomb exploded, with the immediate rush of adrenalin, I had blocked out much of the physical pain. I was in shock, survival mode. But the numbness was gradually beginning wear off. While resting on the cot, I began to relive the burning or stinging feeling in my eyes and on my face and chest. This pain stemmed from the glass embedded throughout my entire body because of the church bombing. I still recall the cutting sensation that I experienced whenever I blinked, or even tried to open my eyes.

Later, they took me into surgery, and they operated on my eyes. The doctors explained to Momma that there were about twenty-six pieces of glass in my face, including my eyes.[25] The word if popped into my mind numerous times. *If* only the girls had moved over to the other side of the room. *If* I had looked straight ahead instead of turning to the right to see the girls the moment the bomb exploded, the glass and debris may not have damaged my right eye as badly. Frankly, I was lucky to be among the living.

Our lives, so carefree that morning as my sisters and I blissfully made our way to worship service, were shattered. I was with Addie from the time that we left home that morning to her last precious moments on earth. As dusk or sunset crept by, I had to face a terrible realization – my sister no longer among the living. Addie was dead.

Figure 11. Shelled out Women's Lounge at the 16th Street Baptist Church. Courtesy of the FBI.

Notes

1 Clare H. Woolston wrote the lyrics to the song "Jesus Loves the Little Children."
2 Sarah Collins Rudolph, "The Gathering: Victims" Family Panel" (lecture, Birmingham Southern College, Birmingham, Alabama, and February 2004).
3 Sarah Collins Rudolph, "Four Women from Birmingham" (lecture, Wright State University, Dayton, Ohio, March 11, 2004).
4 Ibid.
5 Sarah Collins Rudolph (lecture, F.A.M.E., Seattle, Washington, January 15, 2012.
6 Rudolph (lecture, First F.A.M.E).

7 Rudolph, "Four Women from Birmingham"; see also Debra Rubin, "Survivor Recalls Role in Civil Rights History," January 25, 2016, http:njjewishnews.com/article/29677/survivor-recalls-role-in-civil-rights-history.

8 Rudolph, "Four Women from Birmingham."

9 Rudolph, F.A.M.E.

10 Rudolph, letter to Snipe, August 4, 2010.

11 Sarah Collins Rudolph, (lecture POCWA or People of Color Wellness Alliance, Cincinnati, Ohio, November 19, 2016).

12 Sarah Collins Rudolph, letter to author, August 4, 2010.

13 Angela Tuck, "Little Girl Gone," *The Atlanta Journal*-Constitution," September 14, 2013, https:www.ajc.coms/news/little-girl-gone-rUqnlb11WBTfRpQua74 rnM.

14 Steven Levingston, *Kennedy and King: The President, the Pastor and the Battle over Civil Rights* (New York, Hatchette Books, 2017), 429

15 Sarah Collins Rudolph's correspondence to author, dated August 4, 2010.

16 Tonya Ott, Long Forgotten, 16th Street Baptist Church Bombing Survivor Speaks out, *Here and Now (NPR*), January 25, 2013, https://www.npr.org/2013/01/ 25/ 170279226/long-forgotten-16th-street-baptist-church-bombing-survivor-speaks-out.

17 Rudolph, "Four Women from Birmingham"; Ott, "Long Forgotten."

18 Alabama, Tenth Judicial Circuit Court, Thomas E. Blanton, Jr. vs. State of Alabama Trial Transcript, 2001. (Refer to Rutledge's testimony in Chapter 21.) Neither the defense attorneys nor the prosecution posed any direct questions to Samuel Rutledge pertaining to Sarah during the course of Blanton's trial. More importantly, readers should recall that no one ever file attempted murder charges on the behalf of the fifth little girl, as the statute of limitation passed or ran out.)

19 Diane McWhorter, *Carry Me Home*, 525.

20 Alabama, Tenth Judicial Circuit Court, State of Alabama vs. Robert E. Chambliss Trial Transcript, 1977, Birmingham Public Library, Department of Archives and Manuscripts, 67.

21 Rudolph, "Four Women from Birmingham."

22 Rudolph, "Four Women from Birmingham."

23 Ibid.

24 Ibid.

25 Ibid.

Chapter 5. Dear Lord

You go into church to praise God, and you come back out without your sister.[1] — Sarah Collins Rudolph

She aged that night
after
the day had gone
and left her with her thoughts
Is this America? [2]

They say it's some terrorist, some
barbaric
A Rab, in
Afghanistan
It wasn't our American terrorists
It wasn't the Klan or the skinheads
or them that blows up nigger churches…
They say (who say?) …..
Who? Who? Who?[3]

So many questions consumed me in the hours and days following the bombing that killed my sister. While lying in bed, I constantly thought about who bombed our church and why. Who could be so cruel? I wondered who killed Addie. She never harmed anyone. Addie was so sweet. Janie thought of her as a peacekeeper. At first, I didn't know the extent of our loss. Not one to mince words, Mama got straight to the point. "Someone put a bomb under the basement steps of the church," she told me, while we were in the recovery room. She continued, "It killed your sister and three little girls." Although heavily sedated, I cried outward now. Within time, shock gave way to fear, disbelief, and hate.

A deep sadness engulfed me over the next few days about the situation. There were the almost constant bombings in Birmingham: five within ten days in September of 1963 alone, largely in response to integration. One section of town was bombed so often people called it "Dynamite Hill." It seemed like it was just something people was used to — hearing bombs go off. *Why did they hate us*, I often asked myself, too? Still, we never did think that they would bomb the church up.[4]

In *The Gentle Giant of Dynamite Hill*, Helen Shores Lee and Barbara Sylvia Shores wrote a book about their father, Arthur Shores. Men and women like Shores, Rosa Parks, Jo Ann Robison, E. D. Dixon, Virginia Durr, Clifford Durr, and civil rights attorney Fred Gray, who wrote *Bus Ride to Justice*, all advanced civil rights struggles, especially in Alabama.

Many people living in Birmingham recall the church bombing. At the terrible sound of the explosion, James Edward Lay, a veteran and post office employee, ran towards the 16th Street Church. He recalled:

> Well, when I got on the scene, I realized then it wasn't an airplane crash like I thought it was.... I couldn't see nothing but people merely telling me to be careful. I realized then that it wasn't a plane crash. It was something more serious that had happened. I immediately started digging with my hand. I had nothing else....[5]

Condoleezza Rice who was in church at the time remembered:

> 'Services hadn't begun at Westminster that Sunday, but the choir, elders, and ushers were already in the sanctuary. I was there with my mother as she warmed up on the organ. All of a sudden there was a thud and a shudder. The distance between the two churches is about two miles as the crow flies. But it felt like the distance was next door.[6]

Within days of the bombing, Oscar came to visit and brought me a radio. The people on my brother's job took up a collection to purchase it. Their kindness lifted my spirits. After he left, I turned the radio on. The broadcast confirmed the news. All alone now, I cried out aloud.

Figure 12. The "Four Little Girls." (AP)

Figure 13. The "Fifth Little Girl." Courtesy of Sarah Collins Rudolph

I later learned the "four little girls" had fallen on top of each other, stacked like dominoes. Discovering them must have been agonizing for the members of a search party, which had formed almost instantly at our besieged church that grim Sunday.

Selflessness

Our preacher, Rev. John Cross, assembled a volunteer search party that included folks in the Birmingham-Jefferson Civil Defense Reserve. As shared by Shelly "The Playboy Stewart," James Lay later provided gripping testimony about the discovery made by members of this unit and churchgoers. Not wasting a moment, they dug with their hands, knowingly placing themselves in harm's way, if there was a *second* bomb. Rev. Cross testified how they initially felt "something soft" and used "a little more caution" before realizing that it was a body "and pulled that one out, and dug a little deeper, and there was a second one, and a third one, and finally, a fourth one.'"[7] Lay reconfirmed their grisly find:

> After being down on my knees about ten minutes, I was able to pull up a head, which was a female's head. You couldn't tell whether it was a human being or not from a dog's head. I realized it was human beings' body at that time.... I only had one that I was able to recover, and the ambulance was arriving about that time. They were able to recover the bodies, which was more than one.[8]

In the moments before the blast, my friends didn't even have time to attend to personal details. The act of washing my hands symbolically served this function for the group. They did not primp in front of the mirror, as reported. Maybe some speculated to fill in the void or to try to prove their witness. The thought of "sweet" girls dying so cruelly was difficult to bear; the violent blast ripped their clothes off. Addie's shoe was missing. Maxine McNair, the only parent of the deceased who attended church that day, said that I was crying and bleeding profusely.[9]

The bombing decapitated Cynthia. They found her head about two weeks later, according to her sister, Eunice Morris. Fate Morris, who was only 11 when the church was bombed, needlessly berated himself, thinking he "wasn't there" for his sister Cynthia." [10] Mr. Claude Wesley would identify his daughter based on a ring that Cynthia wore, while a piece of cement somehow lodged itself in Denise's skull.[11] Her child's bible remained intact in her purse, though the sheer force of the bomb shattered stained-glass windows throughout our sanctuary; except for the window displaying a likeness of Jesus the Christ: The bomb blew out the face yet the visual outline of the likeness still remained intact.

Figure 14. The Wales Window of the 16th Street Church, designed by John Betts from Wales. Photo credit: Keith Boyer

Johnny Robinson Jr. and Virgil Ware also died that day. A police officer shot sixteen-year old Robinson as he fled.[12] Part of a crowd angered long after the blast, 'Johnnie' had been throwing rocks at passing cars because some drivers yelled racial slurs at them. Referring to the ill-fated event years later, one writer began his article specifying, "Johnny Robinson Jr. was waiting for his sister to bring him a plate of Sunday dinner."[13] Later that day, Virgil was shot as he rode on a bicycle. His brother James was with him, as I was with Addie when she died. Known for his pranks, James thought that Virgil was faking. Two teens left a segregationist rally, feeling puffed up as they rode a motorbike on a deserted road. With his eyes closed, one of them shot Virgil, on a dare. The teens received suspended juvenile sentences, while the officer who shot Johnny was not convicted. All total, six innocent souls had been extinguished before twilight that unimaginable day. The precious lives of black children didn't seem to matter so much that 'Birmingham Sunday.' I just wanted to know why they had to do such a '"vicious thing as to bomb our church, our sanctuary, shedding innocent blood."'[14]

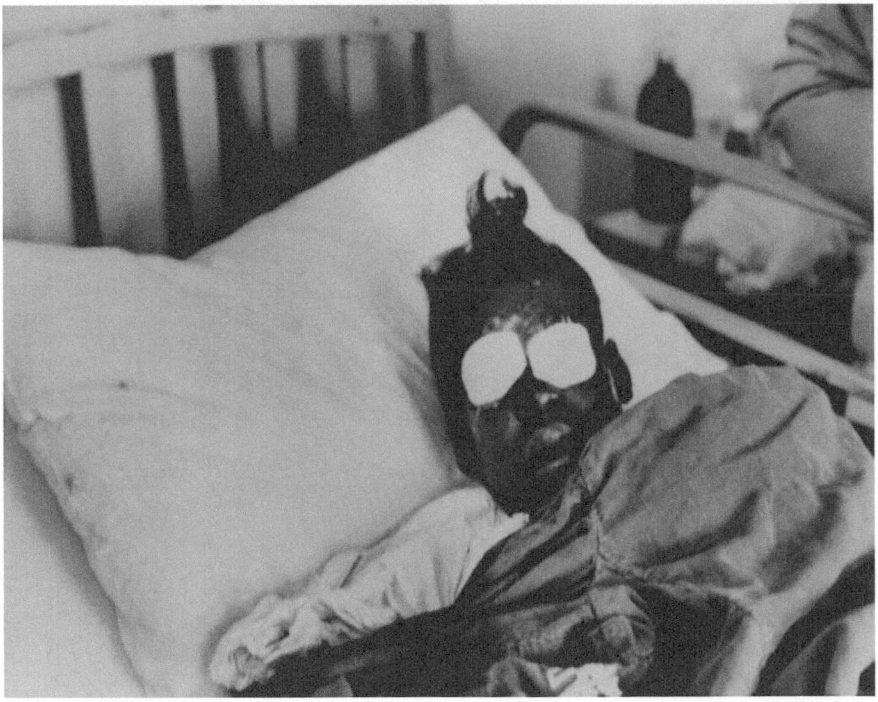

Figure 15. Sarah Collins with patches covering both of her eyes in a hospital bed. Printed in LIFE *magazine in 1963. Getty Images/Frank Dandridge*

Notes

1 Co-hosts Karen Miller-Medxon, Robin Young and Ciku Theuri interviewed Sarah Collins Rudolph on the radio program Here & Now – WBUR.

2 Haki R. Madhubuti (don l. lee), "Maturity," *The Real Dragon Project*, 1977, https://freedomarchives.org/Documents/Finder/DOC28_scans28.ral. dragon. project.1988.pdf.

3 Amiri Baraka, *Somebody Blew Up America & Other Poems* (Philipsburg, St. Martin (Caribbean): House of Nehisi Publishers, 2004), 41.

4. Rudolph, (interview with Satalia).
5 Alabama, Tenth Judicial Court, State of Alabama vs. Thomas Banton Trial Transcript, 227.
6 Condoleezza Rice, *Extraordinary, Ordinary People: A Memoir of a Family* (New York: Crown Archetype, 2010), 97.
7 Alabama, Tenth Judicial Court, State of Alabama vs. Robert E. Chambliss Trial Transcript, 1977, Birmingham Public Library Department of the Archives, 68-69. State of Alabama vs. Thomas Blanton Trial Transcript, 227.
8 Alabama, Tenth Judicial Court, State of Alabama vs. Thomas Blanton.
9 In 1963, an article appeared in print, describing reactions to the 16th Street Church bombing from the perspective of the parents of the four victims.
10 Eunice Morris, "The Gathering" (lecture, Birmingham Southern College, Birmingham, Al., February 2004); Jessica Ravitz, "Siblings of the Bombing: Remembering Birmingham Church Blast 50 Years On," CNN, September 17, 2013 (updated), cnn.com/2013/09/14/us/Birmingham-church-bombing-a…
11 Refer to exhibition of the Sixteenth Street Baptist Church bombing, formerly included at the Birmingham Civil Rights Institute.
12 Taylor Branch, *Parting the Waters: America in the King Years 1954-1963* (New York: Simon & Schuster, 1988), 891. (While Branch indicates that Robinson was shot in the head, numerous other some sources indicate that Robinson a police officer shot him in the back, as Robinson fled from the authorities.)
13 Jon Reed, "Virgil Ware and Johnny Robison: Families Want History to Remember Teen Boys, too," al.com, September 14, 2013 (Updated 01/14/19) al.com/spotnews/2013/09/virgil_ware_and-johnny-robinso.html; Irene Adair Newman's honor's thesis, "Six Notes: History and Memory in Poetic and Musical Commemorations of the Violence in Birmingham on September 15," also referenced Robison and Ware whose names were frequently glossed over, if mentioned, in most narratives about the bombing and related violence. The title of this thesis "was taken from a line in Michael S. Harper's poem 'Here Where Coltrane is.'" The phrase six notes refer to the six murder victims. (Newman wrote the thesis at the University of North Carolina.)
14 Refer to Rudolph's interview in the documentary *Road to Justice: Stories Behind 'Sins of the Father.'"* Made in 2002, the film "Sins of the Father" describes the 16th Street Church bombing from the dilemma of Tom Cherry who would turn state's evidence again his own father, Bobby Frank Cherry.

Chapter 6. Vigil

"Innocent blood has always opened the eyes of the almighty God and always will, even in our generation."
— Rev. Fred Shuttlesworth[1]

"How can you justify being nonviolent in Mississippi and Alabama, when your churches are being bombed, and your little girls are being murdered...[2]
— Malcolm X

"People are always talking about martyrs…But martyrs set themselves up to be martyrs. These children did nothing."
— Mrs. Alpha Bliss Robertson, mother of Carole Robertson [3]

From grieving families to a nation still in shock, the deaths of my sister and friends left people unsettled, sparking vigils, marches, and a wide array of reactions. The blast shook up our community and civil rights leaders who insisted that the President immediately take drastic actions.

Reverend King

In the hours after the bombing, Dr. King and other well-known black leaders would telegram President Kennedy. They were incensed about the murders of the four little girls at our church and raised the distinct possibility for even further violence. King wanted to avoid a bloodbath:

> 'I shudder to think what our nation has become when Sunday school children…are killed in church by racist bombs. The savage bombing of the 16th Street Baptist Church this morning is another clear indication of the moral degeneration of the state of Alabama…In a

few hours I'm going to Alabama. I will sincerely plead with my people to remain nonviolent…however I am convinced that unless some steps are taken by the federal government…my pleas shall fall on deaf ears and we shall see the worst racial holocaust this nation has ever seen after today's tragedy, investigations will not suffice.' [4]

While acknowledging the loss of my friends and the folks injured like me, civil rights leaders such as Roy Wilkins demanded an inquiry,

'[The] National Association for the Advancement of Colored People urges fullest use of federal anti-bombing statute for complete intervention of Department of Justice in Birmingham where four children were murdered and twenty persons injured in the dastardly bombing today of the Sixteenth Street Baptist Church.'[5]

The day after our church was bombed, President Kennedy issued the following statement, which many newspapers nationwide printed:

I know I speak on behalf of all Americans in expressing a deep sense of outrage and grief over the killing of children yesterday in Birmingham, Alabama. It is regrettable that public disparagement of law and order has encouraged violence which has fallen on the innocent. If these cruel and tragic events can only awaken that city and state – if they can only awaken this entire nation – to a realization of the folly of racial injustice and hatred and violence, then it is not too late for all concerned to unite in steps toward peaceful progress before more lives are lost. The Negro leaders of Birmingham who are counseling restraint instead of violence are bravely serving their ideals in their most difficult task – for the principles of peaceful self-control are lease (sic) appealing when most needed.

Assistant Attorney General Burke Marshall has returned to Birmingham to be of assistance to community leaders and law enforcement officials – and bomb specialists of the Federal Bureau of Investigation are there to lend every assistance in the detection of those responsible for yesterday's crime. This nation is committed to a course of domestic justice and tranquility – and I call upon every citizen, white and Negro, North and South, to put passions and prejudices aside and to join in this effort. [6]

Overall, Reverend King didn't just stop with sending telegrams or waiting for the President to respond. He offered condolences to the families, too. Emotions were raw. During this time, Roy had returned home to attend the funeral. He left Birmingham, Alabama in around 1961 to go and live with one of my aunts in Buffalo, N.Y. Like many Black people from Alabama, Roy resettled up North; other people moved to the Midwest.[7] Some left the South to escape from Jim Crow, while other people left searching for better jobs and living conditions, overall.[8] Anyway, when Roy returned home, he was angry about things. He loved Addie; we all loved her. I later learned about a conversation that he had with King who explained to Roy, "'Young man, don't do anything bad.'"[9] Maybe his message helped to calm my brother down. In my opinion, and in the belief of many others, King believed physical violence would not resolve anything and would actually stoop to the level of the people oppressing us.[10] In her autobiography, Rosa Parks gives an example of how King lived by this code:

> 'I remember one SCLC convention in particular. It was held in Birmingham, Alabama, one of the most segregated cities. That's where whites bombed a church and killed four little black girls. I was sitting in the audience, near the stage. Dr. King was closing the convention with some announcements when a white man from the audience jumped on the stage and hit Dr. King in the face with his fist, spinning him halfway around. It took everybody by surprise, and before anyone could react, the man was hitting Dr. King again…
>
> Dr. King yelled, 'Don't touch him! We have to pray for him.' Then he started talking quietly to the man, and he kept talking as the man was slowly led off the stage. There seemed to be more attention devoted to calming the man down than to looking after Dr. King…'[11]

From the example of my brother to his personal life, Rev. King lived by his creed. He visited each of the grieving families after our church was bombed that September. Some have observed:

> 'As a preacher, he was obliged… to face the families in funeral homes and to speak out directly over open caskets. Although King was falling into tactical paralysis… he made no effort to distance himself from the bombing, or to portray these deaths as incidental to the movement. On the contrary, he claimed the mangled bodies. On hearing of plans

for separate funerals, he demanded an explanation from John Cross, pastor of the Sixteenth Street Baptist.'[12]

Within a day of the blast, Dr. King persuaded my parents and other victims' families to have a mass funeral. Carole's parents had already made plans to hold her service on September 17, 1963 at St. John A.M.E Church. Reverend John Cross, pastor of the 16th Street Church, eulogized Carole. Rev. Shuttlesworth also said a few kind words about my dear friend at her funeral service.[13]

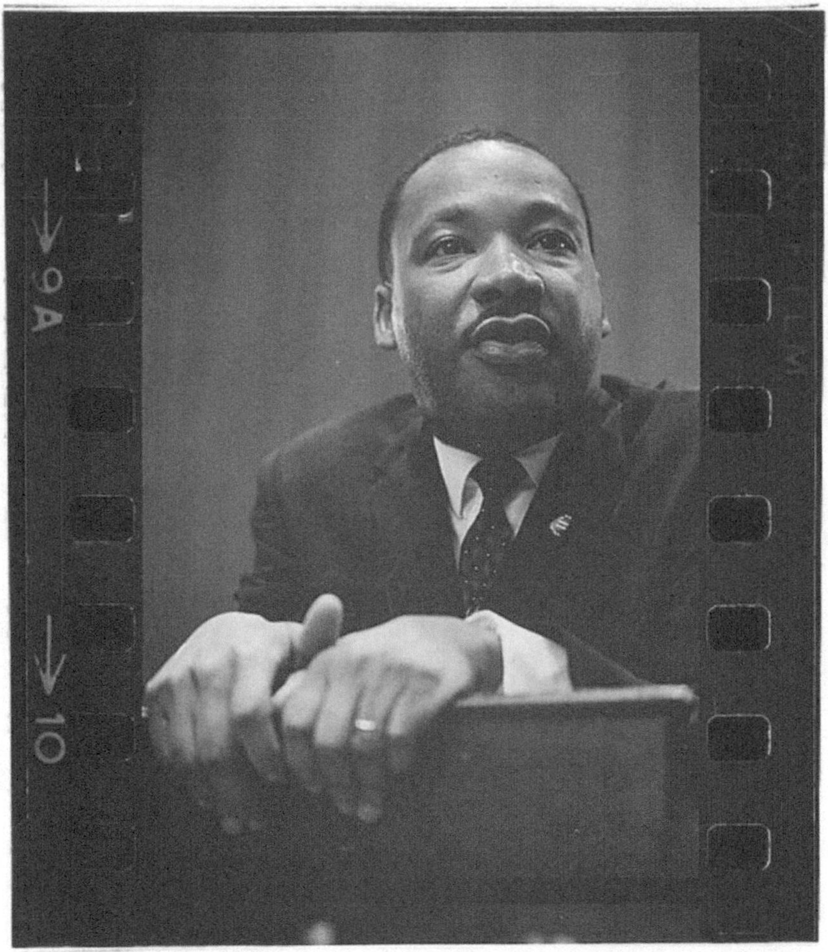

Figure 16. Martin Luther King, Jr. at Press Conference. Library of Congress/Marion S. Trikosko

On Wednesday, September 18, 1963, movement leaders held a joint funeral for my sister Addie, Cynthia, and Denise at the Sixth Avenue Baptist Church where Dr. King delivered the eulogy. According to estimates, about eight thousand people paid their respects; actually, over three thousand people were inside this church, and thousands stood outside.[14] Unfortunately, I couldn't attend their "homegoing" to say my goodbyes in person, however Dr. King's remarks helped me see Addie, Denise, Cynthia and Carole in a different light. He described them as "'martyred heroines of a holy crusade for freedom and human dignity.'"[15] He also talked about the meaning of their deaths:

> And so my friend, they did not die in vain.... And history has proven over and over again that unmerited suffering is redemptive. The innocent blood of these little girls may well serve as a redemptive force. That will bring new light to this dark city.... The death of these little children may lead our whole Southland... from the low road of man's inhumanity to man to the high road of peace and brotherhood. These tragic deaths may lead our nation to substitute an aristocracy of character for an aristocracy of color. [16]

Rev. King criticized folk who "sat on the sidelines," yet benefitted from the struggle; nevertheless, the decision to deploy children in the demonstrations remained controversial.[17] Other civil rights leaders like Malcolm X condemned the bombing of our church and racial violence in speeches and books like *The Autobiography of Malcolm X*, co-written by *Roots* author, Alex Haley. Within two and half months after his lengthy speech in Detroit, where he referred to the four little girls, somebody firebombed his house too during the wee hours in the morning in East Elmhurst, Queens, N.Y., as he rested at home with his wife Betty Shabazz and their children.[18] Sadly, he was assassinated at the Audubon Ballroom in Harlem, N.Y. the following week on February 21, 1965.

I did not hold hard feelings against Dr. King, or anyone in groups like the NAACP, Southern Christian Leadership Conference (SCLC), the National Urban League and the Congress of Racial Equality, which held a march honoring the six slain youths. The deaths of my sister and friends pained activists like Diane Nash who co-founded the Student Nonviolent Coordinating Committee. She was also involved in the sit-ins in Tennessee. Many years after the blast, she recalled her thoughts:

Figure 17. Congress of Racial Equality (CORE) March honoring Negro youth killed in "63 Birmingham bombing, All Souls Church, 16th Street, Washington, D.C. Courtesy Library of Congress/Thomas J. O'Halloran

Her views about the terror attack come from a place of resolve:

Well on the Sunday when the girls had been killed…my former husband and I, Jim Bevel, were sitting in Golden Frank's living room. There was a voter registration campaign going on currently, that we were involved in, and we were crying… we felt like our own children had been killed. We knew that the activity of the civil rights movement had been involved in generating a kind of energy that brought out this kind of hostility… we had one of two options. The first one was… we could find out who had done it, and we could make sure that they got killed…. And the second option was, that we felt that if blacks in Alabama had the right to vote, that they could protect black children. And we…chose the second option.[19]

The church bombing struck a nerve in people far away and nearby, which shouldn't be surprising. After all, 16th Street Baptist Church was also known as the 'People's Church.' On the day of the attack, Charles Morgan Jr., a white lawyer, gave a fiery speech at a segregated meeting of the Young Men's Business Association in Birmingham, Alabama.[20] He later fled for the sake of his safety. In 1963, *Life* magazine published his speech, along with a picture of me. His speech still really hits home:

> 'Who did it? .... The 'who' is every little individual who talks about the 'niggers' and spreads the seed of his hate to his neighbor and his son. The 'who' is every governor who ever shouted for lawlessness... It is courts that move ever so slowly and newspapers that timorously defend the law. It is all the Christians and all their ministers who spoke too late... It is the coward in each of us...'[21]

The bombing of our church impacted *everyday people* and the children, especially black girls like Sharon Robinson who was thirteen years old too at the time of the vicious racial attack; she is the daughter of Rachel Robinson and the legendary baseball player, Jackie Robinson, who famously wore number "42." Less than three weeks before the blast, she had attended the March on Washington with her family. Her father broke the color line in his sport but was dismayed after learning about the deaths of Addie, Denise, Cynthia and Carole. He later organized a rally in Harlem, N.Y. where Malcolm X spoke. As an adult, Sharon Robinson writes about her reaction to the blast in *A Child of the Dream*:

> 'Church bombings are not new. They are used to strike terror. But this attack is so evil. It happens just after Sunday school, before church services. And the victims are innocent girls around my age. The news breaks me down. I'm devastated and insecure. It makes me question the good feelings I'd had from the March on Washington and our wonderful jazz concerts. *Can we win this war?* I wonder.
>
> A few days later, Dad tells us that Dr. King gave the eulogy at the funeral service for three of the girls. He also says that the title of the sermon planned before the bombing was going to be "A Love that Forgives." I hear the words but can't imagine how that is possible. The pain this crime has caused the girls' families, Birmingham, and the movement is unbearable. I've never known this deep level of hate. Where does it come from?'[22]

On September 19, 1963, the President issued yet another statement urging folk to cooperate with the inquiry. (See appendix). The bombing impacted political figures and folk living abroad like Angela Davis who was born and raised in Birmingham, Al. Studying in Paris, France, she was horrified to read the news in the *Herald Tribune*. Absorbing the shock, she pulled away from her oblivious classmates to clear her mind:

> 'Carole, plump, with long wavy braids and a sweet face, was one of my sister's best friends….
>
> …The Wesleys were childless…. I remembered when Cynthia, just a few years old, first came to stay… She was always immaculate, her face had a freshly scrubbed look about it, her dresses were always starched and her little pocketbook always matched her newly shined shoes…. She was a thin, very sensitive child and even though I was five years older, I thought she had an understating of things that was far more mature than mine…
>
> My mother had taught Denise McNair when she was in the first grade and Addie Mae, although we didn't know her personally, could have been any black child in the neighborhood….
>
> No matter how much I talked, the people around me were simply incapable of grasping it. They could not understand why the whole society was guilty of a murder—why their beloved Kennedy was also to blame, why the completely ruling stratum in their country, by being guilty of racism, was also guilty of this murder.[23]

Angela lived in a section of Birmingham known as "Dynamite Hill" because of the bombings that occurred there. We were in grave danger all around Birmingham. People who live in fear or denial often resist change at *all* human cost. Local and state officials like George Wallace and "Bull" Connor played off fears and falsehoods. For instance, Bull had the nerve to suggest that protesters could be behind the bombing. Think about it: Why would folks want to maim, kill their own children?

Peggy Wallace Kennedy later wrote about the bombing, lamenting the loss of my sister Addie and friends, and the injuries that I sustained:

> Deep in my heart I believed they were like me, innocent children with probably little or no concept of the larger forces of history and hatred that would end their lives. They didn't choose the cruel honor of becoming martyrs for a righteous cause….[24]

Addie Mae Collins
April 18, 1949 - September 15, 1963

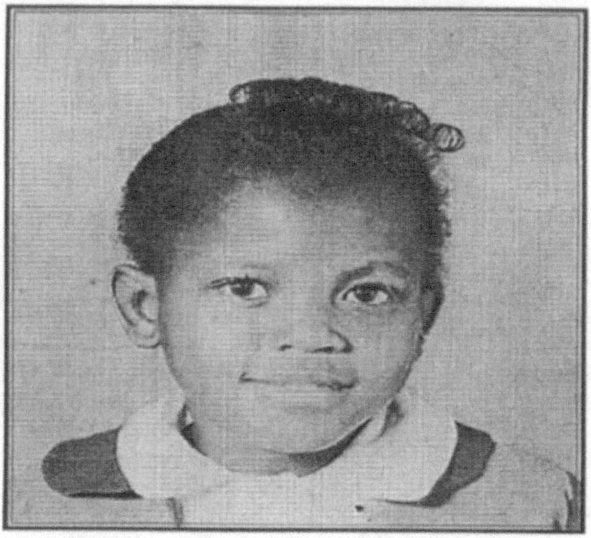

Figure 18. Childhood picture of Addie Mae Collins

In 1963, Peggy was 13 years old, like Virgil Ware, one of the boys killed that day too. "How would mama have felt if it had been me? And what would my father have done to the man that let it happen? Those were questions that I should have asked," Peggy writes in *The Broken Road*.[25]

About ten days before the bombing, *The New York Times* published an article that quoted her dad, Governor George Wallace: He insisted on the need for "a few first-class funerals." I guess he got his wish. But I would like to think that he was not wishing death on innocent kids.

Leaders should measure their words and lead more by example. Yet on April 4, 1968, a peacemaker was assassinated at the Lorraine Motel in Memphis, Tennessee. Dr. King had traveled there to lend moral support to striking sanitation or garbage workers. In '72, during his run for the presidency, Wallace was the victim of an assassination attempt, but he lived. The shooting left him paralyzed, confined to a wheelchair. Before he passed, Wallace visited the Dexter Avenue Baptist Church in Montgomery, Alabama where he asked folks for forgiveness.[26] Was he sincere? *Only God knows.* I only know that I missed my sister Addie.

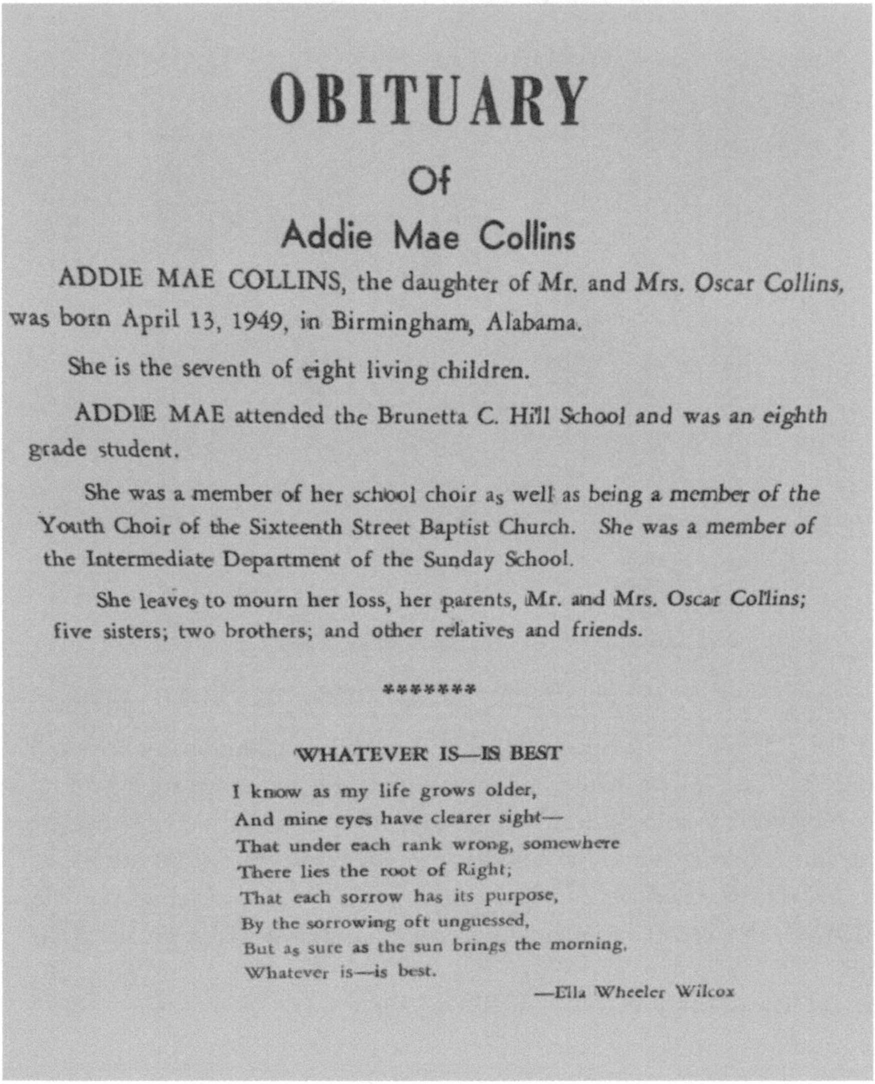

OBITUARY

Of

Addie Mae Collins

ADDIE MAE COLLINS, the daughter of Mr. and Mrs. Oscar Collins, was born April 13, 1949, in Birmingham, Alabama.

She is the seventh of eight living children.

ADDIE MAE attended the Brunetta C. Hill School and was an eighth grade student.

She was a member of her school choir as well as being a member of the Youth Choir of the Sixteenth Street Baptist Church. She was a member of the Intermediate Department of the Sunday School.

She leaves to mourn her loss, her parents, Mr. and Mrs. Oscar Collins; five sisters; two brothers; and other relatives and friends.

****

WHATEVER IS—IS BEST

I know as my life grows older,
And mine eyes have clearer sight—
That under each rank wrong, somewhere
There lies the root of Right;
That each sorrow has its purpose,
By the sorrowing oft unguessed,
But as sure as the sun brings the morning,
Whatever is—is best.

—Ella Wheeler Wilcox

Figure 19. Addie Mae Collins' Obituary. Courtesy of Sarah C. Rudolph

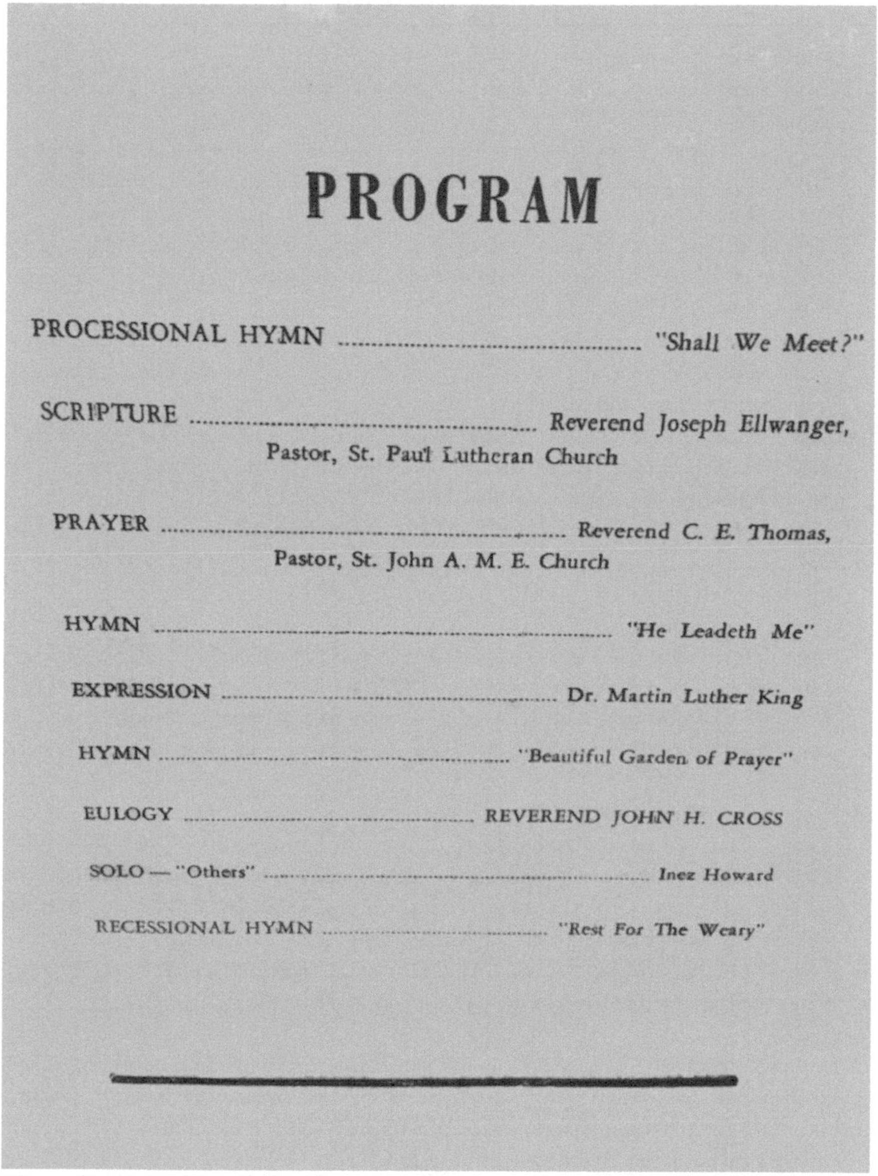

PROGRAM

PROCESSIONAL HYMN .... "Shall We Meet?"

SCRIPTURE .... Reverend Joseph Ellwanger,
Pastor, St. Paul Lutheran Church

PRAYER .... Reverend C. E. Thomas,
Pastor, St. John A. M. E. Church

HYMN .... "He Leadeth Me"

EXPRESSION .... Dr. Martin Luther King

HYMN .... "Beautiful Garden of Prayer"

EULOGY .... REVEREND JOHN H. CROSS

SOLO — "Others" .... Inez Howard

RECESSIONAL HYMN .... "Rest For The Weary"

Figure 20. Addie Mae Collins' Program. Courtesy of Sarah C. Rudolph

Notes

1 Remarks made by renowned civil rights leader, Rev. Fred L Shuttlesworth at the 40th year commemoration service of the Sixteenth Street Baptist Church bombing in Birmingham, Alabama, September 15, 2003.

2 "Message to the Grassroots," *Blackpast.*
3 Carol Nunnelley and Ingrid Tarver, *In Dixieland*, "The Bombing: 7 Years Later," September 13, 1970.
4 Dr. King's telegram to President John F. Kennedy. For further details, refer to https://civilrights.jfklibrary.org/media-assets/the-bombing-of-the-16th-street-baptist-church-
5 See excerpt of Roy Wilkins' telegram to President John F. Kennedy, dated September 15, 1963, https://civilrights.jfklibary.org/media-assets/the bombing-of-the-16th-street-baptist...
6 "Statement by President," September 16, 1963, https://civilrights. jfklibrary.org/media-assets/the-bombing-of-the-16th-street-baptist... (See the John F. Kennedy Presidential Library and Museum.)
7 Isabel Wilkerson, "The Long-Lasting Legacy of the Great Migration," *Smithsonian Magazine*, September 2016, https://www.smithsonianmag.com/history/long-lasting-legacy-great-migration-180960118.
8 Brentin Mock, "The 'Great Migration' was about Racial Terror, Not Jobs," *City Lab*, June 24, 2015, https://www.citylab.com/equity/2015/06/the-great-migration-was-about-racial-terror-not-jobs/396722/.
9 Rubin, "Survivor Recalls Role."
10 John McCartney, *Black Power Ideologies: An Essay in African-American Political Thought* (Philadelphia: Temple University Press, 1992), 91-110. (King deeply believed in a philosophy of non-violence practiced by leaders like Mahatmas Gandhi.)
11 Rosa Parks (with Haskins), *Rosa Parks: My Story* (New York: Puffin Books, 1992), 164-165.
12 Branch, *Parting the Waters*, 892.
13 Taylor Branch noted that Dr. King "could not budge the Robertsons, both schoolteachers, who stoutly resisted the 'grandstand play,' of a mass funeral. 'We realize Carole lost her life because of a movement,' said Mrs. Robertson, "but we feel her loss was personal to us."' Branch, *Parting the Waters*, 892.
14 Taylor Branch, *Parting the Waters*, 892. (Many sources give this estimate.)
15 King, "Eulogy for the Martyred Children," in *A Testament of Hope*, 221.
16 Ibid.
17 Branch, *Parting the Waters*, 892. King did face blame for the church bombing, which he disputed. As Branch notes, "King, refuting the implications of A.G. Gaston and other Birmingham conservatives, maintained that the bombing was the result of too little daring in civil rights, not too much. ...."
18 Malcolm X, "After the Bombing," in *Malcolm X Speaks*, ed. George Breitman (New York: Grove Press, Inc., 1966), 157.
19 Interview with Diane Nash, conducted by Blackside, Inc. on November 12, 1985, for *Eyes on the Prize: America's Civil Rights Years (1954-1965)*. Washington University Libraries, Film and Media Archive, Henry Hampton Collection. (Courtesy Out of the Archives.)
20 "Chuck Morgan," in *My Soul is Rested: Movement Days in the Deep South Remembered*, by Howell Raines (New York: G.P. Putnam's Sons, 1977), 183. Howell Raines interviewed Morgan about the speech. Morgan later explained to him, "'You had

a majority, a county commission, two newspapers, television stations, a myriad of industrial and business leaders; every damn one of 'em had a better forum or audience than I did, and if that ain't an endorsement by silence, I don't know what is."

21 Liz Ronk, "The Girl Who Lived." Time online published the speech and photograph of Collins-Rudolph in 2013. Chased out of town after death threats in 1963, Charles Morgan Jr. later explained why he felt compelled to give the speech to Howell Raines in the book *My Soul is Rested.*)

22 Sharon Robinson, *A Child of the Dream*, 2019.

23 Angela Davis, *Angela Davis: An Autobiography* (New York: International Publishers, 1988), 129-131.

24 Peggy Wallace Kennedy, *The Broken Road* (Bloomsbury Publishing: New York, 2019), 109.

25 Ibid, 110.

26 Gary Alan Fine, "Apology and Redress: Escaping the Dustbin of History in the Postsegregationest South, JSTOR, https://www.jstor.org/stable/43287502?seq=1#metadata_info_tab-contents.

Chapter 7. The Damned Don't Cry

Jesus wept. (John 11:35, KJV)

Leaving behind nights of terror and fear
I rise[1] — Dr. Maya Angelou

In a segregated Birmingham, Alabama, Hillman Hospital, which is now also known as University Hospital, primarily provided care for needy patients — regardless of race — while other facilities like Carraway only served black patients. I would remain at University Hospital, coping with 'terror-filled nights,' reliving the blast in dreams and flashbacks.[2]

I could not attend Addie's joint funeral. I was still in bad shape, but physical pain paled in comparison to the hurt that I felt deep within my soul. I cried my heart out about the bombing. Even men like the Rev. Fred Shuttlesworth wept.[3] Except for maybe Momma, Addie's sudden death shocked everyone. She told some folks that God warned her that one of her kids would die, but to have a child killed in church and another severely injured must have tested her *mustard-seed* like faith. [4]

Tears came easier than sleep did at night, as so much weighed on my mind, including the death of the "four little girls." The twin evils of bigotry and racial hatred cut their lives short here on earth, but I believe that they found a heavenly home. During my hospital stay, the nurses were kind to me. I still cannot recall their names and struggle to remember their faces. It has been so long ago. I remember they used to call me their "little girl." Some nights they brought me ice cream and cookies.

About a month into my recovery, a reporter wrote an article, trying to describe my injuries and state of mind, shared in the excerpt below:

> "Sarah Jean's daily existence now is through sounds: The cheerful greeting of nurses who have made her their pet, the music of the radio, the rustling noises as visitors enter and try to encourage her.... Her right eye is still covered by a patch; her left eye is uncovered, but swollen and she cannot see through it....
>
> Nurses say Sarah Jean has moments of deep despondency, and at other times peps up. But never will she volunteer to talk about the bombing.
>
> 'Don't be discouraged child," a friend told her during a visit yesterday.
>
> 'All right,' she answered so softly you could hardly hear. She sat up in her bed, but bowed her head, as if she didn't want visitors to see her eyes.
>
> 'Sometimes my eyes hurt,' she said, running her fingers back and forth across the bandages....
>
> What does she think about while lying in the hospital bed?
>
> 'About school,' she answered. Her mother, Mrs. Alice Collins, says Sarah Jean is a quiet girl, except among school friends....
>
> Sarah Jean was asked how she feels about the church bombing now that a full month has passed. Her lips moved once but she said nothing — as if afraid."[5]

The reporter got some details right but not everything. Even now, kids still ask if I was afraid when I went into the hospital. Well the answer is yes, I was. I was scared that I would remain blind, forever.[6]

When the doctor removed the patches from my eyes, I couldn't see out of my right eye. I lost my right eye. Gradually, I started seein' out of my left eye.[7] At the beginning of my recovery, I wore bandages on both eyes for weeks. Shards of glass from the stained-glass window and flying debris, left me blindly immediately after the bombing. When the doctor removed the bandages or patches, I could see a trace of light out of it within about two weeks. Tiny pieces of glass remained lodged in my left eye; however, I could see better out of it as the days moved on. The doctors thought I would regain vision in my left eye within a few weeks. They said that it would heal on the count of my youth. I was still quite young at the time of the 16th Street Church bombing.

Sometimes, I cried myself to sleep thinking about Addie, everything really. During those first few nights at the hospital, I scratched myself furiously. It felt like something was crawling all over me. I dug my nails deep into my skin, almost uncontrollably at times. The almost constant itching signaled the onset of a nervous condition that lasted for years.

At first, the bombing caused me to become angry with members of our church. In the days immediately following the bombing, I naively thought they must have had something do with the bombing. My youthful anger was misplaced. When they came to visit me, I would throw the covers over my head, pretending to be fast asleep. Yet, sleep did not come by easily. Sometimes when I managed to catch a nap, someone would tap at the door, suddenly waking me up. The blast left me confused and cranky.

The police claimed not to know who bombed our church, killing the children, even though they were getting tips immediately after the blast. President Kennedy promptly initiated an inquiry. Still, could the police, law enforcement, be involved on any level, or guilty of neglect? Even as a little girl, I believed that someone knew who was at fault from the get-go. I knew people could be cruel to kids based on the past -- like the day Addie and I both ran for our lives, chased away by cruel pranksters near the stadium. I also thought of some of the unpleasant incidents we regularly endured at the local grocery store and even while my sisters and I were selling aprons. Did any of these folks hide behind white sheets, robes or police uniforms come nighttime? I thought about the folk doing the inquiry too. I knew that the bomber was not the bogeyman lying in wait under the bed, or a figment of my imagination.

University Hospital released me near the end of November, but not before my thirteenth birthday on November 10, 1963. The nurses and my family threw me a birthday party at the hospital, but it was not any fun; Addie was not there. Before leaving the hospital, the doctors told Momma to bring me back in February to have my right eye removed. Because if I didn't have it removed, I would go blind in left eye, too.[8]

After I heard the bad news, I did not want to communicate with white people, especially this doctor who was going to remove my eye. I was furious. At twelve years old, how would I look with just one eye? During that phase of my recovery, I also began to have nightmares, constantly. I would wake up, shaking all over, with the memory of the noise from the explosion ringing in my ears. Nurses would come to my room with medicine in the middle of the night. I had a lot of trouble sleeping at night. When morning came, I would drift off to sleep for a while before it was time for breakfast. Afterwards, several different doctors would examine me. This went on for weeks.

To reiterate, the doctors released me from the hospital after about two and a half months. When I returned home, I didn't do chores or anything for the first day or two. Later, Mama sent me to the store. It felt strange walking down the street. I knew it would be something to get used to, seeing life through only one eye. Mama was shrewd. She did not want the church bombing to victimize me. Some routines quickly returned to normal, while other things changed. For instance, when Mama asked me to clean the kitchen or make up the bed, I had to obey. I bathed myself too. Anyway, after my hospital stay, I had to wear glasses – a pair of white glasses, as I recall. I could see good enough to do most everything I had to do. While at home, I watched television and listened to gospel programs and inspirational songs like "Up Above My Head" on the radio: The lyrics go sorta' like this: *Up above my head, I hear music in the air….*[9] Overall, music helped to lift my spirit.

I stayed home for about two weeks before returning to my school. They just threw me back into the classroom: no grief counseling or therapy dogs for me. I went back to school in a terrible condition and mental state. The other children pretended as if they did not notice any change in me. I knew they did. I was uncomfortable, unable to relax. I sat real still. I couldn't focus on schoolwork because *that* day remained in my thoughts. I wondered how anyone could put a bomb in a church where people go to worship and praise God. Hatred had claimed the life of my friends. I counted Addie as a friend too. I missed her, especially when I returned to school.

In Addie's absence, Janie and I became closer. She was just like a little nurse, taking care of me on a regular basis. Whenever Janie saw a piece of glass or something shining on the surface of my face, she dutifully plucked it with almost surgical precision. The sheer force of the blast had embedded glass in my skin. Tiny shards of glass would rise or bubble up to the surface at times.

My last year of elementary school was challenging, mainly due to a teacher who was strict. She had a certain rule of thumb. If students did not get the stitch right, she would punish them.

After the bombing, I just couldn't remember certain things, simple things. For example, one day when it was time to review my work from a sowing lesson, I had forgotten how to create a backstitch. However, the teacher who taught us thought that I was just being a spoiled brat.

"This is not right," my teacher said, as she immediately reached out and smacked me on the back.

"You don't hit me," I quickly responded. "Even my Mother does not hit me like that."

I promptly marched off the school ground, returned home, and told Mama what the teacher did. She became steaming mad. I did not know if Mama was angrier with the teacher or at me for walking out of school. Anyway, Mama took me right back to school. I found out later that she instructed the teacher not to ever hit me. Mama made it clear that if this ever happened again that the teacher would have to answer to her. Following this unfortunate incident, the girls in class drew a little closer to me. After that day, the teacher treated us better. Not all was lost. At that age, most young girls simply want to bond. A national tragedy would also bring us together.

The whole classroom came together the day we learned about President Kennedy's assassination in Dallas, Texas on November 22, 1963. I vividly remember that day. I was in art class, listening to my radio with the volume set low; I was not exactly the role model in all of my classes. Suddenly, the announcer stated that someone had shot President Kennedy. I struggled with the news. I could not tell the teacher because she would scold me for listening to the radio in class, so I shared the report with my classmate, quietly whispering to her.

When the teacher, Ms. Dickerson, noticed us going back and forth she asked, "What's so important that you're talking?"

My friend Rhonda Lee yelled out, "Sarah said they just shot the President!" Rhonda continued, "She was listening to her radio and heard the news."

I was scared Ms. Dickerson was going to fuss at me for having the radio on during class. Instead, she asked me to bring her the radio so that she could listen. Afterwards, she told the class that it was true. Not only did our class hear the bad news, other students knew, as I discovered later during a break. Crying girls filled the restroom, with more coming in with tearful eyes.

I hated that someone killed the President. In my opinion, he was a good man. Racial violence in Alabama and the nation troubled him. In truth, President Kennedy had a checkered record on civil rights. He was mainly concerned about the unsettling violence in the Deep South, especially surrounding the Freedom Riders because of the image it projected in America and overseas. By happenstance or design, President Kennedy was setting the stage for bills that would curb discrimination in America. President Lyndon B. Johnson, who followed him in office, later championed voting rights legislation. I was perplexed. It seemed like people were killing leaders who sought real change. It was a season of violence. Kids didn't escape harm either. I wondered why people had so much hatred in their hearts, when God said in His word that we should love one another (John 15:12). I experienced the brunt of such hatred.

In February of 1964, Mama took be back to the hospital to have my right eye removed. I was in the hospital for several weeks during the recovery process. After the socket healed, the doctor gave Mother the address of a prosthetic provider. We went there for the procedure, and I was fitted with a prosthetic eye.

After that, I faced many new challenges, as my new reality sunk in. I went through a whole lot of pain and nervousness throughout all of that. People didn't understand what I was still going through, because during that time, I didn't receive no counseling, even the second time that I reentered school. They did not counsel me or keep up with me.[10] They didn't see how I was feelin' or anything. Having my eye removed as a child, was like re-experiencing the trauma of the bombing all over again. Returning to school was even harder now. I had to go back the same week of the surgery, not two or three weeks later. I was nervous and feelin' bad. Really feelin' bad, going through something that a child (then 13 years of age) should never have gone through.[11]

This was a difficult time for me. I walked around with the oddest feeling, constantly in a state of panic. I used to think the fake eye would fall out if I moved too fast. It felt too big. I didn't want to play with the children anymore. I looked like a freak, or so it seemed to me. The church bombing left my face disfigured, and there were even more facial marks from my eyeglasses. I didn't want to live like this anymore. On top of this, the hair on one side of my head began to fall out due to all the stress. If a single strand of hair got into my right eye socket, the pain was unreal. The skin around my eye was very sore and still healing. It felt like something was cutting my eyes whenever hair or anything sensitive brushed over this area. I would run to the bathroom or restroom if I were in school — to get it out right away. I rinsed it out because the hair itself felt like tiny particles of glass stuck inside my eye socket all over again. It still irritates me when anything gets in that socket.

School was a chore now. I hated to stand in front of the class. I just knew that my classmates or the children were laughing at me. I used to imagine my fake or prosthetic eye would fall out to the ground and roll around the floor, as my classmates broke out in uncontrollable fits of laughter. I never wanted to be *the joke of the party*, or classroom clown either for that matter. It was so difficult to concentrate. My grades took a nosedive. Before the bombing, they were good, overall. I was an A and B student. In the past, I had even earned an "E" for excellent.

One day at school, I suddenly broke out in bumps or hives all over my face. The teacher took me to the principal's office and called my mother to take me home. She told Mama to bring me back after my face cleared up. I was so glad to get out of school. I hoped my face never got better. I never wanted to return to school at this point.

During the week while I was out of school, I started noticing a deep sadness in my Daddy's eyes. He was a quiet, reserved man. Still, his eyes could not mask the sorrow about the bombing or the death of one daughter and serious injuries of another. Sometimes when my Daddy looked at me, tears slowly streamed down his face. Shortly after this period, he also fell sick but continued to work.

After returning to school, one day I went to visit Dad at his job to ask for an allowance. To my surprise, his boss told me Daddy had fallen ill, again. He had just called a cab to take Daddy to the hospital. When I saw him, my father was on his knees, struggling to breathe. After the cab arrived, I went to the hospital with him. As soon as we got there, doctors put Daddy on a breathing machine. They rushed him to the emergency room. I quickly called Mama who hurried to the hospital. Fortunately, Daddy left the hospital the next morning. The doctors warned him to stop smoking immediately, however he continued. His smoking had begun to irritate Mama, and it may have contributed to their separation before the bombing. Daddy moved away prior to the bombing but always stayed in touch with his family.

The Promise

One afternoon when I got back from elementary school, Mama was talking with visitors. It was an unspoken rule not to interrupt or even sit in the presence of grown up folks, so I made it a point to remain out of sight. After her company left, Mama did something unusual. She confided in me about their conversation. The visitors had privately told Mama to expect compensation for Addie's death and my injuries. After that day, this topic of conversation rarely came up between my Mother and me, but I never forgot about this discussion. It didn't escape my attention that my family had medical expenses because of the bombing.

After the bombing, people from around the country and world sent monies and gifts to the 16th Street Baptist Church, as well as letters of condolences to all the families. All told, the church received about $24,000 for the families, which it divided equally among them. Among other items, the press reported that church leaders intended to establish a fund to support the education of the brothers and sisters of the victims and other members. The same AP story reported on "the setting up of a trust fund to finance the education and medical expenses of Sarah Jean Collins, 12, a Negro girl who lost sight in her right eye in the blast. Her sister, sister, Ad (sic) Mae, 14, was killed."[12] None of this occurred. Eventually, the 16th Street Baptist Church established a scholarship committee, which was beneficial. However, years later when Janie sought scholarship support from the church for one of her kids to attend college, my sister did not receive funding to the best of my knowledge.

Come Rain or Shine

As a family, we did not attend worship services at the Sixteenth Street Baptist Church for much longer after the bombing. The leaders of our church conducted services at the Gaston L.R. Hall Building (located near the corner of Fourth Avenue and 16th Street) while crews repaired the damages. It took about eight months to complete the repairs. After the work was finished, Mama took us back to the Sixteenth Street Baptist Church. There were too many reminders. Furthermore, I did not feel safe there anymore. We still listened to the preached word and sang those hymns about faith. However, those songs did not provide me with much solace or comfort. Every time I heard a loud sound, even a car backfiring, it caused me to shake all over my body at the memory of that awful day. The thought would remain on my mind throughout the service. I sat still in church, staring straight ahead like a zombie, shell-shocked. I wanted to get away from that church. I know Mama sensed my fear, unease. Gradually, we stopped attending the 16th Street Church soon after it reopened, and I was so relieved.

Instead, Mama began to conduct church services at our home. She would begin by praying. We all sang hymns together at the start of the service. With her alto voice, Mama could suddenly burst out in a song like "I'm a Soldier," which gospel great James Cleveland interpreted. Whatever song she chose, we had hymnbooks, and often followed along. Two of her favorite hymns were "Yield Not to Temptation" and "Holy, Holy, Holy." Some days I can picture Mama singing, *Holy, holy, holy! Lord God Almighty! Early in the morning our song shall rise to Thee; Holy, holy, holy, merciful and mighty! God in three Persons, blessed Trinity*!"[13] Her heart-felt singing ushered in the true atmosphere of worship.

When the word of the Lord came forth, Mama would teach us scriptures from the Bible and explain what they meant. With the passage of time, other kids in the neighborhood joined us. The crowd became larger, so Mama rented a small house in the neighborhood to hold services. Reverend Johnnie Burrell heard about our little church; Rev. Burrell and his wife got together and began to help Mama. This couple picked up kids who were not attending church and brought them to worship with us. In time, Mama decided it would be best if Mr. Burrell preached and she became the church superintendent. The three adults pitched together and bought clothes for kids who were in need. Among other things, Mama used monies that she had received from the 16th Church to fund this effort and other activities related to our growing church. They were able to do other things for kids because they started selling fish and chicken dinners on the weekends, while we played baseball near Legion Field. The reverend sold dinners at his barbershop to his regular customers too. The extra income helped us out at our congregation, the Christian Community Congregational Church.

The size of our congregation expanded quickly, so we had to seek another building. We started having services at Foster Grocery Store. We turned it into a storefront church on Sundays. Reverend Burrell rented this space from Mr. Foster during the off-peak hours. We had service there on Sundays until the grocery store closed. City planners made the decision to enlarge the parking lot at Legion Field Stadium, and eventually the grocery store ceased operating. Our congregation continued to rent the space for services. I liked this space because it was located a block from our house near the Legion Field where we played baseball. Anyway, we rented the building for about a year but moved out because Legion Field needed the land for a parking lot.

We found another building on the corner of Seventh Avenue and Twelfth Street and rented it for a few months. The rent was high. The adults sold even more dinners to pay the rent but still could not come up with the rent money on time. Reverend Burrell and Mama had no choice but to abandon this plan. They were forced to suspend church services altogether. Mama later moved away from the neighborhood because Legion Field bought her property to expand their parking lot.

We moved into a newer neighborhood, which had an enormous church about two blocks away from our home. Momma later became a member of that church. She began to look happy once again. I knew it was because she didn't have all the pressures from running her own church, though staying busy helped her with the grieving process too.

Notes

1 Maya Angelou, *Maya Angelou: The Complete Poetry* (New York: Random House, 2015)159-160 Maya Angelou, *Maya Angelou: The Complete Poetry* (New York: Random House, 2015),159-160

2 Sarah Collins Rudolph correspondence with Tracy Snipe on June 12, 2014.

3 Andrew M. Manis, *A Fire You Can't Put Out* (Tuscaloosa: The University of Alabama Press, 1999), 404.

4 Rudolph, correspondence with Snipe; Sarah C. Rudolph, Lecture at Cuyahoga Community College (Eastern Campus), February 26, 2014.

5 Jim Purks, "Sound is World of Negro Bomb Victim," *Corpus Christi Times*, October 10, 1963.

6 Sarah Collins Rudolph correspondence with Tracy Snipe on June 12, 2014.

7 Sarah Collins Rudolph, "Four Women from Birmingham."

8 Ibid.

9 Sister Rosetta Thorpe originally composed this classic. Contemporary gospel artists, notably Kirk Franklin, have interpreted this song.

10 Sarah Collins Rudolph, "Four Women from Birmingham."

11 Ibid.

12 James Purks, "Pastor of Bombed Church Outlines Some of Prospects," *American News* (Aberdeen, South Dakota) December 4, 1963.

13 Reginald Heber wrote the lyrics to "Holy, Holy, Holy" in 1826. Donnie McClurkin also sings an evocative gospel version of this traditional song.

Chapter 8. They Say It's Wonderful

We smile, but, O great Christ, our cries
To thee from tortured souls arise.[1] – Paul Laurence Dunbar

"I went through the worst thing I think any child could ever go through, and I've still got the scars... but every time I try to find a door open, for somebody to help, that door just always is closed for me."[2]
— Sarah Collins Rudolph.

After graduating from elementary school, I attended A. H. Parker High School, starting in the ninth grade. School administrators assigned me to a secondary school with kids from throughout the entire school district, not just my former elementary school, Brunetta Hill. I welcomed this change in my daily life, especially since my peers and classmates never brought up the bombing. It was kinda' like a taboo topic or 'hush-hush,' you know? I just assumed that many of them did not know that my unsightly facial scars stemmed from the church bombing. If only a mask could hide them. Sometimes I saw other kids whispering and pointing in my direction. I would ignore them and keep walkin.' Decades later, when I began to attend our high school class reunions, I discovered nearly everyone knew about "it," but, hardly anyone made "it" the central point of our conversations. Years later, my classmates would honor me as the 'Forgotten Girl' at one of our high school reunions. It was a pleasant surprise. Living in fear and with PTSD can dampen any adolescent's outlook on life, as it did mine. Several years ago, during a speaking event in Cincinnati, Ohio, Donald Washington, a former classmate, introduced me to the captive audience as a bombing survivor; he described what I had endured as a "hellish experience."[3] If only he knew everything, including all the doors that were closed to me as child, teenager, and light years beyond the bombing itself.

In high school, I wanted to fit in, like most young people. Yet, I would experience another personal setback — perhaps related to the discriminate past — one that robbed us of four precious lives. Parker was challenging. Although I studied, I didn't grasp certain concepts as quickly. Algebra was especially trying. I could not solve word problems quickly no matter how hard I applied myself. My concentration dipped, and my grades suffered. I managed to do well enough because I made it to the tenth grade. I received another blessing during this challenging period.

That summer Ms. Steplight got in touch with Mama to inquire if I could go to a camp for the blind located in Hardwick, Vermont. I qualified for the program. I was visually impaired. I did not know anything about Vermont but wanted to go there, so Mama consented. They provided her with my travel itinerary and a plane ticket, as well as some additional information about the summer camp. I flew on Delta Airlines. This was the first time I had flown, and I loved it. The flight was thrilling. And our camp was the best. It was so much fun. We did all kinds of exciting things. We went swimming, hiking and mountain climbing. Once, we even sailed on a boat. The food was also tasty. Seemingly, I gained about twenty pounds within a month. I had fun, guiding the other kids around and fixing hair. I was a team leader. Although the camp was mostly for the blind, they still allowed me to attend. One of the girls there even taught me a little sign language.

Mama allowed me to return to this summer camp for the next two summers since I enjoyed it so much. One year, we traveled on a one-day outing to on an expo in Canada. It marked my first and only trip outside the United States. All told, I had started to feel good about life again.

Stars Fell in Alabama

As my junior year of high school ended, I really focused on my lessons. I had to if I wanted to pass to the twelfth grade, and graduate on time. Like most teenagers, I wanted to socialize. One night I went to a party where I met a guy, Billy Sanders, who asked me to share a dance with him. He was good-looking and *he could dance, wicky wacky.*

It was a magical night in Alabama, as we literally danced the night away. At the time, songs by the ever-popular duo Sam & Dave and Otis Redding's incredible cover of "Try A Little Tenderness" were still all the rage. Aside from dancing, it was so easy to talk to Billy. We talked about anything and everything.

I could not stop thinking about him after the dance that night. I had never dated anyone. After meditating on it for a spell, I gathered the courage to bring up the subject of Billy at home. I asked Momma, "Can Bly, I mean Billy, visit with me?"

Mama thought about it for a spell and replied, hesitantly, "He can come and see you on Wednesday evenings for an hour and a half." Back then, we also used to refer to dating as "receiving company."

Billy was about three years older than I was. I didn't know him during elementary school. However, in time I met his devoted grandmother and grandfather. They raised Billy who was an only child. His parents had died a long time ago.

Billy was my first boyfriend. We dated for several months. Being young and searching for love to fill the void in my life, I got pregnant before the end of the school term. Summer break charged ahead that year. I knew that it would be time to return to school in September.

I did not dare tell Mama I was pregnant, but she noticed that I was not as active as I used to be. One day she directly asked me, "Are you pregnant Sarah?"

"Yes Ma'am," I said.

"Well, I'm not taking you to see no doctor. You see him the best way you can," she bluntly replied.

Shortly after this tense conversation, I got a job cleaning up a restaurant to pay for the doctor bill. My boyfriend worked at Bell South Telephone Company. Billy promised to help me with the medical bills and gave me the money needed for the deposit. During that time, anybody expecting a baby had to have a $50 deposit at the hospital before checking in to give birth. Incoming patients normally made smaller deposits, typically in about $50 increments. Normally, hospital administrators collected $250.00 to offset the cost of the delivery. In general, the cost for hospital care today is far steeper.

Early on during my pregnancy, I went to the clinic for my checkup. I wanted to make sure that I was in good health and that everything was okay.

"Where's your mother young lady," the nurse asked me?

"Oh, she's out of town," I quickly replied. I told the nurse that because Mama made it clear that she was not going to take me to the local clinic. She was angry and disappointed because I got pregnant while unmarried and in high school.

"Well, we really should not administer an examination without your mother's presence, honey. But since she's 'out of town,' I will complete the checkup right now," she continued. After the checkup, the nurse informed me that everything appeared to be fine.

I continued to work at the restaurant until the manager asked me to work on Sundays. I told him I could not work on Sunday because I had to attend church. During our conversation, he stared at me closely. His eyes rested on the ever so slight bump protruding from my stomach.

"I don't want you to come to work again," he told me. "You could hurt yourself or the baby, while lifting heavy plates or mopping the floor."

One night during the fifth month of my pregnancy, I woke up to get a glass of water. On the way back to bed, I tripped and fell. When I got up, I felt the strangest sensation.

"Mama," I screamed out.

She came running. "What's wrong Sarah?"

"I believe the baby is coming now," I sputtered out in complete shock.

Mama raced to the phone and called my sister Flora to drive us to the hospital. Afterwards, Mama wrapped me up in a blanket. Soon after we arrived at the hospital, the doctor shared the bad news. I had a miscarriage. When I discovered that my baby was dead, I sobbed uncontrollably. I had had a baby boy. How could he be dead? Although I was not too far along in my pregnancy, I still wondered if this fall alone caused my miscarriage. Many years later, I learned that there were other mitigating factors, stemming from the bombing that may have contributed to the miscarriage, too.

Mama held me closely in her arms as the terrible news hit home. "Baby, don't cry." She continued, "Maybe, you can have a child later in life. "Don't let this upset you so Sarah."

I was beyond comfort. My mind went back to my sister, Addie. With the loss of this baby, I was losing someone precious, yet again.

Within days of pulling myself back together, I had to break this sad news to someone else who was special in my life, Billy. He came to visit me after I returned home from the hospital. Never one to put off things, I broke down as I shared the terrible news.

"I loss our son," I told Billy, as I began to cry.

Nodding in disbelief, he fought back the tears. Pulling himself together, Billy asked me, "How are you doin' Sarah?"

"Alright," I managed to say. Deep down inside, I felt terrible. I was heartbroken. If I had had a girl, I was going to name her Addie, like my sister. I so wished that our son had lived.

With the passing of time, Mama revealed something else about my condition to Janie who shared their conversation with me some years later. Mama told her that I would probably not ever be able to carry a child to full term because a piece of glass, still wedged in my stomach, stemming from the bombing. The location of the glass makes it too dangerous to move; it remains lodged in the walls of my abdomen.

Anyway, when summer break was over, I went back to school, a welcome change. It was my senior year. I didn't know how I was going to make it through that year. Furthermore, I no longer lived at home, by choice. I knew that my teachers would push me in school, so I studied even harder, praying to graduate. My most difficult subject was Algebra. I was terrible, when it came down to solving the word problems, but I had a good Algebra teacher, which made all the difference. Eventually, I would catch on. I struggled mightily with my concentration and schoolwork ever since the church bombing.

Coping with my life in the years after '63 was challenging. As my last year in high school approached, I went through familiar rituals like taking my senior picture. My once stellar grades had slipped to C's and D's, so I was uptight during senior year to say the least. Somehow, I would manage to complete my education at A.H. Parker High School in 1969.

I thank God who gave me the strength to finish high school.[4] I didn't think that I was going to after all that I had went through. The bombing could have ended my life, but *God kept me.* I was glad to be done with this chapter of my life, still clueless about the future. Even with my childhood dream deferred, I still didn't want time to *pass me by.*

Figure 21. Sarah Collins, High school senior. Courtesy of George C. Rudolph

New Directions

As I think back on the past, life presented me with a sea of changes and many challenges after graduation. First, I did not remain in touch with Billy. I don't know where he is living now or today. Second, after completing school, I tried to find a job. I wanted to attend driving school but needed money to pay for classes, so I began cleaning house for a doctor and his wife to pay for it. I enrolled in the AAA Driving School. I was tired of catching the bus everywhere I had to go and wanted my own vehicle. I wanted to learn how to drive badly, but I didn't catch on quickly due to my nerves. When my lessons were over, the driving instructor said, "You need many more lessons." Failing so, he stubbornly declared, "You could end up killing someone or getting yourself killed on the road."

After this blunt talk, I gave up on driving. I continued to take the bus to my new job. I worked for another physician for about six months and made enough money to rent a room and buy clothes.

One day while I was walking downtown, suddenly, I heard someone call me. I didn't know who it was until the person came closer. It was Doretha, one of my girlfriends from high school.

After talking, I discovered that she worked at Birmingham Stove and Range. She told me that they were hiring. I got directions from Doretha but did not go immediately. I worked for the doctor for another month. I decided that I wanted to move into an apartment but wasn't earning enough money to pay for rent, utility bills and my medical bills. Thus, I went to Birmingham Stove and Range, a local foundry or steel factory, to apply for a job. I promptly completed an application for employment to be able to pay my medical bills too. Surprisingly, they hired me on the same day to work on the skillet line.

This job was easy. All I had to do was to put cast iron skillets inside a machine, clean out the ruff inside and put it into another machine later to get everything shiny. I had to be at work at 7:00 a.m. I regularly took a Yellow Cab at 6:30 a.m. I had a designated or regular driver. While working at Birmingham Stove and Range, I lived in furnished apartment in Norwood, which is a suburb of Birmingham. Fortunately, the rent there was reasonable. Even the location was handy. I could also easily get to the laundromat in the neighborhood. A grocery store was close by, as was the hospital. I worked for this company from 1970-1973.

My job at Birmingham Range and Stove initiated my work in the foundries around Birmingham. I did not make this choice by accident. It was deliberate; my job there fitted the bill. I could hide out doing this type of work.[5] I never wanted to be in the public eye or forced to interact with people on a regular basis. I wanted a job where I could hide my face, as I shared later in life with different audiences during various speaking engagements. As a girl, I used to dream of becoming a nurse. I have always wanted to help others. I also liked the starched, white uniforms Mama used to wear as a nursing aid. Before the blast, I thought about joining the army, primarily to further my education. I remember calling an army recruiter and asking whether a person with only one eye could enlist. The man on the telephone plainly said "no" to my inquiry.

Dearly Beloved

Other milestones would mark these years. Sadly, in 1970, the next-door neighbor found my father on the floor of his home, dead. Fortunately, he had lived to see me graduate from high school. Daddy died from an asthma attack. A quiet man, my Father was never the same man again after the church bombing. I really do believe Addie's death left him broken-hearted.

Like several of the other victims' fathers, my Daddy never lived to see any of the men even indicted for the church bombing, much less see them stand trial. Though he rarely mentioned it, the bombing was particularly hard on my dad and other fathers who may have felt that they were our protectors. Mr. Alvin Robertson, Carole's father, once openly discussed the 16th Street Church bombing in a rare interview. He indicated that the loss of the four little girls was not just about advancing the cause of integration or people getting better jobs:

> 'You know once when I was in a barber's chair a man came in and remarked to someone else that every time he saw a colored guy driving a bus he thought that those four little girls didn't die for nothing… I really wonder if that's what people think, that they think of lives in terms of better jobs. I wonder if people are silly enough to feel that the family should be satisfied that some people are clerking in stores now.'[6]

Further, Mr. Claude Augustus Wesley, Cynthia's father who used to be a school principal, found it "almost unbelievable" that the people responsible for the 16th Street Baptist Church bombing had escaped for years: This outcome always "puzzled" him, according to his adopted daughter, Shirley.[7] By 1970, Mr. Chris McNair saw minimal change in Birmingham. Even years after the bombing McNair wondered, "'have there been enough changes?'"[8] To the best of my knowledge, no one interviewed my dad after the church bombing. We rarely, if ever, really discussed *it*. The wounds were still too fresh, too painful for him.

Looking back, I have fond memories of our father bringing us girls' candy, when my sisters and I were still young. He could *make the sunrise* too in our eyes, so we colored him in shades of love.

Figure 22. The Collins family, circa 1970. Courtesy of Sarah C. Rudolph

Notes

1 Paul Laurence Dunbar, "We Wear the Mask," in *The Complete Poems of Paul Laurence Dunbar* (New York: Dodd, Mead & Company, 1958), 112-113.

2 Carol Dawson, "Sarah Collins Rudolph," *Baylor Magazine*, September/October 2003, baylor.edu/alumni/magazine/0202/news.php?action=story&story=7597.

3 Donald Washington, POCWA Board Member ("Introduction of Mrs. Sarah Collins-Rudolph, Donald Washington, Community Gems: A Night of Elegance, Cincinnati, Ohio, November 19, 2016). Eric H. Kearney, CEO of the African-American Chamber of Commerce and an Ohio state senator, was the emcee.

4 Rudolph, letter to Snipe (not dated or nd).

5 Rudolph, (First A.M.E. Lecture, Federal Way, January 15, 2012).

6 Nunnelley and Tarver, "The Bombing: 7 Years Later."

7 Carol Nunnelley and Ingrid Taver, "Shirley Wesley is Symbol of People's Grieving," *In Dixieland*, September 13, 1970.

8 Ibid. Christopher McNair lived to see substantive changes in Birmingham, Ala. He testified in all three trials pertaining to 16th Street Church bombing. McNair and his wife Mrs. Maxine McNair were prominently featured *4 Little Girls* (1997).

Chapter 9. Lush Life

One Saturday as I was eating lunch inside Shoney's in downtown Birmingham, Alabama, a young man came to my table and asked to join me. I agreed. I said, "Okay," just like that. We quickly eased into a conversation. He seemed like a nice fella'. After this chance meeting, we immediately began dating. After a whirlwind romance, Derrick and I got married a mere year later.

We did not have a big wedding or anything of the sort. We got married at my Mom's house. Reverend Burrell tied the knot between us. Our guests included Mrs. Burrell, the former first lady of our church, my oldest sister Addie Bea and, of course, Mama. None of Derrick's family members attended our wedding. I never bothered to ask him why. I wore a simple dress, not a white wedding gown that many women wear. Derrick sported a casual shirt and dress pants.

Derrick's father owned a popular restaurant, Ole Soul. Derrick would take me there. This lifestyle introduced me to beer and later whiskey. I only sipped on beer — until the pain became unbearable. I worked at Birmingham Stove and Range for three years, but I decided to quit because my father-in-law needed someone to work as a short order cook. I started cooking at Ole Soul for that reason. I would go to work an hour before the restaurant opened to prepare the food. Only one waiter worked there, and we became fast friends. Several years after I began working at Ole Soul, the University of Alabama bought the property. After that deal, I was out of work. My husband worked for the city of Birmingham, sometimes cutting down trees, until he lost his job. With no money coming in, we moved in his with his Dad – a big mistake. I should have recognized the warning signs.

Derrick started staying out until all hours of the night. That is when the beatings began. He would slap me around and tell me to get out of his face. Whenever I got up the nerve to question him about these outings, Derrick would lash out, “I'll come home when I get ready.”

To console myself, I began to drink, especially when I was alone at home. My drink or cocktail of choice was gin and grapefruit juice. I remembered how to prepare this drink. I made it for customers while working at my father-in-law’s restaurant, but now I freely indulged. At first, I would drink a little every now and then. Later, I began to keep a pint of liquor around the house to help “calm my nerves,” or so I had convinced myself. Drinking became like a daily companion. I had my share of *twelve o’clock* tails throughout the day — anything to dull the pain of life that had steered terribly off course. I was becoming a lonely and *sullen gray-face* girl too. The thought of losing my sister, losing my baby boy hurt me. I drank to fix all the broken places within. I had started smoking reefer too. I never dabbled with pills or harder drugs. Somehow, I didn’t allow my drinking to turn me into an alcoholic.

In the meantime, Derrick and I never went out together anymore on dates. The beatings continued regularly. His dad would tell him to let up on me, a little but Derrick always had a quick comeback.

He often fumed, “This is my wife. You ain’t got nothin’ to do with this private matter.”

Luckily, his father could pack his own clothes and spend the night at a motel just to get away from it all. Deep down inside, I wondered what had become of the happy-go-lucky man I met a long time ago. Was it all for show? I was always in the wrong in his eyes, no matter how hard I tried to please that man.

One day, Derrick came home while I was at Janie’s house. Before leaving home, I had cooked supper – a fancy meal, as I recall. I even left it on the stove in case my husband came home hungry. However, when I returned, he immediately started in on me.

“Where you been?” he demanded.

“At my sister’s house,” I guardedly replied, as I tried to go about my business that day.

However, Derrick flipped out on me or flew into a rage and began viciously beating me. I guess my honest reply triggered a switch inside his tiny, little brain. After beating me down, he had the nerve to take me back to Janie's house.

"You're not going back there," she told me. "You're staying here with me."

I followed her advice but never filed a police report or went to the hospital. I only went back to that forbidden house once again to pack up all my clothes. I lived with Janie for several weeks, while looking for another job.

I didn't have much experience, so I tried to find work in another foundry, sort of like my former job at Birmingham Stove and Range. In time, I succeeded. The employment office sent me to a company called Lawler Machines & Foundry, a cast iron and aluminum foundry. They made all types of burglar bars and other gadgets for the city of Birmingham. I began work at Lawler's in 1974 and would remain with the company for the next fourteen years. I was a core maker; the core is the part of the iron mold or aluminum that forms the interior of a hollow casting. I performed a variety of tasks around the shop like cutting aluminum, drilling, grinding, inspecting, and running the cleaning machine.

Anyway, one day during lunchtime, I decided to walk to a park across the street from the plant. And just whom did I run into? Take a wild guess. Derrick. He acted as if he was so glad to see me.

"Can I take you out to lunch sometime?" he immediately asked.

"I beg your pardon," I emphasized

"C'mon Sarah."

"Honey, all of that ended when we got a divorce," I told Derrick, as I strutted away, determined that no *sweet talkin'* man would ever play me for the fool again. I didn't want to revisit that sad, lonely chapter of my life. Besides, I knew love wasn't supposed to be a battlefield, too. In time, the rainwater washed me; later in life, the water from the baptism cleansed me.

Even the mockingbirds, knew why I left Derrick, or why I *made it to the exit*. I'm not one for domestic violence. I filed papers on him long before our chance meeting in the park. I knew I would have *rotted away* if I had remained in any physically abusive marriage. When it comes to relationships, I do not spend time dwelling on the past. I made a vow not to ever let anyone abuse or violate me again in that manner.

Years later, I would see Derrick once again. I ran into him at the Kirklin Clinic, but I haven't laid eyes on him since that day.

Chapter 10. Pursuance

And the Lord said unto Cain, Where is Abel thy brother? And he said, I know not: Am I my brother's keeper? Genesis 4:9, KJV)

This act was not an aberration. It was not something sparked by a few extremists gone mad. On the contrary, it was logical, inevitable. The people who planted the bomb in the girls' restroom in the basement of the 16th Street Baptist Church were not pathological, but rather the normal products of their surroundings. And it was this spectacular, violent event, the savage dismembering of four little girls, which had burst out of the daily, sometimes even dull, routine of racist oppression.[1] – Dr. Angela Davis

After my divorce, I continued to work at Lawler. Into my fourth year with the company, my left eye began to give me trouble. It started burning and tearing often, so I made an appointment with Cooper Green Clinic. The doctor told me that my eye pressure was up. He prescribed eye drops for me. Each time I returned, there was no major change. He even tried a different prescription but to no avail. I went back there for the next several months to monitor the situation but stopped going. I could not afford to keep taking off from work.

As soon as I settled into a routine on my job, the first trial began. Unsurprisingly, the state of Alabama subpoenaed me to testify for the prosecution. Authorities had indicted Robert Chambliss for the murder of Carole Denise McNair on September 24, 1977, and his long-awaited trial began on November 14, 1977.

Even in 1963, the FBI could have thrown the book at Robert E. Chambliss ("Dynamite Bob") but allowed the opportunity to slip away. One author described Chambliss as "a battle-scarred veteran in the underground war for white supremacy and member of Birmingham's Robert E. Lee Klan Klavern."[2] In October of 1963, authorities convicted Chambliss, along with John Hall, of transporting dynamite; however, they got off with a light punishment — a 180-day suspended jail sentence and a $300 fine for the illegal possession of dynamite.[3]

I was incredibly uptight during the trial in November of 1977. Including me, over two dozen witnesses testified for the prosecution. During the trial, Chambliss's niece by marriage, Elizabeth H. Cobbs (later known as Petric J. Smith) was *the* surprise or star witness. Her testimony had people sitting on the edge of their seats. She testified that on September 14, 1963 she had a conversation with her uncle, Robert Chambliss, at his home. That morning, she told him about a recent news story about a "cutting incident" involving a young white female acquaintance. This story angered Chambliss. He told his niece Elizabeth "'"that if anyone had backed him up, that they would have had the G.d. niggers in their place by now."' Further, Elizabeth testified that Chambliss told her "'"that he had enough stuff to flatten half of Birmingham"' and that he declared, "'"You just wait until after Sunday morning, and they will beg us to let them segregate."'[4]

Moreover, she went on to state that about a week later, while sitting on the sofa at Robert E. Chambliss' home, she overheard her uncle mutter something, as he closely watched a news story on television about murder charges that could stem from the Sixteenth Street Baptist Church bombing. According to Elizabeth, he stated, "'"it wasn't meant to hurt anybody. It didn't go off when it was supposed to,"' seemingly talking back to the reporter. [5]

I felt like I was on trial too, when I went on the witness stand to tell jurors what happened on the morning that the bombing occurred. Still living in Birmingham, Alabama I was twenty-seven years old when I testified, no longer a little girl. Overall, it was still painful, overwhelming. I had tried hard to put the disturbing memories of the bombing out of my mind. However, when I took the witness stand, I had to relive that heartbreaking Sunday all over again. With each passing word the hurt and nightmares — they all came rushing back. However, this time it was all worse because the person responsible for killing my sister and friends, and causing me to lose an eye, was sitting in the courtroom within my eyesight.

Arthur Hanes was Robert Chambliss's main lawyer, while Jon Yung, an attorney for the prosecution, questioned me. Mr. Chris McNair and Reverend John Cross testified, too. Mr. McNair bravely identified a picture of his deceased daughter's body, while on the witness stand. Denise wanted her Dad to wait until she left for church; however, he had to leave before her; he served as the superintendent of Sunday school at St. Paul Lutheran Church in Birmingham, Al. According to Mr. McNair, Denise's last word to him were, "'Okay Daddy, go ahead.'" [6] The next time that he saw his daughter Denise was at a makeshift morgue in a hospital. When I finally took the witness stand, I incorrectly stated my age otherwise, the rest of my testimony is accurate; I was not cross-examined, afterwards.

Bill Baxley, the former Attorney General for the State of Alabama, led the prosecution for the state. During his closing argument, Baxley asked a mixed jury of nine blacks and three whites to give my friend Denise a birthday present. She would have had her twenty-sixth birthday on that same day, November 17, 1977. The jury conceded, too. At the close of his trial on November 18, 1977, a jury convicted Chambliss of murder in the first-degree. Judge Wallace Gibson sentenced him to prison for life for the murder of Denise McNair. Baxley strategically decided to press charges against Chambliss for the death of only one of the four girls, Denise, just in case the verdict came back not guilty.[7] Not having access to all the evidence both frustrated and prevented Attorney Bill Baxley from pressing charges against the others suspected of the 1963 bombing. Decades later, he later publicly expressed his frustrations.

Nevertheless, some fourteen years after the bombing, Chambliss was finally going to prison. At his sentencing, Judge Wallace Gibson asked Chambliss if he had anything to say, after asking him to approach the bench.

Chambliss replied, "'Judge, Your Honor, all I can say is that God knows that I never have killed anybody and never bombed anything in my life, and I was not down there at that Sixteenth Street Baptist Church.'"[8]

At the time of his sentencing, I thought that jail was too good for Bob Chambliss. Taxpayer's monies, including mine, would have to be used to keep him alive. The girls he killed didn't get off so lightly. Did Chambliss or his peers ever think of them as God's children, too? They never conceived of black people as brother and sisters.

When he had the chance to testify or speak up during the actual trial, Chambliss flat out refused to take the witness stand, much to the dismay of his lawyers.[9] Eventually, he served his sentence at St. Clair County Correctional Facility at Odenville; on October 28, 1985, they transported him to Lloyd Nolan Hospital where he died the following day.[10] Chambliss died in 1985, while still serving time. He never told on or expressed regret or remorse, as far as I know. After the verdict in the trial of "Dynamite" Bob Chambliss, I stated to the press, "'I know one thing. It was a long time."[11]

In hindsight, I cannot but admire the former Alabama state attorney general who made a vow to seek justice for the four little girls:

> 'They had issued me this card that had phone numbers on it. We didn't have 800 numbers back then. Because I traveled all over the state, I knew I'd be using it every day…
>
> So I sat down the day before I was sworn in and wrote each of those girls' names in each corner of that card. I knew that every time I used that card I would look at those names and remember that I wanted to do something.'[12]

Baxley would persevere despite the death threats and hate mail that he received. However, prosecuting the killer of my sister and childhood friends may have costed him mightily from a strictly political viewpoint. Though he served as the Lieutenant Governor of the state of Alabama (1983-1987), he lost the primary in 1986 in his bid to become the actual governor. Nevertheless, an adventurous law student by the name of Douglass Jones regularly attended Chambliss's trial, skipping classes.[13] Our paths would cross too some a quarter of a century later.

Both Directions at Once

I returned to work still angry about the trial but more determined to forge ahead. I knew deep down inside that Chambliss was not the only guilty party of the church bombing. It should not have taken fourteen years for justice to prevail. I tried hard to push such thoughts aside and focused on my own personal life.

At work, the boss placed a poster or sign in the clock room by the time that I resumed work, after the taxing trial. It indicated the work shift would start at 6:00 a.m., beginning that upcoming Monday. I wondered how I was going to make it to work on time, since the bus did not run that early where I lived. Near the end of the day, I asked my fellow co-workers if anyone was coming from near the Mason City area. A foreman, Tommy, told me that he lived in Powderly, which was a stone's throw beyond Mason City, so I began to commute with him. Around the second week, the company decided that Tommy had to come to work an hour earlier, which meant I had to get up even earlier to ride with him to work. I knew it was time to work on getting my driver's license.

During this period, one day my sister Junie and I went out to lunch. She had her own car. One day after getting behind the wheel, she suddenly got sick and pleaded with me to take over. I attributed this to the lingering stress after the bombing. Junie also endured a terrible ordeal. I still admired my sister. She has pushed through so much. Her deep faith in God and work ethic sustained her over the years. Anyway, my training at the AAA Driving School kicked into high gear. I guess it had to take an emergency for me to realize that I could drive.

After this incident, I picked up the manual again to study for a driver's permit. I was determined to succeed this time around, and I studied for two weeks straight. When I took the actual road test, I passed and got my license. It was a welcome turn of events in comparison to my first attempt. I was a nervous wreck driving back then. I remember the instructor's words after my first attempt: "You failed." I do not accept failure.

I regularly deposited at least twenty-five dollars per week into a savings account to make a down payment on a car. After I had saved three hundred dollars, I went to a car lot and saw a green Nova Chevrolet automobile that I liked. I made a down payment on it. The monthly note was affordable. I no longer had to catch a ride with anyone. The car came on time for me. Two weeks later, the boss asked me to work at one of their other plants, Yellow Hammer. He wanted me to drill and help with packing and shipping at the plant, and I worked there for a week.

When I returned to Lawler, they put me back to work on the core machine. This was my assignment for a while because there was a big order for cores. Things were running smoothly, until my glove caught in the machine one day. I clicked the button but did not initially notice that my glove was stuck. This device almost pinned me down over the top of the machine. Thank God, I was able to hold the machine down and use my free hand to press the stop button. I pulled a muscle in my arm and later got a doctor's slip to have it checked out. I was off work for four days before the doctor released me to return the following week.

Altogether, I had worked at Lawler's for ten years before they moved me to another core room in the same plant. This core room was nicer and larger than the previous one. There were three core machines in the room. At one point, the company hired two new workers. One of these new employees immediately became my manager because this job was a "man's thing." They figured I could not handle the core room, although I had operated it for ten years before new workers came aboard.

I worked anyway to pay my bills. However, they began to move me to the dirtiest and coldest sections of the plant. I noticed that the new boss was not getting his hands dirty. I had been there for fourteen years; still the supervisor assigned those grimy, dusty jobs almost solely to me.

One morning it was bone-chilling cold. Somehow, I still made it to work. The boss assigned me to work on the washer that frigid day, so I went around to where the washers were located. The washers are small irons with holes in the middle. The room where they were located was absolutely freezing cold, so I decided to go back to the room where they kept the core machine. I stood by the heater to warm up.

The boss stared me up and down. "Didn't I tell you to operate the washer?" he asked.

"Yeah, you did. But it's cold around there. And I'm not fixin' to work nonstop."

"What gives you the right to talk to me like that?"

The words came rushing from my mouth in a torrent. "As a matter of fact, I give myself the right. And while I'm at it, I give myself the right to walk out of this plant. I quit!"

I left the company that day and never returned. It was not fair to place a man in charge of me. I believe in equal rights on the job too; besides, I had worked for the company much longer. In far too many instances, women still face sexism and racial discrimination or double standards on the job.

I decided later to put in an application in at Sterilite Plastic. To my surprise, the company called me back the next day and hired me. That job started out great. Management assigned me to sort out dish racks, sponges, and drawers. Later, I also assembled and taped the boxes up for packaging these supplies. I worked in that department for a month before they moved me to another machine that made plastic. That machine was a nightmare! I had to pull the plastic out of the machine when it opened, assemble the boxes, and put labels on them — almost at the same time. Every day the manager assigned me to a different machine, or so it seemed. Sometimes I had to work quickly, or until the plastic closed back into the machine. When this happened, I would have to ring for the mechanic, too. You had to be awfully quick with your hands, especially on jobs like this one. I caught on and liked working there, but when they put me on twelve-hour shifts, I left that job as fast as I could. Altogether, I worked there for about five months.

After I received my check, I decided to place an advertisement in *The Birmingham News.* I had settled on a new idea after leaving Sterilite Plastic. In the advertisement, I stated that I was in business to clean homes. I indicated that I had my own car or transportation and references too, if needed. I received numerous telephone calls in response. I began work immediately, and I worked almost every day. This work was better than my labor at the plants in one key respect. In a way, I was my own boss and could determine my pace.

I began cleaning a condominium for Ms. Ruth. She did not live alone. She lived with a friend, Mr. Singleton. Ms. Ruth walked me through some easy tasks that I did not know how to complete at the time. She asked me if I knew how to operate a dishwasher. I had never used one before. I was glad for her help. Many of the other clients had dishwashers. She also showed me how to operate a self-cleaning oven. Overall, my job as a housekeeper kept me busy. I was a hard worker, so clients would recommend me to their friends, family members. Sometimes I would clean about two homes a day, but not that I complained. Furthermore, when they needed someone to sit with their loved ones, I did this type of work, too.

One of my clients owned a condominium. She wanted to travel to visit her daughter but needed someone to sit with or keep her elderly friend who had Alzheimer's disease. At the time, I did not realize how helpful that assignment would prove to be later. She would be gone for one week, so I decided to take a week off to keep him. This was the first time I had cared for an elderly patient. I learned a lot, keeping him. After attending to this patient, I started doing this type of work too. Between housekeeping and homecare, I was constantly busy.

I cared for many people during those years. Once I had to take care of an elderly white couple. The husband who was sickly had had a heart operation. His wife had serious health issues, too. Someone once found her unconscious in a car. Their son asked me to cook and clean for his parents. I shopped for them and took care of the household chores. About six months after I began working there, doctors diagnosed the husband with lung cancer. His prognosis was not good. They did not give him longer than two months to live, but I began to pray for him, daily. We would hold hands together, his family and me. I asked God to heal him. He did live longer than two months. God let him live six months longer to get his business straight and spiritual house in order. After his death, his wife moved into a private senior citizen's home.

After she moved into this nursing home, I received a call from a woman in Avondale who wanted me to care for her mother-in-law. She just wanted me to come over to ensure that her mother-in-law allowed workers to bring her Meals-On-Wheels deliveries, daily. Administrators designed this program to safeguard the regular delivery of meals. At night, I would also help my client prepare for bed. I made sure that she got her shower in the morning. I would take her to the beauty salon to get her hair done, which turned out to be short-term employment. In the end, my client moved in with her daughter-in-law because she could no longer stay in the house alone anymore. Eventually, they sold her home.

One day, not long after this job ended and I had finished washing my hair at home, someone knocked at my door. It was a white woman from Tuscaloosa. She informed me that one of my neighbors told her I took care of the elderly, which I verified. She told me her father lived up the hill from me and needed someone to cook for him. She had been trying to get her father to move to Tuscaloosa with her, but he steadily refused. He was as they say, "set in his ways." He wanted to live alone. She wanted to know if I would be willing to prepare meals for him on a regular basis. I already cooked food for myself, so this job would be a breeze. She told me the woman that stayed next door to him used to cook for her father but had recently moved to Center Point. Anyway, by the time the neighbor delivered his meal it would be cold. In time, we came up with a plan, and I accepted the offer to prepare three meals a day for her dad.

When my newest client, Vivien, would come to Birmingham, she made sure that her father got his haircut. She would also bathe and shave him. I later took on all these tasks. I was a novice barber. I had to learn quickly because her dad liked to get haircuts, regularly. My employer would call me in advance from Tuscaloosa to get her dad ready for his doctor's appointment. At other times, she simply came to town to take her Dad out to lunch. During these outings, I often spent time with Johnny Mae, one of my previous clients who had moved into a senior citizen home. This was a stable period, as life began to fall in place.

Notes

1 Davis, *Angela Davis: A Biography*, 130-131.

2 Dan T. Carter, *The Politics of Rage: George Wallace, the Origins of the New Conservatism, and the Transformation of American Politics* (New York: Simon & Shuster, 1995), 167.

3 Jeremy Gray, "Chambliss, Hall Convicted of Dynamite Possession, Released on $300 Bond (Oct. 9, 1963)," http://blog.al.com/birmingham-news-stories/2013/10/chambliss_hall_convicted_of-dy.html.

4 Alabama, Tenth Judicial Circuit Court, State of Alabama vs. Robert E. Chambliss Trial Transcript, 1977, Birmingham Public Library, Department of Archives, pages 261, 273, and 275.

5 Ibid., 277.

6 Alabama, "State of Alabama vs. Robert E. Chambliss," 184.

7 William Baxley, interview with author, September 13, 2013, Birmingham, Alabama. (During the course of the interview, Attorney Baxley confirmed with Snipe that if the charges had come back "not guilty" that he would have pressed charges against Robert Chambliss for the murder of the three other victims.)

8 Alabama, "State of Alabama vs. Robert E. Chambliss," 700.

9 Jones, *Bending Toward Justice*, 66-67.

10 Frank Sikora, *Until Justice Rolls Down: The Birmingham Church Bombing Case* (Tuscaloosa: The University of Alabama Press, 1991), 162.

11 Rick Bragg, "38 Years Later, Last of Suspects is Convicted in Church Bombing," *The New York Times*, May 23, 2003, http://www.nytimes.com/2002/05/23/us/38-years-later-last-of-suspects-is-convicted-in-church-bombing.

12 Joe Wilhelm, Jr., "Alabama Attorneys Share Lessons of Justice with JBA," *JAX Daily Record*, February 23, 2011, https://www.jaxdailyrecord.com/article/alabama-attorneys-share-lessons-justice-jba.

13 When the trial occurred in 1977, Doug Jones was still a student attending the Samford University School of Law. In the article "Justice for Four Little Girls," Jones wrote the following: "As a second-year law student, I cut classes and watched from the balcony of the courtroom as the trial of Robert Chambliss unfolded. I never imagined that twenty-four years later I would stand in the same courtroom as the United States Attorney for the Northern District of Alabama and finish prosecuting the Sixteenth Street Baptist Church Bombing cases."

Doug Jones, "Justice for Four Girls: The Bombing of the Sixteenth Street Baptist Church Cases," *Young Lawyer* (American Bar Association Young Lawyers Division), Volume 14, Number 5, February/March 2010, 1.

Chapter 11. Mating Call

One day after driving away from the nursing home, suddenly I heard a loud thud. It grew worse as I drove along, so I turned on my blinkers and pulled off onto the shoulder of road to check things out. It turned out to be a flat tire. My mind was racing ahead, full steam. I had this "thing" about driving, years after the bombing. How in the world was I going get out of this jam? Before I could gather my thoughts, a dark, handsome man walked up to me with a playful grin on his face, as if his smile alone could resolve everything.

He had spotted me pulling off on the side of the road as he was traveling in the opposite direction, and doubled back around to see if I needed help. Quickly sizing things up, he offered his help right on the spot. I kept a spare tire in the trunk of my car. After he retrieved the spare, he got started. His skills were on open display. Clearly, he knew about cars. Before I could catch my breath, he had already finished the job. I later learned that this Good Samaritan was a mechanic by trade. That much he did share with me, as he labored.

"How much do I owe you sir?"

"Nothing at all," I replied.

"Well, I can't thank you enough," I said as I hurriedly got inside my car.

"Look here, can I get your name and telephone number – that is if you don't mind?"

"Can you?" I responded. "I don't give my number out. Anyway, my name Sarah."

"Hello. Pleased to meet you Miss Sarah," he said. "Some call me Roy but my full name is Leroy Cox," he added for emphasis. He was clearly stalling, hoping to engage me in conversation. "But *you* can just call me Leroy," he continued.

Feeling a tug of sympathy for him, I asked Leroy to give me his number, knowing fully that I wasn't going to call him. I figured it was the least I could do. After all, I had tried to pay him for the job, but he refused to take any money.

"Now make sure you stop by the service station to put more air in your spare tire. It doesn't have enough right now," Leroy said. "And get the flat tire repaired. It may still be okay."

"Thank you so much," I said as I climbed back into my vehicle and drove away.

I immediately went to the service station to follow through with his advice. Unfortunately, the mechanic there could not repair the tire, so I ended up calling Leroy, the man who initially helped me. I wanted to know the best place to purchase a brand-new tire. Leroy told me that they sold tires where he worked and proceeded to give me his work address. I went there the following day. I told one of the other mechanics at the shop what size I needed. His co-worker gave me a deal, outfitting me with the new tire. I was glad to put that episode behind me. I had to have reliable transportation in my line of work.

Good Bait

I continued to care for my patients and clean homes. Meanwhile, about a week after I had dealt with my car situation, I received a mysterious telephone call.

"Hello."

"And how are you today?"

"Okay," I said curiously. After pausing I asked, "Who this is?"

"It's Leroy."

"Leroy who," I asked as I began to replay the past few days in my mind. I remembered the kind man who came to my assistance when my tire blew out. It seemed odd to me. How could he possibly know my telephone number? In the end, curiosity got the best of me. "How did you get this number?"

"I wrote it down from off the form," he replied. "You filled it out when you brought the tire to our shop that day. I've wanted to call you ever since." He added, "I thought you would hang up on me."

I hesitated. "Well, thanks for helping me out that day."

"I've had you on my mind ever since Sarah," he said. "Would it be all right to call and talk to you from time to time?" Sensing a minor break through, he continued. "I usually don't have anything to do after I leave work. I just want to be able to talk to someone."

"Well, nothing's wrong with talking," I said.

Anyway, Leroy and I proceeded to talk on a regular basis for the next several months. We would converse almost every night. We were forming a real friendship, so I thought. As time went by, Leroy stopped calling as often. Then the calls stopped altogether just as quickly as they began. I didn't think anything of it. Life had taught me to "keep on pushin.'"

Chapter 12. The Father, the Son and the Holy Ghost

Lift up your heads, O ye gates'; and be ye lift up, ye everlasting doors; and the King of glory shall come in. Who is this King of glory? The Lord strong and mighty, the Lord mighty in battle. Psalm 24: 7-8.

Redeemed. Redeemed. I've been washed in the blood of the lamb.
Redeemed. Redeemed. I've been washed in the blood of the lamb.
(Traditional Song)

Prior to cleaning homes and sitting with older adults, I worked in the foundries in Birmingham, Al. for about thirteen to fourteen years. I was hiding out because I was ashamed. I still felt bad about how I looked, years after the bombing. I often felt nervous, even fearful at times, so I began to do things to try to help ease my anxieties.

Everything the enemy told me to do, I was doin.' I began to drink heavily. I also began to go to parties and started smokin' marijuana, thinking all those kinda' things would help my condition and ease my anxieties. Oh, but when I got through drinkin' and smokin' marijuana, or when all of that wore down, I was still in that bad shape, you know, so I started really attending church regularly once again.[1]

Anyway, I didn't go back to 16th Street Church. I started back going to church, regularly. I called it "visiting churches," you know. I visited churches all around the city of Birmingham; the city has countless churches. Still, I could not find permanent relief for what I was going through. I went through life, some twenty years or more, in that foggy state of mind.[2] Deep down inside, I felt that life had more to offer me.

Invitation

One day my sister called me. Janie told me she was goin' to a church that was on Avenue G. She sounded so excited. I sat up on the edge of my seat, waiting to hear even more of her good news.

"Sarah, you really need to come to the church I attend. It's called the International Lighthouse Church," she said. "God is using Apostle Eric Smith to perform all kinds of miracles." Janie continued excitedly, "God is healing, and the people are being saved in Jesus' name," she exclaimed.

Well, I was happy to hear about all of this and perked up immediately. I said, "Oh, I gotta' try that church."

"Well then, just come on down to Avenue G," Janie replied.

I thought that my sister said Avenue C. I drove there but was unable to find the building. You know how the enemy will try to turn you around from discovering just what you need to find.[3] I called Janie to tell her about my mishap.

"When are you going back," I asked her.

"Tonight," she said.

That was all that I needed to hear. "I'm gonna' make sure that I go with you." I met up with Janie later.

When we got there, the apostle was already preaching. "Repent and be baptized in Jesus' name for the remission of yo' sins," he cried out. "And ye shall receive the gift of the Holy Ghost."

I sat there in silence, mesmerized at the words flowing from his lips. Everything was sounding so good to my ears. I wanted this 'Holy Ghost' more than I wanted anything else.

I had tried everything, but I didn't try Jesus, you know. Ooh and he began to really preach that word, so I thought to myself, 'Look like this is exactly what I need.'

"When you repent and get covered in the blood," he preached, "God will wash all your sins away."

I thought to myself, "It looks like I need to try this right now."

"If you want to repent and be saved and baptized," he said, "just go on upstairs. The saints will get you ready."

He continued, "All you ladies, you go this way," he said, while pointing to the side. He continued, "Men move to the left, ladies to the right," as the saints gathered around.

Sitting in my seat in the pews, I was so excited. Well, I bolted up and ran so quickly that my shoes fell off. I left them right there and ran to the upper room. The saints told me to pray, and I followed their advice, asking God to forgive me for my sin.

"Just keep talking to God," the apostle encouraged me.

I really began to ask God to forgive me. Cause' I had so many sins. I wanted to be washed in the blood. I prayed on. Afterwards, I went on out there in the water and he baptized me in Jesus' name, Glory to God![4]

I felt so good when I came up from under the water that night.

After the baptism, the preacher asked if anybody wanted to join the church. Well, I joined church that same night. Further, I wanted to be with Janie. We liked being together.

Later on, I began to attend this congregation regularly. I would experience a profound change in my life. After taking this step, making this change, God began to heal me of something I had carried in my spirit for about twenty-five years. I recall the moment it all got started. Onc night, as I silently sat in the pews, Apostle Eric Smith motioned for me to come up front.

I sat in about the fourth row. I was looking straight ahead, as the Apostle continued with the service. He began praying, talking to God, and calling out for people to come forward. He looked over at me.

"You," he repeated. "Yeah, you come here right now please," he said motioning toward me. "*Tonight gon' be your night*," he boldly stated, as I gradually moved forward.[5]

"I see you have a nervous condition." The apostle continued." "God is showing me that you have a nervous condition..."

And I said, "Y-yes," just like that. I knew that he had to have received that message from God up above because this man didn't know me from Adam. He didn't know nothin' about me, at the time.

And I said, "Yeah, yeah," just like that.

The Apostle continued, "Well God said He gonna' heal you, right now!" By that time, I had slowly inched my way even closer to him.

"Raise your hands up," he said.

I slowly lifted my hands up, as the preacher began to pray for me, I fell under the anointing. When the apostle reached out and touched my forehead, I literally hit the floor. I had never felt like that before. As the scriptures detail, "The prayers of the righteous availeth much." Honey let me tell you; Apostle Smith *really* prayed for me! And deliverance followed, quickly. As one of my friend's aunt is fond of saying, "'God did it!'"

I was a different person altogether when I got up. I used to be scared to speak in church. But when I got back up off that floor again, I began to run around in the church that night, whoa, Praise God! After I joined church, I immediately got busy there.

After that meaningful night, I realized that I had been suffering from many afflictions since the bombing. Up until the time I joined the International Lighthouse, I had attended so many different churches. Oftentimes people would just stare at my face. The scars on my face may have put folks off. In different scenarios, people acted as if I had a disease or something. I did not allow any of this to hinder my worship. I attended churches that I knew I would not join later. Yet, the International Lighthouse was altogether different. I felt love, total acceptance there. I did not go through so many mixed emotions. As time went by, I came across another, even deeper revelation. If only I had not looked at the people for acceptance, but to God.

Aside from attending church regularly, life changed in other ways too after God healed me. For instance, my fear of driving on the freeway, especially in rainy weather, eased up, noticeably. Talking or testifying in front of congregations, no longer taxed me. In fact, I became a devotional leader, and an usher. I even sang on the choir. I couldn't even sing, praise God! At one time, Apostle Eric Smith's brother was our choir director. One day, he asked me to lead a song. I still remember the song I chose, "This is the Way We Praise Our God." Nothing could stop me from praising God after He manifested himself and became a real presence in my daily life.

Having gained a new boldness, I was not scared to do anything in the church, or in life for that matter, Glory to God! He made a *wonderful change* in my life. I used to sit up in church like a zombie; Before God touched me that night. This awakening let me know that God is real! I know for myself that I never felt like that in the past, thank you Jesus! [6]

As time went on, I went to a tent worship service, too. During this outdoor service, the prophet spoke a powerful word about my past, bringing a crucial aspect of it into greater clarity.

"I see smoke, dust all around you," the Apostle told me.

I listened in silence, as he continued to speak.

"A pillar was supposed to collapse on you," he continued. "But an angel held it upright, sparing your life."

At the time Apostle Smith relayed this message, he still did not know about my connection to the 16th Street Church bombing.

There were other changes too after the apostle prayed for me. I was never one for talking to news reporters. After God touched me, I was ready to face my past, and the future. My face even began to clear up. Many people noticed this change, including my sisters. The overall improvement in my physical appearance was something to witness. It also did wonders for my self-esteem. God was healing or cleansing me, inside and out.

I Hear a Rhapsody

The Birmingham News called me in September of 1988 to ask about my life some twenty-five years after the blast. I invited reporters to come on over to my place. I shared with them that living had been difficult, until I came to accept Jesus Christ as my Lord and Savior. After that, I adjusted better to life's demands and challenges.

Following a series of interviews, other significant changes began to unfold in my world. For instance, one day after the interviews ended, the telephone rang. To my shock, it was Leroy Cox. After we eased into conversation, I fell silent.

"Why you stop callin' me Leroy?" I asked.

There was a brief pause. "I been sick, Sarah. My stomach's been bothering me," he said without going into detail.

I did not press any further. Instead, I began telling Leroy about the Lord, and how the Apostle prayed for me when I went to the International Lighthouse Church. I could slowly hear the excitement building in Leroy's voice as I went on. I shared with him how God had even healed me of a nervous condition and fearfulness.

"Do you want to go to church with me? They're having service this Friday?" I told him.

"Yes," he responded without hesitation. Leroy went that Friday. Almost unbelievably, the preacher baptized him that same day. Leroy liked the church so much that he joined it the next Sunday. And God began to do great things for him, let me tell you! God healed his stomach problem.

I could see a new peace in Leroy, as we began spending more time together. He was so very alert. He had noticed how my hair had begun to fall out, especially on one side of my head and recommended that I visit a beautician, which turned out to be sound advice. The hairdresser began to treat my hair, and it started growing again. To top this off, Leroy would take care of my car whenever anything went south. We were growing closer with each passing day, spending a lot of time together. We were falling deeply in-love.

About a year later, Leroy asked me to marry him. I consented. And we got married on December 16, 1989 at the International Lighthouse Church. Our wedding was lovely. My husband looked dashing in his white tuxedo. Of course, Mama attended, as she appeared alert that day. I introduced her to Leroy years earlier. She saw the possibilities for us, even then. But she had become more forgetful, as her health declined.

Janie made all the gowns and dresses for the wedding. She had the church decorated so nice. I did not send out invitations, but many of Leroy's family members and friends were there. After the wedding, we went to Atlanta for our honeymoon.

Happiness and joy surrounded us. My husband had a zest for life. He was skilled at operating boats. We would stay out in the boat for hours. He took me fishing too. He was great at it. Leroy even taught me how to use the rod and reel. In sum, our life together was splendid.

Notes

1 Sarah Collins Rudolph, "The Message," First A.M.E. lecture
2 Ibid.
3 Rudolph, "The Message."
4 Ibid.
5 Shauna Stuart, "'God Had to do a Work in Me': Sarah Collins Rudolph on Reclaiming Her Story," al.com, September 10, 2018, https://www.al.com/ news/.
6 Rudolph, "The Message."

Chapter 13. Kulu se Mama

In search of our mothers' garden, I found my own. – Alice Walker

Surely, I have behaved and quieted myself, as a child that is weaned of his mother: my soul is even as a weaned child.
—Psalm 131:2, KJV

The year of 1990 stands out for several important reasons. During this phase of my personal life, our family had to rebound from yet another devastating blow.

During that year, I had begun to spend even more time with my Mother. The doctors diagnosed her with Alzheimer's disease; added to this, and an almost crippling arthritis began to take its toll on her body. As her condition grew worse, I became one of Momma's primary caregivers. On the rare day that she felt like getting out, I would take Mama to church. She really enjoyed going to church and would stand up and sing songs, or even testify on her good days. Church members looked forward to her 'rip-roaring' testimonies. At that time, we were still attending the International Lighthouse.

One day the Apostle asked the congregation, "Does anyone want to be baptized in the name of Jesus?"

Mama grabbed my hand. "Take me up front Sarah. I want to be baptized," she insisted.

Apostle Smith would baptize Mama that very day. You should have heard the body of the church applaud and rejoice in the Lord!

While her health held up, Mama worshipped with us in church. She loved to sing. Oftentimes she forgot the name of her favorite song.

Mama would scratch her head with a puzzled look, trying in vain to remember it. Her once serene facial expression would turn serious.

"Pass. Pass… Oh, what *is* the name of that song Sarah?" Mama would ask me.

"Do Not Pass Me By," I would gently remind her.

The church members would laugh and nod approvingly. They loved my Mother, too. After all, how could anyone, not love her? Of course, I knew the words. I embrace the lyrics to this song every day of life. *Pass me not, Oh gentle Savior, hear my humble cry, While on others thou art calling, do not pass me by.*[1]

On September 16, 1990, I attended a special event — the dedication of Addie's very own tombstone at a gravesite service at Woodlawn, or formerly Greenwood Cemetery. Mama's rapidly declining condition did not permit her to go along with me, however several parents of the other little girls were there, including Mrs. Apha Bliss Robertson and Mrs. Gertrude Wesley who described the service a "'lovely.'"[2] Mr. Tom Mullinax kindly donated the tombstone to honor my dear sister Addie. It reads:

SHE DIED SO THAT FREEDOM MAY LIVE![3]

Her grave used to be marked with a wooden cross. Tom Mullinax, who purchased the tombstone for my sister stated, "'a hero deserved a better grave than that.'"[4] Remarkably, officials also honored all four of the little girls "with a state historical marker noting that three are buried in Birmingham's oldest black cemetery."[5] Several dignitaries and invited guests spoke at the brief service, but I didn't say too much. Melanie Jones, who covered the event, wrote, "During the ceremony, Sarah Collins Cox sat stoically beside her sister's new tombstone."[6] Actually, I was breathing a sigh of relief. "'I feel real good that so many thought enough to put a headstone on my sister's grave," I shared with her. I continued, "She had nothing but a piece of wood,'" marking her grave.[7]

At the time, Reverend Cross, who used to serve as the pastor of the Sixteenth Street Baptist Church, thoughtfully commented:

> "We must say to them, 'Thank you Addie Mae, Cynthia, Carole and Denise. Because you have made us grow as a city and a people. We have grown from hatred to love, chaos to community and to become

not a city associated with bombings, but a city associated with progress and entertainment."[8]

Mr. Mullinax invited George Wallace III and Martin Luther King III to "show how far we have come in Alabama by having two individuals on the same program whose fathers played such a pivotal role in the history of the civil rights movement."[9] King wasn't able to attend due to a prior obligation, but Wallace did attend the dedication ceremony. He said, ""I know my father, who was governor of Alabama at the time of the bombing, was shaken by the bombing that resulted in the deaths of these children.""[10]

Within weeks of the gravesite dedication, my emotions quickly shifted from a highpoint to a sinking low. Momma's condition was rapidly worsening. For some time, she could not attend church. Mama had long since stopped speaking. I had so enjoyed talking with Mama and spending time with her at social outings. Honestly, after she had been sick for so long, I believe that she forgot my name, too.

"Do you know who I am?" I would ask her, as she stared blankly ahead. "I'm your *baby girl*, Sarah," I would emphasize to Mama, hoping against hope to trigger a response, or nod of recognition.

Maybe it was the ravages of time, coupled with a cruel brain disease and the pain of losing a daughter. Her body was there, but the soul had begun to slip away with each passing day. I suppose that is why some people refer to this disease as the "long good-bye."

Mama had long ceased to discuss Addie's death, or referring to the compensation that she had waited for so many years in vain. Perhaps, the pain was still real despite the brave front she put up for so many years.

One day they rushed Mama to the hospital. I stood by her side to the very end. When she passed away on October 5, 1990, I was devastated. She gave birth to me and was with me when I experienced two of the most devastating losses in my lifetime -- the deaths of my sister and baby. As fate would have it, Addie was the one child that Mother could not save.

I missed the many intimate conversations that we used to share. As I indicated before, during one such talk Momma told me about the pledge or promise made to help her financially in the wake of Addie's death and my life-threatening injury. Some of her lifelong struggles like this one have become mine. My Mom taught me so much about life. I learned priceless lessons about civil disobedience from her, too. I have come to treasure a calendar picture that shows Momma holding her purse, while standing proudly on the steps of a church, along with other "foot soldiers."

After Momma passed, I wanted to keep myself busy. During this period, Leroy and I began to look for a house that we could call our own. He wanted a home with a large garage, which he could also use to repair cars. One day while I was flipping through the newspaper, I spotted an ad: "House for sale with a very large garage." After checking it out, we got so excited. It was the ideal home for us, with a two-car garage and ample storage space, so we spoke to the realtor. He informed us that three people ahead of us were already in the loop. Still, we signed a contract anyway and deposited our "earnest money" as a down payment. When we got home, we said a special prayer.

The realtor called us a few months later. At the time, we did not realize that they were going to let us get the house. He was calling to tell us how much we had to have for the closing cost soon. Luckily, both Leroy and I had been saving money. We were still short by five hundred dollars. We promptly set that amount aside on the following payday and closed on the house.

To our delight, the house passed inspection. The first task that I completed was to wallpaper all of the rooms. I love wallpaper. It can bring a burst of vibrant, beautiful colors to almost any unadorned room. I also bought curtains to match the wallpaper, while LeRoy measured the windows for installing the blinds. We moved in after I cleaned the house. Once we settled in, LeRoy surprised me. One day later, he brought home the most beautiful black chow. He was jet black and looked like a grizzly bear, so we simply called him Grizzly. He was a good watchdog. For instance, he barked if anyone came nearby while LeRoy was putting his tools inside the garage. Overall, Grizzly helped to lift our spirits.

Notes

1 Fanny Crosby wrote the words to "Pass Me Not, O Gentle Savior" in 1868, while William H. Doane would provide the music a few years later. Several contemporary

artists, including M.C Hammer, have recorded or updated the traditional hymn; Hammer entitled his version, "Do Not Pass Me By" (1991).

2 Melanie Jones, "Bomb's Victim's Grave Finally Gets Stone," *The Birmingham News*, September 16, 1990.

3 Tom Mullinax penned this inscription for Addie Mae Collins' headstone.

4 Ibid.

5 Ibid.

6 Ibid.

7 Ibid.

8 Ibid.

9 Ibid.

10 Ibid.

Chapter 14. Summertime

Let him kiss me with the kisses of his mouth: for thy love *is* better than wine. (Song of Solomon 1:2 KJV)

Some periods in life we just want to savor. After years of turmoil and tumult, I had finally reached such a point in my life. Some weekends, Leroy and I would invite the family over and I would barbecue. He also had a large swimming pool installed in our backyard. The kids really enjoyed the pool, not to mention the snacks and food. Generally, I would prepare the food. A friend complimented me on my ribs and encouraged me to sell food on Saturdays. It sounded like a good idea, so we got together and planned how we were going to execute it. Word got out and Leroy's friends came over to buy my barbecue rib sandwiches. Some of my family members and friends bought sandwiches too. It was a success, and the extra money came in handy. We bought bricks and cement, and Leroy built an even larger barbecue pit.

That summer I also decided to plant a vegetable garden that consisted of greens, tomatoes, red peppers, bell peppers and okra. After we finished, I noticed that the front yard could benefit from some coloring. I went and got some beautiful azaleas and planted them in the front yard. The garden was growing slowly. I noticed my next-door neighbor had a beautiful garden, so I asked her for some tips. She encouraged me to try a different solution. She gave me some of her Miracle Growth to start with and instructed me how to use it. Within a few days, I could see a difference in my garden. I went out, bought some of my own, and used it as she explained to me. I tried it on my flowers, and they grew. I had some of the prettiest and largest vegetables you could ever see. I started putting my vegetables in bags and placed them in the freezer. I also gave much of my vegetables away. After that summer, I had a garden every year for a long time.

Nature Boy

Some days when the weather was not too hot, Leroy and I would go to Rainbow City or Logan Martin to fish. I would catch a few fish but not nearly as many as Leroy usually caught. Let me tell you, that man could really fish. If they were not biting on one side of the lake, Leroy would usually move somewhere else. He would not spend much time in spots where the fish were not biting. Sometimes we would go to another lake altogether and stay there for hours on end, or long as we caught fish. One day we pulled in a huge turtle. It was so funny. I had never seen anything like that before. I told Leroy to throw it back in the water and he did. About an hour later, I caught a great big catfish. An unspoken competition began between us. After I caught the catfish, he went on a tear, reeling in three more catfish, four brim and two trout.

Every time we went fishing, I boasted to Leroy, "I'm going to catch more fish than you today." However, he caught more fish every single time.

I had to change tactics, quickly. "Hey, whoever catches the most fish gets to clean them too," I said.

"Bet," he replied.

My husband often was stuck with this task. Like a good sport, in the end I usually pitched in and helped him out.

On the surface of it, we had discovered love's *magic potion,* as everything had been going great. That is until Leroy went to work one Monday morning. His boss informed him that they were going to have to lay someone off because business had gotten slow. Since he was one of the last employees hired, he was laid off the following Friday. Leroy came home upset.

"Don't worry. You are an excellent mechanic. And you gotta' a garage. Maybe you can tool around the garage until something better comes along," I encouraged him.

Leroy shrugged his shoulders and sighed deeply, but I could tell that I had planted a seed. He quickly set up shop, and it didn't take long for him to find a customer. He rebuilt a motor for one man. I had never seen someone break down a motor and put it back together with all new parts. I found this work to be fascinating. I would sit and watch him for hours. Leroy could really put a motor together. He bought a cherry picker from the flea market to make his work easier. It was amazing to see him crank or raise the car up, after he placed the newly rebuilt motor in the vehicle and bolted it into place.

As the word spread, people flocked to Leroy's garage to get their cars repaired. Then again, success does not always come without a price tag. I no longer appreciated the way that Leroy was keeping the garage. It became increasingly untidy. I knew this job could be grimy at times, with oil stains everywhere; however, at some point it became ridiculous. I found myself constantly picking up paper and tin cans, removing oil stains. Leroy had purchased chemicals to put on the oil spills but to no avail. Never one to shy from work, I used to cart off smaller car parts so that I could maneuver around the garage in order to create more space in the garage. I believe in cleanliness and order.

There were many cars near or on our property, which led to undesired attention, as people began to take notice. Finally, the city became involved and cited Leroy for various infractions. Officials came over and told us that Leroy could not repair cars in the neighborhood because it violated the zoning ordinance. To his credit, he tried to get the area rezoned. This was a difficult task due to the residential restrictions, so he abandoned this effort and switched to the tactic of going to the homes of his clients to repair their vehicles. This option did not work either because people in the other neighborhoods would only complain about the noise level. Always enterprising, Leroy had to find other jobs. He tried a few options, ranging from carpentry to mowing lawn and repairing appliances. In general, the living was not quite so easy anymore. We still had bills to pay.

Chapter 15. The Believer

One particular Sunday LeRoy decided to accompany me to church. On that morning, Apostle Eric Smith preached on tithing (Malachi 3:8-12). After we left church that day, Leroy declared that he was going to follow these teachings. From that point onward, he began to tithe ten percent of his earnings. God began to pour out blessings on Leroy who was getting jobs left and right. People were donating cars to him. Once again, he parked all the cars in front of the yard. He bought a mobile home and a wrecker and placed gates all around the front of the house, wishfully thinking that the authorities would not be able to spot our home from the street. Is anything we do in life ever really hidden, especially when we are trying to walk in the light?

Leroy's business was booming, so he completed carpentry work on our house. He remodeled our home and built a porch upstairs. Repairs aside, slowly people began to take note of all the cars again. Word got back and eventually officials from the city began to complain about the cars parked on the street; they demanded that Leroy move them. He parked some of these cars at the homes of our different neighbors, while he drove other vehicles to the homes of his friends for safekeeping. In time, he began to work in his garage once again. This decision quickly proved to be a disaster. Junk started piling up worse than ever before. Perhaps he should have looked to buy a shop in a business zone; hindsight is 20-20. In truth, finances were still a question mark. To make things worse, Leroy's "friends" started sitting around while he worked on cars. Some of the fellas even brought alcohol with them to our house.

Everything went downhill from there. Nothing was ever the same again. After a period, the beer cans began to pile up around the garage. One day I went into the garage as soon as Leroy and his friends left. I just could not believe my eyes—oil stains were on the side of the garage, whisky bottles, wine bottles, and oily rags were everywhere. The garage was in tatters, a complete mess. I never thought things would get that bad.

Leroy drank moderately when we first met, but drinking had become his pastime. The garage had become the gathering place or a hangout for my husband and his drinking buddies. I constantly had to ask him to keep the space tidy. Occasionally, he tried, but the garage never stayed clean for long.

Leroy stopped going to church altogether, as he began to spend more time in the garage than our home. He had a phone and refrigerator put into the garage. Why, he even installed a bathroom in the garage! He practically had everything that he needed there. He only came into the house to eat or go to bed.

I used to think that we were such a unique pair or couple, but Leroy and I rarely spent time together anymore; instead, alcohol became like his best friend. Beer cans lined the inside of the refrigerator inside the garage. Leroy bought a can crusher and saved his beer cans. Always enterprising, when he collected enough cans, he sold them. He used this money to purchase even more beer!

Don't Explain

My husband was neglecting his work and responsibilities around the house. When our heating system failed temporarily, we did not have enough money to purchase another unit. We had to burn coal and wood. At first, he was good about getting coal and wood ordered. We never had to worry about staying warm, but it got to the point where Leroy even stopped following through with the orders. We would soon suffer the consequences.

We had a bad snowstorm in March one year. We did not have enough money to order coal or wood, so I decided to go to the coalhouse to pick up two sacks of coal and some wood. I wanted our house to be warm after the storm. After I got home and put the coal and wood away, Leroy arrived later with a big sack.

"What's that?" I asked him.

"When the storm comes in, I want to make sure I have me something to drink."

Leroy had purchased a half-gallon of liquor. I didn't say nothing. Not a peep. I ended up starting the fireplace that day. The house was warm and cozy.

Before I had fully woken up the next morning, LeRoy casually sauntered into our home with a woman and two little boys -- *my fault, I fear.* I couldn't allow myself to go *there*. Anyway, this woman, I believe her name was Tina, stayed up the hill from us. We became fast friends that day, as Tina volunteered that her heater had stopped working. It was freezing cold at her house. After chitchatting with her, I cooked a meal for all of us on my coal stove. We had black-eyed peas, fried chicken, and cornbread for dinner. Later that day, the snow melted a little, and we walked to the store. Tina and her sons were good company. After the storm, she called her father who picked Tina and the boys up and took them to his house.

After that winter snowstorm, Leroy hooked up another heater in our home. I did not want to repeat that scenario again. However, not all the storms of life were behind us. One cold night, Leroy's cousin called me.

"You need to come and get your husband," he said. "Leroy's sittin' inside his car fast asleep with the motor running," he blurted out.

"Where's the car?"

"At Vice Hill Apartments."

Leroy was inside his car, still drunk and asleep when I arrived. I banged on the window. Within a few moments, he opened his eyes. I repeated this action, trying to keep his attention.

"What you want?" Leroy mumbled, while he was still drunk. "What do you want?" he repeated. His eyes were beet red.

"Open this car door," I shouted back.

He complied and slowly staggered out the car, almost tripping or losing his balance. He leaned on me, and we walked home together. His breathe was heavy or stale with the smell of liquor. As soon as we got home, he went back to sleep. Eventually, he sobered up.

"We need to talk," I said later.

I continued. "Why have you been drinking so much lately? Don't you remember when you were sick the last time?" I reminded him, "God healed you my dear. I didn't think you would start drinking again."

I began to tell my husband about the unclean spirit. "He walketh through dry places, seeking rest, and findeth none. Then he saith, I will return in my house from whence I came out. And when he cometh in, he findeth it empty, swept and garnished. Then it goes out and brings along seven other spirits even worse than itself, and they come and live there…."' (Matthew 12: 43-45). Ultimately, the man is in worse shape than he was at the start.

I later explained to Leroy, "You need to go back to church. Ask God to forgive you." I went on. The word says, "Because if we confess our sins, he is faithful and just to forgive our sins and to cleanse us from all unrighteousness" (John 1:91).

Leroy found his way back to church for a season. Still, he did not get serious with God about his problems. He wasn't ready to stop drinking. Most days when LeRoy got home, he could not wait to get in the garage to pop open a can of ice-cold beer. He thought drinking was the answer to his problems. However, this lifestyle created a rift, breach between us. I watched joy and laughter all *slip away* from our marriage, leaving an almost unbearable strain behind. The fleeting thought *where are the clowns* when we need them most was not lost on me.

Leroy used to exhibit many great qualities. He was so protective of me in the past. I used to think the world of him, but he was changing, becoming more like a stranger to me with each passing day. Everything was changing.

Chapter 16. Little Old Lady

Leroy continued to find odd jobs as a mechanic, while I stayed busy too. I kept my job providing an elderly man with meals. God blessed me with another patient to take care of in the meantime. Her name was Mrs. Penelope Garrett. I was her caregiver. Penelope turned out to be one of the nicest persons that I have ever had the opportunity to know. Although we were born in and shaped by different eras, she provided me with priceless lessons about life.

I worked two days a week for Mrs. Garrett. She lived nearby me, which made our working arrangement simple. She needed someone to take her shopping and to places like the bank and beauty salon since Mrs. Garrett's hearing was failing her. While I worked for her, she also began to complain about her sight, so I took her to the eye doctor.

After one visit, in a moment of deep despair Penelope declared, "I can't see. I wish I wasn't alive."

"Don't ever wish that you were dead because you don't know who will need you while you're living," I replied instantly. "Right now, God's using you to be a blessing in my life. While you have breath in your body, just thank the Lord. And always remember, someone out there is in much worse condition than you are."

Afterwards, I told her about my past and the bombing. Penelope was speechless. In time, we became good friends. We would call each other and talk for hours. She keenly remembered things from her childhood days. If I must say so myself, she had an excellent memory; especially for someone who was ninety-six years old. She was a cut-up, hilarious. We would sit back and laugh about some of the stories she shared with me.

Her skill as a storyteller was unmatched. Knitting came easily to Mrs. Garrett, when her eyesight did not bother her. She kept a clean house and worked in the garden as a pastime when she had the energy. Mrs. Garrett only asked for help when she was not up to certain tasks.

One day, Mrs. Garrett asked me to cut the grass. Even though it was not one of my usual tasks, I told her that I would certainly try. As I began to mow the lawn, observing me out of the corner of her eyes, she said, "That's not the right way Sarah. Let me show you how."

Mrs. Garrett made her way over to the lawnmower and began to show me how to mow the lawn "correctly." She was surprisingly strong and nimble. Even now, I smile to myself when I remember who *really* taught me this skill.

Mrs. Garrett no longer had any children. The one son she had died many years ago, but some of her nieces and a granddaughter lived just outside of town. Occasionally, I would talk to them on the telephone when they called the house. Later they came to Birmingham, and I got the chance to meet all of them. They were so happy to see me in person, and I was happy to meet them, finally.

Sometimes when Mrs. Garrett and I shopped for clothes, she grew fed up looking for clothes that suited her. Mrs. Garrett rarely found an outfit that she liked. She wanted clothes that were not too fancy for a "seasoned citizen." Further complicating matters, Mrs. Garrett was tiny, even shorter than I was, I might add. We were quite the pair walking together around Birmingham – young and old, one black, and the other white.

One day when I did not have to work, Mrs. Garrett fell ill. When the meals-on-wheel person came to deliver her meal, they found her on the floor unconscious. Emergency personnel rushed her to the hospital where she slipped into a coma for about two weeks. I would go there and pray for her almost daily. Once when I arrived, she was struggling to take breathes. As I sat nearby, a stillness fell over her. I immediately asked the nurse on duty to come check on her.

"I'm glad you were there with her," the nurse said. "At least she didn't die alone."

The nurse asked for my name. She later informed the family that I was there when Ms. Garrett took her last breath. Now, I didn't attend the funeral, as I find the idea of funerals hard to take --- the funerals that I have attended and the services that I could not attend. Anyway, after the funeral Ms. Garret's family told me all the fond memories that she shared with them about us. I was surprised at all the wonderful times that she treasured and remembered. As they were leaving, her family members promised to give me something they knew Ms. Garrett would have wanted me to have when they returned.

Dealin'

After the death of Mrs. Garrett, I began to refocus on saving my marriage. I longed for the happier times that LeRoy and I shared together in the beginning. In the meantime, I found other work.

Leroy's drinking had returned full force. He also started staying out all night. Often when I was leaving home for work, he would be returning to go to bed. Usually, he was still hanging out. We barely communicated at all. It got to the point where I would not see Leroy for three, four days or more at a stretch. I was uptight and worried sick. I could not take it in anymore and finally spoke up one day.

"If you don't want to stay here and help out with the bills, you may as well move in with whoever you stayin' with," I screamed out at Leroy. He did not say anything.

"I don't need help to do badly. If you can't help out around here, just leave."

After my outburst, not much changed. Leroy still spent a lot of time in the garage. The garage light remained on all night. The bills continued to pile up every month. In time, he did straighten up a little and got a job. He worked for three weeks until he got sick. He went to Carraway Emergency, complaining of sharp stomach pains. This intense pain would last for five minutes at a time and suddenly stop. The doctors there were not able to diagnose what was wrong with Leroy. The next time that he had an episode, Lee went to Cooper Green Hospital. Their doctors were also clueless. Racked with stomach pain, the chills would follow suit. Poor Leroy was in this bad condition for nearly two months, on and off. One day it got so bad I told him to make an appointment at Brookwood hospital. He made an appointment that same day.

After examining him, the doctor told my husband to call his family because they were going to hospitalize him. They suspected that there was an issue with his arteries. Further tests verified that this was the problem, so Leroy stayed overnight, and the physicians released him from the hospital the next evening. After that day, he did not have any more problems and went back to work. I thought everything was going to work out after this episode. In fact, things got better, temporarily.

As time went by, the subject of transportation came up. Leroy thought we needed another car. I was not convinced that we needed a car. I went along anyway. When we got to the car lot, eventually I spotted a red Cavalier that I liked. I had never bought a new car before in my life. I really wanted everything in my credit to check out. By the next day, I was driving off the lot with that car.

After I purchased the car, Leroy initially changed for the better. When he returned to work, he made sure that I had everything that I needed. He also started being more attentive once again, which may have saved my vision.

Chapter 17. Soul Eyes

His eye is on the sparrow and I know He watches me.
–Dale Reichel

Can't find what you can't see…?[1]
—Michael S. Harper

Almost as if on cue, one day Leroy asked me, "When was the last time you had your eyes checked Sarah?"

"It's been a long time," I said. My eyes had started to bother me again. But I had slowly grown used to the pain and discomfort.

"You need to go. I know your glasses need to be changed by now."

I made an appointment at America's Best Eye Care. Besides, they offered a free eye exam and two pair of glasses. After the eye exam, the nurse continued, "Do you want to get your eye pressure checked?"

"No," I said.

"It's only ten dollars more. It's important," the nurse replied.

"Okay, go ahead and check it," I said.

After the procedure ended, I knew instantly something wasn't right. The nurse consulted with the ophthalmologist who informed me that my pressure was fifty. He immediately wrote a prescription for me to get some eye drops to reduce the pressure and referred me to a doctor who specialized in glaucoma-related problems. He gave me the address and instructed me to let them know that I was on the way.

I recall his dire warning: "Don't stop anywhere until you get there."

I still don't remember the name of the doctor who checked my eye pressure on that day but credit him for acting swiftly. My eye pressure was sky high. His diagnosis and recommendation helped to save my left eye. Decades after the church bombing, I could have lost my vision without any warning. In some respect, that conversation with Leroy was my warning.

Following the bombing, doctors would determine I had glaucoma. About a decade later, physicians detected that I also had a cataract in my left eye. I may have had it for a while before the official diagnosis.

I began to check in with an eye doctor regularly the following week. Dr. Aiden Sullivan worked at the Callahan Eye Foundation. When I met him that first day, he was pleasant and happy to see me. The doctor had terrific bedside manner.

"How did you lose sight in your right eye?" he asked me.

"Years ago, at the Sixteenth Street Baptist Church," I replied. I proceeded to tell him about the bombing, thus my journey with Dr. Sullivan began. He sprang into action. He began to treat me with three kinds of eye drops. Initially, I had to come back every month. He told me that it was important to use the eye drops as directed. I only had vision in my left eye. It was critical to maintain it. Dr. Sullivan wanted to make sure that I did not go blind. Each month that I went back, my pressure was lower. Occasionally, when it spiked up, Dr. Sullivan would change the number of drops or put more drops into my eye. In time, my pressure went down to sixteen. I only had to return about once every four months.

If anyone needs a good glaucoma doctor, I highly recommend Dr. Sullivan. He is excellent. He used to refer to me as his "Miracle' Baby" – I guess on the count of my youthful age at the time of the bombing. The second miracle is that I did not lose my vision. Years removed from childhood, it is hard to imagine that any doctor, much less a white physician, could make me feel somewhat at ease despite of everything in the past. I still remember the trauma that I experienced, especially in the months after doctors removed my right eye.

In the past, I used to have to put drops in my eyes four times a day as a part of my routine – once in the morning, a different kind two times a day in the afternoon, and another type before bedtime. I stuck to this routine for decades. I don't have to put drops in my eye now. The doctor informed me to use Refresh Optive Lubricant when it burns.

I still have a piece or fragment of glass in my left eye from the church bombing, but Dr. Sullivan does not want to bother it because it is just sitting in one spot. He refuses to remove it surgically, fearing that something could go wrong and that I could end up blind. When this piece of glass starts to impair the sight in my left eye, I guess the good doctor will consider removing it; my vision is decent despite the piece of glass that remains there. However, I still suffer with glaucoma in my left eye.[2] Dr. Sullivan also reconfirmed that I have a cataract.

About nine years ago, I began to experience serious problems with my left eye. The eye doctor recommended surgery, and I complied. Finally, in June of 2012, my doctor performed an emergency operation. Dr. Sullivan installed a shunt to drain the excessive fluid from my left eye and decrease the level of my eye pressure. This eye does not bother me as much since the surgery. He still checks it every four months to see if the shunt is draining properly.

For a while, the vision in my left remained about the same at first after surgery. Had I not had the surgery, my sight would have gotten worse. Following surgery, my vision was very blurry but improved with time. My left eye is less red. It does not burn all day long, as it used to prior to this surgery. However, some things never change. I still gotta' remove my prosthetic eye and soak it in water every night. This has been my ritual or routine for over fifty years.

I wonder if the person who went around calling herself the "fifth little girl" during the period leading up to the 50th anniversary would want to endure this daily grind. As I recall, Doug Jones, who led the team that prosecuted Blanton and later Cherry, informed me about someone who appeared on the scene just in time for the commemorative activities. Will the *real* Sarah Collins Rudolph stand up? Don't laugh! Sometimes even I gotta' chuckle.

As is often said, imitation is the best form of flattery. I guess the imposter wanted to bask in all the commotion, the glory of the story, but would she want to trade places if she really *looked* at my life? Would she want to see the picture that confronts me every day that I look in the mirror — before I apply or put on my makeup? Would she still want to walk in my shoes, even for a mile? Would she want to fight the battles I have had to fight, pushing through the fears and trauma as a child and an adult? I would like to have met her, if only for a few minutes. We could have engaged in "real talk." I would have been more than willing to share a history lesson or two with her. As I've said before, "Every day I'm reminded of the bombing, just looking in the mirror and seeing the scars in my face. I'm reminded of it every day."[3]

For all the imitators, I am *the* fifth little girl and I still have battle scars to prove it. Some of the burn marks on my body have never faded away entirely, despite the cream and ointments that I've used over the years. Despite the passing of time, they haven't disappeared altogether. Some may find pictures of me without makeup on and with an eye missing from my right eye socket or orbit disturbing, yet this is my reality check when I'm blessed to wake up in the mornings; and the last image I process before turning in for the night. It's a whole lot to think about, trust me.

On the other hand, some have asked me, "How do you feel about only being able to see out of one eye as a result of the bombing?" Well, if you really *looked in my life,* far beyond the lectures and interviews, you would see that I still feel blessed, though I only see outta my left eye. I can get around without having anyone to lead me, as I once gladly led the blind years ago at summer camp. God knows that I was still glad to be a helping hand.

Notes

1 Michael S. Harper, "American History," poetryfoundation.org/poems/42831/American-history-56d221785...

2 Emma Lindsey, "Southern Discomfort," *The Guardian*, September 7, 2002, https://www.theguardian.com/theobserver/2002/sep/08/features.magazine137

3 Tanya Ott, "Long Forgotten."

Chapter 18. Echoes of a Friend

In the sweet by and by,
We shall meet on that beautiful shore.[1]

The dream is the truth.[2] – Zora Neale Hurston

At the beginning of 1998, my family decided to move Addie's body or remains from Greenwood Cemetery to Elmwood Cemetery because of neglected state of the cemetery. My husband encouraged me to pursue this action. Despite his over the top drinking and the difficulties that we were having in our marriage during that period, nonetheless, Leroy gave me helpful advice. He could be fiercely protective of me at various times. Anyway, as January proceeded, Junie selected the mausoleum, while I worked on getting the casket. At first, we did not have enough money to cover all the expenses. Thank God, a lady came forward after learning about the story in the press. She volunteered to help after learning about this part of our story. Outlets such as *People* magazine covered the story.[3] Some folk planned a fundraising program, "Fighting for You," and took up donations to help us move the body.[4] But we were taken aback by a surprising turn of events, after the body was exhumed:

> 'A baffling discovery was made last week when Addie's sister, Sarah, ordered her grave opened….
>
> But when workers opened the Addie's grave, they were horrified to find nothing. They dug 2 feet deeper, then 2 feet wider. Still nothing. No body was there to accompany the gray marker…'[5]

I personally received a surprising call from a journalist or reporter with *People* magazine. She confirmed this news. To our astonishment, my sister "'Addie was not there.'"[6] Later on, one observer would write, "Addie Mae Collins is a key figure in American history.... How could the body of an iconic figure simply disappear without a trace?"[7]

The story of Addie's missing body generated press coverage with the local media in Birmingham and throughout America in papers like *The Los Angeles Times* and *The Washington Post*, as it occurred right before the Martin Luther King holiday. One writer observed, "But today as the nation commemorates King's birthday, Addie Mae Collins is more than a martyr. She is also a mystery."[8] The reporter also indicated that after viewing a documentary about the four victims of the blast at the 16th Street Church, a guide told visiting tourists about the discovery:

> 'Tara Walton, a tour guide, announced that one of the victims was missing. Many people gasped. Walton said talks had been underway to bring all four girls back to the church, to rebury them together in a special memorial area, but that those talks were now indefinitely on hold.'[9]

Well, a reburial never took shape, with Addie's body missing – an underlying viewpoint among some beginning during the late 1990s. The four girls were never reburied in a 'special memorial area' by the church. They were never buried in the same cemetery. Nevertheless, the thought of a her body missing troubled me; some people vandalize and destroy graves, motivated by hatred: Barriers are erected around the graves of some revered civil right activists for this reason. Referring to a visit that I made to Greenwood with Janie, Harriet A. Washington put forward a bold theory in the book M*edical Apartheid*, which had to be considered:

> 'But Janie Gaines and Sarah Cox know from experience that black cadavers tend to disappear. In January 1998, the sisters frowned as they surveyed the crumbling headstones, trash and tangled weeds strangling Greenwood, the Birmingham, Alabama cemetery which their family had long ago laid their sister, Addie Mae Collins. It was thirty years before her sisters could bear to visit her grave, and when they saw its neglected state, they immediately arranged to have Addie Mae moved to another, better-maintained cemetery. However, workers who

> opened the grave recoiled in shock: It was empty, devoid of casket and corpse. Addie Mae's body, like so many buried in black cemeteries throughout the South is missing. No one can know with certainty who took the body or why, but many are convinced that her body joined the untold thousands of anonymous black cadavers on anatomists' tables.'[10]

Janie couldn't revisit Addie's grave; the hurt was too deep, as she said. I also told the media, I had been "'going there, talking to her for years,'" merely to discover Addie wasn't there: "'I knew her spirit was with the Lord, but I never thought that her remains weren't there.'"[11] I have shed many a tear for my sister. At times, I went to her grave with flowers in hand, especially on her birthdays, as I still do. Addie was born on April 18, 1949.

Still, the story of my sister's missing body was confusing, for many years. At the time, some writers considered it a "second" tragedy in relationship to the deadly bombing, and on par with other racially charged episodes. In the distant past and more recently news reporters noted that designated workers made yet a second attempt to locate Addie's remains:

> 'Workers dug in front of the headstone, but the plot was empty. They tried a few feet away in another spot. They found a rusty casket — and inside — the corpse of an elderly person with dentures. Think of that. Rudolph hasn't known the exact location of her sister's remains for 18 years.'[12]

I can say with absolute certainty that my 14-year-old sister *did not* have false teeth, so that corpse could not possibly have been our Addie. Over the years, members of my family and I refused to let this matter die, though the outcome did not seem promising. We were determined to find our sister's remains, as most families would want to do given the circumstances. As Janie remembers, a wooden cross, nearby a tree, marked Addie's final resting place. My family did not have the funds to purchase a headstone at the time of her death in '63.

Caught up in this dilemma, LeRoy, Janie, and her daughter Sonya and I sought further explanation from Poole's Funeral Home, which had conducted Addie's burial. We asked Ms. Poole or the lady at the funeral home to provide us with the location of Addie's plot. Afterwards, the funeral home gave us a general map, indicating where they laid Addie to rest.

Having buried two of the four girls in same cemetery on the same day, Poole's Funeral Chapel has had an elaborate history in civil rights struggles in Birmingham, even before the '63 bombing.[13] At either rate, Ms. Poole told us that the papers with the map showing Addie's exact gravesite or burial place was missing, and possibly burned in a fire. The record was in this fire, so she did not have any idea where Addie's remains were located. We started going to different places like the local library, for example. We thought that perhaps we could find where she was located but still did not come up with where her remains were.[14]

After we couldn't do anymore, we managed to get a lawyer, John Hall, who provided us with legal counsel.[15] At the end of the day, we tried to sue Poole's Funeral Home; however, the family had to drop this claim, or so the judge later ruled. We no longer knew specifically know where Addie was buried but desperately wanted to locate her moral remains. To my knowledge, no one ever checked with the fire department to verify if there was a fire, as the funeral home declared.

After filing a lawsuit on the behalf of our family, I later received a letter labeled "Working Interrogatories, Request for Productions of Document." Eventually, officials took depositions from representatives of the funeral home, but several factors led the judge to dismiss our claim. First, no one had indicated that Addie's remains were missing in over thirty-five years. From a legal standpoint, the deaths of several potential witnesses and other circumstances weakened our claim. Furthermore, Poole's Funeral Home had filed for bankruptcy.

We later filed a claim against the city of Birmingham. We believed that the city was the only remaining party that could have played a role in the dislocation of Addie's body. When we attempted to sue the city, officials claimed they did not possess any records and that they were just responsible for the cemetery's maintenance. Still, the city was not the sole party responsible for the maintenance and upkeep of Greenwood Cemetery since '63.

Without the exact location of Addie's grave, no one had the right to dig up other gravesites, trying to locate her remains. Other families had buried their loved ones in this graveyard too. We faced tremendous hurdles. Ultimately, the legal system forced us to dismiss the case because we lacked any sound evidence or proof of where to find Addie's remains. We could not hold the city solely responsible for this second tragedy.

Attorneys drew up a letter, confirming that after full disclosure, I would agree to dismiss the claim. According to our lawyer, we had few other options. They were probably gonna' throw our case out of court anyway.

Not knowing about Addie's grave both pained and frustrated me for years. At the time, I often wondered why things ended on this note. The mere idea of not being able to find her body wounded my spirit. I thought that surely a "civil rights martyr" deserved better treatment, even in death.[16] Besides, Addie was *our* sister. I was determined to do right by her under these circumstances; more than likely, she would have sought answers too, if she had lived on instead of me.

To begin to make amends, on August 23, 2003, Attorney John Hall sent a letter, proposing the idea of creating a memorial for Addie, which then city attorney, Thomas Bentley, III responded to promptly:

> "Your letter calls on Birmingham officials to respond to the unfortunate and tragic circumstances of Addie Mae Collins' death and "loss" or her mortal remains with a suitable memorial. Because of the proximity and connection of the Civil Rights Museum to Kelly Ingram Park, I am also forwarding the letter to the Director of that institution. Of course, the same can be said of the 16th Street Baptist Church. It is not by (sic) role as a public employee to comment on the merits of this endeavor. However, I must wish Ms. Collins' family success in honoring her memory."[17]

Until several years ago, everything seemed to be at a standstill. But I kept talking about the need to locate Addie's remains, definitively. In the fall of 2014, I even wrote a letter to President Barack Obama about my mission to find Addie's remains, as well as my quest for restitution. I didn't receive a response. Finally, during the fall of 2016, hope appeared.

Years ago, I would dream about Addie for the first and only time to date. In this vision, she was standing behind some shrubs. "I was right here all the time Sarah," she whispered to me. Then I woke up. This vision would turn out to be prophetic, telling. In the meantime, *I'll keep dreaming.*

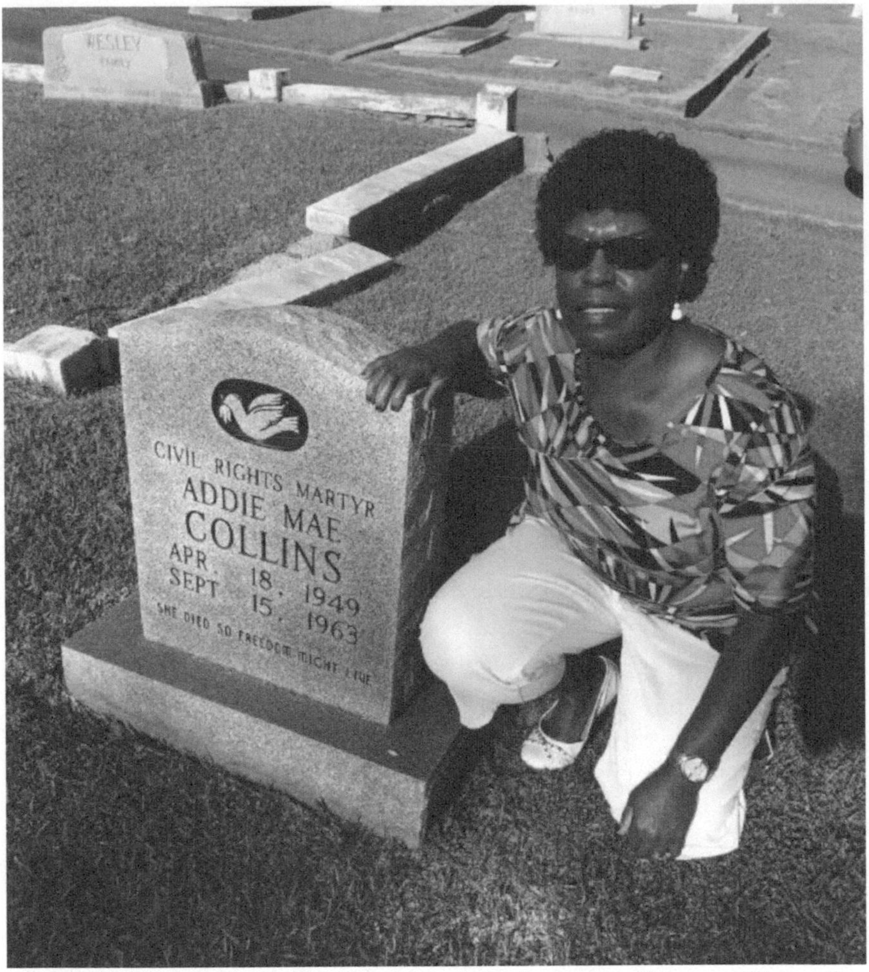

Figure 23. Sarah Collins Rudolph at Addie Collins's gravesite. Courtesy of George C. Rudolph.

Notes

1 S. Fillmore Bennet wrote the lyrics to this hymn. See the following for further reference: "In the Sweet By and By – Lyrics, Hymn Meaning and Story – God Tube," https://www.godtudbe.com/popular-hymns/in-the-sweet-by-and-by/. (This staff notes that "in the New Orleans Jazz tradition 'Sweet By-and-By' is a standard hymn played in so-called 'jazz funerals.'")

2 Zora Neale Hurston, *Their Eyes Were Watching God* (New York: Harper Collins Publisher, 1965), 1.

3 "The Day the Children Died," *People* Magazine.

4 Rudolph, "Four Women from Birmingham."

5 Ibid.

6 Rudolph, "Four Women from Birmingham."

7 The artist formerly known as faith, "Where is Addie Mae Collins," Uncategorized, October 17, 2014, https://fnmunford.wordpress.com/ 2014/10/17/where-is-addie-mae-collins.

8 J.R. Moehringer, "A Child Lost to Racial Hate Lost Again in Birmingham," January 19, 1998, http://articles.latimes.com/1998/jan/19/news/mn-9918.

9 J.R. Moehringer, "A Child Lost to Racial Hate"; J.R. Moehringer, "Body of Victim in 1963 Blast at Alabama Church is Missing," January 19, 1998, https://www.washingtonpost.com/archive/politics/1998/01/19/body-of-victim=in 1963-blast-at-alabama-church-is-missing.

10 Harriet A. Washington, *Medical Apartheid: The Dark History of Medical Experimentation on Black Americans from Colonial Times to the Present* (New York: Double Day, 2006), 119.

11 J. R. Moehringer, "A Child Lost to Racial Hate" and J.R. Moehringer, "Body of Victim in 1963."

12 Brian Pia, "Addie Mae Colllins may be Buried on the Other Side of Her Tombstone," October 27, 2016, https://abc3340.com/news/abc-3340-investigates/abc-3340-news-investigates-search-for-addie-mae-collins.

13 For further details, refer to "Poole's Funeral Chapels," https://www.poolefuneralchapel.com/about-us/history.

14 Rudolph, "Four Women from Birmingham."

15 Ibid.

16 Moehringer, "A Child Lost to Hate." (In another twist of fate, the historic Greenwood Cemetery — some history books also refer to it as Woodlawn Cemetery — is located nearby the Birmingham-Shuttlesworth International Airport, renamed in honor of the Rev. Fred Shuttlesworth, a civil rights icon and pioneer.)

17 Thomas Bentley III (Assistant City Attorney, City of Birmingham, Department of Law) letter to John C. Hall, Esq., September 10, 2003.

Chapter 19. After the Rain

Coping with medical emergencies and the ordeal of learning about Addie's missing body seemed to bring Leroy and me closer together. Our marriage appeared to be on the mend. That is until a brand-new set of issues crept up—namely a car of all things. About a year after I bought the Cavalier, Leroy convinced me to trade it in for a better car. He pointed out that the car had depreciated and that the cushion on the car seat was beginning to wear thin. We did not need to get another car immediately, but I went to the car lot to see what was available. We looked around. I spotted a black Monte Carlo that I liked. I did not think the dealership would allow me to buy this car; besides, I was happy with the Cavalier. I provided the necessary credit information and talked to the salesclerk, while the dealer inspected the Cavalier. The car salesperson approved everything, so I traded the Cavalier in for a Monte Carlo -- another big mistake.

After I changed cars, Leroy changed. Within a week, he stayed out all night with my car. We quickly fell into that old frustrating pattern again. I would get up to go to work, looking outside, up and down the road, waiting and hoping he would come soon. He was constantly late. Sometimes, I would arrive to work an hour late. However, I knew that I could not continue to put my job at risk. Something had to give.

Finally, one day I hollered at him, "stay outta' my car, Leroy."

Every action has a reaction, consequence. With his pride wounded, my husband stopped helping me out with the car payments overnight. He was blind to how such strong-arm tactics were chipping away at our marriage and his wedding vow to honor and cherish me.

When Leroy finally went back to work, he began to experience problems with his legs. His boss wanted to know why such a young man had all of these ailments. "Ask my husband," I told him.

Honestly, I did not know the answer. Leroy missed several more days from work. I guess his boss just got tired with all of the excuses and told LeRoy that he had to find someone willing to work regularly. His boss had to let him go. I didn't blame the man.

I was in a desperate fix financially. I had to come up with money for my car payment, insurance and house note, not to mention the utility bills. I stayed on bended knees, praying for a financial blessing. To make matters worse, Leroy began to stay out all night once again. He had moved out without taking his clothes. He would go away from home for five days and return for two. This pattern continued for months, until I spoke up one day. Our marriage had become a masquerade. I could no longer take his disrespect and lack of commitment.

"You may as well go ahead and take your clothes and stay with whoever you livin' with," I told my husband. He shrugged his shoulder and kept stepping.

Even after this heated exchange, nothing changed. I moved on, inwardly. During this period, I received a phone call from Mrs. Garrett's granddaughter. She told me to meet her at the "Grand's house." Grand was their nickname for their grandmother. When I got there, she apologized for taking so long to arrive and promptly handed me an envelope. I opened it curiously. To my surprise, the envelope contained a cashier's check for two thousand dollars. I was overjoyed. I hugged her. I just could not stop thanking her. "You're a Godsend," I told her.

I put the money to use immediately. I paid my bills and put the rest of it in a bank account, however money alone could not resolve all my problems.

One morning I got on my knees and cried out to the Lord. "God you see all things and you know I've tried to be a good wife to LeRoy for the ten years we have been married." I continued, "When we got together Leroy said *You* brought us together God. He prayed for a saved wife, but Lord I can't take this any longer. I need you to help me because I just cannot do this alone. Help me in Jesus' name," I prayed. I couldn't cry out any longer.

After I got up off my knees, I drove to the post office to mail in a bill payment. I parked in front of the post office – in a spot where I wasn't supposed to park. As I walked away, somebody shouted out, "Sarah Collins," and seconds later more excitedly, "Sarah Collins!"

I just knew that voice and looked back, quickly. *Flashback*, could it be George Carlson Rudolph? No way, I thought to myself.

"Hello George," I said.

I just couldn't believe my eyes when I saw George, my classmate. We both graduated from A. H. Parker High school, in the class of '69 to be exact. Go Thundering Herds!

Years earlier, I ran into George as I was traveling around town. In fact, it was several days before I was to marry LeRoy Cox. I had a million things on my agenda at that time, but still shared a passing conversation with George. It is all but impossible not to talk to him. A likeable person and gentle man in my eyesight, George practically knew everybody in our class. He would ask former classmates to sign or initial their photographs in the yearbook, whenever he ran into them. He used to travel around town with the yearbook in his car, when it was in good condition.

George was always well mannered and friendly when we were in high school. While talking to him in the parking lot of the post office, I quickly realized not much had changed.

"I have my yearbook at home," George said. "Do you want to see pictures of some of our classmates today?"

"Yeah, I think I would like that. First, I gotta' move my car. It's parked illegally."

My conversation with George made me long for the carefree days of high school. After all, life was much more difficult than Algebra. At either rate, I wanted to see the yearbook. I thought George had the yearbook with him inside of his car. However, he no longer drove around with it anymore. It had gotten old and was falling apart.

"Just follow me to my house," George said.

Minor Mishap

After we both drove away, I mistakenly followed the wrong car. How silly of me, I later thought to myself when a stranger bounded out of the car. I apologized to the baffled driver. As soon as I got home, I called George. Fortunately, he gave me his number before we drove away.

"Hey George, you'll never guess what happened." Before he could answer I blurted out, "I followed the wrong car."

George did not seem at all surprised. "Just meet me back at the post office."

"Alright," I said.

Once we got beyond this mishap, I drove back to the post office to meet up with him. After I arrived, George explained how he honked the horn after he saw me turn down the wrong way. To tell you the truth, I was concentrating so hard I did not hear anything. Driving was still serious business for me.

After meeting up with him for the second time that day at the post office, George showed me the pictures in his yearbook. As we chatted, he continued, "You know one of our classmates passed away recently."

"Sure 'nough," I said. That really got my attention.

I later learned that when one of our classmates dies or passes away, George respectfully writes 'Deceased' next to that person's name in his yearbook in honor and memory of the individual.

"You're too good of a lady to be enduring such things," he said.

I didn't respond. After this conversation, George began to call me on a regular basis. We would talk for a long time. I told him I needed help, but also time to heal.

Around this time, my husband ended up moving in with some woman, and we got a divorce. I used some of the money that Mrs. Garrett had left behind for me to pay for the divorce. I had it stashed in the bank.

I had always thought Leroy and I would grow old together, but we did not. It was painful to realize that ten years of marriage had ended, but one person alone can't hold a marriage together. Occasionally, I still reflect on what Leroy told me in the beginning.

"I'm glad to meet a Christian lady. Someone who I can trust," he continued. "I've been praying for a Christian wife."

Leroy thought I was going to be weak or a push over, on the count of my upbringing. He believed that I would always put up with his behavior. However, this was hardly the case. He found out, "The Lord giveth, and the Lord taketh away" (Job 1:21, KJV).

Chapter 20. In a Sentimental Mood

After the divorce, my life changed but faith kept me intact, or moving forward. During this time, George and I talked often, almost daily. Our conversations were soothing. He was polite, charming. I was beginning to have deep feelings for him, even during a time of uncertainty in my life. I had just ended my marriage and hesitated before jumping into another relationship. I had been down a loveless road once before and did not want to go there again. Just the mere thought of getting married again was a "no-no" for me. Please not another husband; not anymore marriages, I tried to convince myself, but my heart refused to listen. Seeking clarity, I began to talk and *really* listen to God.

I was always fond of George, even while we were in school. As I said before, we were in the same grade at A. H. Parker High School and graduated in the class of 1969. George always used to speak to me. Some students, even adults, often shied away from me. The bombing had left my face messed up, but George did not look at me as if I was a monster. I used to be so self-conscious because of all the visible scars.

An only child, he came from a very stable background. His father was a preacher, while his mom was a homemaker. Mr. Rudolph served on the ministerial staff at the Sixth Avenue Baptist Church. Grieving families held a mass funeral for three of the little girls at this church, during the turning point of the Movement. In fact, Rev. Rudolph was active in civil rights struggle and took steps to try to integrate the police force, inspiring Rev. Fred Shuttlesworth as one writer pointed out:

'After the Reverend George Rudolph unilaterally appealed to the city hall for black police on June 21, [1955] and the *Birmingham World* and *Birmingham News* again editorialized on the issue, Shuttlesworth was inspired to become involved. Soon after Rudolph's appeal, Fred drafted a petition to the city commission.' [1]

As an adult, I met Reverend Rudolph and his wife, Mrs. Elizabeth Rudolph, shortly after George and I became better acquainted. George attended the funeral service for the little girls, even though he was a kid at the time. He stood outside among the crowd. Like other people, he remembers hearing the bomb go off, while clear across on the other side of town that September day. I was amazed and touched by the thought that he attended the mass funeral, even though he did not know Addie, any of the other girls, or even me at the specific time. At one point, his father Rev. George Rudolph served as president of a neighborhood watch group during the height of the conflict in the '60s.

Figure 24. George C. Rudolph in uniform, circa 1970.

After graduating from Parker in '69, George decided to join the army, almost right after school. I can still relate to his picture in uniform as the person who befriended when we were still in high school. The military deployed George to Vietnam from September of 1970 to July of 1971 where he fought in the Vietnam War. He was a member of the U.S. Army. As a veteran, he regularly wears his Vietnam jacket, especially when we travel. At any rate, we renewed our friendship some thirty years later.

George pursued me and we happily exchanged vows after a brief courtship. Every so often the good Lord sends us someone at the time when we least expect. Oftentimes we do not always accept whom He sends our way. On the other hand, too often we settle for whom and what he does not give us. In George Carlson Rudolph, I have found my soul mate and the love of a lifetime. The mutual understanding, respect, and support that we both share for each other is priceless.

My One and Only Love

George and I got married in 2000. In fact, it was on my birthday, November 10. I instantly became a mother to his son, George Carlson Rudolph Jr., or 'Lil' George as we used to call him. He was still a child, when we got married, so I ended up raising a son after all, with all of its demands and blessings too. Singing is one of my son's gifts.

The wedding ceremony was a strictly low-key affair. George and I exchanged vows, wearing blue jeans. We never bothered to tell the guests in advance about our planned wardrobe or attire, so folk showed up, dressed up to the nines! Except clothes don't really matter. I found love in George at a time in life, when I least expected it. He cherishes me for who I am. He could care less about the scars, or even the fact that I have a prosthetic eye. One is ever so fortunate to find true love once in a "blue moon." And in George, I have found *a love of my own.*

After our marriage, I helped my husband to take care of his elderly parents. I used to comb his mother's hair and prepare her meals; now George combs my hair on occasion. Until a few years ago, George and I took turns spending the nights at his aunt's home. Katie Shorter, George's paternal aunt, is in her late nineties but lived alone for years. She remembers my Dad from his days working at the restaurant. She recalls my visits there when I was a little girl. Who would have guessed that our paths would cross again, decades later?

George and I also share mutual friends like our classmate Jamaal; he converted to Islam and later took on this name. My testimony about the church bombing moved Brother Jamaal who voluntarily worked in the prisons. He invited me to share my story with the inmates, and I took him up on the offer. I made a trip with him to St. Clair's Correctional Institute where one of the men convicted of the church bombing was imprisoned. Anyway, I talked about my story of survival and shared my testimony with the prisoners. Our differences in faith did not matter to my classmate; nor did it seem to matter to inmates who listened intently.

George and I actively participate with our other friends from high school in class reunion-related activities. We've traveled out of town to cities like New Orleans, La. This network has also led to several speaking engagements nationally. During several related interviews, George has spoken out, sharing that my story of surviving the blast in Birmingham and dealing with PTSD is comparable to enduring a warm like Vietnam.

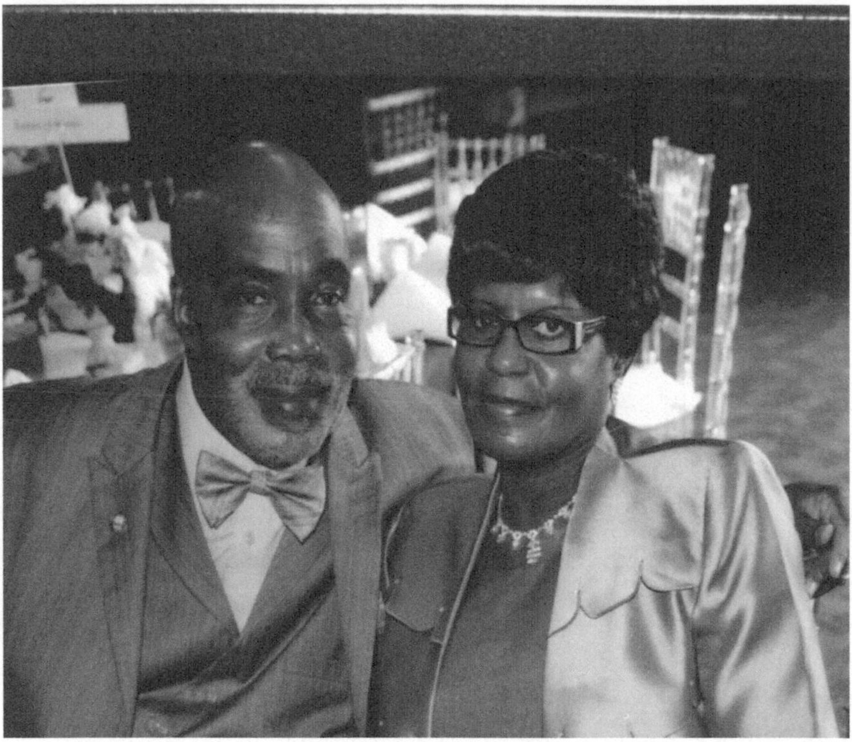

Figure 25. George C. Rudolph and Sarah Collins Rudolph together.

Notes

1 Andrew M. Manis, *A Fire You Can't Put Out: The Civil Rights Life of Birmingham's Reverend Fred Shuttlesworth* (Tuscaloosa, Alabama: The University of Alabama Press, 1999), 82.

Chapter 21. Resolution

"Like the tragedy in Dallas that fall, the Sixteenth Street Baptist Church bombing had ceased to feel like a murder case and had become a piece of culture, abstract yet powerful and permanent, as haunting as the work John Coltrane recorded two months after the crime."[1] — Diane McWhorter

There cometh a woman of Samaria to draw water: Jesus saith unto her, Give me to drink.
(For his disciple were gone away unto the city to buy meat.)
Then saith the woman of Samari unto him, How is it that thou, being a Jew, asketh drink of me, which am a woman of Samari? For the Jews have no dealings with the Samaritans. (John 4: 7-9, KJV)

For many are called, but few chosen. Matthew 22:14 (KJV)

Like many unions, my marriage to George has not come without trials. But our love grows stronger with each passing year. Speaking of trials, within months after we exchanged vows, Thomas Blanton's trial began.

The period before Chambliss' trial in 1977 through 2001 was like a time of 'irresolution' for my relatives, and undoubtedly other victims' family members. During this long interval, I came to admire the efforts of attorneys Doug Jones and William Baxley. Still, during an interview with *The New York Times*, I shared my reservations about the court case:

> 'There will never be any closure for me. Every time I go back into the bathroom and put makeup on, it always comes back to me. The scars on my chest and arms and my face will always remind me.'[2]

It had taken almost thirty-eight years to bring Blanton to trial. His trial began on April 25, 2001. Judge James Garrett presided. Just think of what Carole, Denise, Cynthia and Addie could have accomplished, if they had lived that long here on earth! Twenty-nine witnesses testified against Blanton, including Samuel Rutledge and myself. (My testimony at Thomas Blanton's trial is in the appendix.) I've included part of his testimony because of the heroic role that he has played in this story.

Q: What church did you attend at the time?
A: 16th Street Baptist Church.
Q: Mr. Rutledge, do you remember the morning of September 15th, 1963 when there was an explosion at the church?
A: Yes, sir.
Q: Were you at church that morning?
A: That morning I was there.
Q: Do you recall about what time you got there?
A: About 9:30 or 10:00 for Sunday school. Yeah.
Q: And what did you do? Did you attend a Sunday school class there?
A: Every Sunday. Yes, sir.
Q: What part of the church building were you in that morning around 10:20?
A: It was in Sunday school on the 16th Street side right above where the bomb went off. We was having Sunday school class. And when the bomb went off everybody got quiet. And someone asked the statement, what was that. Said that was a bomb.

MR. Robbins: Judge, we would object to that.

THE COURT: I'll overrule it.

A: So we got up and slid down the steps where we went up in the back to our Sunday school class over the plaster.
Q: Now you say--
A: And when we got there –
Q: You said that you slid down the steps?
A: Yeah. We couldn't walk down it because the plaster had covered it up from the bomb.
Q: Okay. So you just had to slide on the plaster?
A: On the plaster down the steps. So I went to the door where I come into to go down the steps. Wasn't no steps. So I was so excited. I leaped… down on the pavement. Hit the ground right in front of where the bomb went off…. Passed the hole. Looked in it. They said

> come away there might be another one…Went to the front of the church, the pastor had us round there. Said, well we're glad it didn't kill nobody….[3]

Mr. Rutledge also testified that the bomb destroyed his car, a white 1958 Oldsmobile, both blowing out the windows and forcing the trunk open. He reaffirmed, "I had to junk it. Couldn't be fixed."[4]

Neither the prosecution team nor the defense attorneys asked Mr. Rutledge questions concerning me because the focus was on the deaths of the four girls, I suppose. No one ever file attempted murder charge. My life almost ended, too. However, I would have the chance to testify.

When I attended Blanton's trial, I could only see the back of his head because of where I sat. Still, I found it difficult to look at his face or into his eyes when I testified. In the back of my mind, I thought so this is one of the men suspected of killing the four girls, sitting here in the same room with me! I had to hold my peace: Hold it together—mind, body, and soul. Suddenly, the song flooded my mind "Victory Shall Be Mine," *if I just hold my peace*. When I approached the witness stand to speak about the events leading up to that horrible day, I knew that God was with me, as I relived each moment in a sense. I couldn't have done it without the good Lord. I took the stand after the bittersweet testimony of Mr. Christopher McNair, Denise McNair's father. [5] I explained what happened in the women's lounge before and in the terrifying seconds after the blast. My actual testimony in 2001 at the Blanton trial was very consistent with my witness in 1977.

At the conclusion of the trial, a jury pool of eight white women, three black women and one black man deliberated for about two and half hours before reaching a verdict to convict Thomas E. Blanton, Jr. of murdering the four little girls.[6] Doug Jones was elated with the jury's verdict and could barely control his emotions inside the courtroom gallery after the jury foreperson read the verdict on May 1, 2001. He exchanged heartfelt hugs with some of the families of the slain girls. But my celebration was somewhat muted. Judge Garrett asked Blanton if he had anything to say before he rendered or decided the sentence. As widely reported by the media, Blanton said, "I guess the good Lord will settle it on judgment Day."[7] The judge would sentence him to four life terms in prison.

Jurors noted that the secretly recorded tapes of former Klansman Thomas Blanton made it possible for them to convict him of the 16th Street Baptist Church bombing. Members of the jury recounted that they went back over the tape and listened to make sure they had heard enough. Jurors repeatedly listened to it.

The tape was a recording from an FBI device planted in a kitchen wall, documenting a conversation between Blanton and his wife at their home. In this 1964 recording, Blanton told his wife that he was present at a Klan meeting when the men planned the bombing. Prosecutors presented this tape recording as key evidence. There were several other critical factors, too. For instance, Blanton made some incriminating statements about the church bombing while driving in a car with an FBI informant. Members of the jury listened to the tapes from the vehicle. Several sidebar comments that Blanton uttered on tape convinced jurors that he may not as have built the bomb but still conspired with the Sixteenth Street Church blast.

I have often wondered why it took so long for the state of Alabama to convict Blanton. I had so much anger inside about the bombing and the judicial process itself. I had lost so many people who were near and dear to me. Thirty-eight years was an awful long time for him to walk around as a free man, when there was significant evidence against him. Witnesses died during this precious time, while the memory of other bystanders had grown fuzzy. I also thought about how racially divided the city of Birmingham was during the 1960s. Had the trial taken place then, most likely the jury would have been all white and male. Would they have declared Blanton "guilty" during the 1960s? According to Hoover, the chance of this happening was "remote." But, did he have the moral right to make this decision, as a leader of an agency within the Department of Justice (DOJ)?

Family members rejoiced after his long-delayed conviction, while hoping for a similar outcome in the pending trial. Mama and Daddy had passed on by then. What if they had only lived to see the day? What *would* they have possibly thought? Men like my father, Chris McNair, Claude Augustus Wesley, and Alvin Robertson were a rarity. My mother, Maxine McNair, Gertrude Wesley, Alpha Robertson were all standout women.

I still wonder what would have happened if the FBI had chosen to present *all* of the critical evidence about Blanton, and other suspects like Frank Cash and Bobby Frank Cherry to Bill Baxley in 1977.

One Up, One Down

I waited patiently for Cherry to stand trial. He was sixty-nine years old when the state grand jury indicted him on four accounts of first-degree murder, nearly thirty-seven years after the church bombing. He was an old man by then. Just looking at him made me wonder how he was able to sleep at night for years with the blood of innocent children on his hands. When I watched the nightly news on television, I would see Cherry carrying a plastic bag filled with pills, I presume. I wondered if they were to help him to sleep at night. I learned later that the authorities housed Cherry on the medical floor of Jefferson County Jail. He suffered from a heart condition, diabetes, and claustrophobia.

Cherry lived in Birmingham until the late 1960s before moving to Mabank, Texas. He worked on different odd jobs too. He returned to Alabama to face unrelated charges for rape and sodomy. Cherry had posted bond and was living with relatives in Shelby County, when he learned of his indictment.

The state issued the murder indictment against him on May 17, 2000. In a surprising later turn, even Cherry's own son turned state's evidence against him: Fox (FS) created a movie about the father-son relationship, *Sins of the Father*, told from the viewpoint of Tom Cherry. The movie starred Tom Sizemore, Richard Jenkins and Ving Rhames.[8] I also later shared my viewpoint about everything in *The Road to Justice*, a documentary that also dealt with the aftermath of the church bombing.

The judge postponed Cherry's court date several times, however on Monday, July 16, 2001, Jefferson County Circuit Judge James Garret ruled that he was mentally unfit to be tried on murder charges from the church bombing. Still, Judge Garrett scheduled another hearing for Cherry on August 10, 2001. The Alabama Department of Health was to evaluate his mental competency at this hearing. If the judged ruled Cherry mentally competent, lawyers could prosecute or charge him for the bombing. When the judge made this comment, I knew there was hope. I didn't believe God brought this legal matter this far to let it die.

Mickey Johnson, who was Cherry's lawyer, said that his client had vascular dementia therefore could not assist in his own defense, as is required by the law. In July, four mental health experts testified that Cherry had this condition but differed on the severity of the illness. Judge Garrett carefully weighed this evidence before ruling Cherry should not stand for trial. He requested that mental health experts complete additional testing at the Taylor Hardin facility in Tuscaloosa, Alabama to determine whether Cherry could later regain competency. In December of 2001, two Taylor Hardin experts testified that Cherry was faking his bad memory and concluded that he was competent for trial. Defense Attorney Mickey Johnson indicated that he would not put his client through further competency testing. He decided to let the issue rest and focus on defending his client.

I prayed that they would find Cherry competent to stand trial. He was the last living suspect directly tied to the blast. Separate juries had convicted Chambliss and Blanton of the 16th Street Church bombing, leading to the deaths of the four little girls. I believed that Cherry's trial would bring the families even closer to the bar of justice. Thankfully, God answered our prayers.

Cherry's trial began on Monday, May 13, 2002. During that week, members of the jury heard testimony from prosecution witnesses, including two members of Cherry's immediate family, his granddaughter Teresa Stacy Cherry and Willadean Brogdon, one of his former wives. Jurors would also hear tapes that Mitchell Burns secretly recorded, which linked Cherry with Chambliss and Blanton.

Just how could Cherry or other Klansmen brag about the deaths of four young girls who did not get the chance to live out their dreams, I thought silently? Girls who could have become doctors, lawyers, artists or entered whatever profession they chose; instead, the heartless choice of men acting on racial hatred, mainly in retaliation for the integration of schools in Birmingham, brutally ended the lives of *four precious souls*. I loved Addie and my friends, as did so many people. For any individual or hate group to take their lives away caused much sorrow. Their killers could only see skin color, but true love comes in all forms, all colors.

I took the witness stand to testify on Monday, May 20, 2002. I was the last actual witness to testify for the prosecution. Doug Jones, the lead prosecuting attorney, questioned me along the following lines:

Q. Ms. Rudolph, where do you live?
A. In Birmingham.
Q. How long have you lived in Birmingham?
A. Fifty-one years.
Q. And did you come from a pretty big family?
A. Yes.

Q. Brothers and sisters?
A. Yes. I have brothers and sisters. I had –
Q. Did you have several brothers and sisters?
A. Yes.
Q. Junie and Janie.
A. Yes, I did.
Q. Addie Mae one of your sisters?
A. Yes.
Q. Where did you grow up here in Birmingham?
A. 6th Court West.
Q. Were you living on 6th Court West Sunday morning, September 15, 1963?
A. Yes, I was.
Q. Did you and your sisters go to church?
Q. Yes. We went to church that morning.
Q. Where did you regularly go to church?
A. Went to the 16th Baptist Church.
Q. And was there a special youth service planned that morning?
A. Yes, it were.
Q. And who all went to church with you?
A. Janie and Addie. We walked to church that morning.
Q. You walked to church with Janie, your older sister and Addie?
A. Yes.
Q. And Addie was younger or older than you?
A. She was older.
Q. Let me show you State's Exhibit Number 35. Do you recognize the young lady in that picture?
A. Yes.
Q. Who is that?
A. That's Addie.
Q. That's Addie Mae Collins?
A. Yes.
Q. And she was much older than you?
A. She was two years older than me.
Q. So you and your sisters, were you supposed to have any role in the youth service that morning?
A. Yes. We was supposed to sing in the choir.
Q. You were going to sing in the choir?
A. Yeah
Q. Was Addie going to sing in the choir?
A. Yeah.

Q. What about Janie?
A. She was, too. She was in the choir.
Q. How far a walk was it that morning?
A. We had to walk from 1st street to 16th Street.
Q. Pretty good ways?
A. Yes.
Q. Once you got to the church, where did you go and where did the other girls go?
A. We went downstairs to our class in the basement. Class was already in session, so we stayed and we went into the ladies' lounge.
Q. Now, did Janie go with you into the ladies' lounge or just Addie Mae?
A. Just Addie.
Q. Were there other girls in the ladies' lounge?
A. Yes. When we got there, wasn't but three girls came in.
Q. Who came in?
A. Denise McNair, Carole Robertson, and Cynthia Wesley.
Q. Did you know all of them?
A. Yes.
Q. Where they supposed to participate in the youth program also?
A. Yes, they did.
Q. What happened in the ladies' lounge that morning?
A. Well, I was looking out the door, Carole and Denise and Cynthia, they came in to go to the restroom. So we were sitting in the ladies' lounge already, so when they came out of the restroom, Denise asked my sister to tie her sash.
Q. Where were they standing?
A. They were standing right there by the couch over by the window.
Q. Were all four of them standing there?
A. Yes.
Q. What did you do at the sink?
A. I was over there at the sink washing my hands.
Q. Did you turn around and see someone tying a sash?
A. Yes. I looked back and Addie was tying Denise sash.
Q. Addie was tying the sash on Denise's dress?
A. Yes, she was.
Q. What happened then?
A. Well, they began to talk. And when I turned around to listen to the conversation, I heard this loud noise, boom. And I didn't know what happened.
Q. Were there things that occurred and came on top of you in the ladies' lounge?

A. Yes. Glass went into my eye and cut me in my chest and all over my face.
Q. Was there debris on top of you?
A. It was just around me. It didn't get all on top of me. It was around.
Q. Were you injured?
A. Yes.
Q. Could you see?
A. No. I was blind in both my eyes.
Q. Have you seen State's Exhibit Number 52 before?
A. Yes, I've seen that.
Q. Is that a picture of you?
A. Yes.
Q. In the hospital?
A. Yes.
Q. Where (sic) both your eyes are covered where glass went into your eyes from the explosion?
A. Yes, it did.
Q. Now, did you lose, permanently lose, the sight in any eye?
A. Yes. I lost my right eye. My left eye is damaged right now. I have glaucoma in my left eye.
Q. Ms. Rudolph, after the explosion and you couldn't I assume could not, see anything in the ladies' lounge from your injuries and what all was going on: is that right?
A. That's right.
Q. What did you do?
A. I began to call Addie.
Q. What did you say?
A. I said, Addie, Addie, Addie.
Q. Did your sister ever answer you?
A. No, she didn't.
Q. Did you ever see your sister alive again?
A. No, I never did.

MR. JONES: That's all we have, Your Honor.
MR. JOHNSON: No questions.
THE COURT: You may step down.

Next witness.[9]

Some of his questions really took me back to that Sunday at the 16th Street Church, nearly bringing me to tears. For the most part, we were all so excited about singing in the choir that Youth Sunday. Just the thought that I was *never gonna see* Addie, Denise, Cynthia, or Carole again, at least not on this *side of the mountain*, was crushing; like being hit with a ton of concrete bricks. *It's hard to explain*, to put into words really, the devastating pain of losing Addie.

I permanently lost vision in my right eye, as well as my childhood innocence, but hating those men was not going to bring the girls back or healing for the soul. It took a long time to heal after years of self-medicating with alcohol and reefer, not to mention marital woes. I had to learn to forgive to heal. Besides, God forgave me for my trespasses. How can I call myself a Christian and not forgive, when God chose to forgive me of my trespasses? With that thought, I began by forgiving Chambliss, and others involved in the blast; I believe God forgives when one repents, yet, true repentance comes from the heart: I loathe saying this but if they did not repent, "The wicked shall be turned into hell, as described in Psalm 9:17. I believe hell is real; it's not imaginary, made-up, or invented.

The closing arguments in Cherry's trial began on Tuesday, May 21, 2002. A jury of three white men, three black men, and six white women began deliberating on whether Cherry murdered the four girls at the 16th Street Baptist Church. The jury deliberated two hours and twenty minutes before returning on Wednesday, May 22 at 6:00 p.m. without a verdict, as we anxiously waited. The deliberations continued for several hours into the next day — about six hours, roughly.[10]

While crying, the forewoman delivered the verdict that Cherry was guilty of murdering the four little girls at the 16th Street Church. It was May 22, 2002, shortly after 1:30 p.m. As she continued to read the second and third counts, Cherry looked stunned, helpless. Later, Judge Garrett asked if he had anything to say at which point Cherry insisted, ""This whole bunch have lied all through this thing."" Evidently, he was referring to the team of prosecutors who led the state's case. Cherry later added, ""I've told the truth. I don't know why I'm going to jail for nothing."""[11]

Judge James Garrett sentenced Bobby Frank Cherry to consecutive life sentences on four counts of first-degree murder for the deaths of the four girls. In 2001, Blanton received the same sentence. Authorities took Cherry to the Jefferson County Jail where he remained until his transfer to a state prison. I don't know why Cherry claimed that folks lied on him. The evidence was stacked against him. His trial should have occurred years earlier. Cherry lived freely for many years before he was locked up. On October 29, 1985, he died of cancer after serving six years at the Kilby Correctional Facility in Montgomery, Alabama.

After the trials, especially the court case that terminated in 2002, reporters from Alabama, and others from as far away as Great Britain, questioned me about the outcome. Even now, some still pose similar questions. They ask questions like "how are you now?" Reporters also wanted to know if *I* had forgiven the men sentenced for killing the four girls. Even now, I still wonder why journalists pose this question of forgiveness to me, instead of the men convicted of the brutal crime? Nevertheless, I hope Cherry got in touch with God before he died so that his soul maybe ready to meet the good Lord on Judgment Day: Cause they also gotta' stand before God to be judged. (Hebrews 9:27)[12]

During quiet moments, I wonder if any of the men accused, and later convicted of the '63 church bombing, ever replayed *that* awful day all over again. Sadly, we never got the chance to have our Youth Sunday program because mean-spirited people did not value our lives, our dreams. Their unthinkable deeds brought pain into the lives of so many people. At times, life was almost unbearable for the survivors, without and with psychological counseling. In time, our faith helped to deliver us from evil, as my sister Junie shares in the upcoming book the 16th Street Baptist Church bombing, *Saving the Best Wine for Last.*

I didn't make direct eye contact with Chambliss, Blanton, or Cherry during their respective trials. I was focusing on correctly answering the questions that the lawyers posed to me. Like other family members, I had waited a long time—almost forty years – for the three trials. I still question why we had to wait. Did people in positions of power and influence not take the brutal murder of four African-American girls to heart? Why else would it take so long for the accused to face serious charges? Just think of all the time that was lost. I wish the law had tried and convicted these criminals while they were in the prime of life.

When I testified at Chambliss' trial in 1977 at the age of 27, I still had a lot of anger and resentment, at times bordering on hatred, inside of me about the death of the girls. It took fourteen years to bring him to trial, which did not seem fair to me either. Moreover, Blanton and Cherry went unprosecuted for decades, while another suspect, Herman Cash, died. Chambliss and Cherry both served a little time and died in prison; Blanton died during his nineteenth year of incarceration. Like I stated,

> 'They put these men in jail when they had one foot in the grave… They had been living free for so many years. Addie and them didn't get the chance to enjoy life. Their lives were taken when they were 14 and 11.'[13]

In Bobby Frank Cherry's obituary, published by *The Washington Post*, the reporter observed,

> 'Mr. Cherry and the three other Klansmen were suspected within days of the bombing. They were known for their violent behavior. But the case faltered after 1965, when FBI Director J. Edgar Hoover refused to pursue it.
>
> Twelve more years would pass before Alabama Attorney General Bill Baxley completed a seven-year investigation, which resulted in the conviction of Chambliss, who was considered the gang leader. The case received renewed attention in 1993, when an FBI agent in the Birmingham office recovered more than 9,000 FBI documents and surveillance tapes that had not been shared with prosecutors.[14]

In other words, the evidence was suppressed. The FBI did not fully disclose the contents of its investigation about the bombing, perhaps leading to delayed convictions. It makes me wonder about the inquiries behind other major civil rights crimes or cases. Anyway, I still wonder if everyone who was directly involved with or conspired with bombing our church has had to give a full account. I look forward to pouring through even more information pertaining to the bombing of the 16th Street Church with the declassification of even more files.[15]

A group of young people that I once spoke to inquired, "Is there a silver lining, or otherwise positive aspect to my life-long experience?" Even including my trials, *and the answer is yes.* I can't go around holding hate in my heart for the people who bombed the church, killing the innocents. God knows who bombed us. The Lord knows if there were more people, other than the ones that went before the bar of justice. Knows them by names. After God saved my life, in time He stopped me from seeing things in the natural. The Lord wants me to grow, spiritually, so I can't hold hatred inside my heart. I had to let it all go. His word says in Romans 12:19 "'Vengeance is mine; I will repay saith the Lord." To repeat, God forgave us, so I have to do the same.[16] (John 1:9) Eventually, society held people responsible for taking the lives of four children –

hateful, jaded men who refused to see us as children of God, or even to recognize our humanity. Folk in positions of authority must share some of the blame for fostering a climate of hate in cities like Birmingham and other places like Neshoba County, Mississippi.

Anyway, folk want to know how I feel about Birmingham now, and whether or not the city has changed since the '60s. My answers have not altered much. Birmingham has a warm, homey atmosphere, which is why I have lived there so long. If not for the bad influences, our city would have progressed further, even sooner. Remember, some thought Birmingham could become the 'Atlanta of the South.' Crime is an issue in this city like in other places in America. We have many churches, good hospitals but fewer good public schools. So many of our school districts are just as segregated, if not even more, as in the distant past. Nevertheless, I think Birmingham is a nice place to live. Still, I'll always have memories of *that* day. When I look in the mirror, I still see traces of the evidence—glass marks on my face and cuts all over my body. I will have to live with all of this for the rest of my natural life. I'm still living with other side effects. I have flashbacks when I hear loud, sudden noises like a car backfiring for instance, as I noted earlier. And learning to drive on the highway was a major feat for me. Occasionally, I still get anxious when I'm on an airplane, and it's about to land. The landing gears and loud noises can be unsettling. However, I try to fight off such anxieties.

About two years after the last trial, my sisters and I participated in "The Gathering: Civil Rights Justice Remembered," a symposium on major civil rights cases held on the campus of Birmingham Southern College. During the course of this awesome event, someone asked me, "'Mrs. Rudolph, had you given up hope? Or do you still have hope?'"

I replied, "I didn't give up hope. I was always waitin' for that time to come, because it was just takin' so long. And I really didn't want my sister to die in vain." All along, I prayed for a just outcome. I know my prayers were not in vain. With my sisters Junie and Janie nearby, I continued on:

> 'But I have to say this. I know I thanked them once before, Doug Jones and his team, for how they worked so hard to get justice. I'll always remember that phrase he would say, 'Justice delayed didn't mean justice was denied.' So I just thank God that justice prevailed.'[17]

Attorneys Bill Baxley and Doug Jones fulfilled a mission, too. Each brought passion, commitment to cases involving the church bombing.

They asked Eunice Morris the same question too. Eunice and I had become close during the trials and offered moral support to each other. It was only natural. After all, we both lost a sister. At either rate, when the facilitator posed the question of hope to Eunice, she replied:

> 'I mean you can move on, because hatred shouldn't live in your life. It'll ultimately destroy you. I remember when I was sitting in the courtroom with Mr. Cherry, and I was waitin' for him to show some type of remorse…about what he did. And then I looked at the jury, and the jury looked like to me, that that was one of their…children. They was...relivin' it, 40 years ago. And, I sit there, and I remember when this verdict came in, and I grasped Sarah's hand, you know. Forty years and looked like it was just yesterday. But it was never too late. All the evidence came forth, to me, just on time.' [18]

Eunice Morris perished in the years following the trials in 2001 and 2002. The bond of our friendship meant the world to me, as did her witness. As soul sisters, we encouraged and gave hope to each other.

Notes

1 McWhorter, *Carry Me Home*, 569.
2 Kevin Sack, "Survivor of Birmingham Church Bombing Has Few Expectations for Trial," *The New York Times*, April 24, 2001.
3 See excerpt of Samuel Rutledge's testimony at the Thomas Edward Blanton's trial in 2001. Notably, neither the defense attorney nor prosecution posed questions to Rutledge pertaining to Sarah Collins Rudolph during his testimony.
4 Ibid.
5 T.K. Thorne, *Last Chance for Justice: How Relentless Investigators Uncovered New Evidence Convicting the Birmingham Church Bombers.* (Chicago: Lawrence Hill Books, 2013) 196.
6 Ibid, 177 and 207.
7 Jeffrey Gettleman, "Ex-Klansman Convicted in 1963 Alabama Church Blast," *Los Angeles Times*, May 2, 2001, latimes.com/archives/la-xpm-2001-may-02-mn-58306-story.html.
8 Anita Gates, "Television Review: A Father's Guilt, A Son's Wrenching Decision," *The New York Times*, January 4, 2002, nytimes.com/2002/01/04/movies/television-review-a-father-s-guilt-a-son-s-wrenching-decision.html?searchRes…

9 See Sarah Collins Rudolph's full testimony at the trial of Bobby Frank Cherry in Birmingham, Alabama in 2002. Cherry was pronounced guilty at the conclusion of the trial.

10 Doug Jones, "Justice for Four Little Girls: The Bombing of the Sixteenth Street Baptist Church Cases," *The Young Lawyer*, Volume 14, Number 5, February/March 2010, 2.

11 Thorne, *Last Chance*, 243.

12 Rudolph, letter to Snipe, dated June 12, 2014.

13 Joseph D. Bryant, "Reparations for 1963 Church Bombing Survivor."

14 Yvonne Shinhoster Lamb, "Birmingham Bomber Bobby Frank Cherry Dies in Prison at 74," *The Washington Post*, November 19, 2004, https://www.washingtonpost.com/wp-dyn/articles/A61428-2004Nov18.html.

15 "Baptist Street Church Bombing — FBI," www.fbi.gov>history>famous>cases>baptist-street-c...

16 Rudolph, letter to Snipe, dated June 12, 2014.

17 Rudolph, "The Gathering."

18 Eunice Morris, "The Gathering."

Chapter 22. For Her Ladyship

I am my Sister's keeper![1] –Anna Julia Cooper

Jesus, keep me near the cross,
There a precious fountain —
Free to all, a healing stream —
Flows from Calv'ry's mountain.
In the cross, in the cross,
Be my glory ever;
Till my raptured soul shall find
Rest beyond the river.[2]

The years between the blast and the trials led to a time of "irresolution" for myself and other siblings like Addie Bea whom I've never discussed publicly.[3] To say Ad-Be, her nickname, had a rough way to go is putting things mildly. Tenderhearted like her namesake, things began to pass my eldest sister by in the prime of life. Over time, she became like one of *the lonely people*. It's not hard for me to imagine slipping into this state. Still, I was able to *keep it together* as the "fifth little girl" and into adulthood.

Ad-Bea will always hold a special place in my heart. As a little girl, I admired her. She was gorgeous and had big dreams. Really, pictures don't do her any justice. Strong-willed and lady-like too, she had a delicateness about herself yet a steeliness too, like a 'magnolia'. She showed promise, as did all my sisters whom I have bonded with at different points in life. We've all had to overcome obstacles to survive in the aftermath of the bombing; *only the strong* don't always survive. Life has a way of deferring American dreams. But we don't give up on them despite the painful past.

Ad-Bea attended the 16th Street Church, as a young adult. In fact, she was there on the day that the four little girls were murdered. No one could find or locate her for hours on end. As a young adult, Addie Bea moved to Buffalo, New York, yet beauty offers no passport.

I never visited her in New York, but I strongly suspect that she was in an abusive relationship, strained marriage based on her words and deeds. I have traveled down that lonely road before, and I vowed never to purchase a return ticket. I knew my sister well. *Something happened* there. Addie Bea was a sensitive soul, much like her namesake. To tell the truth, I don't believe that Ad-Bea ever got her younger sister's death. How can one, I mean?

How do we really begin to count the *all* the Sixteenth Street Baptist Church bombing victims and folk still suffering from trauma. They range from members of my family, quite possibly to others who left Alabama — not to mention the fearful child in me who sat in the 16th Street Church like a zombie in a trance, still in shock, months after the bombing.

Sometime after A-Bea returned to Birmingham from Buffalo, we decided to have her committed. We had few choices. She hurt herself badly, after having an awful fit, and nearly bit her thumb off her hand. It ain't easy to reveal such closely guarded details about someone that I knew and loved. Still, I want people to know just how much the church bombing tore my family apart, decades beyond the actual event.

Only the Lord knows how the bombing disturbed Ad-Bea, perhaps leading to her eventual breakdown. Although institutionalized, she was still crystal-clear, especially when it came to certain aspects of the past. The facility where she lived was out of town, but I would visit her there. Occasionally, I brought her home with me for the weekends.

In September of 2003, our dear cousin Roy (who was from North Carolina) and other relatives on my Dad's side of the family came down South to Birmingham, Al. on a chartered bus.[4] My relatives wanted to visit the Birmingham Civil Rights Institute. Addie Bea and I went with them for the visit, as I had brought her home that weekend to meet our people. When they began to get off the bus to go inside the facility, Addie Bea said she was tired. She didn't want to go inside, preferring to sit on the bus instead, so I told them that I would sit inside the bus along with my sister. I'd already seen practically everything in the museum. Besides, I didn't want my sister to sit alone. Since the Sixteenth Street Church is directly across from the Birmingham Civil Rights Institute, when Addie asked to go to the restroom, we walked over to the church.

Just as we were about to descend the stairs, Addie Bea hollered, "I don't want to go down there! "Death's down there," she rambled on.

She was *still* terrified. Addie Bea refused to move an inch. I declare, it nearly broke me down on the spot. For years, I had lived her anxieties about the 16th Street Baptist Church, after the bombing. Deep down, I knew how she felt. But for the twins, grace and mercy, I too could be threading a thin line between madness and reality. When I look back on the past, "MAY BE" the greatest victory and the key to survival lays in letting go, releasing this pain.

Later, Addie Bea's name would prove to be a source of confusion. Once, a rumor circulated that Addie Collins was alive, not killed in the bombing at church. According to that account, Addie was merely living out of town. I know. This may all be hard to grasp, considering all the official stories making the rounds about the murder of the four little girls. Still, folks heard the two names Addie and Collins mentioned together and mistakenly jumped to the conclusion that the "civil rights martyr" was, alas, alive. Some began to think that Addie was not killed in the church bombing but had merely moved away. And that someone had made up an elaborate tale or hoax. I beg to differ. No one made up this story or designed it only to elicit sympathy.

More specifically, I heard about an episode on a local radio talk show. I can't recall the name of the program or host. Somebody called in to say they didn't believe my sister died in the bombing at the 16th Street Church because "Addie Collins" had been seen, spotted laying low in a mental facility in Alabama.[5] Now, plenty of folks didn't know I had two sisters named Addie — Addie Bea and the sister that was killed named Addie Mae. This entire story could be comical at times, if it wasn't so tragic.

Sadly, Addie Bea Collins transitioned on July 20, 2004: May she rest in peace, along with her sister and namesake, Addie Mae Collins.[6] At the time, my sister was living with her foster mother in Aliceville, Alabama.

Still, some of my memoires of Addie Bea are tied to church. The 16th Street Church itself has achieved recognition as a national landmark and a UNESCO World Heritage Site.[7] Our church played a central role in Birmingham, especially during "The Movement." Tens of thousands of people still visit this sanctuary every year to pay homage and to worship.[8]

People from across the country and around the world travel here out of respect and admiration. For example, Daniel Ayalon, a diplomat from Israel, visited the church several years ago.[9] I kept the story from the newspaper about his stay in Birmingham, Alabama. During his brief visit to our city, Ayalon said:

> "'It is our sacred duty not only to commemorate the victims, but also send a message from Birmingham, from the Sixteenth Street Baptist Church, a message all across American [sic] and all across the world, (of) no more with hatred, no more with fanaticism.'" [10]

Leaders from countries like South Africa have also visited the city of Birmingham, including Archbishop Desmond Tutu and the former President, F.W. de Klerk.[11] During his official visit, Tutu stated, "'the courage of civil rights protesters who helped end segregation in Alabama inspired opponents who overthrew apartheid in South Africa.'"

The 16th Street Baptist Church and its leaders often waded into unchartered waters during our freedom struggle. It maintains a distinct place in the city of Birmingham under the leadership of the Reverend Arthur Price, Jr. Personally, I've attended this church on different special occasions over the past two decades, more or less.

Upon reflecting about the bombing and loss of life, Reverend Jesse Jackson once said, "We transformed a crucifixion into a resurrection."[12] However, for years, I sidestepped going to this church, at all cost. It was not unlike Calvary, Golgotha for us. Families suffered great losses there, for the benefit of the nation. However, I used to avoid even driving near this sanctuary, until I moved into a neighborhood close by the Sixteenth Street Church. At one point, the community near the church became crime ridden. I moved away after someone broke into my home.

I'm not nearly as torn apart when I visit this church now. I've even spoken at the 16th Street Baptist Church within the past several years and I've attended many of the memorial services. When I think about it, the church itself never left me with all bad memories. Instead, it was the bombing and the fear, real or imagined, that something could occur again that kept me away. Church burnings occurred periodically during the 1980s and 1990s; in the not too distant past such troubling incidents occurred in New Orleans, Louisiana. Anyway, as a young girl, I didn't feel safe or even wanted to attend worship service at the 16th Street

Baptist Church immediately after the blast. PTSD kept me entrapped in the shadows and hiding out of plain sight – that is until the good Lord saw fit to bring me fully into the light of day. Like still waters, the love for my sisters Addie and Addie Bea run deep. Grief could have kept me in a way, predicament but I choose to continue to walk in the *beautiful light.*

Notes

1 Anna Julia Cooper, "Womanhood: A Vital Element in the Regeneration and Progress of a Race, in *A Voice from the South* (Xenia, Ohio: The Aldine Printing House, 1892), 32; https://docsouth.unc.edu/church/cooper/cooper.html.

2 Written by Frances J. Crosby, the melody to the hymn "In the Cross (also known as Near the Cross") was composed by William H. Doane.

3 Of note, Sarah first brought up this sensitive topic with me either after we had known each other for about six years. The subject began rather casually, as we awaited Junie's late arrival at an airport in Pennsylvania on September 14, 2010. Sarah, June and I lectured at Dickinson College the following day, September 15, 2010.

4 Sarah Collins Rudolph, letter to Tracy Snipe, April 25, 2014.

5 Ibid.

6 Ibid.

7 "Sixteenth Street Baptist Church National Historic Landmark," httpss://www.birminghamal.org/listings/sixteenth-street-baptist-church-national-historic-landmark.

8 Kyle Smith, Gail Cameron Wescott and David Cobb Craig, "The Day the Children Died," *People* Magazine, August 11, 1997, 88. Reporters note that the Sixteenth Street Baptist Church has roughly 80,000 visitors annually.

9 Jesse Chambers, "Israel Diplomat Honors Victims," *The Birmingham News*, November 14, 2012.

10 Ibid.

11 Barnett Wright, "An Indelible Mark on History," *The Birmingham News*, January 6, 2013.

12 Jesse Jackson, a prominent civil rights leader and a former presidential contender, made this observation in relationship to the 16th Street Baptist Church bombing in Spike Lee's Oscar-nominated documentary, *4 Little Girls.*

Chapter 23. Ascension

"I'm in Birmingham right now, but they don't even know me."
— Sarah Collins Rudolph [1]

My sister Janie and I appeared on a major news broadcast during the thirtieth anniversary year of the bombing. It was one of our first major public appearances nationally. Connie Chung, who co-anchored the *CBS Evening News* years ago, interviewed us. Speaking publicly about the bombing has been a process. In the past, I rarely gave interviews but made an exception for *People* magazine in 1997. When I look at the picture of Junie and me that *People* published with the article, "The Day the Children Died," I can clearly see the weight of everything etched on my face. During the late 1990s, film director Spike Lee also called to interview me for *4 Little Girls*. After thinking it over and talking with my husband LeRoy who provided me sound advice on most occasions, I passed on his request for an interview for different reasons; I learned that some earnings from the film would go toward college scholarships.[2]

As I recall, Spike Lee also spoke to a local television station in Birmingham during this period. He stated that all the families approved of his documentary film production, or something to that effect. I didn't ask my immediate family members who participated in this ambitious project their overall thoughts about their experiences. One of my sisters made a passing remark about me in *4 Little Girls*, a documentary that situates the church bombing and the stories of the families impacted by this tragedy in civil rights history. It helped to spread and publicize the story, especially to a younger generation of viewers who had not lived through the struggle. The footage of the four dead children disturbed me.[3] After watching the movie at a local theatre, my blood pressure shot up. I could tell that some of the scenes brought back memories of it all to Janie who appeared in *4 Little Girls*, along with Junie. Later, Janie and I would watch the movie in Birmingham. She nearly drove off the road on the quiet drive back home. Anyway, I passed on yet another request.

Many years ago, Gail King (who now co-anchors *CBS This Morning*) reached out to on the behalf of the *Oprah Winfrey Show*, I believe. In 2002, it was a staple in daytime television. As a television host, Oprah Winfrey has tackled so many difficult, challenging topics. However, I still opted not to appear on the show. During my telephone conversation with Gail, I suggested Janie who accepted the invitation. Overall, the notion of appearing on national television seemed daunting at that point of my life and battles with PTSD. But I'm in a different place now and would be open to sharing my insights in this type of format. Following the trial, *The Oprah Winfrey Show* ran an episode on forgiveness that featured Janie, along with Teresa Stacy Cherry. Her grandfather was convicted of the bombing. Between the Blanton trial in 2001 and Cherry's trial in 2002, our country and others would grapple with terrorism on a vast scale.

Like many other people across the nation and around the world, I was speechless after the events of September 11, 2001. On "9/11," terrorists targeted the World Trade Center and the Pentagon and nearly averted striking a third target after a struggle occurred aboard an aircraft that crashed-landed.[4] When I saw the first plane fly into the Twin Towers of the World Trade Center, I just could not believe what I was seeing.[5] I ran to the telephone, called my friend Kathleen and told her to look at the news on Channel 6. And while I was watching the news like millions of other viewers, the second airplane crashed into the other twin tower. I was so scared. Initially, I thought the first plane had a mechanical error, mistakenly hitting the World Trade Center, until I saw the next plane do the exact same thing. I was saddened to observe what happened that day, resulting in a staggering loss of life. No one should have to die in that manner. One day, I hope we will find out how to love one another, instead of acting on hatred. God is *love*. It's time out for all the hate. Before anyone kills, think about all the consequences. Terrorism leaves hurt behind. Besides, God gave life, and it is up to Him alone to take it.[6]

Incidentally, days before the terror attack on September 11, 2001, President George W. Bush, issued a public statement (or Proclamation

7460), pertaining to the bombing of the 16th Street Baptist Church and the deaths of my friends, challenging folks to fight against racism:

> 'One of the darkest days for the cause of civil rights was September 15, 1963, when a bomb exploded in the basement of the Sixteenth Street Baptist Church in Birmingham, Alabama. The blast ended the lives of four young African-American girls, and ultimately demonstrated the tragic human costs of bigotry and intolerance…
>
> NOW, THEREFORE, I, GEORGE W. BUSH, President of the United States of America, by virtue of the authority in me by the Constitution and laws of the United States, do hereby proclaim September 9-15, 2001, as National Birmingham Pledge Week. I call upon the people of the United States to mark this observance with appropriate programs and ceremonies'….[7]

The year after 9/11, I accepted an invitation from the Congress of Racial Equality (CORE) to travel to New York City. In 2002, CORE presented me with an award, my first honor. I was so surprised to tell the truth. *The Birmingham News* wrote an article about this event, noting:

> Sarah Collins Rudolph and Doug Jones will receive the Congress of Racial Equality's Harmony Award, given annually to highlight examples of race reconciliation…. (Niger)Innis said the two were selected to show how far Birmingham and the nation have come in race relations since the civil rights era. [8]

I traveled to New York City along with my friend Kathleen to accept the award in 2002. She happens to be white. We were very close during that period of our lives. The bombing did not lead me to discriminate against and hate all white people. Hatred destroys. Attorney Doug Jones and I spoke at CORE's banquet. CORE honored Jones as well as the four girls. Chanda Temple, the news reporter covering this event wrote, "Reports of the bombing often focused on the four girls, often without mention of Rudolph." I further added, "'it looked like I was the one who always got left behind. It was somewhat hurtful. Just because I was injured, they just shoved me to the side.'" I added, "'sometimes I think I was spared simply because it wasn't my time…'"[9]

In 2003, I also began to address the issue of restitution in detail, as I shared with Carol Dawson during an interview with *Baylor Magazine*:

> 'I'm angry about all I've been through. People aren't concerned, you know. It hasn't been a bad life, but I just feel like I'm not right yet. You see people who get help for this or for that, but the time hasn't come when anybody gave me any.'[10]

In 2004, I participated in two different major forums: the Victim's Family Panel at a major forum, *The Gathering: Civil Rights Justice Remembered* in Birmingham, Al. and "Four Women from Birmingham" in Dayton, Oh.[11] Focusing on major civil rights-related court cases like the Vernon Dahmer trial, there was a separate panel for lawyers and the media too in Birmingham. This panel included defense attorneys and prosecutors like William Baxley, former Lt. Governor and State Attorney General in Alabama and Doug Jones, a former U.S. Attorney. Journalists included Howell Raines, Diane McWhorter, Frank Sikora, Rick Journey, Chanda Temple and Jerry Mitchell of *The Clarion-Ledger* in Jackson, Mississippi.[12]

The next month I spoke on a panel at Wright State University. Dr. Tracy Snipe, who attended the 40th year memorial program at the 16th Street Church, invited me to talk at this college. Tracy and I spoke over the telephone during the fall of 2003. Junie put us in contact with each other. The Saturday following the memorial service program, he met Rev. Fred Shuttlewsorth and Junie at a breakfast program held in the basement of the Sixteenth Street Church, mainly for members of the renowned Benedict Choir.[13] From what I understand, their voices filled the space beautifully at the commemoration program, *setting the atmosphere* with covers of songs like "My Everything (Praise Waiteth)" by Richard Smallwood & Vision.

Shifting back to our WSU visit, I enjoyed meeting Dr. Roberta Boyd and staff members like Jennifer who met us at the Dayton International Airport. The generous staff managed to exceed our expectations during the brief visit, providing us with a security detail and a special musical arrangement of songs near the start of the official program. Dr. Boyd presented each of the four guests with a corsage, and as soon as we stepped foot on to the stage, the audience gave us a standing ovation.

Figure 26. Sarah C. Rudolph and Junie C. Williams lecture at Wright State University (WSU). March 2004. Courtesy of WSU.

The next year Junie and I would also share the podium together at the University of the District of Columbia in Washington, D.C. We addressed a large gathering and later received citations on behalf of city council. It was my first trip to the capitol. After the event, we toured the city and took pictures near the White House.

Years later, on the 45th anniversary year of the 16th Street Church bombing, attorney Doug Jones presented me with the "Lifetime Achievement Award" from the Birmingham Pledge Foundation. It was my one of my first public receptions at this church. At the presentation, the former U.S attorney reminded everyone, "'there were five little girls in that lounge...Sarah is truly an inspiration.'"[14]

Jim Rotch wrote the "anti-racism statement" associated with the pledge because he thought that people, especially those who were not of age at the time of the '63 bombing, should learn about the story.[15]

> **I believe** that every person has worth as an individual.
>
> **I believe** that every person is entitled to dignity and respect; regardless of race or color.
>
> **I believe** that every thought and every act of racial prejudice is harmful…
>
> Therefore, from this day forward **I will** strive daily to eliminate racial prejudice from my thoughts and actions.

I will discourage racial prejudice by others at every opportunity. **I will** treat all people with dignity and respect… knowing that the world will be a better place because of my effort.[16]

During the program in 2008, I stated that four little girls "came to Sunday school and never made it home,"' so we should "never forget their sacrifice" for the good of the nation, while in 1963 Dr. King stated, "The split blood of these innocent girls may cause…Birmingham to transform the negative extremes of the dark past into the positive extremes of the beautiful future.[17] Immediately following the memorial service, Christopher McNair explained to a news reporter, ""'it's always painful,"' while his wife Mrs. Maxine McNair stated, "'you take a deep breath and go on."'[18] On an uplifting note, days later, Tracy and I visited Mr. Samuel Rutledge. We would both speak with him again within a year.

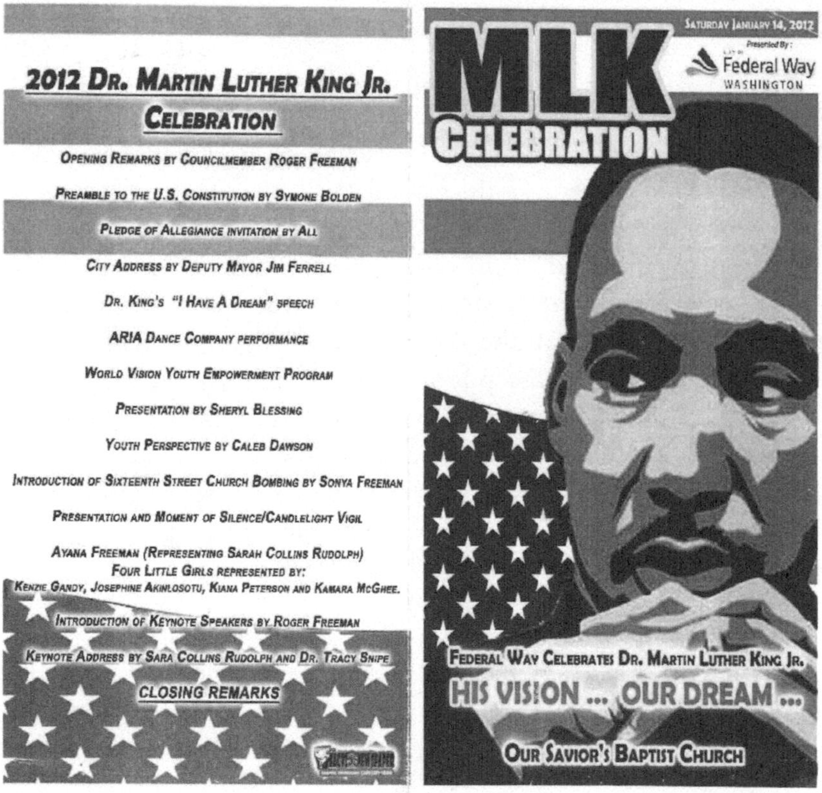

Figure 27. MLK Celebration in Federal Way, Washington. Courtesy of City Hall.

Figure 28.Sarah C. Rudolph along with WSU students in March of 2012. Beginning with top left Sherita Jackson, Chad Lovins, Moneeka Gentry-Stanifer, Phil Logan, and Michael Tyler; bottom left Allison DeSimio, Collins Rudolph and Rebekkah Mulholland. Photograph courtesy of Chad Lovins

During the next several years, I lectured extensively about the blast at schools such as WSU, while in 2010, Junie and I joined Dr. Snipe for a presentation held at the National Conference on Race and Ethnicity (NCORE) in Baltimore, Maryland entitled "Unsung Heroines, Untold Stories." On September 15, 2010, we lectured at Dickinson College in St. Carlisle, Pennsylvania. About a year and half later, Dr. Snipe and I traveled to the Pacific Northwest in 2012. Roger Freeman invited us to speak at the Martin Luther King Celebration program held in Federal Way, Washington. During that trip, I also gave a message at the historic First African Methodist Episcopal Church out in Seattle, Washington. Two months later, I met up with WSU students in Birmingham, Al. [19] During our meeting, I asked them specific questions about the four girls who died in the attack. They answered my questions thoughtfully. Students should learn this history.[20] Before we departed, I gave each one of them small gifts — for correctly answering my questions. I gladly left, empty-handed. I'm happy they are furthering their education, too.

In September of 2012, we spoke at the University of Nebraska in Omaha and at the Medical Center. Beginning in 2013, we picked up the pace, lecturing at the University of Nebraska (Lincoln) and the Cleveland Community (Tri County). Tracy arranged and lectured with Junie, Janie and me, including at the Martin Luther King event in Lincoln. He also arranged for me to speak to teachers from Atlanta at the Birmingham Civil Rights Institute, during this increasingly busy period. I also lectured at churches and schools in Birmingham and in other cities in Alabama.

On September 28, 2012, I spoke on a panel at the American Bar Association (ABA) conference in St. Louis, Missouri: "Lessons in Leadership from the Civil Rights Movement: First Person Accounts Panel." The presentation at the ABA was somewhat interesting. People responded on social media in real time during our speech in front of a live audience that day. I was on the same panel with D'Army Baily, (the founding president of the National Civil Rights Museum in Memphis, Tennessee) and Frankie Muse Freeman (a lawyer who once served on the U.S. Commission on Civil Rights).[21] Judge Bernice Bouie Donald, (who moderated our panel at the ABA) invited me to participate in this forum after she personally attended a lecture at University of Nebraska (Omaha) where I spoke, along with Junie and Dr. Snipe in September of 2012.

Meditations

Two months later, I woke up early one morning on a mission, and *I didn't have no doubt.* It was about a week before Thanksgiving, as I firmly recall. Something led me to go to City Hall to speak to Mayor William Bell and the members of Birmingham's City Council too. I wanted to express my opinion about several issues, well before the 50th anniversary year of the bombing. For one, I was still paying out of pocket for medical costs and injuries related to the bombing, which did not seem fair to me. When I was a child, my parents shouldered most of these expenses. As an adult, I had to pick up or continue where they left off. No one ever honored the promise made to my Mama. Although we were victims of terrorism, families impacted by the '63 bombing never received compensation. We dealt with the cost and emotional trauma for decades. Furthermore, I had been coping with a bout of depression following my eye surgery in earlier in 2012. The doctor even prescribed medication for me.

I didn't want the city of Birmingham to gloss over my connection to the bombing. My last-minute decision to talk to then Mayor William Bell and members of city council even surprised George who accompanied me to City Hall. A reporter happened to be there. Later, *The Birmingham News* published a follow up story. The news reporter, Joseph D. Bryant, quoted me directly several times. Bryant pointed out other facts like my current job working as a domestic with a local cleaning service located in Birmingham, Al. He explained why I sorted out city and state leaders:

> 'I had been going through a lot of changes trying to find help,' she said, adding she has been told she is ineligible for relief funds because of the age of the crime. 'Everybody I go to, the door is shut.'
>
> Rudolph said it is proper to ask current city leaders for some help to bring relief from the damage done in part because of actions from former leaders…
>
> 'The police were doing what Bull Connor told them to do. If all that hadn't come about, that church wouldn't have been bombed,' she said. 'It looks like it shouldn't take 50 years for something that happened in 1963…'[22]

Finding the courage to share even more of my story publicly, after years of keeping so much inside wasn't easy. Yet, this choice allowed me to cross paths with other individuals who grasped what I was trying to convey, especially concerning restitution. In terms of social media, the feedback that I received was mainly positive, although not uniformly. This wasn't the first time that I mentioned the topic of compensation or steered the conversation towards how the racial climate in Alabama may have contributed to the deadly bombing itself in 1963. To recap, I really began to speak up about this painful topic in an interview that I gave with Carol Dawson in *Baylor Magazine*, complemented by the article "Lessons from the Civil Rights Movement," focusing on the youth.

> 'It was the church's first official Youth Day, honoring the young people who'd recently poured onto the streets to become the surprise revolutionary strong arm of the movement…. In the previous months, they had been marching, singing freedom songs…'[23]

I have worked through some of the anger since this interview in 2003, but my overall position remains the same. In addition, I myself, and family representatives, have written to American presidents about restitution and the subject of Addie's remains, when this subject matter was still in question.

I felt better after speaking out to the press about these issues. Stephanie Engle contacted me shortly after *The Birmingham News* article in November of 2012 appeared in print. She lives outside of Birmingham proper but took an overall interest in the story; within months, we encouraged elected officials at the local, state and even national levels to consider long-term issues related to the families of the victims of the '63 blast and other victims of hate crimes, especially in the state of Alabama. I spoke to groups in cities like Montgomery, Alabama.

During this period, my views about reparations and restitution only deepened. I read more about the government's response to the Tulsa Riots or Tulsa Race Massacre of 1920 (also known as the "Black Wall Street Massacre") and the case of thousands of Japanese who were sent to internment camps in America at the height of World War II.[24] These tragic cases makes one think seriously about the injustices suffered by black people living in Florida too, as depicted in Jonathan Singleton's film *Rosewood*. Nevertheless, restitution for the bombing survivors and victims' family is a subject that deserves serious consideration.[25]

Notes

1 Joseph D. Bryant, "The Fifth Little Girl," *The Birmingham News*, November 25, 2012.

2 Jessica Ravitz, "Siblings of the Bombing: Remembering Birmingham Church Blast 50 Years On, CNN, Updated September 17, 2013, www.cnn.com/2013/09/14/us/birmingham-church-bombing-anniversary-victims-siblings/index.htl; Patty Satalia, Conversations at Penn State University; see website address too. (In "Siblings of the Bombing," Rudolph notes that she also declined Bill Cosby's team request to write a play based on her in 2012. Cosby's spokesperson visited her in Birmingham, Al. to pitch the idea. In the past, Rudolph usually denied such requests and interviews. After taking time to heal and self-reflect, she is more open to such requests.

3 Matt Patches, "As the Birmingham Bombing Turn 50, Spike Lee Reflects on the Dark Road to '4 Little Girls' (Q &A)," *Hollywoodreporter.com*, September 13, 2013, https:"www.hollywoodreporter.com/news/as-Birmingham-bombing-turn50-629177. (In this article published by the *Hollywood* Reporter, Spike Lee discussed

the agonizing choice that he made regarding his decision to show the postmortem photographs of the four little girls.)

4 On September 11, 2001, a fourth commercial plane, departing from Newark, New Jersey, crashed in Somerset County (Shanksville, Pennsylvania). For a dramatic recreation of the doomed United Airlines passenger plane, refer to the film "Flight 193."

5 Rudolph, letter to Snipe, April 25, 2014.

6 Ibid

7 L.S.A., List of C.F.R., https://books.google.com>books. (George W. Bush Proclamation 7460). See Proclamation 7460 of September 8, 2001 (National Birmingham Pledge Week, 2001), 260-261.

8 Chanda Temple, "Civil Rights Group CORE will Salute Victim, Prosecutor," [2002] *The Birmingham News.*

9 Ibid.

10 Carol Dawson, "Sarah Collins Rudolph," *Baylor Magazine*, September/October 2003, baylor.edu/alumni/magazine/0202/news.php?action=story&story=7597.

11 G. Douglas Jones, letter to Sarah Collins Rudolph, January 27, 2004. (Birmingham Southern College hosted *The Gathering* on February 12th &13th 2004. Bill Baxley led the team of lawyers who prosecuted Robert Chambliss in 1977, while Doug Jones led the prosecution for the trials held in 2001 and 2002, respectively.)

12 *The Gathering*: Lawyers Panel and *The Gathering*: Media Panel. (Birmingham-Southern College, located in Birmingham, Al. held this event.)

13 According to the official website for Benedict College located in Columbia, S.C., the Benedict College Gospel Choir continues to be the premier such choir in the country. This historically black college is also ranked as one of the top-ranking baccalaureate colleges nationwide by Washington Monthly (www. Benedict.edu).

14 Greg Garrison, "Survivor Honored on Anniversary of the Birmingham Bombing," The Birmingham Times, September (2008).

15 Garrison, "Survivor Honored."

16 "BIRMINGHAM PLEDGE: SIGN IT – LIVE IT- SHARE IT," www.tolerance.org/sites/default/files/general/Birmingham%20Pledge%20Form%202016.pdf.

17 Garrison, "Survivor Honored"; King, *A Testament of Hope*, 222.

18 Ibid. (During a brief conversation later that evening, Mrs. Maxine McNair urged me to continue to integrate historical events into the curriculum like the church bombing -- despite the somberness of the content—and to continue to screen documentaries like *4 Little Girls* and *Angels of Change*.)

19 WSU students also participated in the Students & Stewards program of the Faith & Politics Institute 12th Congressional Civil Rights Pilgrimage.

20 Rudolph, letter to Snipe, April 24, 2014.

21 The Honorable Bernice Bouie Donald also moderated a second panel, "Lessons in Leadership from the Civil Rights Movement: Legal Issues Panel." The second panel featured Barbara R. Arnwine, Elaine R. Jones, Theodore M. Shaw and Paulette Brown.

22 Bryant, "The Fifth Little Girl."

23 Carol Dawson, "Sarah Collins Rudolph," *Baylor Magazine*, September/October 2003, baylor.edu/alumni/magazine/0202/news.php?action= story&story=7597. For additional perspectives on this story, also refer to Gayle Yancey's "Lessons Learned from the Civil Rights Movement," also published by *Baylor Magazine* in 2003; Baylor.edu/alumni/magazine/0202/news.php?action=story&story=7585.

24 Diane McWhorter, "Civil Right Justice on the Cheap," *The New York Times*, September 15, 2013, nytimes.com/2013/09/15/opinion/Sunday/civil-rights-justice-on-the-cheap.html; "Facts and Case Summary – Korematsu v. U.S., uscourts.gov/educational-activities/facts-and-case-summary-kormatsu-v-us; Barbara Palmer, "Stanford Alumnus Seeks Reparations for Survivors of Deadly 1921 Tulsa Riot," Stanford News, February 16, 2005, Charles J. Ogletree, "Tula Reparations: The Survivors' Story," Boston College Third World Law Journal, Vol. 24 Issue 1 (2004), lawdigitalcommons.bc.edu/twlj/vol24/iss1/4/; news.standford.edu/news/2005/february16/Tulsa-021605.html; C. Jeanne Bassett, "House Bill 591: Florida Compensates Rosewood Victims and Their Families for a Seventy-One-Year-Old Injury," Florida State University Law Review (Volume 22/Issue 2. Winter 1994), ir.law.fsu.edu/cgi/viewcontent.cgi?article=14987 content=lr.

25 Joseph D. Bryant, "Reparations for 1963 Church Bombing Survivor Difficult, but Not Impossible, Experts Say," Updated March 7, 2019; Posted April 18, 2013, al.com/spotnews/2013/04/post_911.html; see also Stephanie Engle's position paper on reparations for victims' families of the 1963 Birmingham Church bombing.

Chapter 24. Black Pearls

To obey is better than sacrifice.
—1 Samuel 15:22 KJV

Leader: Addie Mae Collins, Denise McNair, Carole Robertson, and Cynthia Wesley, born Cynthia Morris, we honor your names because you are always referred to collectively as the 4 Little Girls but you were each unique, beautiful individuals with personal dreams and aspirations.
All: We honor your names….
Leader: Addie Mae, Denise, Carole and Cynthia, we honor your names because we confess that when you were taken we did not understand why you had to die for we see through a glass darkly but now we assured that all things work together for the good to them that love God, to them who are the called according to His purpose.
All: We honor your names. –Gaile Pugh Gratton Green[1]

From the outset of 2013, the pace of life gathered speed, as the nation recalled Birmingham's special place in the Civil Rights Movement.[2] Representatives Terri Sewell (D-AL), (R- Spencer Bachus) and Senator Richard Shelby (R-Ala), as well as the entire Alabama congressional delegation, led the effort to honor the four girls with a congressional gold medal (H.R.360). This was the first time that private citizens had received this honor since 9/11.[3] In 2013, I took part in many speaking engagements related to the 50th year memorial of the blast. For example, in January, I presented the keynote MLK address at the University of Nebraska (at Lincoln), along with my sisters Janie and Junie, while Dr. Tracy Snipe served as the facilitator. Prior to this trip, NPR interviewed me about the fiftieth anniversary year of the bombing and topics like restitution or compensation.

I've always believed that the state government or some party should compensate the families of the four girls and the victims of this terror attack. Although the Victim's Compensation Act did not finally take effect until 1983, we lived through homegrown domestic terrorism. I was a victim and survivor of the church bombing. I believe that the tone or atmosphere fostered by some officials added to an atmosphere of lawlessness, contributing to the eventual terror attack. Remember, Bull Connor used to patrol the streets of our city, riding a white tank.

That terrible day in September, I lost an eye, not to mention my sister and best friend. Moreover, I still suffer with PTSD and other health-related issues. As George stated in an NPR interview:

> "'If you look back at the people in the trade towers, each of those victims got paid. The families, they got paid…But my wife, she didn't get anything. She should get compensated.'"[4]

Some exceptions aside, I have had to pay for doctor visits, glasses, eye check-ups and other expenses. My husband's job insurance covered some of my expenses when he worked. However, George retired years ago. I don't receive his medical benefits, as I mentioned during an NPR interview in January of 2013 and on other subsequent occasions.

In February of 2013, James Ware and I gave a talk to students at a Barrett Elementary School about the life-changing series of events that occurred in Birmingham, Al. on September 15, 1963.[5] I am glad that the city of Birmingham is acknowledging his brother Virgil and Johnny Robinson, more and more. This Black history program gave us the chance to provide youth in a local public school with a vital history lesson. I discussed the bombing and explained how I tried to deal with the trauma. I would give a similar lecture at a church in March of 2013.

My visit to Reed's Temple (Church of God in Christ) in Griffith, Indiana was quite special. About a day or so before my presentation at Reed's Temple, a local anchor affiliated with NBC News interviewed me in their Chicago studio. Afterwards, I shared my story or testimony with the congregation, Pastor David Reed, First Lady Iris Reed, and members of the assembly presented me with several special gifts, including an 'Addie Doll.' First Lady Iris read an article in *Baylor Magazine* about how

I spent my thirteenth birthday in the hospital and wanted to revisit this chapter of my life. She also wanted to present a meaningful black history program, especially for the youth and to focus on ways to combat and overcome violence: Mrs. Reed later informed a newspaper reporter, "I want the world to know more about Sarah and her story of courage, resilience, fortitude and faith in God." [6]

During the very first half of 2013, Fate Morris, who was Cynthia's biological brother, and I communicated often. We became involved in the effort to bring public awareness to the issue of reparations or restitution for bombing victims, and victims' family members, too.[7] We gave joint interviews to the AP and to the local media, which ordinarily wouldn't be the simplest thing to do with anyone given the importance of this topic. However, our paths had crossed many years ago; we were both in the same graduating class at A. H. Parker High School. Years earlier, the news that the church bombing killed his sister disturbed him as young boy, and later in his adult life. At first, Fate did not fully grasp his sister's fate on the actual day of the bombing. [8] I questioned the idea of awarding a congressional gold medal and still have other views about this topic. At first, I opposed this idea. Let me explain. To me, awarding the four little girls a medal after their deaths was like putting a band-aid over a wound that has not entirely healed. Don't get me wrong. Giving them the medals *was* the honorable thing to do, but it is just a *first step*. I realize that some families may think differently, but we deserved restitution, not just a glossy medal.[9] As I stated in an interview during the height of the debate,

> 'I can't go to the store and pay for my doctor's bill with a Congressional Gold Medal.... No, they put a bomb in that church and killed my sister...I'm letting the world know, my sister didn't die for freedom. My sister died because they put a bomb in that church and they murdered her.'[10]

Fate, who rarely speaks above a whisper, addressed the issue of restitution too. Aside from losing a sibling in a terror attack, we share other experiences like the issue of recognition, for instance. Aside from Cynthia's violent death, the circumstances surrounding her last name left hurt him. The Wesley's took Cynthia in as a little girl, and raised her, so the world knows her by the name "Wesley."[11] I can still relate to him when it comes to the issue of acknowledgement. For years, people forgot about me, too. During the lowest point of my life, I used to wish that I had died along with my sister and friends. But I had so many things to work out. In contrast, those four girls -- they were each at a different place. No one is perfect. Yet, they were truly *angels of change.* As for Addie, she was like a *pearl in my world*; they were all black pearls.

Nowadays, compensation for the victims and survivors of tragedies like the Sixteenth Street Church bombing does not appear to be on the agenda, especially since the 50th commemoration is over. For years, so many officials have pointed to the statute of limitations, which doesn't help survivors like me. Before 9/11, the church bombing was one of the worst acts of terrorism on American soil. Imagine widows, widowers, and orphans of 9/11 going around the nation asking for compensation some fifty years later for their medical expenses and ongoing suffering. Granted some first responders to 9/11 like firefighters, EMTs, and the police had to rely on the courts (and later members of Congress and the media), they received help.[12] Many of the children or survivors of rescue workers killed during 9/11 receive scholarships to further their schooling.[13] Congress members overturned President Obama's veto, allowing victims of 9/11 to sue the government of Saudi Arabia. No such benefits exist for victims and survivors of the '63 bombing. The statute of limitation disqualifies us. As Carol Dawson of *Baylor Magazine* wrote in a feature article, "applications to the FBI Victim Funds have proved futile: such cases are retroactive only to 1983."[14] However, I continued to address this fact while sharing my story in other settings.

On April 15, 2013, I spoke on a panel at the University of Virginia (Center for Politics) along with other civil rights activists from Virginia like Edwina Allen Isaac, Rita Mosley, and Catherine Scott, as well as Joan Bland from the state of Alabama. A child activist, Bland had been engaged in "The Movement" from the age of 11 and bore witness to the events of "Bloody Sunday." Several of the panelists were civil rights activists as young folks. The forced closing of Robert Mussa High School (known as Moton High School) compelled some of these women to forgo their education early on. Dr. Patrice Grimes who teaches in the School of Education at the University of Virginia moderated our panel, "Voices of the Civil Rights Movement."[15]

Earlier that day, a terrorist attack near the finish line of the Boston Marathon rattled the nation. I could relate to the victims and survivors of this vicious attack and immediately began to pray, for everyone. I was the victim and a survivor of a terror attack too, so I live and experience such events differently. It was another reminder of senseless violence. The organizers decided not to cancel the event, which was fine by me. The members of the panel all received a standing ovation at the end of this program.

About two weeks after returning from the event in Charlottesville, Virginia, I later expressed my thoughts about the Boston Marathon in a letter that I wrote to Tracy:

> 'While the people was out racing and having a wonderful time, there in the street was the enemy, waiting and watching to destroy the peoples' fun. It was time for him to snatch away all of the laughter, joy. For all of the people that died and who were maimed, may God give you peace.
>
> The devil meant it for evil, but the Lord will turn it around for your good. Your loved ones are in heaven. For those who survived and are still alive, may the joy of the Lord be with you, forever. This all reminds me of the bombing of the 16th Street Church. When we got together to have a wonderful day, the devil creeped in to wreak havoc and destruction, but don't worry. The battle is not over; the Lord's got the last words.
>
> The people that bombed the church, they got to stand before God. Many of the bombers should know that one day they got to stand before God and give an account of every evil deed that they have done.
>
> So people, please rejoice because great is your reward in heaven [to] *all* them that suffer on this earth.'[16]

In April and May of 2013, legislation honoring my four friends passed the House and later the Senate, largely thanks to the efforts of Representative Terri Sewell and the Alabama delegation.[17] On May 24, 2013, President Barack H. Obama signed a bill (H.R. 360) honoring Addie, Cynthia, Carole and Denise.[18] Legislators awarded my peers with the Congressional Gold Medal some fifty years after their deaths. The President signed the bill in the Oval Office to much fanfare; family members and dignitaries surrounded him. I watched it all on television. I was not in the congressional chambers when the U.S. Congress passed this act earlier in honor of my peers. I declined both select invitations but regretted my decision not to go. I should have made some decisions for myself, or even prayed more for direction, instead of weighing so heavily on the advice of others at the time.

I was not there when President Obama signed the bill honoring the four girls, but I admire his tribute to them in *The Audacity of Hope*. As a senator, he visited the 16th Street Church while on the Congressional Civil Rights Pilgrimage. In 2011, I also took part in the Congressional Civil Rights Pilgrimage in Alabama, sponsored by the Faith & Politics Institute.[19] Congressman John Lewis regularly traveled with and co-led this annual pilgrimage. The delegation often tours states in the Deep South. During the 11th trip, I spoke to the group at the Birmingham Civil Rights Institute. It is still not stress-free for me to speak at the 16th Street Church; I truly learned so much during the entire pilgrimage. We toured the National Voting Rights Museum and Institute and the Brown Chapel A.M.E. in Selma, as well as the Southern Poverty Law Center (SPLC) in Montgomery, Alabama. Honestly, I found the Civil Rights Memorial in front of the SPLC, designed by Maya Lin, to be inspirational. Years before I traveled with the group, then Senator Obama visited the 16th Street Church when he traveled to Alabama to give a speech at the Birmingham Civil Rights Institute too. Clearly, his visit to the church moved him, as he expressed at length:

> After the tour, the pastor, deacons, and I held hands and said a prayer in the sanctuary. Then they left me to sit in one of the pews and gather my thoughts. What must it have been like for those parents 40 years ago, I wondered, knowing that their precious daughters had been snatched away by violence at once so casual and so vicious? How could they endure the anguish unless they were certain that some purpose lay behind their children's murders, that some meaning could be found in immeasurable lost. Those parents would have seen the mourners pour in from all across the nation, would have read the condolences from across the globe, would have watched as Lyndon Johnson announced on national television that the time had come to overcome, would have seen Congress finally pass the Civil Rights Act of 1964. Friends and strangers alike would have assured them that their daughters had not died in vain... And yet would even that knowledge be enough to console your grief, to keep you from madness and eternal rage—unless you also knew that your child had gone on to a better place?
>
> My thoughts turned to my mother and her final days.... I carried such thoughts with me as I left the church and made my speech. Later

> that night, back home in Chicago, I sat at the dinner table, watching Malia and Sasha...I thought of Sasha asking me once what happened when we die — 'I don't want to die, Daddy,' she had added matter-of-factly — and I had hugged her and said, 'You've got a long, long way before you have to worry about that,' which had seemed to satisfy her. I wondered whether I should have told her the truth, that I wasn't sure what happens when we die... Walking up the stairs, though, I knew what I hoped for — that my mother was together in some way with those four little girls, capable in some fashion of embracing them, of finding joy in their spirits....[20]

Building on some experiences like the speech that I gave to the Congressional Civil Rights Pilgrimage delegation in 2011, and other lectures that I gave about the bombing during that period, Dr. Snipe and I also lectured at the National Conference on Race and Ethnicity (NCORE) in New Orleans, Louisiana during the late spring of 2013. The title of our talk was "Girl Forgotten." Dr. Snipe, Junie and I lectured at NCORE for the first time years earlier; our session was well-attended. During our first presentation at this conference, which we titled 'Unsung Heroines, Untold Stories,' I spoke about restitution and finding Addie.

Local and national, as well as the international media interviewed me during the summer of 2013. For instance, I shared my story and concerns with the Reverend Jesse Jackson on his radio show, "Keep Hope Alive." I still had reservations about the Congressional Gold Medal award. Months earlier, this part of the story made world news in countries such as Ireland, while the BBC World Service interviewed me about the 50th year memorial.[21] To be sure, Rev. Jackson believed that perhaps some were using the awarding of the gold medal to the "four little girls" merely to score political points; Joseph Bryant of *The Birmingham News*, who had written several articles related to the 50th year memorial of the deadly church bombing that included this aspect of the story would also remark:

> 'Jackson has mentioned a petition to Congress for restitution as a possibility. He said officials are attempting to use Rudolph and the 1963 commemoration to contrast the Old South to the progressive New South. But what Rudolph need is substance over symbolism...'[22]

In the end, I did decide to attend the Congressional Gold Medal Ceremony in Washington, D.C. I traveled to the capitol after speaking with Representative Terri Sewell who, among other elected officials and representatives, faithfully worked to award the gold medals posthumously to the four girls. As I later explained during an interview with Diane McWhorter, "'what changed my mind is that I love my sister. She can't talk for herself but I can."[23] Members from all four families, dignitaries, and invited guests attended this special ceremony.

The Congress of the United States
requests the honor of your presence at a
Congressional Gold Medal Ceremony
in honor of

Addie Mae Collins, Denise McNair,
Carole Robertson, and Cynthia Wesley

on Tuesday, the tenth of September
two thousand thirteen
at three o'clock in the afternoon

Statuary Hall
United States Capitol
Washington, District of Columbia

The favor of your reply is requested by the fifth of September
BoehnerRSVP@mail.house.gov

Figure 29. Congressional Gold Medal Ceremony Invitation. Courtesy of George C. Rudolph.

I spoke to several reporters before and at the conclusion of the Congressional Gold Medal Ceremony in Washington, D.C. The gold medal is a tremendous honor the four little girls and one of many ways to acknowledge their sacrifice. They gave a lot to the city of Birmingham, our nation and fully deserved this award.

Throughout the year of 2013 and during Empowerment Week in early September, I reconnected with friends like Donzaleigh Abernathy. I had met her years ago, in around 1991, as I recall. An actor and author, she is the daughter of Juanita Abernathy and the late Rev. Ralph Abernathy, former pastor of the First Baptist Church in Montgomery, Alabama and co-founder of the Southern Christian Leadership Conference (SCLC).[24] Reverend Abernathy's role in the Movement (from the fledgling Montgomery Bus Boycott to the Poor People's Campaign), cannot be understated. His congregation, the First Baptist Church, sheltered endangered civil rights activists at the height of the Movement.

Donzaleigh has been writing a movie script about that Sunday, morning or September 15, 1963, and other events in the civil rights struggles from her perspective.[25] She is very smart, and a beautiful person. I am so excited about what God is doing in all our lives.

Towards the end of that week, I attended the unveiling of the Four Spirits Memorial in Kelly Ingram Park on Saturday, September 14, 2013. This life-like monument honors Denise, Addie, Cynthia and Carole. Kelly Ingram Park was the key staging ground for so many demonstrations at the height of the Birmingham Campaign, so this setting is ideal. There were countless foot soldiers or "non-violent revolutionaries" among the throngs of people at the event. The memorial takes its title from Birmingham native Sena Jeter Naslund's novel *Four Spirits*; this book centered on the fatal church bombing. The Rev. Joseph Lowery, a former SCLC president, gave a rousing speech at the debut. Few can work a crowd like Rev. Lowery. Before concluding, he quoted the lyrics from a Beatles' song for good measure. His speech tapped into the spirit of 'The Movement,' and the day itself. Anyway, I think that the memorial is a great way to recognize the four girls. Still, I wish that it had depicted Addie a little differently in relation to her peers.

After the unveiling, along with family members, I later attended a private reception at the Birmingham Civil Rights Institute. Gaile Green wrote a lovely tribute to my friends. Carole Robertson was her cousin.

Family members and invited guests read the litany at the end of the short program. Relatives representing each of the different families, lit candles honoring the four girls, as audience members read the litany. As we departed, the organizers of this even gave us beautiful souvenir candles, etched with the likeness of the four girls.

Elizabeth MacQueen, who was from Birmingham, Al., designed a memorial honoring them at the request of Four Spirits Inc. While I've voiced my thoughts about how it depicts Addie; overall, the memorial helps to ensure that we don't forget what the four little girls sacrificed. This public memorial also includes pictures of the late Virgil Ware and Johnny Robinson. Tina Allen's photograph is included, among other famous people connected to the bombing and Birmingham's history. My friend Tina was a gifted sculptor; her sculptures were huge in size or dimension. Subjects of her work included the author of *Roots*, Alex Haley. Tina also planned to work on a sculpture in tribute to the four girls and me. We talked about this amazing idea. I would love to have seen the finished project. However, Tina, who was close to her Dad, died after he passed away. She did not get the chance to carry out her vision.

More Precious than Bronze

At one point during the commemoration service in Washington, D.C., officials gave me with a bronze medal duplicate of Addie's congressional gold medal. I deeply appreciated this gesture but valued something else even more – arriving at a resolution about my sister's remains. This had become my mission, and a conversation that I continued long after the resolutions ended. Addie was more valuable to me than silver and gold. She was a child with *a heart of gold*. She was *my friend*. I miss her so *I've been lookin'…'* As George has stated, my family is no different from others in that we wanted to properly bury or put away our loved one.

Circumstances didn't allow my family to purchase a tombstone in 1963. Since the late 1990's, we had both written and spoken to various government officials about the topic of my sister's remains. It was like a festering wound. The medals are pleasing, but next to making it into the kingdom, one of my priorities in life was verifying her mortal remains.

The period after the 50th memorial caused me to long for Addie even more. She never had the chance to grow up, to explore her talent as an artist. In fact, two of the girls were musically inclined. Carole studied the clarinet while, Cynthia played the saxophone. With her lively personality and flair for the dramatic, Denise surely could have lit up the silver screen if she pursued acting. Just to think of all the fun times we could have shared as teens, adults, or now in what would have been the golden years.

Notes

1 The Litany, "We Honor Your Names," included with the permission of attorney Gaile Pugh Gratton Green. Carole Robertson was her first cousin. Green wrote "We Honor Your Names" to coincide with the 50th year commemoration of the 16th Street Baptist Church bombing and first shared it publicly shared it with the families of all four victims present in a special ceremony at the Birmingham Civil Rights Institute. At the end of the ceremony, the family and assembled guests lit candles in honor of their loved ones.

2 Barnett Wright, "An Indelible Mark on History," *The Birmingham News*, January 6, 2013; Joseph D. Bryant, "Gold Medal for 'Four Little Girls' Gains Majority," *The Birmingham News*. (Refer to the appendix for the full text of H.R. 360)

3 Joseph D. Bryant, "Sister, Brother of Two of 'Four Little Girls' Reject Plans for Gold Medal, Surprising Advocates," April 11, 2013, al.com/spotnews/2013/04/sister_brother_of_two_of_fourh.html.

4 Tonya Ott, "Long Forgotten, 16th Street Baptist Church Bombing Victim Speaks Out," *All Thing Considered*, NPR, January 15, 2013, https://www.npr.org/2013/01/25/170279226/long-forgotten-16th-street-baptist-church-bomb.

5 Marie Leech, "'Fifth Little Girl' Honored," *The Birmingham News*, February 13, 2013.

6 Sue Ellen Ross, "Survivor Bring History Life," *Post-Tribune*, March 15, 2013. (While booking Sarah Collins Rudolph for this speaking engagement, Iris Reed expressed her desire for the bombing survivor to be able to reach out to youth in their congregation and young people in the greater Chicago area in the wake of the random handgun related death of Hadiya Pendleton.)

7 Jay Reeves, "Kin of '63 Church Bombing Victims Split Over Medal," AP, April 12, 2013, http://www.sandiegouniontribune.com/.

8 Jessica Ravitz, "Siblings of the Bombing: Remembering Birmingham Church Blast 50 Years On," CNN, September 17, 2013, http:/www.cnn.com/2013/09/14/us/Birmingham-church-bombing-anniversary-victims-siblings/index.html.

9 Jay Reeves, "Sarah Collins Rudolph, '63 Alabama Church Bombing Survivor, Seeks Funds, Refuses Award," Blackvoices, April 10, 2012, http://www.huffingtonpost.com/2013/04/10/sarah-collins-rudolph-alabama-church-bombing...; "Ku Klux Klan Bombing Survivor Opposes US Congressional Medal Ceremony: Victim of 1963 Alabama Church Bombing Wants Restitution, not Medal of Honor" April 15, 2013, http://www.irishtimes.com/news/world/us/ku-klux-klan-bombing-survivor-opposes-us-con...(Collins-Rudolph asked for $6 million dollars. Prior to the beginning of the 50th memorial year

commemoration, under the office or auspices of Mayor William Bell, the city of Birmingham offered to provide Rudolph with $10,000 for a series of lectures. However, she did not accept this proposal).

10 Joseph D. Bryant, "Sister, Brother of Two of 'Four Little Girls' Reject Plans."

11 Ibid.

12 Kristen Saloomey, "'We will Fight': 9/11 Families Renew Bid to Sue Saudi," AJ, January 19, 2018, https://www.aljazeera.com/news/2018/01/fight-911-familes-renew-bid-sue-saudi-180119063953735.html; Chris Baynes, "US Court Allow 9/11 Victims' Lawsuits Claiming Saudi Arabia Helped Plan Terror Attack," *Independent*, March 29, 2018, https:www.independent.co.uk/news/world/Americas/Saudi-arabia-9-11-victims-lawsuit-us-court-allowed-twin-towers-terror-attack-september-a8279

13 "9-11 Related College Scholarships," College Scholarships.org, www. College scholarships.org/scholarships/September-11th.htm.

14 Carol Dawson, "Sarah Collins Rudolph," *Baylor Magazine*, September/October 2003.

16 Glenn Crossman of the University of Virginia (Center for Politics) helped to coordinate or put on the event.

16 Rudolph, letter to Snipe, April 25, 2014.

17 "Senate Unanimously Passes Gold Medal Bill to Honor the 'Four Little Girls,'" Press Release, May 9, 2013, https:/sewell.house.gov/media-center/press-releases-senate-unamimously-passes-gold-medal-bill-honor-four-little-girls.

18 "Congresswoman Sewell Joins President Obama at the Bill Signing Ceremony for the Congressional Gold Medal Bill to Honor the 'Four Little Girls,'" Press Release, May 24, 2013, https://sewell.house.gov/media-center/press-releases-congress woman-sewell-joins-president-obama-bill-signing-ceremony.

19 Sarah, Junie, and I joined the delegation that year by invitation. Sarah gave a brief talk at the Birmingham Civil Rights Institute during the pilgrimage that year, while her sister Junie spoke at the 16th Street Baptist Church.

20 Barak Obama, *The Audacity of Hope: Thoughts on Reclaiming the American Dream* (New York: Three Rivers Press, 2007), 224-226.

21 "Ku Klux Klan Bombing Survivor Opposes US Congressional Medal of Honor," April 16, 2013. (SOURCE?)

22 Joseph D. Bryant, "Reparations for 1963 Church Bombing Survivor."

23 Diane McWhorter, "Civil Justice on the Cheap," *The New York Times*, September 15, 2013.

24 Donzaleigh Abernathy – IMDB, https://www.imdb.com/name/nm0008651. According to this site, Abernathy 'won the Tanne Foundation 2012 Artist Award for her work as an actress and for her script, 'Birmingham Sunday.''

25 Rudolph, letter to Snipe, April 24, 2014.

Chapter 25. Psalm

By the rivers of Babylon, there we sat down, yea, we wept, when we remembered Zion. We hanged our harps upon the willows in the midst thereof. (Psalm 137: 1-2, KJV)

He restores my soul (Psalm 23:3, NKJ).

God will wash away all our tears…
He always has…He always will. —John Coltrane

On September 15, 2013 I attended the 16th Street Church. Rev. Arthur Price instructed the Sunday school lesson titled "A Love that Forgives."[1] Congresswoman Terri Sewell and Rev. Jesse Jackson later led the wreath laying ceremony, while Reverend Bernice King offered moving prayers:

> 'We thank you father for the tremendous progress we have made in 50 years, that we can sit in the safe confines of this sanctuary being protected by the city of Birmingham when 50 years ago the city turned its eye and its ears away from us.'[2]

Still, my heart was heavy that Sunday at the 16th Street Church, as an AP picture of me reveals.[3] But I was there in honor of my friends. I spoke to the press near the site where bombers placed the dynamite. I explained, "'God spared me to live and tell just what happened on the day.'"[4] I returned to church later that afternoon. Hundreds of people, of all races, attended the commemoration, which C-Span covered live.[5]

Figure 30. Sarah Collins Rudolph with Rev. Jesse Jackson. Courtesy Collins-Rudolph

Ambassador Andrew Young spoke, while Attorney General Eric Holder questioned the U.S. Supreme Court's ruling in the Shelby decision, vowing, "This is a fight that we will continue."[6] President Obama wrote:

> Today, we remember Addie Mae Collins, Denise McNair, Carole Robertson, and Cynthia Wesley who were killed 50 years ago in the 16th Street Baptist Church bombing. That horrific day in .... quickly became a defining moment for the Civil Rights Movement. It galvanized and broadened support for a movement that would eventually lead to the passage of the Civil Rights Act of 1964.[7]

Diane McWhorter's op-ed published by *The New York Times* noted:

"The sometimes-impressive anniversary tributes stand in contrast to how little glory the bombing victims themselves caught... So when Congress awarded the girls... the Congressional Gold Medal... it was ... a shock that Ms. Rudolph responded, no thanks. 'I'm letting the world know, my sister didn't die for freedom...'My sister died because they put a bomb in that church and they murdered her.' Declining to attend President Obama's signing of the resolution... she stated her preference for compensation 'in the millions....'

.... In the wake of the attacks on the Boston Marathon and the World Trade Center, an outpouring of financial aid for the victims expressed a belief that their suffering was a sacrament of our democracy. Yet Sarah Collins Rudolph – maimed by native-born terrorists in our nation's great internal struggle – has been expected to deal with protracted medical and cosmetic issues, to say nothing of other forms of anguish, on a domestic worker's wages....

.... We can put a man on the moon. Should it really be that difficult to find justice, if not a measure of security, for our black young – including, at long last, the 'fifth little girl'?"[8]

Soultrane

Two days later, during my interview with Amy Goodman, Aaron Mate stated, "Mrs. Rudolph you have been denied compensation. Initially, the Congressional Gold Medal wasn't going to — it didn't include you. Do you feel as if history has forgotten what happened to you?" I said,

Yes, I feel forgotten. Like yesterday, I should have been resting...for what I went through on the weekend, but I had had to go get up at 6:00 and still go to work when if there was money that... had been given to me I wouldn't have to do this... I know the four girls should get all the praise... they was killed [but] ... I'm still suffering....[9]

Years later, I pointed out to yet another journalist, "'They didn't do nothing for me. They never gave me restitution for what I went through.... I felt like they was treating me like I put the bomb in the church.'"[10] Recognition came slowly from a far, and later on in Alabama.

Figure 31. Sarah Rudolph presented with keys to city of Cincinnati. The Birmingham Time.

That autumn local officials from Cincinnati presented me with the key to the city. Karen Imbers, Deborah Kelly and Mary Lynn Tate of the law firm Ulmer Berne LLP helped to arrange the event. The local YWCA Women's Gallery also opened "The 50th Anniversary the Civil Rights Movement, 1963-2013." Artwork included Trelan Jones' "Four Girls."

In November of 2013, I traveled to New York, along with Dr. Snipe. We lectured at the Brennan Center for Justice, organized by civil rights attorney Nicole Austin-Hillary. After a film screening of *4 Little Girls*, we participated in a Q&A at the New York University Law School. We later toured the National September 11th Memorial & Museum. When I think of terrorism, it still upsets me. Exodus 20:13 states, "Thou shalt not kill?"

In December of 2013, ESPN interviewed me for a documentary on the N-Word, which aired the next year. During the filming, I met writer and sportscaster Jemele Hill. The film shows me walking into the 16th Street Church, lighting a candle along with hip-hop artist Common.

People, mainly of the white race, used this word to make Blacks angry and to try to make us *feel bad.*[11] It is a hateful word. Some adults and youths, especially, use this word or variations of it in conversation, and even in jest. Entertainers like the late rap artist and actor Tupac Shakur have altered its spelling to take back power and deflect from the sting of this word. Dick Gregory's autobiography includes this word as its title.[12] But, I've never liked this expression because it was used when referring to everyday people and great women and men throughout history and in entertainment like Sammy Davis Jr., Victoria Adams Gray, Fannie Lou Hamer and Malcolm X. It's time for people to stop taking this word so lightly. Blacks were killed, spat on, hung on trees, laughed at — while being called by the N-word. It's never been a laughing matter.

I used to stay on 1517 8th Avenue North, or close by the 16th Street Church.[13] One day while I was out walking, a white man asked me, "Do you have a cigarette?"

"No, I don't smoke," I said politely.

"I wasn't talking to you, nigger," he sharply replied.

I didn't say nothin' to him but headed home to get something. When I came back looking for him, he was gone. Thank goodness for the both of us. Now, I wanna' think that the *God in me* would have won out, but honestly, I had reached the breaking point. The 'n-word' is not a happy one.[14] Besides, I never liked living near the church. It reminded me too much of the past. I moved away after someone broke into my home. If you review the trial transcripts of some of the key witnesses during the courtroom trials of Chambliss and Cherry in particular, you will discover the ease at which *that* word was a part of the makeup of the individuals who stood accused of bombing the church. Cherry once confided to a witness that he "'lit the fuse that blew up the nigger church.'"[15] After having survived a bombing, instigated by people who thrived on racial hatred, this word carries a negative energy force.

During black history month in 2014, Dr. Snipe and I lectured at the Cuyahoga Community College (Tri-County Campus) and at their Metro campus in Cleveland. These two events were special because I met my niece Arleena Collins, Roy's daughter, for the first time. We've have remained in contact, even after her dad died several years ago.

In March of 2014, the People's Organization for Progress invited me to participate in a women's history program held at the Abyssinian Baptist Church in Newark, N.J.[16] Lawrence Hamm heard my radio interview on *Democracy Now*, with host Amy Goodman, that previous September. He introduced me that night. Let me tell you, even I wanted to meet this woman, Sarah Rudolph! George and I were so impressed with everything and the scope of the program. Snipe also addressed the audience during the Q & A session. Coincidentally, while on this trip, we learned that his aunt, Josephine, worked at the Addie Mae Collins Child – New York NY Child Care Center, for years. Several decades ago, Junie visited the Addie Mae Collins Head Start.

At the end of the program in Newark, I met a young lady, Victoria Pannell (a NAN Youth Move National leader) who attended the event. An honor student as well as an aspiring actress, the junior high school student was also affiliated with the National Action Network (NAN), founded by Reverend Al Sharpton who also hosts "Politics Nation" on MSNBC and a nationally syndicated radio show, "Keeping it Real." Ms. Pannell was doing another great service. She helped with an on-line petition initiated by the Reverend Toni Depina to try to ensure that people injured in the bombing, like myself, received restitution for their pain and suffering and to cover medical expenses.[17] During our stay in New Jersey, I finally met up with another student who had previously reached out to me on-line about an idea for a project. A good drawer like Addie, this young man wants to create a children's book devoted to games that Addie and I played as kids. He reached out to me, further inquiring about this terrific idea. George and I met him during my stay in Newark. Many young people are smart, talented and they have been a blessing in my life. I often pray that the Lord gives them wisdom.[18] Granted some of the events that we're witnessing now are disturbing, it is refreshing to realize that youth are now marching in full force again, and also exploring new ways of connecting with civil rights history – including the usage of the internet and social media.

Notes

1 Associated Press, "In Alabama, 'A Love that Forgives,'" POLITCO, September 15, 1963, https://www.politico.com/story/2013/09/alabama-church-bombing-annivesary-096817.

2 Jay Reeves, "Church Marks 50th Anniversary, Ku Klux Klan Bombing Killed 4 Girls in 1963," *USA Today*, September 16, 2013.

3 Ibid.

4 Ibid.

5 "16th Street Baptist Church Bombing Commemoration Ceremony, September 15, 2013," C-Span, September 15, 2013, https://www.c-span.org/video/?83835-1/16th-street-baptist-chuch-bombing-commemoration-ceremony; Associated Press, "In Alabama, 'A Love that Forgives.'"

6 Associated Press, "In Alabama, 'A Love that Forgives.'"

7 "Statement from the President on the 50th Anniversary of the 16th Street Baptist Church Bombing," *The White House*, September 15, 1963, https://Obama whitehous.archive.gov/the-press-office/2013/09/15/statement-president-50th-anniversary-16th-street-baptist-church-bombing.

8 Diane McWhorter, "Civil Rights Justice on the Cheap," *The New York Times*, September 15, 2013.

9 "Stain on the Legacy of Birmingham: 1963 Church Bombing Survivor Struggles to Pay Medical Bills," *Democracy Now*, September 17, 1973. Amy Goodman, Radio interview with Sarah Collins Rudolph.

10 Mary Milz, "Church Bombing Survivor Recalls Horrific Day in 1963, WTHR, January 19, 2020, https://www.wthr.com/article/church-bombing-survivor-recalls-horrific-day-in-1963.

11 Rudolph, letter to Snipe, April 25, 2014.

12 Dick Gregory, *Nigger* (New York, Pocket Books, 1973).

13 Rudolph, letter to Snipe, April 25, 2014.

14 Ibid.

15 Cherry's trial transcript 2002. See testimony of one of Cherry's wives or relatives. One of his grandson's also testified that he never used racial epithets against African Americans, excluding the word "nigger."

16 The POP planned the program, "Mrs. Sarah Collins-Rudolph, 'The Fifth Girl,'" which took place in Newark, New Jersey on the evening of March 27, 2014. This organization also honored several African-American women, living in New Jersey and New York, including retired educator Willa Cofield, Mildred C. Crum who was the first African-American woman councilwoman in Newark; civil right leader and lecturer Theodora Smiley-Lacy; and Claudette Colvin who lived in New York. Claudette was unable to attend the program that evening.

17 Toni Dipina, "Petition: The Fifth Little Girl who was Severely Injured in the 1963 Birmingham Church Bombing Deserves Restitution…NOW!," https://www.change.org/p/the-fifth-littel-girl-who-was-severely-injure... (Rev. Toni Dipina initially led this charge. Along with several colleagues and friends, she once worked on a documentary pertaining to Sarah Collins Rudolph's life story. At either rate, 2589 supporters had signed the petition, still shy by roughly 97, 411 supporters several years ago).

18 Rudolph, letter to Snipe, dated June 2014.

Chapter 26. Love

Justice is what loves looks like in public.
—Dr. Cornel West

Tell the children I love them
—Sarah C. Rudolph

One day you are going to be able to say to your children, your great grandchildren, 'I was in the same room with Sarah Collins Rudolph,' because of the significant history she represents for all of us.[1]
—Glenn Ellis

I enjoy communicating with young people in Alabama and nationwide. From grade school pupils to graduate students, I share this story with the youth, faithfully. I also listen to them closely. Occasionally, they even write me poems and letters, and I respond in some instances. I believe that I connect with youths on this level because of the trauma that I experienced as the *fifth little girl*. By the grace of God, I've *made it* too. Engaging with the youth reminds of the magnitude of Dr. King's dream, and the deep meaning of songs like "We Shall Overcome." The letters that students from Orangewood Elementary School in Phoenix, Arizona wrote to me after their lesson during Black History Month in 2014 were very moving. Clearly, they studied this lesson. I've taken the liberty to include some of their letters and my replies; their insights and questions give me a ray of hope for our *children's grandchildren*.[2]

Dear Sarah Collins Rudolph,
I heard of your story a couple of weeks [a]go in Mr. Tucker's class (my history teacher). I just wanted to tell you that we remember you and

we care about you. I am very sorry that you suffered in the bombing of the 16th St. Baptist Church. I am also very sorry that you lost your sister Addie Mae Collins. I am also sorry that you got hurt with the bombing of the church. I think the civil rights movement was very important because it just does not seem fair that they can separate people by their skin color. Gladly, it isn't much of an issue where I live, although it can be an issue in certain areas. We need to stop this. I am a thirteen-year-old girl named Ana Karen and I go to Orangewood School. I wish I could meet you some day because I think you are so brave and amazing. Please write back if possible.

Dear AnaKaren,
Thank you for writing me; you have great wisdom and knowledge. I say this because when you say that people should not be separated by their skin color, you are so right. I wish they knew that when this world began.

Dear Sarah Collins Rudolph,
It was a class project to write you because everyone was curious. Honestly, I would have done it if it wasn't an assignment. I have a lot to ask and say, but I don't know how to word everything. I'm not going to tell you I'm sorry for what happened. I think the bombing at 16th Street Baptist Church and you coming forward made America realize a lot. Honestly, the change wouldn't have happened, if these events didn't.... To me you are an inspiration...You made me realize ... other stories America tries to hide... Your pain should have been recognized.... I hope you are able to retire, and go on vacation with your husband. Just remember people have your back, and there is more to come. Instead of I'm sorry, I'll say thank you.

Love, Ashely

Dear Ashley,
Thank you for writing me and asking the question concerning my health... The noise from the bomb really keeps me jumping when I hear a loud sound. When I drive, I am so afraid of traffic. I know I have to get out and work.... Pray that one-day God will heal...me and others.

Dear Mrs. Sarah Collins Rudolph,
I am writing this letter to show my appreciation for your sacrifice at the 16th Street Baptist Church. It is truly an honor to be writing to you.

My name is Molly… Lately, we have been studying civil rights, and we spent a day in class learning about you. You are an important part of history. I hope that these letters make you feel honored and appreciated because that's rightfully deserved… Your sacrifice is not forgotten and is indeed respected. I want to express my sadness that you have suffered for many years.
With great gratitude,
Molly

Dear Molly,
I hope that you are feeling fine and having a great year. Your letter made me feel honored and appreciated. Thank you so much for [your] kind letter. May God bless you….

Dear Mrs. Sarah Collins Rudolph,
My name is Juba… For the past few weeks, we have been learning about the civil rights movement. We learned all about Dr. Martin Luther King Jr., Jackie Robinson, and you. Before we started learning about civil rights, I never knew about you but now that I have learned about you, I think more people should know and learn about you. I want you to know that you are a great person and will never be forgotten.

Sincerely, Juba

Dear Juba,
I hope that you are having a wonderful day. Thank you for writing me. I am glad you are learning about civil rights in Mr. Tucker's class and learning about King and all the other great people. Some gave their lives for us to have our rights as citizens of the United States. Thank you so much for your beautiful words of love.

Love you- Sarah Collins Rudolph

I see hopeful signs with this generation. But I don't want to give the false impression that *all* students are on the same page, especially when it comes to the subject of race-relations. Years ago, an audience member, a teacher I believe, inquired "How would you approach my high school students who still harbor overt racist attitudes"'?[3] My gut reaction was that when we reconsider the matter racism is still too widespread now.

But I thought about the question for a few extra moments before I explained, "You know. God made all of us." I continued,

> 'When he made us, he made us all in his image. When he made us, He did not have any respect of person. *He loved us all.* And when we look at the world in terms of black and white, its plain wrong. I do not believe that God wants us to look at it this way. God wants us to look at the fact that we are all human beings. The laws of the land should treat us all the same way. He made us all in his image, so why should we love blacks just because we are black and hate white people, or vice versa. We did not make ourselves. They have to realize the fact that we did not make ourselves black, just like a white person does not make himself or herself white. They just gotta' accept us as we are.'[4]

Broadly speaking, I believe that some folks won't change until they learn this important lesson. *His* word tells us about the need to walk in love (Ephesians 5:2). When you really know about love, you don't look at the color of skin, or anything else. Furthermore, in John 1:3 we read that the Lord made everything, including people. Without His input, nothing else could exist.[5] In my opinion, it's a lesson that students and adults should reflect upon further and I emphasize it while on the road.

In April of 2014, my traveling would continue with the "Love Wins Tour,' initiated by Rev. Toni DiPina and Frank Jordan who shared an affiliation with the Boston Red Sox. At one point, Toni was working with some people on a documentary about the bombing of 16th Street Baptist Church and my life as survivor. She worked briefly with an on-line campaign for me to acquire funding to offset my ongoing medical-related expenses. Anyway, this tour included several stops in the New England region, including a pivotal meeting with students at Burncoat Elementary School. Overall, George and I enjoyed our stay in Boston. It made me more fully appreciate the expression "Boston Strong," to which I would add, "Boston Loves." This city showered us with love during our brief stay there.

There were so many highlights from the 'Love Wins Tour.' George and I attended services at the Rockdale Congregational Church on Sunday, April 27, 2014 where Reverend DiPina was one of the pastors. Several days later, I was the special guest of honor at a Community Leadership Breakfast, hosted by the Boston Red Sox and the Boston

Area Church League. Other highlights of the trip included meeting Harvard University law professor Charles Ogletree. There were lighter moments like attending a baseball game at Fenway Park as honored guests where we sat in the guest seating. During a break in the action, they announced and showed a picture of George and me on the jumbo television screen. After the game, we got the chance to meet David 'Big Papi' Ortiz and other players on the roster of Boston Red Sox baseball team. In some ways, this episode was reminiscent of the happier days during my childhood, enjoying outings on the baseball field with Addie.

On a somber note, during a tour of the city, we drove to Boylston Street where a vicious act of terror occurred on April 15, 2013 during the Boston Marathon Bombing. As a victim and survivor, I can relate. I wish the survivors of this horrific incident, as well as folks affected by 9/11, a speedy, soulful recovery. One of the airplanes involved in 9/11 departed from Logan International Airport in Boston, Massachusetts.

The concluding day of the 'Love Wins Tour' included a program in Andover, Massachusetts at the Andover Newton Theological School. Dr. Nancy Nienhuis provided the welcome and introduction for the program, "An Evening with Mrs. Sarah Collins Rudolph." Reverend Brandon Thomas Crowley, Senior Pastor of the Myrtle Baptist Church recited a prayer. The Lovetones, a group affiliated with Myrtle Baptist Church, sang many songs linked to the civil rights movement such as "Ain't Gone to Let Nobody Turn Me Round" and one of my favorites, "We Shall Overcome," which is how I felt that day. After my talk about the bombing, we had a reception at the Wilson Library.

The city of Boston and state of Massachusetts gave me several citations and honors during this tour. On Tuesday, April 29, 2014, the Boston Red Sox and Boston Area Church presented me with the 2014 Legacy Award in recognition of my efforts to "promote peace and reconciliation by sharing my story with the youth and teaching them that even through tragedy and struggle there is always hope during the journey of life…." The Suffolk County District attorney also presented me with a citation noting that my "message of faith and forgiveness now inspires individuals and communities across the globe…." Further, the Boston City Council proclaimed "April 29, 2014 as Sarah Collins Rudolph day in the City of Boston…" in a resolution that they presented to me. On a final note, the Commonwealth of Massachusetts the House of Representatives Black and Latino Legislative Caucus presented me with a citation. It simply stated, "Congratulations to Sarah Collins Rudolph lone survivor of the 16th Street Baptist Church bombing in Birmingham, Alabama in recognition of you being an Ambassador of Peace not just in the African American community but also across all races with the message that faith and forgiveness leads to knowledge and peace…" After all the festivities, George and I would return home exhausted, but on a spiritual high.

Shortly after our return home, Miles College awarded Addie with an honorary doctorate degree some fifty years after we lost my sister in the '63 bombing. Denise, Cynthia, and Carole would also receive this rare honor. The thought of calling my sister "Dr. Addie Mae Collins" still amazes me. I guess that students would also refer to her as such. I smile to myself. Mama must be smiling in heaven too, rethinking about her choice to name her daughters 'Mae' and 'Bea.' MAYBE we have done our mother and father proud. Meanwhile, I also received letters, poems and a list of imaginative questions from pupils at Burncoat in Worcester, Massachusetts following my return to Birmingham, Al.

Based on my lecture in Worcester, some of the students had follow up questions for me, which is usually a sign of keen interest. Firstly, they posed the question, "How were you able to go on living, knowing that your sister Addie was gone?" I wrote back that I had to continue to go on living. I missed my sister Addie, a lot. Honestly, I still think about her, even to this day. I explained how I believe that God wasn't ready for me yet because He had something else for me to do.

They also inquired, "Did it ever cross your mind that perhaps [the misfortune] should have happened to you instead of your sister?" I shared that I never thought that it should have been me. I was not ready to meet God. I had to repent of things that happened in my personal life. Addie was an "angel of change," and is now in heaven with God!

Finally, they inquired, "If you could go back and save the four girls, would you, or would you not have risked your own life, and how?" I explained, "Yes," I would have tried to save them. However, I would have to have known where the bomb was located. *If I could turn back the hands of time*, if I had known that someone had placed a bomb under the stairs next to the window where they were standing, I would have said to them "Let's get out of here right now! There is a bomb, and it's about to go off where you all are standing. Run fast…"[6]

Within several days of jotting my answers to their questions down, George, Dr. Snipe and I later addressed a large group of students from Winona State University. Students from Minnesota were taking part in a civil rights pilgrimage. Professors John Campbell, Thomas Tolvaisis, Alexander Hines and community spokesperson Joe Morse led a large delegation. Their visits included stops in Birmingham, Alabama and Philadelphia, Mississippi. We shared some major news with this group. With my consent, George reached out to Thomas Blanton during the spring of 2014. Surprisingly, he responded. At the end of one his handwritten letters to me, Blanton wrote "God bless your sister Addie Mae Collins." He closed with the remark, "Your Friend." (See appendix)

During the summer of 2014, some schools around the country like Miami University of Ohio were remembering the fiftieth anniversary of Freedom Summer, as the nation recognized the passage of the Civil Rights Act of 1964. Several events were held in Jackson, Mississippi. But anyway, my sister Junie spoke at Miami years ago. Folks have cited the bombing of our church and death of the "four little girls" as critical to the passage of civil rights laws. The killing of Chaney, Goodman and Schwerner or three civil rights workers in Mississippi, combined with other high-profile deaths, all added to the passage of the Voting Rights Act (1965) during the administration of President Johnson. Personally, I wondered why racial progress resulted in so much death and violence.

Alabama state troopers also savagely beat Jimmy Jackson and other protesters following a voting rights demonstration in Marion, Alabama. James Bonard Fowler, an Alabama state trooper, shot Jackson who was trying to protect both his mother and grandfather too after a skirmish with the police. Jackson's death sparked more protests and the march from Selma to Montgomery to promote black voting rights. The Rev. Dr. King pleaded with folks to come to Alabama to fight for a just cause. At Dr. King's King request for committed volunteers following Bloody Sunday, Viola Liuzzo traveled all the way from Detroit, Michigan, risking her life because she felt so passionate about a cause. She would be killed or assassinated in cold blood on March 25, 1965 — or on the day that she personally transported marchers. I later met her daughters Mary and Sally in 2014, or on the official opening day of the National Center for Civil and Human Rights in Atlanta, Georgia. From the four little girls to folks like Jimmy Lee Jackson, Viola Liuzzo and Rev. James Reeb, hatred claimed too many lives. My visit to the Southern Poverty Law Center

(SPLC) in Montgomery, Al. and its memorial drove this point home. It is past time for the hatred and injustice to cease.

We must realize that the earth is just a dressing room to take off everything that is ungodly. When we do this, we can be ready to dwell in the land made by God's own hand. I am writing about heaven—a place where justice, love and forgiveness will reign. A place where *no wars, no hatred will be tolerated.* In this "New Jerusalem," all people will be treated the same regardless of race or creed. When we do well and love one another, as God has called us to do, He is pleased. God is a god of love, not hate. When you receive His spirit on the inside, you can love too.

In the meantime, we must do better here on earth. When I read about the senseless killings and hate crimes, sometimes based solely on the color of a person's skin or who they worship, it disturbs me. I am referring to ordinary people who harm each other, as well as the disturbing cases of too many young black peoples, dying at the hands of the police in America. We owe it to all young people to leave the world safer for them to negotiate than it was during the '50s and '60s.

I have increased my faith, gaining strength attending Perfecting the Saints Ministry where I still read the announcements and gladly serve as an usher. I'm also a licensed evangelist. After I eventually retire, I hope to lend a hand by serving on a board with other members, dealing with projects like building repairs, for instance. Our congregation is led by Apostle Donald Lewis; his wife, Joanne Lewis is the First Lady.[7] Aside from when I'm on speaking engagements on the road or feeling under the weather, I try not to miss church. Cause in the words of Apostle Lewis, I don't want to "'miss out on my dissertation,'" so I regularly attend the Lighthouse Church in Birmingham, Alabama. I also visit the 16th Street Baptist Church on special occasions like the 51st anniversary year of the bombing, for example. Several years ago, Rev. Arthur Price, the current pastor of the congregation, made a statement that perhaps points to *a new day in Birmingham*, while recognizing the four little girls:[8]

> 'Birmingham is a different Birmingham, a changing Birmingham, so very different than what it was 51 years ago. We stand as witnesses to everyone who will hear, that God's grace and mercy is available to all as we continue to seek peace and cohesion on our nation and globally. May we always remember Cynthia Wesley, Carole Robertson, Denise McNair and Addie Mae Collins.'[9]

On September 15, 2014, I spoke at the memorial service at the 16th Street Church. In September of 2013, Doug Jones and I shared reflections at a breakfast event in the church basement.[10] Jones tried two of the suspects. He also describes both trials in *Bending Toward Justice: The Birmingham Church Bombing that Changed the Course of Civil Rights.*

Later the Honorable Congressman John Lewis (D-Georgia) invited me to accept an award on his behalf from the National Press Club in Washington, D.C. I was surprised and humbled by his request. I deeply admired Lewis who placed his life at risk many times during 'The Movement,' including the perilous journey across the Edmund Pettus Bridge in Selma, Alabama on March 7, 1965. Lewis and Hosea Williams led some 600 marchers on "Bloody Sunday."[11] After our trip to the capitol, George and I traveled to Houston, Texas and later to Somerset, New Jersey where I gave a speech to the New Brunswick chapter of the NAACP. In Houston, the Honey Brown Hope Foundation would honor Texas State Representative Senfroni Thompson and me.

Some look back to "The Movement" as a model for activism, even now. When possible, I'm willing to lend my perspective or voice. For instance, in October of 2014, I participated in a 'Day of Remembrance' in the nation's capital that focused on the questionable killing, mainly of black people in confrontations with the police. Throughout the rally sponsored by Spirit House, speakers read off the names of hundreds of victims. During this event, I shared my experiences growing up in Birmingham, while George briefly discussed our then ongoing efforts to relocate Addie's body; I gathered so much vital insights firsthand on the struggles people face today, especially young people of color. On the other hand, I believe they can also learn more about past struggles, by reflecting on events like the church bombing. This rally reinforced the reality that some still have little respect for the dignity of the lives of black people. If bigots had more respect, my friends would not have lost their lives in a black church, or under any circumstances.

In terms of present-day problems, I can grasp some of the thinking behind platforms like #Black Lives Matter. Police brutality and private citizens, individuals taking the law into their hands was a pressing issue in Alabama during the 1960s, and it still resurfaces now; law-abiding or upstanding police officers in America aside, this continues to be a vexing problem in our country and worldwide. We need societal changes. I take this into account while marching and voting in memory of my peers.

Notes

1 Ashley Caldwell, "Survivor of 1963 Birmingham Church Bombing Talks Loss of Sister, Friends," *The Philadelphia Tribune*, September 25, 2018, www.Phillytrib.com>news>survivor-of-the-church-bombing...

2 This expression harkens back to Stevie Wonder's classic song, "As" on the groundbreaking album, *Songs to the Key of Life*. Students from schools in Massachusetts also wrote letters and poems honoring Sarah Collins Rudolph in conjunction with her "Love Wins Tour" in the Northeast.

3 Rudolph, "Four Women from Birmingham."

4 Ibid.

5 Rudolph, letter to Snipe, June 12, 2014.

6 Rudolph, letter to Snipe, June 14, 2014.

7 On June 19, 2014, Perfecting the Saints Ministry church held "A Vessel of Honor Conference," hosted by Evangelist Charlean Cook, Donald Lewis and Joanne Lewis.

8 Ariel Worthy, "Sarah Collins Rudolph Revisits 16th Street Baptist Church."

9 Greg Garrison, "Sixteenth Street Baptist to Mark 1963 Bombing," September 10, 2014.

10 On Friday, September 13, 2013, Congresswoman Terri A. Sewell hosted the Community Breakfast Honoring the Four Little Girls at the Sixteenth Street Baptist Church. Jones and Collins-Rudolph provided "Historical Reflections of September 15, 1963."

11 John Lewis and Hosea Williams, SCLC leaders, courageously led this march. Numerous protesters suffered grave injuries that day at the hands of Alabama state troopers. Bloody Sunday received worldwide press coverage, galvanized the civil rights movement, and ushered in a new era of immediacy for voting registration.

Chapter 27. Compassion

bestowed with the compassion
to convert the fertile soil of future deeds
into inspiration for the entire human race….
a deliberate creation,
never allowing the pains of life
to compromise dedication….
catalyst and root of the movement
the scar and motivation of an unnamed nation,
the universe's
universal……soulmate.[1] (Sierra Leone)

It is a sad story, but there is joy that came out of it.[2]
— Sarah Collins Rudolph

It is well with my soul.[3]

Years after the bombing, I want society to remember *I'm a survivor*, not just a victim. I also want people to know that there is a path to surviving, enduring upheavals like the one I've endured as the fifth girl. For me, the route to survival begins with compassion, forgiveness, looking at the spiritual self. It does not require alcohol and marijuana, none of that stuff.[4] I took that indirect route, trying to numb the pain; however, I have a brand-new outlook. Nowadays, I look forward to spending more time with my immediate family and working on a few projects.

Years ago, my niece Sonya Jones made plans to open the Addie Mae Center Youth Center at a local church. She later decided to change the name to the Addie Mae Collins and Sarah Collins Youth Center to honor me also; Janie's youngest daughter also helped to put together a reception in my honor at the Birmingham Botanical Gardens in 2004.[5] Sonya faced challenges funding the center and did not get to realize or finish this ambitious project, but there is always hope for tomorrow. I would like to see more emphasis placed on such centers and less on the selling or commercialization of 'The Movement,' as other activists and foot soldiers have stated.

I share my story about the 16th Sixteenth Street Church bombing to remind Americans about an event that also indirectly led to the passage to major voting rights legislation. I also try to convey the importance of voting in my lectures and interviews like my "Conversations at Penn State University."[6] That particular outing occurred in January of 2015, when the nation was planning events to remember the 50th anniversary of the passage of the Voting Rights Act of 1965. Dr. Snipe and I lectured at PSU to an overflow audience. Later that year, I participated in a major civil rights film festival in Washington, D.C.

In February of 2015, George and I received an invitation to attend a private screening of the film *Selma*, directed by Ava DuVernay, at a local theatre in Birmingham, Al. We were the only two people in the audience. Creative liberties aside, the four little girls were not walking down the stairs discussing Mrs. King's sense of fashion, as depicted. Still, the opening scene was jarring. George and I nearly jumped out of seat when the bomb detonated. Only moments earlier, the four little girls were engaged in light-hearted conversation. There was no *fifth* little girl with them in the opening scene or frame.

Later that month, Dr. Snipe invited me to participate in another WSU program, "Daughters Rising from the Dust: Children of the Civil Rights Movement, Speak Out!" Our panel featured the daughters of civil rights activists and pioneers. The participants included Ilyasah Shabazz, Rene Evers-Everette, Mary Liuzzo Lilliboe, Angela Lewis, and Joanne Bland. President David Hopkins welcomed us. The previous day, Dean Kristen Sobolik welcomed Junie who also participated in the three-day event. Despite the heavy snowfall outside, several hundred people still showed up for our panel. It was an unforgettable evening that began on a high note. Directed by Jeremy Winston, the renowned Central State University Chorus treated us to freedom songs, spirituals, gospel music and a popular tune; I enjoyed their cover of the Stevie Wonder hit, "Love's in Need of Love Today."

Dr. Kimberly Barrett, formerly the Vice President of Multicultural Affairs of Community and Engagement at WSU, would describe our select panel as a "'"once in a lifetime event"' of six distinguished guests presenting individual "'"stories of triumph over tragedy."'[7] We all shared stories about our families and addressed topics like voting, race relations, education and policing. For instance, Rene Evers (executive director of the Medgar & Myrlie Evers Institute) was a young girl young when her father, Medgar Evers, was assassinated. According to Rene, as a child, Medgar's father (James), told him not to move off the sidewalk for anyone.[8] Raised by her mother Betty Shabazz, as a child Ilayasah only has fleeting memories of her dad as a child. After our presentation, I was impressed with the books set up in her display, like the novel *X*. As a little girl, Angela Lewis learned of her father, James Chaney. She was born ten days after he was murdered; prior to his death, Chaney was in Oxford, Ohio, training students.[9] He was one of the three civil rights workers slain in Mississippi during Freedom Summer. Angela explained that her dad was uneducated and from a poor family, but his motto was "use what you have."'[10] Finally, Joanne Bland recounted witnessing the events of Selma's Bloody Sunday on March 7, 1965. Joanne saw firsthand the terrible events of that day: looking back on this ordeal, she explained, "'I didn't realize how damaged I was until I started to talk about it."'[11]

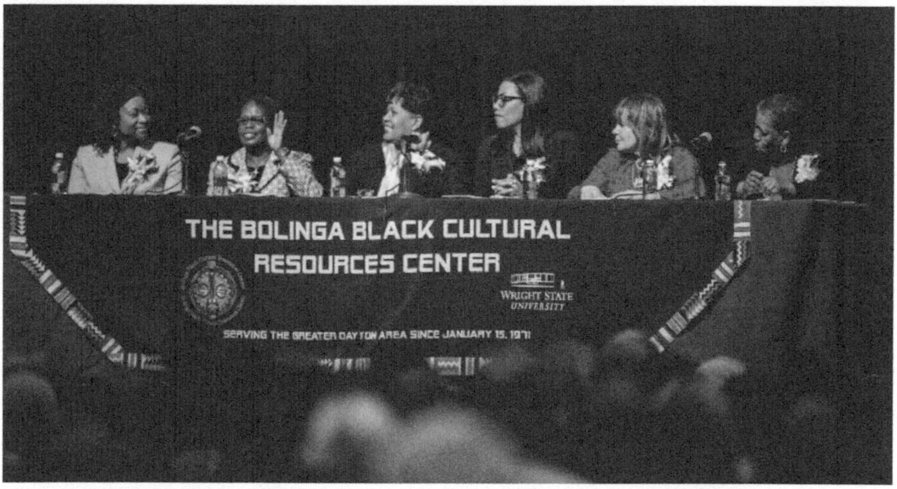

Figure 32. The Phoenix Project Program. Pictured left to right; Angela Lewis, Sarah C. Rudolph, Reena Evers-Everett, Ilyasah Shabazz, Mary Liuzzo-Lilleboe and Joanne Bland

I can relate to her sentiments. As a kid, Joanne went to jail thirteen times for demonstrating in Alabama. As an adult life, she later became friends with Mary Liuzzo Lilliboe whose mother Viola Liuzzo, a white woman, was murdered by members of the KKK just outside of Selma, Alabama. Mary reminded audience members that Rev. King petitioned Americans with the Holy Bible in one hand and the constitution in his other hand.[12] When it was finally my turn to speak, I discussed Mama's involvement in civil rights struggles in the city of Birmingham during the 1950s and 1960s. I shared some of my personal experiences and ended by stating, "'It's time for authorities to stop shooting our young black people'" because they should not look at us as merely "second-class citizens."[13] I also stressed that it's far time for Blacks to stop killing each other, too. In fact, it's time for *all* of the killing to stop.[14] If only people would take the time to consider one of God's greatest commandments: *Love thy neighbor as thyself.* At the closing of this fantastic evening, about a dozen or so WSU students, mostly associated with the Ohio Student Association (OSA), serenaded us with a song that hailed SNCC legend, Ella Baker; she was sorta' like the glue that held SNCC together. Students activists from across the nation would learn the lyrics during a series of workshops held in Jackson, Ms. in 2014 in tribute to Freedom Summer.

Sitting on the same panel and exchanging ideas with Mary, Joanne and all the other speakers was wonderful. I understand and could relate to their feelings of loss. George and I met Mary and her younger sister, Sally Liuzzo, at the grand opening of the National Center for Civil and Human Rights in Atlanta, Georgia. Its stain glass memorial to the four little girls is just breathtaking. Anyway, at breakfast the next morning, Mary and I, along with our small party, struck up a brief conversation about two letters that I had received from Blanton. He referred to Gary Thomas Rowe Jr. in both letters. In an obituary, one writer noted that the name "Gary Rowe "first appeared in public after the killing of Mrs. Liuzzo, a 39-year-old wife of Detroit teamsters official and a mother of four who had come to Alabama to help in the Selma-to-Montgomery civil rights marches in the spring of 1965."[15] The name of Gary Rowe was once associated with the assassination-style death of Viola Liuzzo. Before the year ended, I shared the stage with Mary Lilleboe again.

In February of 2015, I also attended a special service at a church in North Carolina and traveled to Buffalo, New York to attend an original play about the 1963 bombing, written by Marie Hall Mullen.[16] A native of Birmingham, Alabama, Marie has lived in Buffalo, N.Y. for decades. According to Marie, Addie was one of her childhood pals. At one point during the process of revising the original play, she interviewed me. I told Marie about a voice I heard yelling, "Somebody bombed the 16th Street Church" in the moments after the blast. She later changed the name of the play to "Somebody Done Bombed the 16th Street Baptist Church." Presented by a cast in Buffalo, mainly comprised of members of the Mount Olive Baptist Church Theater Ministry, the second half of this play included a restaged funeral scene and a version of King's 'Eulogy for the Martyred Children.' At the premier, Ronald Brown who played King penned the eulogy in his own words. One reviewer wrote:

> 'In addition to a jarring, point-for-point re-enactment of the scene in the church basement based on Collins Rudolph's recollections, the play also recreates the funeral for three of the girls that was held three days after the bombing.'[17]

Marie rewrote this eulogy for the Alabama premier. Mayor William Bell and his wife, Dr. Sharon Carson Bell, showed up among other guests.

A newspaper reporter wanted to know if I would be able to "handle" the funeral scene in the play, especially since I did not attend Addie's funeral. I informed the journalist that I knew how to get up and leave, if it became a bit much.[18] However, I sat through that entire scene in Buffalo, and in Montgomery, Alabama. To reiterate, while I was in Buffalo, N.Y. in February, I also briefly reunited with Roy.

In March of 2015, I was not able to attend activities related to the 50th commemoration of the Selma to Montgomery Marches honoring the foot soldiers and the events related to Bloody Sunday. I recognized the historical value of this solemn occasion.[19] Years earlier, I traveled to Selma, Alabama as a guest speaker with the Congressional Civil Rights Pilgrimage, backed by the Faith & Politics Institute and Congressman Lewis. On the 50th anniversary of the march, President Obama noted the four girls, while giving a speech about Selma's role in the struggle:

> As John noted, there are places and moments in America where this nation's destiny has been decided. Many are sites of war…Others are sites that symbolize the daring of America's character – Independence Hall and Seneca Falls…

> Selma is such a place. In one afternoon, 50 years ago, so much of our turbulent history—the stain of slavery and anguish of civil war; the yoke of segregation and tyranny of Jim Crow; the death of four little girls in Birmingham; and the dream of a Baptist preacher—all that history met on this bridge.[20]

During June of 2015, I took part in the March on Washington Film Festival in Washington, D.C. Along with Mary Liuzzo Lilleboe and Yvette Johnson, I spoke on the panel, "Ordinary People, Extraordinary Deeds." Festival producer Isisara Bey and various other coordinators planned the program and screened excerpts from *4 Little Girls*, *Home of Brave* and *Booker's Place*. As later arranged by the staff, Mary and I also lectured at the Association for the Study of African American Life and History (ASALAH) conference held in Atlanta, Ga. in September.[21]

During the film festival in the capital, I also spoke on a roundtable moderated by Suzanne Malveaux. Other panelists included former U.S. Attorney General Eric Holder and Claudette Colvin. I became upset as I went back in time to the heart-wrenching moment that I lost my four friends. As I rose from my seat, I began to cry, while telling our story and talking about my injuries and struggles. Claudette reached back to comfort me. I shared how unjust laws led to the mistreatment of black people in America from the Slave Codes to the Black Codes to Jim Crow. Before taking the stage, I spoke with Mr. Holder, concerning my quest for restitution, pertaining to the bombing; we also gave him a copy of a letter that I once wrote to President Obama about this matter. Family members and representatives have spoken with and written President Ronald Reagan and other state leaders but all to no avail, thus far.

When it comes to the question of restitution, I find the response of government officials at the local, state, and national levels to be lacking. On a personal level, I'll continue to press forward on this issue, as long as I have strength left in my body: I also feel obliged to move forward on this issue in memory of both my mother and sister, Addie.

Blue World

September 15, 2015 marked the actual fifty-second anniversary of the Sixteenth Street Baptist Church bombing. That day Janie, Junie and I attended a memorable breakfast event, and later on, participated in a special program, "Ties that Bind Two Holy Cities" in Charleston, S.C.

Figure 33. Circle of Survivors; pictured from left to right, Polly Sheppard, Sarah C. Rudolph, Janie Junie C. Williams, Janie C. Simpkins and Felicia Sanders. Courtesy of Blondelle Gadsden.

It was our first trip to the "Port City." We went there to meet and comfort family members of the 'Divine 9' (or 'Blessed 9' as I call them) and uplift the body of the church; like countless people across the nation, around the world, we mourned with all nine of the grieving families.

The day after we arrived in the Palmetto State, we met many of the victims' family members, including two survivors, Felicia Sanders and Polly Sheppard.[22] The depth of strength that they've demonstrated is so worthy of respect, admiration; the victims' families heartfelt remarks at the bond hearing, within days of a deadly terror attack, touched many. But I gained an even deeper insider's view of the magnitude of their loss, as we broke bread together that Tuesday morning on the campus of the College of Charleston. After leaning in and listening to their individual stories, we offered them words of encouragement — words of hope, too. After all, we had some earthly idea of the middle passage-like experience that they were experiencing and what they are still possibly going through and processing, yet must overcome. Recovering from an unthinkable act of racial terror ain't ever no *easy walk* — for anybody.

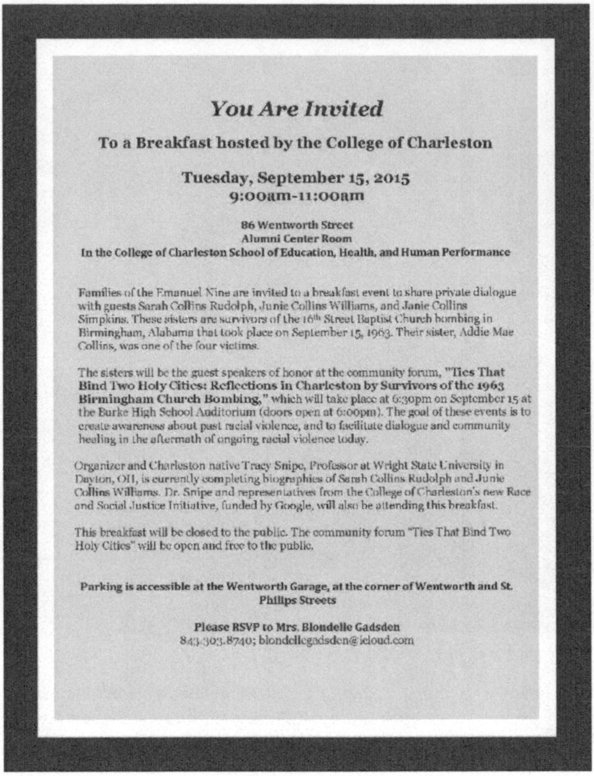

You Are Invited

To a Breakfast hosted by the College of Charleston

Tuesday, September 15, 2015
9:00am-11:00am

86 Wentworth Street
Alumni Center Room
In the College of Charleston School of Education, Health, and Human Performance

Families of the Emanuel Nine are invited to a breakfast event to share private dialogue with guests Sarah Collins Rudolph, Junie Collins Williams, and Janie Collins Simpkins. These sisters are survivors of the 16th Street Baptist Church bombing in Birmingham, Alabama that took place on September 15, 1963. Their sister, Addie Mae Collins, was one of the four victims.

The sisters will be the guest speakers of honor at the community forum, **"Ties That Bind Two Holy Cities: Reflections in Charleston by Survivors of the 1963 Birmingham Church Bombing,"** which will take place at 6:30pm on September 15 at the Burke High School Auditorium (doors open at 6:00pm). The goal of these events is to create awareness about past racial violence, and to facilitate dialogue and community healing in the aftermath of ongoing racial violence today.

Organizer and Charleston native Tracy Snipe, Professor at Wright State University in Dayton, OH, is currently completing biographies of Sarah Collins Rudolph and Junie Collins Williams. Dr. Snipe and representatives from the College of Charleston's new Race and Social Justice Initiative, funded by Google, will also be attending this breakfast.

This breakfast will be closed to the public. The community forum "Ties That Bind Two Holy Cities" will be open and free to the public.

Parking is accessible at the Wentworth Garage, at the corner of Wentworth and St. Philips Streets

Please RSVP to Mrs. Blondelle Gadsden
843.303.8740; blondellegadsden@icloud.com

Figure 34 College of Charleston Breakfast Invitation

Hearing their stories firsthand moved my husband and others who were present to tears during our morning event. We listened to stories about mothers, sons, daughters, and granddaughters who unknowingly were on the battlefield that Wednesday evening. Dr. Snipe attended another reunion where Sharon Oakley relayed how their "loved ones" bowed down on bended knees to pray at the end of bible study with their eyes closed and "woke up in glory." Near the end of our session, Marlene Jenkins, informed the entire group that she traveled to South Africa after the racial violence in Charleston. At the time, she gained another dimension about the alleged shooter's surname and was able to see this American tragedy from another viewpoint. At the end of our event, I left feeling as if we were members of one big family, sorority.

After communing with our newfound friends, later that morning, then WCSC news anchor Debi Chard interviewed my sisters and me. Afterwards, George, Janie, Junie and her husband Christopher Williams and I toured Emanuel. Structurally, the ground floor is also quite similar to the layout of the 16th Street Church basement, prior to its renovation.

At the start of the evening program at Burke Magnet High School, historian Bernard Powers provided a commentary, while Junie, Janie and I later spoke – some of us delving more into undisclosed details. [23] At the end of our session, we received proclamations from the city. Blondelle Gadsden stated, "'I don't know how they do what they're doing,'" but "'I've been able to draw some of my strength from just watching them, and seeing them try to make everyone else understand that things will be alright.'"[24] Notably, a rather sizeable delegation from Thornton Township, led by Frank Zucharelli and mainly facilitated by Alergnon Penn, timed its trip to overlap with our event. Frank noted that their group was nominating Emanuel for the Nobel Peace Prize. [25]

About a month before traveling to Charleston, I wrote a free form, open letter in tribute to the nine victims or "saints" of the Charleston Massacre at the historic Emanuel African Methodist Episcopal Church. I refer to the title of this letter or poem as the "Blessed Nine." It reads:

> They are called 'Blessed Nine' for a reason. [Namely], they no longer live in a country where people are judged by the color of their skin. They no longer live in a country where they murder innocent people. They don't have to get up and see people sleeping in the streets, when this is a rich country and [folks] can be helped. They no longer have to listen to the cry of the poor asking for better wages to live on. They don't have to see the beating of black people by police caught on camera. They don't have to see the rich bragging about the money they have in the bank. They don't have to see drugs [being] smuggled into our country by strangers. They no longer have to see blacks, both young and old, being shot down and tazed because of the color of their skin. They don't have to hear about bombings, the setting of fires or murders in our churches. They don't have to see the pictures of people dying in Africa because of hunger and thirst. They are with the Lord and we must know that they are happy and praising God. In Him we live ...We [are] nothing without Him. Thank God for their mansion![26]

I didn't share my open letter with our attentive audience on that outing. I am my Father's daughter, so I still can be a little reserved at time. However, I'm glad that my sisters and I were able to help share our stories in Charleston, South Carolina. By the end of trip, along with Blondelle Gadsden, we had shared the grand idea of family members and members of the congregation visiting the Sixteenth Street Baptist Church in Birmingham, Alabama.

Peace on Earth

I also participated in various programs during March and April of 2016. For instance, Glen Ellis invited me to Philadelphia, Pennsylvania for a series of speaking events. George and I have been friends with Glenn for a long time. I knew his family when I was a student at Brunetta C. Hill School. They lived across the street from this elementary school, but Glenn graduated from Parker several years after we finished high school. During my visit to Philadelphia, Pennsylvania, members of city council presented me with the famed Liberty Bell. Later that month at an event in Allentown, Pennsylvania, organizers of the "Stories that Shaped Our Nation" selected me as one of the civil rights icons in the 2016 class.[27] While there, I met Airicka Gordon-Taylor, co-founder of the Mamie Till-Mobley Memorial Foundation. A cousin of the late Emmett Till, Airicka is also one of the Freedom Memorial's former icons.[28] At the end that April, I traveled to California for the first time. Attending *Honoring Our Legacy* (a civil rights play and gospel musical) was one of the highlights of a fellowship-sponsored trip to San Diego, California, as was my individual presentation at a high school where Frank Jordan brought voter registrations forms to stress the importance of voting to students.[29] A local newspaper also printed a story about me emphasizing,

> Sarah is a living legend that is currently cleaning homes to pay the ongoing medical bills that still remain as a result of the bombing.... Through a life long journey of prayers, faith, and the eventual forgiveness of her attackers she has found peace, joy, and the knowledge and truth that love wins.[30]

I traveled to Florida and Texas that summer and later to Cincinnati, Ohio in autumn. In Florida, I attended a play and several NAACP-related functions, including an evening gala in Longview, Texas.[31] The People of Color Wellness Alliance (POCWA) sponsored my Ohio trip. Years earlier, the law firm Ulmer Berne arranged for me to address kids at North Avondale Montessori School. POCWA also designed a series of talks for me to discuss how trauma effects people, especially kids.

STATE OF ALABAMA
BOARD OF PARDONS AND PAROLES

-SARA COLLINS RUDOLPH
[redacted]

PAROLES HEREBY GIVES YOU WRITTEN NOTICE THAT THE FOLLOWING PRISONER WILL BE CONSIDERED FOR PAROLE IN AN OPEN PUBLIC MEETING OF THE BOARD AT 301 S. RIPLEY STREET, MONTGOMERY, ALABAMA ON 08-03-2016. SIGN-IN SHEETS ARE AVAILABLE WHEN DOOR OPENS AT 7:30 A.M. AGENCY OPERATIONAL BUSINESS WILL BEGIN AT 8:00 A.M. AND HEARINGS WILL BEGIN AS SOON AS POSSIBLE THEREAFTER.

THE VICTIM NAMED IN THE INDICTMENT, A VICTIM'S REPRESENTATIVE, OR IF THE VICTIM IS DECEASED AS A RESULT OF THE OFFENSE, THE VICTIM'S IMMEDIATE FAMILY, AS DEFINED BY THE BOARD'S OPERATING RULES, OR, IN THE EVENT THERE IS NO IMMEDIATE FAMILY, A RELATIVE OF A VICTIM, MAY SUBMIT HIS/HER VIEWS IN WRITING IN ADVANCE OR BE HEARD IF PRESENT AT THE TIME HIS/HER CASE IS CALLED. IN MOST CASES, BOARD DECISIONS WILL BE RELEASED UPON COMPLETION OF THE HEARING TO THOSE PRESENT. HEARING RESULTS ARE ALSO POSTED ON THE BOARD WEBSITE.

WEAPONS ARE NOT ALLOWED ON THE PREMISES AND CELL PHONES MUST BE TURNED OFF (OR ON VIBRATE) DURING THE HEARINGS.

NAME
BLANTON THOMAS EDWIN JR
216691
R/S:W/M DOB:06-20-1930
ST CLAIR CORRECTIONAL FAC
MINIMUM RELEASE DATE 99-99-9999

TIME IN CONFINEMENT
YEARS/MONTHS/DAYS
015-00-27 AS OF 05-13-2016
AN ADDITIONAL 41 DAYS HAS ACCRUED.

SEE FOLLOWING FOR CONVICTION INFORMATION:

JID	COUNTY	SENTENCE DATE	CASE #	CONVICTION	SENTENCE YY MM DD	
LAP	JEFFERSON	05-01-2001	CC2000-002216	MURDER	LIFE	CS
LAP	JEFFERSON	05-01-2001	CC2000-002218	MURDER	LIFE	CS
LAP	JEFFERSON	05-01-2001	CC2000-002219	MURDER	LIFE	CS
LAP			?000-002220	MURDER	LIFE	CS

AMER ;ISTANCE (334)353-8067
VICT ... (334)242-8050
VICTIM WAITING ROOM AVAILABLE
FOR FREQUENTLY ASKED QUESTIONS VISIT OUR WEB SITE
HTTP://WWW.PAROLES.STATE.AL.US

Figure 35. Letter to Sarah C. Rudolph. Board of Pardons and Parole.

Two key events marked the second half of 2016. I got the shock of my life when I received a letter from the Alabama Board of Pardons and Parole, requesting my appearance. We didn't know that Thomas Blanton was sentenced to life but *with* the possibility of parole. The Parole Board had scheduled his hearing for August 3, 2016. This letter rattled me. At the end of his 2001 trial, the judge sentenced Blanton to four consecutive life terms, so I never have thought he would see the light of day.[32] During his sentencing, most prisoners were automatically eligible for parole after serving fifteen years in jail, it seems. As the hearing loomed, I was of two minds. I knew that the time that Blanton had spent in prison would not bring our girls back. I still concluded that his sentence should remain intact. Besides, by the time of their convictions, most of the men actually convicted of bombing our church already had already lived most of their lives freely, without having to answer for this horrific crime. Some were nearly knocking on death's door, like I've stated in the past: in fact, Frank Cash, one of the main suspects, died before being held accountable.[33]

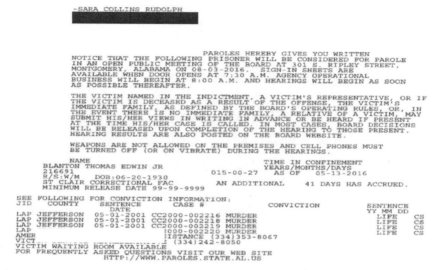

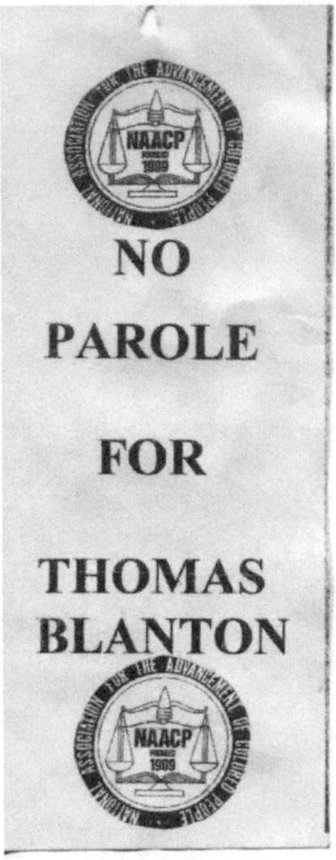

Figure 36. Birmingham's chapter of the NAACP flyer

Prior to giving my statement, my husband George, Dr. Tracy Snipe and I sat in an area next to the room where the hearing occurred. We sat by Tom Mullinax who had befriended Mrs. Alpha Robertson; Tom had vowed to speak up on her behalf for Carole. Family members, the media, members of the Jack and Jill Club and Birmingham chapter of the NAACP filled the courtroom. One spectator, Teritia Kirkland, later revealed to Dr. Snipe, "I thought the man [Blanton] was dead.... This is history."[34]

After sitting in a room for about forty minutes, the families were ushered into an adjacent courtroom, as the parole board hearing finally began in Montgomery, Alabama. None of Blanton's relatives attended the hearing to my knowledge. Once the hearing began, statements read by Lisa McNair and Carole's older sister, Diane Brockington, took me back in time yet again. I could relate to almost every word. I had lost my sister, too. They both stated that the board should deny Blanton's early release. Lisa tearfully explained board how the bombing left "'a legacy of pain" in her family.[35]

Diane also revealed that members of Jack and Jill of America Inc., an organization devoted to promoting leadership among black kids, had just elected her little sister Carole as president of the Birmingham chapter. But the bombing aborted her potential in life, robbing Carole of the chance to show leadership skills. Diane also noted that her sister had attended a conference on racial healing the weekend before the 16th Street Baptist Church bombing.

As I took the stand, the weight of it all hit me. Basically, I was testifying for the fourth time, yet still found it difficult. I told the board of the hatred that had built up inside of me because of the church bombing. I had to pray and turn to God to rid myself of the hate. Due to time limitations, I only spoke for about five minutes. I could have talked for much longer.

Doug Jones spoke on the behalf of Cynthia Morris Wesley's family. He cited the message on her grave: "She loved all but a mad bomber hated her kind." Jones said to the effect, "Children's lives do matter."[36]

After hearing statements from Jones and other key witnesses, the board issued its ruling in a little over a minute: about eighty seconds to be exact. The board denied Blanton parole. After the hearing, I briefly spoke to the media. Upon further questioning, I shared the fact that we had communicated with Blanton about two years prior to this hearing. George decided to write Blanton with my approval. To our surprise, he replied. In two handwritten letters, Blanton denied any responsibility for the 16th Street Church bombing; he never apologized to me, instead citing Bible verses. Blanton pinned the blame on Gary Thomas Rowe, Jr., an FBI informant with a complicated past. (See letters in appendix).

I was relieved after the hearing ended. I could finally sleep in peace again, as best I can. It is impossible to dredge up memories related to the bombing in such an intense setting without also reliving the trauma and nightmares. I cannot begin to describe all the emotions and memories the hearing brought back. We didn't know what the board would decide. The loss of the 'four little girls' and statute of limitations aside, the fact that no jury ever tried anyone for the attempted murder on me as the 'fifth little girl' shouldn't go ignored or buried in the historical records.

Transcendence

Within weeks of the hearing, sadly, Mr. Samuel Rutledge died. During my interview with Shauna Stuart of *The Birmingham News*, I replayed my brief conversation with Rutledge, a deacon at the 16th Street Church. I met him again during the 1970s. He stuck up a brief conversation with me at the Smithfield Library in Birmingham, but when I was an adult.[37]

> "He came off the street and he asked me, 'Hey, do you know who I am?' I said, 'Naw.' He said, 'I'm the one that came to church that Sunday and bought (sic.) you out.' And I said, Oh, thank you. Thank you so much.' You know, I never did see who it was because I was blind. Glass got in both of my eyes."[38]

After his death, I reached out to a local television news station in Birmingham. I described Mr. Rutledge as my 'personal hero.'[39] He truly was. He risked his own life when he jumped down into the basement to rescue me, demonstrating bravery and compassion. He didn't know me from Adam. Another bomb could have detonated or blown up in his face. Rutledge never received the recognition that he fully deserved. My husband and I attended his funeral service at the 16th Street Church on September 10, 2016: May his soul rest in peace. Surprisingly, the following month would mark another major shift or turn in this story.

In October of 2016, a television news station in Birmingham ran a series of investigative stories about the likely resting place of my sister remains, theorizing that "Addie Mae Collins… may be buried on the other side of her tombstone at Greenwood Cemetery in Birmingham, quite possibly "several feet behind her headstone." Advanced Radar Technologies, an underground radar company that later volunteered its service, would put this lone, single theory to the test. [40] John Hall who also represented our family in a past claim, reached out to the company.[41] I am so grateful to him. For many years, I had been determined to move my sister's remains mainly because of the overall neglect and occasional vandalism at Greenwood Cemetery. The television coverage also noted:

> 'Vandals broke tombstones and raided some of the graves. Skulls and bones littered the ground. In fact, the cemetery operators declared bankruptcy in 1986 after 10 lawsuits alleged that graves here were being recycled.'[42]

After this particular news story hit the local airwaves, I explained, "'It would make me more happy to know where she's at instead of being lost. Because she's a civil rights martyr and should be found.'"[43]

Finally, in the spring of 2017, we received promising news. I was there with George and John Hall the day that one of the experts, Randy Field, explained "what our equipment is telling us is that the object that appears to be a child's coffin based on the size of area we located."[44]

After years of turmoil, I was overjoyed.[45] "'I'm so happy we found where Addie's grave is located. I'm just really happy,'" I stated to press.

George shared, "'I want to cry, you know? I'm just overwhelmed. It's very emotional.'"

A DNA match should resolve everything, yet I want my sister to be at rest. As an extended family, we may still reconsider this option. For now, I want Addie's body to stay at Greenwood Cemetery; Cynthia and Carole remain buried there too, while Denise's body was transferred to Elmwood Cemetery, years later. As a matter of fact, Alabama's Historic Registry currently designates Greenwood Cemetery as an historic cite, mainly due to the grit and determination of Attorney John Hall.[46]

Feeling Good

For years we fought for voting rights and this fight has reaped benefits. In the city of Birmingham, voters would elect former attorney Randall L. Woodfin as mayor in a run-off against then Mayor William S. Bell in late November of 2017.[47] In December voters, especially black women, would turn out in record numbers to help elect Doug Jones in the special Senate election. At his invitation, I appeared on the campaign trail with Jones and former Vice President Joe Biden earlier that summer. Biden pointed me out, as I sat quietly in the audience. Prior to this election, I encouraged friends and families to get out and vote on social media. People fought, died for us to exercise this prized right.

In time, Biden appeared at 16th Street Baptist Church. He spoke at a memorial event. He stated, "The same poisonous ideology that lit the fuse at 16th Street pulled the trigger at Mother Emanuel and unleashed the anti-Semitism, anti-Semitic massacre in Pittsburgh and Poway.'"[48]

I've traveled around the country along with George, and Dr. Snipe occasionally, lecturing in auditoriums like the Madame Walker Theatre complex in Indianapolis, Indiana. I returned to Georgia, New Jersey, South Carolina, New York, Illinois, and California. I've visited Iowa and Arkansas. In New Jersey, I spoke to a group of attorneys connected with the New Jersey State Bar Association's Minorities in the Profession Section).[49] I have traveled to Richmond, Va. too where I was the guest of honor at the 18th Annual Virginia Black History Month Gala. I cannot stress enough how all of this was beyond my imagination as a young girl involved with civil rights struggles. I have also viewed several plays that include snippets of my life story. About a year or so before the 50-year anniversary of the blast, Bern Na Dette Stanis, a talented actress who gained fame as Thelma Evans on the ever-popular show, "Good Times" visited me in Birmingham, Al. to discuss putting on an actual full stage theatrical production of my life story in conjunction with Bill Cosby's representatives; however, the contractual terms didn't suit me. Timing is crucial, as is the right set of conditions.

On a personal level, I'm still tackling other matters, including the issue of restitution. I would like to see this issue addressed in a fair way, even years after the deadly bombing, taking into consideration my life-long injuries and challenges. I'm also troubled by the recurring church burnings and shootings that occur more than they should in black communities, whether by the police or randomly. All the violence in our synagogues, mosques and houses of worship has to cease, as I shared in response to a question posed to me in an interview.[50] Why should any child or little girl in the United States of America have to repeat the trauma similar to what I went through? Haven't we learned our lessons? We gotta' *save the children*; the young women and men. We can accomplish this with an action verb, *love*. Then, we have to remake certain laws, too.

So many years after our church in Birmingham was bombed, killing four beautiful girls, the act of forgiveness was pivotal for me to move beyond the devastation. I often share this point and the importance of voting. Four Godly children and many others lost their lives, creating this possibility. The "hard" circumstances surrounding them in death was not without purpose. We were blessed to have them in our lives. Their presence alone changed me forever.

Not all the changes in my life were good, or came without setbacks. Personally, I went through a *severe* test to earn this testimony. My point is this: After you've tried everything else and everything has failed, try Jesus. I used to stress this point at the end of my talks. *I'm a witness* who lived to testify about an unforgettable day in history. When the bomb exploded, I called on the *Son of the Living God*; and I still call his name. Everything is gonna' be *all right now*. It took forever for me to feel good again, and to live my life *like its golden* or precious. After enduring years of trauma, I urge folk to seek counseling, though I did not take this route.

I'm gonna' close this story with a point that I shared with an audience years earlier in Seattle, Washington. You know, before my healing, I used to be shy to speak. But anyway, I was in such high spirits, as I shared the message. I know my speech ain't always so "fancy," like on that day. Yet *when the spirit of the Lord* is at work, does it really matter? As if on cue, the worship song during that service that particular Sunday morning at the First African Methodist Episcopal Church (F.A.M.E) was "Do Not Pass Me By, Oh Gentle Savior," Mama's favorite. I revealed to the assembled:

> "You know … what Jesus done for me. I supposed to *been* dead. He [the apostle] prophesied to me that I supposed to been dead when the bomb went off.... I seen the cars outside that was tore up from the bombing, and yet God kept me on my feet. The windows blown out across the street.... The windows in the church was blowed out. And by me bein,' I think I weighed at least about 60 pounds [or so], He didn't let me fall. I was still on my feet.... I looked at the papers after the bombing, and I seen the cars that was torn up just from the vibration of this bomb. And I know then that *God is real....*
>
> We got to praise God. He is good. Hallelujah. Thank you, Jesus, thank you Jesus, thank you Jesus!"[51]

Having overcome *many dangers, toils and snares*, I am still calling for a "change" in our nation. I want the people to realize that *love is greater than hate.*[52] Hatred destroys. It cruelly bombs a refugee camp overseas; bombs a church in Alabama, killing four sweet girls and decades later, a federal building in Oklahoma City, then killing nineteen innocent children.

Through it all, survivors must discover the will to live. And I am a survivor. I've 'rested' my heart, my soul from all this violence by praying. "I stay in the word of God." I wanna' leave hope, love, and the struggle to attain social justice, racial equality as my civil rights legacy. Meanwhile, I truly do believe *someday*, we will be together, walking hand in hand: my sister Addie and me and Cynthia, Denise, and Carole: *Oh, deep in my heart, I do believe* love must overcome someday. Why not today?

Notes

1 In February of 2015, Sierra Leone (known as Lucy Owens) wrote 'Mitochondrial Eve,' an original poem in recognition of principal daughters of the Civil Rights

Movement. The daughters or honorees at this WSU-sponsored program included Ilyasah Shabazz, Angela Lewis, Joanne Blend, Reena Evers-Everette, Mary Liuzzo Lilleboe, and Sarah Collins Rudolph.

2 Simon Moya-Smith, "Birmingham Remembers 4 Little Girls 50 Years after Infamous Church Bombing," NBC News, September 13, 2013.

3 Horatio Spafford wrote the lyrics or words to "It is Well with My Soul," while Phillip Bliss composed the music to the hymn.

4 Jasmine Guy, *Afeni Shakur: Evolution of a Revolutionary* (New York: Atria Books, 2004), x. (Afeni Shakur raises a similar point in the biography written about her: "'I want to talk about how you can survive without destroying yourself in the process and that when you do survive there's something left…some spirit left for the next day.'")

5 Chanda Temple, "The Fifth Little Girl: 1963 Church Bombing Survivor to be Honored with Benefit Dinner," *The Birmingham Times*, July 16, 2004. Sonya Jones acknowledges both of her aunts, Sarah Collins-Rudolph and Addie Mae Collins. Jones tried to establish a cultural center honoring her aunts (Shauna Stewart)

6 "Heard on Campus: Sarah Collins Rudolph, 16th Street Church Bombing, January 26, 2015, http://news.psu.edu/sotyr/342001/2015/01/23/campus-life/ heard-campus-sarah-collins-rudolph-16th-street-bombing. (Rudolph and Snipe addressed a capacity crowd at Penn State University's Speaker Series forum. Sarah Collins Rudolph also appeared on the program "Conversations from Penn State.)

7 Kimberly Barret (lecture, "Daughters Rising from the Dust," WSU, February 18, 2015).

8 Rene Evers-Everette (lecture, "Daughters Rising from the Dust," WSU, February 18, 2015.

9 Angela Lewis (lecture, "Daughters Rising from the Dust," WSU, February 18, 2015.)

10 Ibid.

11 Joanne Bland (lecture, "Daughters Rising from the Dust," WSU, February 18, 2015).

12 Mary Liuzzo Lilleboe (lecture, "Daughters Rising from the Dust," WSU, February 18, 2015.

13 Sarah Collins Rudolph (lecture, "Daughters Rising from the Dust, WSU, February 18, 2015).

14 Sarah Collins Rudolph (lecture, "Daughters Rising from the Dust," WSU, February 18, 2015).

15 Michael T. Kaufman, "Gary T. Rowe Jr., 64, Who Informed on Klan in Civil Rights Killing, Is Dead," *The New York Times*, October 4, 1998, http://www.nytimes.com/1988/10/04/us/gary-t-rowe-jr-64-who-informed-on-klan-in-civil-ri...

16 "Somebody Done Bombed the 16th Street Baptist Church," *Homewoodstar.com*, July 15, 2017, thehomewoodstar.com/events/somebody-done-bombed-16th-street-baptist-church. (*The Homewood Star* reported that Mullen's production was "one of the top ten plays of 2015 in Western New York.")

17 Colin Dabrowski, "52 Years Later, Birmingham Church Bombing Echoes in Buffalo," February 27, 2015, https:/buffalonews.com/2015/02/27/everybody-should-know-52-years-later-birmingham-ch…

18 Dabrowski, "52 Years Later, Birmingham Church Bombing Echoes."

19 See program notes from "Non-Violent Revolutionaries: 50th Anniversary Foot Soldier Reunion (Selma 1965)."

20 Barak Obama, "Remarks by the President at the 50th Anniversary of the Selma to Montgomery Marches," The White House (Office of the Press Secretary), March 7, 2015. https://obamawhitehouse.archives/gov/the-press-office/2015/03/07/remarks-president-50th-annivesary-selma-montgomery-marches.

21 The theme for the film festival was "Trouble the Waters: Inspire the Nation." In addition to appearing on the same panel in Washington, D.C. Rudolph and Lilliboe spoke on a panel at the Association for the Study of African-American Life and History ASALAH conference in Atlanta, Georgia in September of 2015, sponsored by the March on Washington Film Festival program.

22 On September 15, 2015, several faculty members and administrators at the College of Charleston invited families of the Emanuel Nine to an intimate breakfast event with Sarah Collins Rudolph, Janie Collins Simpkins and Junie Collins Williams.

23 Karina, Bolster, "Ties Binding Two Holy Cities Connects Charleston to Birmingham, AL.," WCSC, September 15, 2015, https://destinytopeace.com/ties-that-bind-two-holy-cities. (As Bolster further noted, "the discussion was part of an event by the College of Charleston to raise awareness about the race and social justice issues across our nation."

24 Ibid.

25 Karina Bolster, "Mother Emanuel Embraces Process for Nobel Peace Prize Nomination," WCSC, September 17, 2015, https://www.live5news./com/story/30050125/mother-emanuel-embraces-process-for-nobel-peace-prize-nomination."

26 Sarah C. Rudolph spontaneously wrote this 'free-form' open letter on around August 12, 2015, while she was in Birmingham, Alabama.

27 The Board of Directors of the Freedom Memorial promotes programs like *Stories that Shaped a Nation.* Besides Rudolph and Lisa McNair, the 2016 icons class included Addie Mae Collins, Denise McNair, Carole Robertson, Cynthia Morris Wesley, Sarah Collins Rudolph, Terri Sewell, Claudette Colvin, Diane Nash, Marian Wright-Edelman, Alice Walker, Charlayne Hunter Gault, Toni Morrison, Rita Moreno and Joan Baez. (See previous footnote about honorees)

28 Sarah Collins Rudolph honored as "5th Little Girl," Email from Icon Logistics Committee, April 16, 2016.

29 "Immediate Press Release: Sarah Collins Rudolph Honored in San Diego, Saturday, April 30th, 2016." Media outlets highlighted Frank Jordan's efforts too.

30 "The Fifth Little Girl," *The Cincinnati Herald*, October 18, 2013.

31 "Through the Storm We Rise," Longview Branch NAACP 58th Annual Scholarship and Image Awards Gala," Friday, July 15, 2016.

32 See file or clipping related to Blanton Parole and sentencing.

33 Joseph D. Bryant, "Reparations for 1963 Church Bombing Survivor."

34 Kirkland shared this comment with Dr. Snipe prior to the beginning of the Board of Pardons & Parole proceedings on August 3, 2016.

35 "A Legacy of Pain: Birmingham Church Bomber is Denied Parole," by Merrit Kennedy. August 3, 2016. https://www.npr.org./.../a-legacy-of-pain-birming ham-church-bomber-is-denied-parole.

36 Jones spoke at the proceedings in Montgomery, Alabama on August 3, 2016.

37 Stuart, "'God Had to do a Work in Me.'"

38 Ibid.

39 "Man who Pulled Survivor from 16th St Baptist Church Laid to Rest," ABC 33/40, September 11,2016, https://abc3340.com/news/local/samuel-rutledge-laid-to-rest.

40 Brian Pia, "Addie Mae Collins May Be Buried on the Other Side of Her Tombstone," ABC 33/40, October 27, 2016, https://abc3340.com/news/abc-3340-news-investigates-search-for-addie-mae-collins; Brian Pia, "Missing Remains of 1963 Church Bombing Victim Believed to be Found," ABC 33/40, May 3, 2017, https://abc3340.com/news/abc-3340-investigagtes/addie-mae-collins-mystery-solved.

41 Pia, "Missing Remains of 1963 Church Bombing Victim."

42 Pia, "Addie Mae Collins May be Buried on the Other Side"

43 Ibid.

44 Pia, "Missing Remains of 1963 Church Bombing Victim."

45 Ibid.

46 Pia, "Missing Remains of 1963 Church Bombing Victim."

47 Of note, in July of 2017, Chokwe Antar Lumumba assumed office as the mayor of Jackson, Ms. while Atlanta, Ga. Mayor Keisha Lance Bottoms assumed office in January of 2018. Voters elected Steven Reed mayor of Montgomery, Al.

48 Arlette Saenz, Caroline Kenny and Chandelis Duster, "'Hate is on the Rise Again'" Joe Biden Delivers Impassioned Speech on Race in Birmingham," CNN, September 25, 2019, www.cnnn.com>2019/09/15>politics>joe-biden-birmin...; Charles M. Blow, "Joe Biden is Problematic," The New York Times, September 15, 2019, www.nytimes.com>2019/09/15>opinion.joe-biden.

49 Rudolph lectured at the New Jersey Law Center in New Brunswick, New Jersey, co-sponsored by the center's Diversity Committee.

50 *The Birmingham News*. (See article about Rudolph during the 53rd anniversary.)

51 Rudolph, "The Message."

52 Rick Journey, "16th Street Baptist Church Bombing Survivor says Love is Greater Than Hate," WBRC, September 15, 2016, http://www.wbrc.com/story/33107627/16th-street-baptist-church-bombing-survivor-says-love-is-greater-than-hate.

Epilogue: Traneing In

"'I know that there are bad forces that bring suffering to others and misery to the word, but I want to be a force which is truly for good.'"
–John W. Coltrane

"Music would have saved that boy. A few tones from Miles would have made him whole. Too bad nobody didn't put a violin or a saxophone in his hands – and had him listen to Trane play *A Love Supreme*."[1] (Hannibal Lokumbe)

The Fifth girl came from the Fifth element. Hate can't stop what is Heaven Sent." – Jermaine Jones, artist and poet

The Birmingham bombing and Charleston Massacre both crystalize the intersection of musical politics and popular culture, embodied by a Coltrane classic, "Alabama." Other musicians, filmmakers, visual artists, writers and poets have also memorialized these two distinct tragedies.

Singer-song writer Richard Farina paid tribute to the 'four little girls' in "Birmingham Sunday," also covered by Joan Baez and more recently, Rhiannon Giddens. 'High priestess of soul' Nina Simone alluded to the bombing in "Mississippi Goddam," while composer Aldophus Hailstork commemorated the '63 bombing victims in *American Guernica.* Inspired by former U.S. Attorney Doug Jones, the group Chatham County Line created "Birmingham Jail," while Paul Simon's record "A Church is Burning" and Amy Leon's "Burning in Birmingham Bait" allude to the bombing: The socially-conscious song "Ball of the Confusion," by the Temptations, takes on broad themes, as does Bruce Springsteen's "We are Alive."[2] Several original band members of the Motown-based group hail from Birmingham.[3] In the genre of gospel music, Marvin Sapp's "Never Would Have Made It," gives "remembrance to the four little girls lost," while the R. J. Phillips Academy of Baltimore, Maryland presented "I Can't Think of Sunday" in "memory of Addie Mae and her friends": In 2012, UAB choir director Kevin Tuner composed "You Don't Know What I Could Have Been" in tribute to the four bombing victims.[4]

Langston Hughes's "Birmingham Sunday," Dudley Randall's "The Ballad of Birmingham" and Michael S. Harper's "American History" all invoke the blast in poetry. Singer Jerry Moore recorded the "Ballad of Birmingham," while Harper later paid homage to the six slain children and Trane in "Here Where Coltrane Is." Furthermore, in "Lady Day and John Coltrane," poet Gil Scott-Heron honors Coltrane and the legendary Billie Holiday, deemed one of the 'first ladies of jazz' along with Sarah Vaughn and Ella Fitzgerald.[5] Moreover, attorney Gail Pugh Gratton would write "We Honor Your Names" as a litany to the "four little girls" (including her cousin Carole), while visual artist Jermaine Jones lauds the fifth little girl Sarah in the poem "The Fifth Element."

Something About John Coltrane

Dancers and thespians have honored the four girls and Trane too whom biographer Lewis Porter describes as one of the "great musical talents of the twentieth century."[6] Superbly interpreted by students in the Stivers School for the Arts Dance Department (located in Dayton, Ohio), dancer-choreographer DeShona Pepper Robertson's "4 Denise, Carole, Cynthia and Addie Mae," is a revelation; indeed, a breathtaking example of poetry in motion, validating the healing power of dance.[7] Robertson performed with the Dayton Contemporary Dance Company (DCDC) whose broad repertory includes famed choreographer Eleo Pomare's *Las Desenamoradas*. Based on Federico Garcia Lorca's "The House of Bernarda Alba" (danced to Trane's "Ole"), critic Anna Kisselgolf of *The New York Times* deemed *Las Desenamoradas* Pomare's masterpiece.[8] Further, Alice Coltrane's mesmerizing electronic score, "Something About John Coltrane," provides the opening music to "Cry," a dance created by Alvin Ailey, founder of the Alvin Ailey American Dance Theater (AAADT). Judith Jamison who originated the role and Donna Woods are among the famous interpreters of a dance that Ailey choreographed as a "gift" to his mother, Lula Cooper. Ailey created the tour-de-force dance in honor of "'all black women everywhere, especially our mothers,'" while Laura Nyro's sentimental "Been on a Train" and the tune "Right On, Be Free" (sung by the Voices of East Harlem choir) both complement Alice Coltrane's work.[9] At one point during the song "Right On," the lead vocalist passionately sings *mother, mother save your child*: a sentiment that still resonates universally.

Several recent plays are centered on the '63 church bombing. They include *A Love that Forgives* and *Somebody Done Bombed the 16th Street Baptist Church.*[10] Playwright Christina Ham's *Four Little Girls: Birmingham 1963* is in the vanguard of such plays. On September 15, 2013, Phylicia Rashad directed a reading of *Four Little Girls* in the capitol.[11]

Writers such as Paul Curtis (*The Watsons Go to Birmingham*), Anthony Grooms (*Bombingham*), Sena Jeter Naslund (*Four* Spirits) and Denise Lewis Patrick (*No Ordinary Sound*) all allude to the Birmingham bombing. The latter book is also included in the American Girl book series. Noble prize-winning writer Toni Morrison would situate the deaths of the four innocents in the plot of *Song of Solomon*. Morrison employs the bombing "as part of the rationale for her main characters forming a black vigilante group."[12] A member of the 'Seven Days" contemplates the following:

> Every night now Guitar was seeking little scraps of Sunday dresses — white and purple, powder blue, pink and white, lace and voile, velvet and silk, cotton and satin, eyelet and grosgrain. The scraps stayed with him all night.... Guitar's scraps were different. The bits of Sunday dresses that he saw did not fly; they hung in the air quietly, like the whole notes in the last measure of an Easter hymn.
>
> Four little colored girls had been blown out of a church, and his mission was to approximate as best he could a similar death of four little white girls some Sunday, since he was the Sunday man. He couldn't do it with a piece of wire, or a switchblade. For this he needed explosives, or guns, or hand grenades. And that would take money. He knew that the assignments of the Days would more and more be the killing of white people in groups, since more and more Negroes were being killed in groups. The single, solitary death was going rapidly out of fashion, and the Days might as well prepare themselves for it....[13]

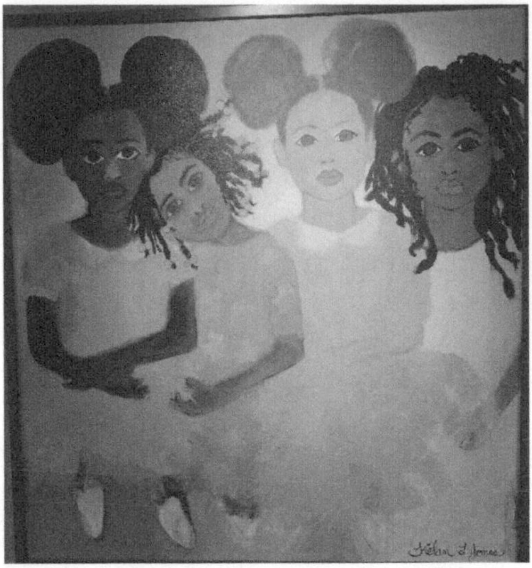

Figure 37. Four Girls by artist Trelan Jones. Courtesy of Scott Kadish.

Writers, sculptors, and visual artists have also defined key events in civil rights struggles. John Petts "The Welsh Window" depicts a black Christ, while John Henry Waddell's "That Which Might Have Been: Birmingham 1963" evokes the essence of the youths, as does Elizabeth MacQueen's Four Spirits Memorial. Samuel K. Armstrong imaginatively illustrates Sarah (embraced by her sister), along with the other three girls.

Directors Kenny Leon (*The Watsons go Birmingham*), Ava Duvernay (*Selma*), Robert Dornhelm (*Sins of the Father*) and Kerri Edge (*4 Little Girls: A Dance Film*) all point to the lethal bombing.[14] Spike Lee's films often integrate jazz music into the plot or commentary, as he skillfully does in *4 Little Girls*, which features the song "Alabama" (as does the film *X*).

The influential critic Stanley Crouch once wrote, "Jazz predicted the civil rights movement more than any art in America." [15] Indeed, cultural forerunners Miles Davis and Coltrane "were formed by and helped to inform the burgeoning civil rights movement of the late 1950s and 1960s", and emerged as "global icons."[16] Coltrane's "Alabama" and "Reverend King" channeled a manifesto, without the benefit of lyrics, as he helped to reconfigure the *winds of change* too.[17] Frank Kofsky who wrote *Black Nationalism and the Revolution in Music* noted Trane was 'quite impressed' with Malcolm X. Similarly, Kofsky envisioned Coltrane as a political force and would write in the names of Malcolm X and John

Coltrane for the President and Vice-president in the contested elections of 1964.[18]

Figure 38. J. Coltrane in 1963. Dutch National Archives/ Victor Hugo Van Gelderen

Ashley Kahn also points to Trane's increasing political awareness.

> 'Though Coltrane's spiritual sensibility set him on a more pacifistic course, he allowed himself to be more outspoken in the titles of his songs. The dirge-like 'Alabama,' recorded in 1963 after the infamous bombing of a black church in Birmingham that killed four schoolgirls, left little doubt as to the choice of his inspiration….'[19]

In *Spirit Catcher* John Fraim labeled "Alabama" as one of Coltrane's "darkest most melancholy pieces," stating it echoed King's 'Eulogy': "After reading the text of the speech on an airplane," Coltrane wrote the instrumental "using the speech's rhythmic inflections; Fraim noted, "juxtaposed against the heavy-handed melancholy of 'Alabama' on *Live at Birdland* is the forward-looking composition 'The Promise.''' [20]

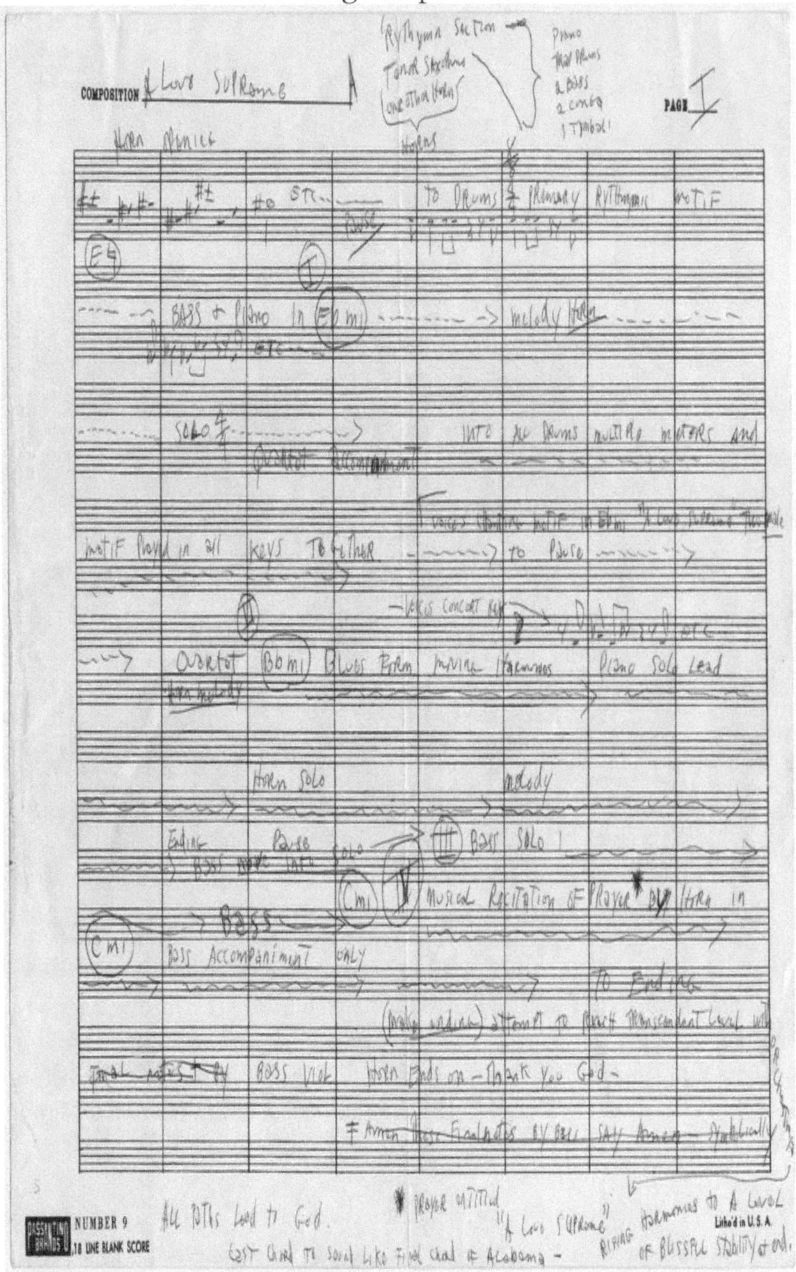

Figure 39Coltrane's Musical notes to A Love Supreme. Author: John Coltrane (See the Smithsonian Collection)

In the documentary film *The World According to John Coltrane*, Alice Coltrane maintains John's "music reflected the times of the 1960s in a different way, which was definitely not more militant but spiritual." She contends that songs like "Peace on Earth" and *A Love Supreme* reveal this positioning.[21] "Alabama," which John Coltrane recorded with Jimmy Garrison, Elvin Jones, and McCoy Tyner, comes out of a more pointed politicized climate. A plaintive tune, there are moments of lightness in "Alabama," until the last few measures of the memorable composition, which almost comes across as a lament or wailing near the end.

In contrast, the stark, politically nuanced "Reverend King," included on the album *Cosmic Music* (1967), reflects discord in a mass movement that incorporated civil disobedience and civil unrest. Within the next few decades, other celebrated musicians in the jazz world such as Miles Davis composed music honoring political figures like Nelson Mandela ("The Full Nelson") and Bishop Desmond Tutu ("Tutu").[22]

Aside from Trane, many other artists have memorialized Rev. King, including the stellar Irish rock group U2 ("Pride") and Stevie Wonder ("Happy Birthday.") In the dance world, after Rev. King's assassination in 1968, Karel Shook and Arthur Mitchell founded the Dance Theatre of Harlem (DTH) in New York. Mitchell was the first black principal dancer in the New York City Ballet (NYCB) and a frequent muse of the legendary choreographer George Balanchine who collaborated with the well-known musician Igor Stravinsky, whom Coltrane deeply admired: Balanchine's fellow Russian émigré created the music for Ag*on.*[23]

Inspired by Dr. King's the "Drum Major Instinct," Hope Boykin, a principal dancer with the Alvin Ailey dance company, choreographed "r-Evolutionary Dream." Additionally, dancers would celebrate Coltrane's work too. Reviewing the dance "A Love Supreme," created by Belgian choreographer Anna Teresa De Keersmaeker and Salva Sanchis, a critic noted, "The dance is a study in craft… It is masculine and powerful, and the next time I'd like to see it with four women."[24]

As a tribute to the five little girls in the church basement, years ago I also attempted to choreograph "Ode to Birmingham: A Contemporary Ballet" to the composition "Alabama."[25] The first movement of this dance informally began with an actor reading from Rev. King's "Letter from Birmingham City Jail." The lead dancer portrays King confined in a jail cell, while other dancers join him, dramatizing the actual speech in movement. Six dancers and one actor rounded out the cast in the first section or movement; the dancer portraying King wore blue coveralls; another dancer represented the clergy, while another dancer portrayed Bull Connor. Dancing on point, three women represent the a*ngels of change* and the biblical figures Shadrack, Meshack and Abendnego whom King references in "Letter from Birmingham City Jail."[26] As the score or music to "Alabama" slowly begins, the scene of the second movement figuratively shifts to the Sixteenth Street Baptist Church basement, as the children gather, eagerly waiting for their Sunday school lesson and the church program to officially begin. For many different reasons, all valid in retrospect, a larger ensemble would not get the chance to present the second movement, mainly due to too many cancelled rehearsals and perhaps an overly ambitious agenda.

During this demanding period, I applied for a grant from the Ohio Humanities Council (OHC) to launch a symposium on John Coltrane in 2004-2005. Ultimately, the project was not funded during that stage.

Figure 40. "Ode to Birmingham: A Contemporary Ballet." Courtesy of WSU.

Figure 41. "Ode to Birmingham." Courtesy of WSU.

Figure 42. "Ode to Birmingham." Courtesy of WSU.

While I tried to stage "Ode to Birmingham" and co-organize "Four Women from Birmingham," I consulted with Sarah, as I expanded the role of the 'fifth little girl' in this dance. I also taught a new seminar in the political science department at WSU, "Politics and the Music of John Coltrane." At the end of this grand project, to my surprise and delight Sarah asked me to collaborate with her on a memoir.

The genesis of "Ode to Birmingham" dates to my field research during the summer of 2003. I took the first of many trips to Alabama, visiting key repositories of civil rights-related struggles in Birmingham, Montgomery, and Selma. I spoke at-length with Christopher McNair at his local photography studio. In addition, I visited the Martin Luther King, Jr. National Historic Site in Atlanta, Georgia. Later that summer, I met and conversed with Elvin Jones who headlined a jazz concert in Chicago, IL. While attempting to organize a John Coltrane symposium to coincide with the 50th anniversary of the release of *A Love Supreme*, I once briefly spoke over the telephone with Michelle Coltrane and Ravi Coltrane, and a representative or agent of the McCoy Tyner.[27]

During my first trip to Alabama, I had a memorable encounter with the Rev. Fred Shuttlesworth and invited him to lecture at WSU. As a precursor to the event "Four Women from Birmingham," he spoke to students in my class on John Coltrane in early March of 2004. Students listened attentively as the preacher spoke with passion and conviction about his several near-death experiences and encounters with members of the KKK. Shuttlesworth was the pastor of Bethel Baptist Church. He also staged protests with other leaders like Rev. King and Rev. Abernathy and led young children, including Sarah Collins, in various marches. Reverend Shuttlesworth would later relocate to Cincinnati, Ohio where he served as the pastor for the Greater New Light Baptist Church. However, Birmingham and the state of Alabama would honor one of the preeminent civil rights leaders in America. During an era when Confederate statues are increasingly being removed or toppled from public squares throughout the United States of America, a statute of Shuttlesworth remains prominently displayed near the entrance of the Birmingham Civil Rights Institute; this institution also awards the annual Fred L Shuttlesworth Human Rights Award. Past recipients include the late Rev. C.T. Vivian, Eleanor-Holmes Norton, and James Clyburn.

Attaining

Born in Hamlet, North Carolina in 1926, faithful parents reared John Coltrane in the African Methodist Zion church. He spent his formative years in Highpoint, N.C, growing up in a middle-class home. Both of Coltrane's grandfathers preached. His mother, Alice Coltrane, would later find employment as a domestic in Philadelphia, Pennsylvania; the family had fallen on difficult times after the deaths of several family members, including Coltrane's father and namesake, John R. Coltrane who worked as a tailor and casually played several musical instruments. His mother sang and played the piano. At her son's request, Alice bought John his first saxophone when he was thirteen. [28] In 1943, Coltrane also moved to Philadelphia as a teen and began his formal musical education at the Orenstein School of Music. He would join the Navy reserve after graduating from high school. Coltrane played while enlisted. He later made his professional debut in 1945. He acquired his apprenticeship and collaborated with musicians Charlie Parker, Dizzy Gillespie, Red Garland, Duke Ellington, Miles Davis and Thelonious Monk, and Sun Ra. Later influences would include the free jazz style of play popularized by musicians such as Albert Ayler and Ornette Coleman. Reminiscing about her husband, the pianist and harpist Alice Coltrane once mused, "As he developed himself more spiritually, we saw it more musically."[29]

A relentlessly curious Coltrane embraced minimalism, modal music, Indian classical music, Japanese music and various styles of African music: He also listened to the chanting in Buddhist temples; Coltrane's reach extends to styles contemporary classic music, rock, pop and funk, according to different sources.[30] In the avant-garde phase of his career, Trane recorded with bassist Jimi Garrison who was an original member of the 'classic quartet,' Pharoah Sanders, Rashied Ali and Alice Coltrane who stated, "there was no way he could go back." John Coltrane lost numerous fans. Nevertheless, Trane had a long lasting influenced on innovative musicians such as minimalist composer La Monte Young.[31]

The famous jazz musician and Sarah Collins Rudolph (the obscure civil rights heroine and icon in the making) grew up in different eras and under vastly differing circumstances. As a child, Sarah was not a jazz aficionado but grew to understand the significance of compositions like "Alabama." Coltrane grew up in the Southern black church, rich in the traditions of charismatic worship. In the latter phase of his career, he drew musically from the intensity of such experiences. From her early years as a member of the 16th Street Church on to her adult life, Sarah's reliance on God anchored her. Aside from experimenting with alcohol and marijuana as a young adult, faith has guided the bombing survivor who never received counseling. She experienced a spiritual rebirth that resulted in a *wonderful change.* Trane experienced a spiritual reawakening too, following a long struggle with drugs, including a heroin addiction. Within days of kicking this habit, he composed his 'magnus opus.'[32]

A Love Supreme

Along with Miles Davis' *Kind of Blue*, *A Love Supreme* occupies rarified status in the world of jazz. Tony Whyton wrote it's one of the "greatest jazz albums" ever recorded.[33] Trane biographer Lewis Porter and Alice Coltrane also admired his works. John Coltrane, who composed the song "Naima" for his first wife Naima Coltrane (nee Juantia Grubbs), would collaborate with his second wife, Alice McLeod Coltrane. In the liner notes to *A Love Supreme*, Coltrane describes his religious reawakening and shares a poem or "psalm written to God." According to John Fraim, "Trane's life progressed...like sections of his *A Love Supreme* — from 'acknowledgment' to 'pursuance' to 'resolution' and finally to 'psalm.'"[34]

The chapter "Acknowledgement" opens *The 5th Little Girl*, yet the themes of 'pursuance' and 'resolution' resonate in the Sarah Collins Rudolph story, along with other motifs like the fight against inequality and lessons on forgiveness. The Sunday school lesson on the day of the blast was entitled "The Love that Forgives" (Genesis 45: 4-15, KJV). In short, this lesson later guided Sarah who struggled to repel the forces of hatred after the devastating loss. On a grander community scale, artists created a body of work, honoring four *angels of change* who would receive the Congressional gold medal posthumously in 2013.

At the age of forty, Coltrane would die of liver cancer at a hospital in Long Island, New York on July 23, 1967. Famed drummer Elvin Jones, formerly a member of the John Coltrane Quartet, later described Coltrane in angelic terms in the documentary *The Legacy of John Coltrane*: His heartfelt account of Trane points to the spiritual core of the much-esteemed jazz musician and Jones' beloved friend:

> 'He was just a spiritual man. In my reflections... he was like an angel on earth. It struck me that deeply...This is not just an ordinary person.

I'm enough of a believer to think very seriously about that. I've been touched, in some way, by something greater than life.'[35]

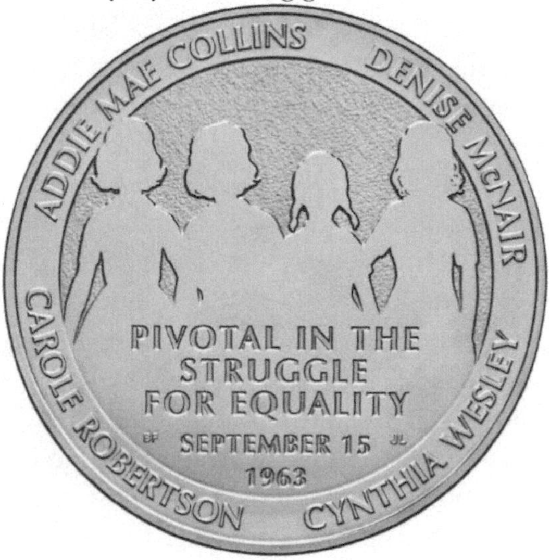

Figure 43. Medal -16th Street Baptist Church Bombing Victims. Library of Congress.

The Coltrane Legacy

Many later years after having a vision, in 1982 Archbishop Franzo Wayne King and Mother Marian King co-founded a church in San Francisco, California where some members revere John William Coltrane as a saint. Nicholas Baham describes the Saint John Will-I-Am Coltrane Church as "a place for jazz pilgrims, devotees of the late jazz legend John Coltrane from diverse corners of the earth" who are dedicated to social justice: "Whatever their social station, the pilgrims and devotees arrive and wait patiently for the 'Coltrane Liturgy,' the integration of orthodox Christian liturgical practice and improvised jazz music," according to the author.[36] (Coltrane family members have opposed this church and his deification.) Nonetheless, the African Orthodox Church would canonize Trane who earned a Lifetime Grammy Award (1992) and the Pulitzer Prize (2007).

Coltrane is widely recognized as an iconic figure in jazz and one of the most influential artists of his generation, thanks largely to seminal albums like *A Love Supreme* and his body of work. Readers who revisit his discography after completing *The 5th Little Girl* may hear some of Coltrane's lesser-known works, as well as his signature compositions, differently. The definition of a modern American heroine, Collins-Rudolph is a civil rights icon. Some use the word icon to describe even banal achievements in music or popular culture; nevertheless, the term 'icon' befits Rudolph. Until recently, mainstream society has not always universally recognized the "fifth little girl" as such in the annals of history: Notably, Millennials and members of "Gen Z" view the civil rights or human rights activist and Birmingham native in this light.

From the opening lines of *Crucifixion Resurrection* and *A Love that Forgives*, which both premiered in Philadelphia, artists and playwrights are invoking Rudolph's historical role.[37] This trend has magnified since the 50th year remembrance of the church bombing, even abroad. The BBC, for example, interviewed Sarah in 2013. Several years later, she discussed the 1963 bombing with an acclaimed Trinidadian-British journalist and actor in the documentary "Martin Luther King Jr. by Sir Trevor McDonald," set for release near the 50th anniversary of King's death.

Organizations and groups such as Tranestop, the Coltrane Cultural Center and the John W. Coltrane Cultural Society (founded by Coltrane's cousin, Mary Lyerly Alexander) all promote the legacy of the late jazz saxophonist. Moreover, the Friends of John Coltrane, a group based in Hamlet, N.C. sponsored the first John Coltrane International Jazz and Blues Festival. Additionally, Dr. Anyabwile Aaron Love of Temple University would coordinate the inaugural John Coltrane Symposium in Philadelphia, Pennsylvania, convened at The Church of the Advocate. In sum, though he died relatively young, Trane left a vast body of music behind typified by recent albums like the compilation *The Coltrane Legacy*.

Amen

The jazz trumpeter and classical musician Hannibal Lokumbe alludes to Coltrane in *Crucifixion Resurrection: Nine Souls a Traveling*. This work imaginatively narrates the lives of the Emanuel Nine, but by way of the 'four little girls.' In July of 2017, Hannibal opened *Crucifixion Resurrection* at Mother Bethel A.M.E. Church. The former Philadelphia Orchestra composer-in-resident also showcased his song on trumpet honoring Collins-Rudolph, 'Ode to Sister Sarah.' He premiered this composition at the National Constitution Hall with the 'fifth little girl' in attendance. Afterwards, Sarah participated in a panel, along with Lokumbe and Steven Levingston, a Pulitzer-Prize winner and non-fiction editor at *The Washington Post*. Jeff Rosen would moderate the session, "Remembering Birmingham: Civil Rights and Constitutional Change at the National Constitution Center." Recognition of the 'four little girls' still occurs, as exemplified by the work of artists such as photographer Dawood Bey, a past recipient of a MacArthur Foundation Genius Grant. His work *The Birmingham Project* memorializes the six youths slain in Birmingham.

We should never overlook Sarah, the four girls, Johnny, and Virgil. Observers also assert that "we must never forget the Mother Emanuel Nine or Jennifer Pinkney and her daughter, Felecia Sanders and her granddaughter, and Polly Shepherd." Artist LeRoy Campbell presented Emanuel 9 family members with his "Bible Study" and 'Encouraging the Survivor," original works of art honoring the Charleston Nine.[38]

Along with Daniel Simmons Jr., Sarah was a guest of honor at the premiere of *Crucifixion*; hindered by an untimely delay, Hannibal treated the son of the late Reverend Daniel Simmons Sr. to a special encore. Steve Prince who attended this show collaborated with Hannibal in the promotional artwork for *Crucifixion Resurrection*; his design "4 Emanuel" reconfigures the 'four little girls' as black women, holding up the gospel banner in homage to the Emanuel 9. In relationship to the production, Prince also created banners depicting the Emanuel 9 victims as saints.

Other creative works pertaining to the tragedy also include *Mother Emanuel, An American Musical Play*. In 2016, this show opened to solid reviews at the New York Fringe Festival.[39] Graphic artist Gil Shuler's iconic palmetto dove design pays tribute to the Emanuel Nine.[40] Steve Jordan's "Peace of Nine" touches on the debate about the Confederate flag, while Leo Twiggs's batik drawings entitled "Requiem for Mother Emanuel" masterfully evokes the Emanuel 9 tragedy.[41] "Emanuel: Love is the Answer," featured yet a second collaboration between William Starrett (artistic director of the Columbia City Ballet) and artist Jonathan Green whose colorful visual creations replicate Gullah traditions on the Sea Islands. Months prior to its world premiere, Adam Parker wrote,

> 'The multimedia production is by the South Carolina Ballet, an enterprise of Columbia City Ballet. It will include projected videos and images: Green's colorful Gullah-inspired paintings, Jenny Horne's now-famous General Assembly speech calling for the removal of the Confederate battle flag from the Statehouse grounds, comments from great spiritual and political leaders such as Martin Luther King Jr. and Mother Teresa, and more.'[42]

On April 15, 2017, the Charleston International Airport installed a poignant permanent exhibition that memorialized the Emanuel Nine:

> The memorial is 400 square feet and contains two five-foot-high stained-glass windows showing Mother Emanuel and nine white doves symbolizing the victims. There is also an oil painting donated by local artist Jonathan Green showing nine birds and a photography exhibit chronicling the community response to the Mother Emanuel massacre. In the center of the space is a Bible open to Mark 4:13-20, the scripture used during the Bible study before the shooting. Rev. Clementa Pinckney's bible and one bible from another of the victims are also in the case.[43]

Musicians have honored and memorialized the Emanuel 9, as have others. Legendary gospel singer, Pastor Shirley Caesar, would cover the Nashville based tune "Mother Emanuel" as an instrument for healing.[44] Furthermore, Joan Baez sang at the third commemorative program in Charleston for the Emanuel 9. Baez led the crowd in several freedom songs and shared her version of "The President Sang Amazing Grace," featured on *Whistle Down the Wind*, her Grammy-nominated album. Zoe Mulford, who attended this event along with Baez, originally wrote and sang this tune. Jeff Scher provided illustrations for Mulford's children's book, *The President Sang Amazing Grace*. In the realm of architecture, a select committee later chose the work of architect Michael Arad, who designed the National September 11 Memorial in New York City, from among a list of distinguished entrants for its Emanuel 9 memorial.[45]

Several years ago, the documentary *Emanuel* (narrated by the Oscar-winning actress Viola Davis) premiered nationwide. Davis and all-star NBA point guard Stephen Curry were executive producers, while actress Mariska Hargitay served as a co-producer of a documentary that would also involve on-screen interviews, mainly with family members of the Emanuel 9 — reflecting on the catastrophe and stories of survival.[46]

According to Hannibal, Rudolph is "a living treasure of history."[47] Increasingly, artists, mass media, and the public are reconfiguring her significance in the wake of 50th anniversary of the blast, the Charleston Massacre and the current climate. Reading *The Fifth Little Girl…The Sarah Collins Rudolph Story* and reimagining the composition "Alabama," which Coltrane references in the musical notes that accompany *A Love Supreme*, may provide listeners and readers with another vehicle for reinterpreting Rudolph's heroism within the context of the lethal church bombing — an event that fundamentally altered the movement's course.

Sarah Collins Rudolph's universal story of redemption provides yet another critical interpretation to a long missing individual chapter in the chronicles of the American Civil Rights Movement. The narrative arc of her story of loss and reconciliation is turning the page to a new chapter, as the sole or "soul" survivor of the five little girls in the basement lounge rises beyond the margins of history. Hence, the importance of telling this story, largely from her firsthand recollection. Sarah reemerges 'bearing scars,' yet relatively 'unscathed.' Beyond just our nation, the world is bearing witness to her historical and literary transformation. In short, Sarah Collins Rudolph is both 'restituting' and redefining a larger-than-life story.

Notes

---

1 Hannibal Lokumbe, *Crucifixion Resurrection: Nine Souls a Traveling.* Written by classical composer, jazz trumpeter and activist Hannibal, the show premiered on presented on June 17, 2017 at Mother Bethel African Methodist Episcopal Church in Philadelphia, Pennsylvania.

2 "16th Street Baptist Church Bombing," en.wikipedia.org/wiki/_16th_Street_ Baptist_Church_bombing. In a lengthy article or blog site, the writer examines the Birmingham church bombing from many different angles, while commenting extensively on the plays and films it later spawned. (Also, refer to choir director from UAB; youtube.com/watch?v=BA9re8JjsFU(Four Little Girls…).

Numerous artists from different genres have memorialized the 16th Street Baptist Church bombing and the four little girls. Some creative works also extend to the perspectives of the families of the so-called perpetrators like Darrah Cloud's play "Stick Wife," according to Koki Notambu. Ursula Rucker's song "For Women" examine the would be lives of the four victims. The extensive article entitled "The Horrific Birmingham Bombing that Killed Four Black Girls on September 15, 1963," written by Natumbu, is an invaluable source in many respects; it references artists who later memorialized the bombing. His article and website reference many other historic sources and commentary within the context of 1963.

3 Thomson Gayle, "The Temptations," *Encyclopedia.com*, https://www. Encyclo pedia.com/people/literature-and-arts/music-popular-and-jazz-biographies/temptations. (Coincidentally, the Tony-nominated play, "Ain't To Proud to Beg — The Life and Times of the Temptations," had a successful run on

Broadway. Three of the core band members have Birmingham roots, including Paul Williams, Eddie Kendricks and Dennis Edwards, while Melvin Franklin was born in Montgomery, Al. Along with producer Norman Whitfield, this group forged the 'psychedelic soul' movement.

4 Chris Williams, "I Can't Think of Sunday," September 15, 2014, http://destinytopeace.com/i-cant-think-of-Sunday; Greg Garrison, "UAB Gospel Choir Director's Song Gives a Voice to Sixteenth Street's Bombing Victims," February 4, 2012, .al.com>living>uab_gospel_choir_directors_son.html; "UAB Gospel Choir Honors 16th Street Baptist Church Bombing Victims with New Single, " *Christian News Wire*, Christiannewswire.com/news/5653318819.html.

5 Irene Adair Newman, "Six Notes: History and Memory in Poetic and Musical Commemorations of the Violence in Birmingham on September 15, 1963" (Honors Essay, University of North Carolina, 2014, https://docplayer.net/42701739-Six-notes-history-and-memory-in-poetic-and-musical-commemorations-of-the-violence-in-Birmingham-on-September-; Miles Davis, *Miles Davis*, 43.

6 Lewis Porter, *John Coltrane: His Life and Music* (Ann Arbor, Michigan: The University of Michigan Press, 1980, 1.

7 Located in Dayton, Ohio, Stivers School for the Arts is a "public arts magnet school" designated to serve grades 7-12.

8 Anna Kisselgoff, "Eleo Pomare, Dancer and Rebel, Dies at 70," August 13, 2008, https://www.nytimes.com/2008/08/14/arts/dance/14pomare.html.

9 Thomas F. DeFrantz, *Dancing Revelations* (Oxford; Oxford University Press, 2004), 182-185. Originated by Judith Jamison, "Cry" is one of the most popular dances in an Ailey repertory, which also include classics such as "Revelations." Judith Jamison led the AADT from 1989–2010. Currently, former dancer-choreographer, Robert Battle leads the AADT. (For further information, also refer to the documentary "Ailey Dances," hosted by Judith Jamison, which also features "Cry" and "Revelations," Ailey's universally acclaimed dance. According to Thomas F. Defrantz, Alvin Ailey also dedicated dances to subjects ranging from Ernest Hemingway to Harriet Tubman to Malcolm X. (p. 167)

10 *A Love That Forgives* is an original production by ChildhoodsLost Foundation based in Philadelphia, Pennsylvania. The staged play centers on the 16th Street Baptist Church bombing. This production, which features an all-youth cast, tells the story of the fateful day from the perspective of the bombing survivor Collins-Rudolph. (While Marie Hall Mullen wrote a play about the blast and chose the title based on what Sarah once shared with her, another aspiring playwright from Philadelphia wrote a play about the custodian of the story of the story, prior to knowing about Sarah.) *A Love That Forgives* premiered in Philadelphia, Pa. in July of 2017.

11 Rick Dildine, artistic director of the Alabama Shakespeare Festival (ASF) and executive director Todd Schmidt wrote about this productions and Christine Ham's play about Nina Simone in a recent AFS playbill; Stacy A. Anderson, "Phylicia Rashad Takes on Directing Role to Mark 50th Anniversary of Alabama Church Bombing," September 15, 2013, AP via ca. yahoo.news.com (See also goodblacknews.org/tag/Phylicia-rashad/.

12 Timothy B. Tyson, "About the 1963 Birmingham Bombing," https://www.english.illinois.edu/amps/poets/m_r/randall/birmingham.htm.

13 Toni Morrison, *Song of Solomon* (New York: Vintage International, 1977), 173.

14 "Excerpts of 4 Little Girls: A Dance Film," Queens World Festival, March 19-29, 2020, https://www.queensworldfilmfestival.com/films/details.asp?fid=719.

15 Filippo Deorsola, "The Influence of Jazz on the Civil Rights Movement," February 10, 2017, https://wwww.fdmusic.live/....jazz....civil-rights-movment/....the-influenc-of-jazz-on-the (Blog: History and Music)' Nat Hentoff, "How Jazz Helped Hasten the Civil-Rights Movement," wsj.com, Updated January 15, 2009, https://www.wsj.com/articles/SB123197292808321 7.

16 Farah Jasmine Griffin and Salim Washington, *Clawing at the Limits of the Cool: Mile Davis, John Coltrane, and the Greatest Jazz Collaboration Ever* (New York: St. Martins Press, 2008), 25.

17 Ashley Kahn, A Love Supreme (New York: Viking, 2002), 76.

18 Chaka Khan evokes the names of Trane, Dizzy Gillespie and Stevie Wonder in her version of "And the Melody Still lingers On (A Night in Tunisia)"; Thomas Barker, "Music, Civil Rights, and Counterculture: Critical Aesthetics and Resistance in the United States, 1957 -1968, Ph.D Dissertation, Music Department University of Durham, 2016, pdfs. Semanticscholar.org/f138/cd16d4a8eafd85bb0384cb31191ea3e6d78c.pdf.

19 Kahn, *A Love Supreme*, 76.

20 John Fraim, *Spirit Catcher: The Life and Art of John Coltrane* (West Liberty, Ohio: The GreatHouse Company, 1996), 154-155; Ashley Kahn, *A Love Supreme: The Story of John Coltrane's Signature Album* (New York: The Penguin Group, 2002), 76. Kahn cites pianist McCoy Tyner: ""The song 'Alabama' came from a speech. John said there was a Martin Luther King speech about the four girls getting killed in Alabama. It was in the newspaper — a printed medium. And so John took the rhythmic patterns of his speech and came up with Alabama."' Moreover, Cole Porter writes, "Coltrane reportedly based the opening recitative of his "Alabama" on some words by Martin Luther King, but I have studied two speeches sent to me by Woideck and have not found a connection." *John Coltrane,* 331; Frank Kofsky, Black Nationalism and the Revolution in Music (New York: Pathfinder, 1970), 223; Frank Kofsky, John Coltrane and the Jazz Revolution of the 1960s (New York: Pathfinder, 1970), 223, 228 and 419.

21 "The Legacy of John Coltrane," directed by Bobby Bryan and produced by Richard Saylor.

22 Miles Davis (with Quincy Troupe), *Miles Davis: The Autobiography* (New York: Simon & Shuster, 1990), 109.

23 Agon featured Mitchell and Diana Adams. Balanchine paired Mitchell with ballerina Suzanne Farrell in "Slaughter on Tenth Avenue" and the electrifying pas de deux of *Agon.* Stravinsky created the score for *Apollo* and *Orpheus*, too. Mitchell also originated the role of Puck in the NYCB's version of the William Shakespeare play *A Mid Summer's Night Dream.* (Virginia Johnson, formerly a principle dancer, currently leads the DTH.)

24 Roslyn Sulcas, "Coltrane by De Keersmaeker, Freewheeling but Structure Intact," *The New York Times*, September 26, 2017, https://www.nytimes.com> arts>anne-teresa-de-keermaeker-a-love-supreme. Penelope Freeh, "Supreme Interpretation: Penelope Freeh on *A Love Supreme*, October 13, 2017, walkerart.org/magazine/supreme-interpretation-penelope-freeh-on-a-love-supreme.

25 The choreography turned out to be truly collaborative, as I worked closely with students in WSU's ballet program.

26 In this part of the dance, I was attempting to portray the progression of events, beginning with Reverend King's confinement to jail on "Good Friday" and the Children's March in the spring of 1963 to the church bombing during the fall.

27 During the fall of 2003 and the spring of 2004, I was attempting to put together or assemble a symposium on John Coltrane in Dayton, Ohio to coincide with the 40th year mark of *A Love Supreme*." The symposium would have focused on two other works, "My Favorite Things" and "Alabama. Recorded in December of 1964 and released in 1965, the thirty-three-minute tour de force became an instant hit. The Classic Quartet once performed the entire groundbreaking album live in Antibes, France in 1965.

28 Ashley Kahn, "Biography – John Coltrane," https://www.johncoltrane.com/biography; "John Coltrane" *BHA*, http://www.myblackhistory.net/John_Coltrane.htm; Shirley Griffith and Steve Ember, "John Coltrane, 1926-1976: The Famous Saxophone Player Helped Make Modern Jazz Popular Around the World," People in America, *Voice of America*, November 6, 2010, https://learningenglish.voanews.com/a/john-coltrane-1926-1967-the-famous-saxaphone-player-helped-make-modern-jazz-popular-around-the-world-106823604/114223.html; Porter, *John Coltrane*, 1-17.

29 For further elaboration on this critical aspect of Coltrane's musical journey, refer to "The World According to John Coltrane," directed Bobby Byron and produced by Richard Saylor.

30 Notably, *The Word According to John Coltrane* was directed by Bobby Byron and produced by Richard Saylor. This documentary references the fact that Coltrane viewed music as a "means to enlightenment," involving an exploration of the soul and his experiences.

31 Ibid.

32 Archbishop King and Mother Marian King would both play fundamental roles in establishing a church bearing John Coltrane's name that would later become affiliated with the African Orthodox Church bearing John Coltrane's name; the Saint John William Coltrane Church was initially established in San Francisco, California in 1969, according to author Nick Baham. Members have integrated musical suites from *A Love Supreme* into the church service or liturgy, normally played on the first Sunday of each month. For additional insights about the congregation and the life and odyssey of Coltrane, refer to Nicholas Baham's *The Coltrane Church: Apostles of Sound, Agents of Social Justice.*

33 Tony Whyton, *Beyond a Love Supreme: John Coltrane and the Legacy of an Album* (Oxford: Oxford University Press, 2013); Martin Johnson, "'A Love Supreme' at 50," *The Wall Street Journal*, November 25, 2015.

34 Readers may also want to refer to the more recent documentary *Chasing Trane.*

35 See also *The Legacy of John Coltrane*, directed and produced by Burill Crown.

36 Nicholas Louis Baham III, *The Coltrane Church: Apostles of Sound, Agents of Social Justice* (Jefferson, North Carolina: McFarland & Company, Inc., 2015), 2.

In *The Coltrane Church*, Baham discusses the history and evolution of this church, beginning in 1965; Baham also explores its "engagement with the Black Panther Party in the 1960s, the 2009-10 Oscar Grant Movement against police brutality, and the 2011-12 Occupy SF movement [which] inextricably links them to 50 years of a broader history of struggles…" (p. 5) Ibid. See also "Saint John Coltrane African Orthodox Church," https://www.atlasobscura.com/places/saint-john-coltrane-african-orthodox-church-skb. (Tantamount to the church's mission is the goal to "help followers recognize sound as the preexisting wisdom of God." Members have integrated suites from A *Love Supreme* into their worship, too.)

37 During Black history month in 2019, the Omega Baptist Church, located in Dayton, Ohio also presented a skit pertaining to the fifth little girl. Angela Lewis wrote the skit. Later during the service, Pastor Joshua Ward based the sermon largely on Sarah's inspiring testimony detailed in a feature news story, "'God Had to do a Work in Me…'", published by *The Birmingham News*. Rev. Joshua Ward centered his sermon on Romans 8: 28. For the full context of the skit and sermon, refer to the following website address: http://admin.mediafusionapp.com/live/embedPlayer.php?contentld=69189.

38 Herb Frazier, ed., *Morning Glory: Ninety Seconds Changed a Church* (Charleston, S.C.: Emanuel African Methodist Episcopal Church, 2016), 7. Contributors to this work include Rev. Dr. Norvel Goff, Sr., Dr. Maxine Smith, Willie Glee, Elizabeth (Liz) Alston and Hon. William Dudley Gregorie. The proposed African American International Museum will likely include references to the Charleston Massacre. The proposed Emanuel Memorial should complement the museum that city official hope open not much further beyond 2021, pending fund-raising drives.; "Native of Charleston, World Renowned Artist Leroy Campbell Returns, "*The Chronicle*, June 17, 2017, www.charleton.net>even>native-of-charleston-wordl-ren... (See also Jennifer Berry Hawe's recent book, *Grace Will Lead Us Home: The Charleston Church Massacre and the Hard, Inspiring Journey to Forgiveness*.)

39 "Mother Emanuel, An American Play," https://www.motheremanuelthe play.com/press.

40 Alison Graham, "Palmetto Dove Image Spread around City After One Year," *The Post and Courier*, June 22 2016 (Updated November 2, 2016), Postandcourier.com/features/palmetto-dove-image-spreads-around-city-after-one-year/article_0…

41 Adam Parker, "Leo Twiggs first South Carolina Artist to Win Prestigious Society 1858 Prize," *The Post and Courier*, August 11, 2018, postandcourier.com/features/leo-twiggs-first-south-carolina-artist-to-win-prestigious—society/article_c72fe60c-9bf9-11e8-8b26-0f70bc812c31.html.

42 Adam Parker, "South Carolina Ballet Production to Celebrate Human Spirit in Response to Emanuel AME Shootings," PostandCourier.com, March 9, 2017, https://wwww.postandcourier.com/features/south-carolina-ballet-production-to-celebrate-human-spirit-in-response/article2b2c579a-050a-11e7-b686-93b7b96cbf2.html; Adam Parker, "Requiem for Mother Emanuel," Columbia City Ballet to Explore Church Shooting Putting Attack in Context Art of Love and Unity," *The Post and Courier*, June 17, 2016, https://www.postandcourier.com/features/arts and travel/requiem-for-mother-emanuel-columbia-city-ballet-to-explore-church/article c0846ac8-8177-559d-bgd89-8367cc24b02b.html; Paul Bowers, "Mother Emanuel Shooting was a Loss for the Gullah/Geechee," *Charleston City Paper*, June 22, 2015, https://www.charlestoncitypaper.com/charleston/mother-emanuel-shooting-was-a-loss-for.

43 "Mother Emanuel Nine Memorial Unveiled in Charleston International Airport," *The Christian Recorder*, April 18, 2017. https://www.thechristianrecorder.com/mother-emanuel-nine-memorial-unveiled-in-charleston-international-airport.

44 See also the original cover of Nashville's "Mother Emanuel." Several individuals affiliated with the Led Zepplin band first covered this song.

45 Journalist Anne Branigin of *The Root* provides a rather detailed description of the proposed memorial carried, as also described by *The New York Times*: "Sections of the church's parking lot would be transformed into two meditative spaces, one a stone memorial courtyard, the other a grassy survivor's garden. Together they would speak to the suffering and resilience of a church that has outlasted two centuries of persecution through its practice of faith and forgiveness.

The focal point of the memorial is a pair of sleekly curving high-backed pews, carved of white marble that would welcome visitors from Calhoun Street like outstretched arms."

46 Maurice Wallace and Tony Tian-Ren Lin, "Like 'Green Book,' the New Charleston Church Shooting Documentary is Troubling," *The Washington Post*, June 21, 2019, beta.washingtongpost.com/religion/2019/06/21/like-green-book-new-charleston-church-shooting-documentary-is-troubling/.

47 Remarks made by Hannibal Lokumbe at the beginning of the requiem, *Crucifixion Resurrection: Nine Souls a Traveling* at Mother Bethel Church in Philadelphia, Pennsylvania on Saturday, June 17, 2017. See also Shaun Brady, "On its Two-Year Anniversary: Remembering the Charleston Church Shooting Through Art and Music," *PhillyVoice*, June 12, 2017, htpps:www.phillyvoice.com/on-its-two-yar-anniversary-remembering-the-charleston-church.

Afterword

And Jesus said, Somebody hath touched me; for I perceive that virtue is gone out of me. (Luke 8:46, KJV)

We have come over a way that with tears have been watered.
—James Weldon Johnson, J. Rosamond Johnson

Mine eyes have seen the glory of the coming of he Lord; He is trampling out the vantage where the grapes of wrath are stored.
—Julia Ward Howe

God in His infinite wisdom orchestrates events in our lives to help us to see how awesome He is and will always be. I've always tried to stay in the shadows of events and situations that occurred around me, yet on July 10, 2015 this wasn't to be the case. I traveled to the capitol of S.C. with family members to witness the removal of the Confederate battle flag. This all occurred weeks after a warmly greeted visitor murdered our sister Myra and eight other parishioners after their bible study session on (Luke 8:5-8) at Mother Emanuel. As we were leaving Columbia, I got a call from a CBS affiliate, asking that we meet a reporter for an interview. My niece Denise Quarles agreed to do the interview. I accompanied her.

Afterwards, a gentleman introduced himself to us. He had learned that we were related to Myra Thompson, Denise's mother.[1] We shared information and agreed to meet later. Our brief conversation would later lead to getting to know three of the Collins sisters — Sarah, Janie, and Junie — and establishing relationships that we hope last for a lifetime. Needless to say, I look forward to watching Sarah Collins Rudolph as she readily steps into and asserts her rightful place in American history.

Figure 44. Picture of Blondelle Gadsden. Courtesy of Gadsden.

Despite the June 17, 2015 tragedy at Mother Emanuel A.M.E. Church in Charleston, South Carolina, the Lord's grace abounds, continuously enveloping us. Notwithstanding the very scope of the calamity that afflicted us, the Creator granted us the opportunity to interact with so many people who share the deep emotions that this unthinkable loss has bestowed upon family members of all nine of the victims. I have a new sense of just how traumatic an ordeal like the bombing was for Sarah Collins Rudolph and her family. I now recognize that the trauma goes beyond what they endured because of the Sixteenth Street Baptist Church bombing on Sunday, September 15, 1963. At the time of the bombing, I was only seven years old and news was not as detailed and, in your face, as it is nowadays. I knew of the incident only because it happened in a church setting and the Rev. Dr. Martin Luther King, Jr. was involved in attempts to bring the perpetrators to justice. Both Dr. King and his wife Coretta Scott King took to the pulpit at Mother Emanuel during the crux of the Civil Rights Movement. But never in my lifetime would I have imagined that I would have such a personal connection to Junie, Janie, and Sarah in the way that I have today. God has a way of providing what we need when the chips are down, and that is what He did when the family members of both tragedies were able to meet, embrace each other's sorrows, and talk about the road to healing.[2]

That these horrific crimes were committed in black churches by white men who felt a need to create a greater divide in the world among people of different races and ethnicities still saddens me. Yet in another breath comes a "sweet inspiration," one that allow us to move beyond the hurt, tears, and disappointments so that we can see a new day. For the Collins family, this was a much tougher struggle than it has been for my family in one major respect; the state and federal resources that society has provided for the families of the Emanuel 9 tragedy have made the situation easier to bear but not completely bearable for many of us to this very day.

Fast forward to Saturday afternoon on October 27, 2018, when we read a headline about eleven Jews who were murdered, and seven other people injured, while attending Shabbat at the Tree of Life synagogue in Pittsburgh, Pennsylvania. This incident hit home for me. While my family and I wrestled with all the heartache of losing Myra, two Rabbis from Temple Beth-El in Great Neck, New York, embraced us through it all. They came to visit us the week after the incident at Mother Emanuel; Rabbi Meir Feldman and Rabbi Tara Feldman came to Charleston, S.C. There was an immediate connection between my family and both Rabbis. So much so, that they invited us to come to Great Neck to talk with their members about forgiveness.

Given the dire circumstances, the act of forgiveness was difficult for many to fathom, yet some family members of the nine victims insisted on this principle at the bond hearing for the murderer of our loved ones. Of all the words spoken in the wake of the senseless execution-style murders of Rev. Clemente Pinckney, Rev. Daniel Simmons, Rev. Sharonda Singleton, Rev. DePayne Middleton Doctor, Susie Jackson, Cynthia Hurd, Ethel Lance, Tywanza Sanders and Myra Thompson the word *forgive* resonated globally, leaving many hearers in disbelief.[3] Some wondered, asked how various families members could forgive someone who had executed such a 'heinous crime.' Are they that weak? Are they crazy? And so forth, were the comments from many, while others struggled to understand our intent or actions.

Forgiving brought some 'closure,' allowing us to move ahead. On a brighter note, this act brought many special visitors to Emanuel like the Collins sisters and the rabbis. Without fail, we have entreated everyone to return. My family members and I visited the Tree of Life Center in Pittsburgh, Pa. Our motto at Emanuel is that we're the church of open doors; we've always welcomed visitors, which hasn't changed. Emanuel means *God be with us*: We know that His presence will remain with us.

As I have noted, I owe thanks to many. In extending this gratitude, I would be remiss if I didn't note that the sisters, and other families of the Sixteenth Street Church bombing, may have been a catalyst for the accommodations that we would later receive; families who labored for years, keeping the story of the bombing relevant. We are perhaps the fortuitous, unintended benefactors of their unrequited pain and untold suffering that no family should have to bear: therefore, I owe gratitude, respect, and love to three fierce women of God — chosen to carry a message — who are still alive because our Father lives within them.

Figure 45 Mother Emanuel, Courtesy of Blondelle Gadsden

Notes

1 The gentleman whom I met that day was Dr. Tracy Snipe, a native Charlestonian. He had returned to the South Carolina State House grounds to witness this event.

2 Along with faculty and staff members at the College of Charleston, Tracy and I coordinated a citywide community forum. It would serve as a "balm" for many.

Healing and lessons in forgiveness can comes in platform like this event which Emanuel 9 Survivors Polly Shepperd and Felicia Sanders attended, along with other family members. Several years after her terrifying ordeal, Sanders would publicly share, "'I can breathe again,'" during an interview televised locally. The mother of Tywanza Sanders and niece of Susie Jackson had attended a workshop in Tennessee that helped her to arrive at this critical point.

Forgiveness can also be intertwined with or a part of the healing process. It continues to be critical in our stories. As Dr. Marjorie E. Baker, a retired professor from the Department of Social Work at WSU notes, "When I first began studying forgiveness well over a decade ago, I noted something that Oprah Winfrey said that I believe to be true: 'If you don't heal the wounds from the past, if you just try to bandage them, you will continue to bleed.' For some, pondering this alternative might be a motivator that leads to the desire to forgive. But, above else, … forgiveness is both a choice and a challenge. And, as a supporter of the individual's right to self-determination, it is my belief, that whatever and individual's choice is regarding the personal and delicate matter of forgiveness, it is to be respected." (Marjorie E"Forgiveness: What It Is, What It Isn't," *Dayton Daily News*, August 5, 2012).

3 My sister left behind her husband Reverend Anthony Thompson, two adult children (Denise Quarles and Kevin Singleton) and many other relatives and loved ones, as did the eight other members who perished. Her husband and son have written about the aftermath of this unspeakable tragedy, as have family members of some of the other eight victims, including Reverend Sharon Risher and Chris Singleton.

Appendix

Sympathy Letters to Family of Bombing Victims

Note: Citizens living across the U.S. and abroad too sent letters to the parents of Addie Mae Collins and other victims in the days and weeks following the Sixteenth Street Baptist Church bombing. Additionally, sorority chapters also wrote in support of the Collins family.

September 22, 1963
Manhattan, Kansas

Dear Mr. and Mrs. [redacted],

We would like to express our sincere sympathy concerning the death of your daughter [redacted]. It is tragic that there should be people in this world that would have the indecency to take the life of an inocent child. May God bless you and help you in this time of need.

Sincerly,
The 9th Grade
Sunday School Class
First Methodist Church
Manhattan, Kansas

RECEIVED
SEP [illegible] 1963

[redacted]
57-27 Catalpa Ave.
Ridgewood 27, N.Y.
October 4, 1963

Dear Mrs. [redacted]:

Enclosed you will find a check for five dollars which is what we collected from our junior dept. boys and girls here in Ridgewood Presbyterian Sunday School to try and let you know in our own little way that we white folks up north here feel terrible about what happened and can only pray for those who did this awful thing. Our prayers are with you and your little girl in the hospital that you may get over this with Gods grace and mercy and that one day we may truly know "Peace on Earth, and Good Will Towards All Men".

I am also enclosing a check a personal check for ten dollars from our general supt. of our Sunday School Mr. [redacted] of 142-25 Pershing Crescent, Jamaica, L.I.,N.Y. with his prayers for all of you and the rebuilding of your faith and your church.

Yours Truly in Christian Love

[redacted]

Apto. Aéreo 12014
Bogotá D. E. 1
Colombia, South America
September 28, 1963

[redacted]
c/o 16th Street Baptist Church
Birmingham, Alabama

In the blessed Name of Jesus Christ I greet you, Mr. and Mrs. [redacted] and family,

It was with great sadness that I read the heartbreaking account in TIME magazine of the murder of your dear [redacted] and the other five Negro young people in Birmingham, and of the destruction of the house of our God, the injuries to the many, and the shock and breavement which you all suffered. Please accept my heartfelt sympathies.

But it was with the greatest admiration that I read of the Christ-like attitudes manifested by your pastors. How great will be your reward in heaven, and on earth, if you as a church can learn from your saintly pastors those lessons first taught by our blessed Lord Jesus which have obviously taken root in their hearts -- and I trust in yours as well. Stand by them!

Our nation has suffered so much from prejudice, --the hateful attitudes which associate with all of a given group the unpleasentnesses and crimes of members of that group. Our archenemy, Satan, would like for you to "get even" with the murderers by "taking it out" in any way you can with any and every white person. But Jesus has prayed for you, that you will stand firm in this hour of breavement and supreme temptation. Guard your hearts from hatred, and know that amongst those of other races there are many, many whose hearts go out to you in your great loss.

I myself attended Chicago public schools 14 years, always with one or more colored classmates. Amongst these were some very dear friends.

In the bonds of Calvary love,

[redacted]

The Thirteen Aides Charity Clu
4027 West 21st Street,
Los Angeles, California,
January 14, 1964

Dear Mrs. [redacted],

The women of this club wanted to help make [redacted] Christmas a happy one. Please excuse the delay of this gift, Fifty-dollars ($50.00). We hope this little gift will help bring a ray of sunshine into her life.

May God bless you and your family. Hoping to hear from you as soon as possible.

Yours sincerely
The Thirteen Aides Chari
President- Mrs. [redacted].
Vice Pres.... Mrs [redacted].

IMMEDIATE RELEASE SEPTEMBER 19, 1963

Office of the White House Press Secretary

THE WHITE HOUSE

STATEMENT BY THE PRESIDENT

The tragic death of the Negro children in Birmingham last Sunday has given rise to fears and distrust which require the cooperation and restraint of all the citizens of that city.

I have received reports from the leading Negro citizens concerning the situation this afternoon. Next Monday I will confer at the request of Mayor Boutwell with white civic leaders who want to give us information concerning the steps which the city has taken and plans to take to reestablish the confidence of everyone that law and order in Birmingham will be maintained.

In addition, I have today appointed General Kenneth Royalland Col. Earl Blaik as a committee to represent me personally in helping the city to work as a unit in overcoming the fears and suspicions which now exist. They will go to Birmingham in the next few days to start on this work of great importance.

In the meantime the Federal Bureau of Investigation, as well as the local authorities, is making massive efforts to bring to justice the persons responsible for the bombing on Sunday and previous incidents.

I urge everyone to cooperate with them in this effort and that all citizens of Birmingham and Alabama will give these processes of law enforcement a full opportunity to work. I urge all citizens in these next days to conduct themselves with restraint and responsibility.

####

Figure 46. Statement by President Kennedy, September 19, 1963.

OFFICE OF THE MAYOR
CITY OF BIRMINGHAM

WILLIAM A. BELL, SR.
MAYOR

January 8, 2013

Ms. Sarah Collins Rudolph
619 Tomahawk Circle
Birmingham, Alabama 35214

Dear Ms. Rudolph:

You are hereby appointed as consultant to the City of Birmingham. As consultant, you will serve on a speakers bureau giving personal accounts of your experiences during the Civil Rights struggle during the 1960's as we observe the 50th Anniversary of the movement. Mr. Erskine Faush, my Chief of Staff will serve as your coordinator for this appointment. He will also advise and coordinate your participation in the year-long observance. You will be expected to participate in a minimum of 4 forums during this period. Your fee for this service will be $10,000.00, which will be paid on a periodic basis as invoices are submitted and approved.

You acknowledge and agree that the City of Birmingham has the right to deduct from the total amount of consideration to be paid to you under this agreement all unpaid, delinquent, or overdue license fees, taxes, fines, penalties and other amounts due the City of Birmingham. Under the terms of this appointment, either party may cancel by giving the other party a two-week written notice. If the terms of this appointment are acceptable to you, please indicate by signing below and returning this letter to my office.

Sincerely,

William A. Bell, Sr.
Mayor

ACCEPTED:________________________ **DATE:**__________

Approved as to form: ____________ Date: January 14, 2013

WAB/TB/kew

Cc: Erskine Faush
Terry Burney

Mrs. Sarah Collins Rudolph
Mr. George Rudolph

January 17, 2013

Hon. Mayor William Bell
Birmingham City Hall
710 North 20th Street
Birmingham, AL 35203

Re: Consultant Fee Agreement Offer

Mayor Bell:

I am in receipt of your proposed Speaker's Consultant Agreement dated January 8, 2013; relative to the yearlong Commemoration of the 50th Anniversary of the Civil Rights movement.

However, after careful consideration, I respectfully decline your offer based on the following reasons:

1. It has been frequently stated that, "Justice delayed does not have to be justice denied." The truth is that justice has only been *partially served in Birmingham.*

2. As you are aware, I have sought restitution as a victim of the bombing from the City of Birmingham. I am now seeking restitution from the City through the murder of my sister, Addie Mae Collins.

As a victim of the bombing, I was left disfigured; my goals shattered – unattainable Mr. Mayor.

3. In recent meetings I have been told there was no connection between federal authorities and local authorities: that there was no way to connect the dots regarding collusion. I realize that former judges were appointed by the US Government and that the FBI is also a Federal entity. So, do I readily expect Federal judges to implicate Federal investigators? No. Nor did I ever imagine a dual justice system would survive 1964, but I was sorely mistaken.

But, with evidence, truth is illuminated, and perseverance endures.

4. A fair solution is attainable and long past due for the families that have suffered unbearable loss on Sunday, Sept. 15, 1963; compounded by arrogant denial from attorneys and city officials. Deliver justice fully to Birmingham.

Regards,

Sarah Collins Rudolph

Sarah Collins Rudolph

H.R.360

One Hundred Thirteenth Congress of the United States of America

AT THE FIRST SESSION

Begun and held at the City of Washington on Thursday, the third day of January, two thousand and thirteen

AN ACT

To award posthumously a Congressional Gold Medal to Addie Mae Collins, Denise McNair, Carole Robertson, and Cynthia Wesley to commemorate the lives they lost 50 years ago in the bombing of the Sixteenth Street Baptist Church, where these ….

Be it enacted by the Senate and House of Representatives of the United States of America in Congress assembled,

SECTION 1. FINDINGS.

The Congress Finds the following:

(1) September 15, 2013, will mark 50 years since the lives of Addie Mae Collins, Denise McNair, Carole Robertson, and Cynthia Wesley were suddenly taken by a bomb planted in the Sixteenth Street Baptist Church in Birmingham, Alabama.

(2) The senseless and premature death of these 4 little Black girls sparked "The Movement that Changed the World".

(3) On that tragic Sunday in September of 1963, the world took notice of the violence inflicted in the struggle for equal rights.

(4) The fact that 4 innocent children lost their lives as they prepared for Sunday School shook the world's conscience.

(5) This tragedy galvanized the Civil Rights Movement and sparked a surge of momentum that helped secure the passage of the Civil Rights Act of 1964 and later the Voting Rights Act of 1965 by President Lyndon B. Johnson.

(6) Justice was delayed for these 4 little Black girls and their families until 2002, 39 years after the bombing, when the last of the 4 Klansmen responsible for the bombing was charged and convicted of the crime.

(7) The 4 little Black girls are emblematic of so many who have lost their lives for the cause of freedom and equality, including Virgil Ware and James Johnny Robinson who were children also killed within hours of the 1963 church bombing.

(8) The legacy that these 4 little Black girls left will live on in the minds and hearts of us all for generations to come.

(9) Their extraordinary sacrifice sparked real and lasting change as Congress began to aggressively pass legislation that ensured equality.

(10) Sixteenth Street Baptist Church remains a powerful symbol of the movement for civil and human rights and will host the 50th anniversary ceremony on Sunday, September 15, 2013.

(11) It is befitting that Congress bestow the highest civilian honor, the Congressional Gold Medal, in 2013 to the 4 little

H.R.360—2

Black girls, Addie Mae Collins, Denise McNair, Carole Robertson, and Cynthia Wesley, posthumously in recognition of the 50th commemoration of the historical significance of the bombing of the Sixteenth Street Baptist Church.

SEC. 2. CONGRESSIONAL GOLD MEDAL.

(a) PRESENTATION AUTHORIZED.—The Speaker of the House of Representatives and the President Pro Tempore of the Senate shall make appropriate arrangements for the presentation, on behalf of Congress, of a gold medal of appropriate design to commemorate the lives of Addie Mae Collins, Denise McNair, Carole Robertson, and Cynthia Wesley.

(b) DESIGN AND STRIKING.—For purposes of the presentation referred to in subsection (a), the Secretary of the Treasury (referred to in this Act as the "Secretary") shall strike a gold medal with suitable emblems, devices, and inscriptions to be determined by the Secretary.

(c) AWARD OF MEDAL.—Following the award of the gold medal described in subsection (a), the medal shall be given to the Birmingham Civil Rights Institute in Birmingham, AL, where it shall be available for display or temporary loan to be displayed elsewhere, as appropriate.

SEC. 3. DUPLICATE MEDALS.

The Secretary may strike and sell duplicates in bronze of the gold medal struck under section 2, at a price sufficient to cover the costs of the medal, including labor, materials, dies, use of machinery, and overhead expenses, and amounts received from the sale of such duplicates shall be deposited in the United States Mint Public Enterprise Fund.

SEC. 4. STATUS OF MEDALS.

(a) NATIONAL MEDALS.—The medals struck under this Act are national medals for purposes of chapter 51 of title 31, United States Code.

(b) NUMISMATIC ITEMS.—For purposes of sections 5134 and 5136 of title 31, United States Code, all medals struck under this Act shall be considered to be numismatic items. Speaker of the House of Representatives.

Vice President of the United States and President of the Senate.

CONGRESSWOMAN TERRI A. SEWELL

September 19, 2013

Mrs. Sarah Collins-Rudolph

Sarah

Mrs. Collins-Rudolph:

Thank you for the grace, dignity and pride you showed during the 50th Commemoration events. From the Congressional Gold Medal presentation at the U.S. Capitol to your special presence on Sunday at 16th treet Baptist Church for the 50th Anniversary, the quiet dignity and peaceful spirit of you and your family was an inspiration to all.

Please know that I was honored to sponsor the Congressional Gold Medal bill and that I will carry the legacy of the Four Little Girls in my heart forever.

Enclosed please find a photo of the Gold Medal presentation with Members of the Congressional Black Caucus during the Birmingham program at 16th Street Baptist Church. While I know that a Gold Medal can never replace the lives lost or the injuries suffered, I hope your family will accept this highest civilian honor in the spirit it was offered from a nation humbled by your sacrifice and grateful for the progress made because of such sacrifices. Please know that Addie Mae will live on in the hearts and minds of the American people.

All the best,

Terri Sewell

TERRI A. SEWELL
Member of Congress

Mrs. Sarah Collins Rudolph
619 Tomahawk Circle
Birmingham, AL 35214
sarahcollinsrudolp@att.net

October 7, 2014

President Barak Obama
The White House
1600 Pennsylvania Avenue NW
Washington, D.C. 20500

Dear Mr. President:

I hope you are having a blessed day. My name is Sarah Collins Rudolph. I was in the ladies' room along with my sister Addie and friends Denise, Carole, and Cynthia when a bomb exploded on Sunday, September 15th, 1963 at the 16th Street Baptist Church in Birmingham, Alabama. They all died instantly. I still miss them very much.

First of all, I want to express my appreciation to you for signing the bill to present the Congressional Gold Medal posthumously to my dear sister and friends. I would like to thank you Mr. President and the members of Congress for giving them the highest honor. I regret that I wasn't able to be a part of that special occasion. At the time I was still working to draw attention to the life-sustaining injuries that I've been suffering from since 1963. My mother was promised restitution or compensation for the family's losses and my serious injuries. She died waiting.

Mr. President, I was twelve years old when I was hurt in the bombing. My body was showered with glass and debris. The doctors were able to save my left eye but had to remove my right eye in February of 1964. Life hasn't been easy since then but I thank God for saving me, injuries and all. I want to share something else with you.

When Addie was first buried, my family wasn't able to purchase a headstone. Years later a tombstone was donated in Addie's honor, describing her as a civil rights martyr. Well over a decade ago, my family decided to remove Addie remains. We wanted to move her to a mausoleum because the cemetery where she was buried was not kept up regularly. When the body was exhumed, we found out that it wasn't Addie's remains; our sister didn't wear dentures. We later reached out to the funeral home and the city of Birmingham for a legal explanation. The funeral home was at a lost since the record of where Addie was buried was destroyed. It was probably burned. The funeral home kept its records in a building next to it, however that building caught on fire some time ago. No one can tell us where Addie's body was moved. After the recent memorial service for the four girls, I explained this fact again (See article). We've also pointed out this travesty to people in different branches of government.

I realize that you are hard at work, Mr. President. Still, my family would be grateful if your administration could help to address this grave misdeed regarding Addie. It would give us a sense of closure, easing heavy hearts.

Sincerely, Sarah J. Rudolph

Sarah Collins Rudolph

Cc: Eric Holder, United States Attorney General

Unforgettable
It's amazing that in the quest and bragging on good sight, that even at times heroes can be overlooked. When all of the smoke cleared behind the bombing of the 16th Street Baptist Church, four little Girls were honorably recognized for their sacrifice and inspiration, but one though seared lay for years in cold and dark shadows. After suffering great physical loss, the emotional damage from racist act paled sometimes in comparison to the minimizing of pain from her own. After years that seemed to be lost in the weeping of the night, only one God could assure the very restoration of joyous years lost.
And I will restore to you the years that the locust hath eaten, the cankerworm, and the caterpiller, and the palmerworm, my great army which I sent among you. And ye shall eat in plenty, and be satisfied, and praise the name of the Lord your God, that hath dealt wondrously with you: and my people shall never be ashamed. (Joel 2:25, 26 KJV)
The God who simply and categorically can't lie declares that after our years of reproach and abandon, there shall be jubilee. From the depths of my heart as Artist of "Through Many Dangers" and owner and CEO of Anointed Homes Art, I now dedicate the project in the honor of Mrs. Sarah Collins Rudolph. Our living Rosa Parks. Our Lazarus whom Christ himself has pulled from the sting of death, to be a living testimony of His power and the very strength and undying perseverance of the Movement. I'm honored to know you Sarah and Blessed beyond measure as I prepare to Preach, Teach, Testify and tell my Kids and

SARAH COLLINS RILEY

The witness called on behalf of the State, after first having been duly sworn to speak the truth, the whole truth, and nothing but the truth, took the witness stand and was examined and testified as follows:

DIRECT EXAMINATION

BY MR. YUNG:

Q State your full name, please.

A Sarah Collins Riley.

Q Are you married?

A Yes.

Q Was your name Sarah Collins Riley prior to your marriage?

A Yes.

Q How long have you lived in Birmingham, Mrs. Riley?

A Twenty-six years.

Q Is that all your life?

A Yes.

Q Were you living in Birmingham on September 15, 1963?

A Yes.

Q I will ask you whether or not you were a member of the Sixteenth Street Baptist Church, here in Birmingham, on that date?

CIRCUIT-169

-91-

* Alabama, Tenth Judicial Circuit Court, State of Alabama vs. Robert E. Chambliss Trial Transcript, 1977, Birmingham Public Library, Department of Archives and Manuscripts (Sarah Collins Riley's testimony).

A Yes, I was.

Q On September 15, 1963, I will ask you whether or not you went to the Sixteenth Street Baptist Church?

A Yes, I went to the Sixteenth Street Baptist Church.

Q Did you go with your family?

A Yes, I did.

Q Did that include your sister, Addie Mae Collins?

A Yes.

Q What time, if you recall, approximately, did you get to the church?

A I can't recall exactly the time, but I know it was something about 10:00.

Q Did you go to Sunday school that morning?

A Yes.

Q I will ask you if you remember where you were at 10:15 to 10:30 a.m., inside the Sixteenth Street Baptist Church?

A I was in the ladies' lounge at that time.

Q Where was that located in the church?
Upstairs, or downstairs?

A It was downstairs, in the basement of the church.

Q How old were you at that time?

A Ten years old.

Q Ten years old?

A Yes.

CIRCUIT-169

-92-

Q You say you were in the ladies' lounge, down in the basement?

A Yes.

Q Was anyone else in there with you?

A Yes, there was.

Q Who was in there, if you recall?

A It was Cynthia Wesley, Denise McNair, Carole Robertson, and my sister, Addie Collins.

Q And yourself?

A Yes.

Q Was anybody else in that particular room at that time?

A No.

Q I will ask you if you recall whether anything happened at about 10:21, or 10:22, a.m. that morning, while you were in the ladies' lounge?

A Yes, it did.

Q What was it?

A It was a bomb.

MR. HANES, JR.: We are going to object to the use of the word "bomb," Judge, and move to exclude it.

THE COURT: Well, I sustain the objection. Of course, it does call for a conclusion of the witness, and I exclude and instruct the jury not to consider that statement of the witness.

CIRCUIT-169

-93-

Q Well, if you would, just tell the jury what happened, without saying what caused it to happen.

THE COURT: Was there an explosion?

A Yes, there was.

Q Do you recall exactly what you were doing at the time that the explosion occurred?

A Yes, I can. I was over to the wash bowl at the time.

Q Washing your hands?

A Yes.

Q Do you know where the other four girls, that you have named, including your sister, were at the time?

A Yes. They were standing over by the window.

Q Did you see your sister immediately prior to the explosion?

A No.

Q Did you see Denise McNair?

A No, I didn't.

Q What were they doing the last time you saw them before the explosion?

A They were standing up around, talking.

Q Were all four of the girls together?

A Yes, they were.

Q What, if anything, was your sister doing?

A My sister was tying Denise McNair's sash on

CIRCUIT-169

-94-

her dress.

Q Your sister was tightening the sash on Denise McNair's dress?

A Yes.

Q Is that the last time you have ever saw your sister?

A Yes.

Q Have you ever seen Denise McNair since that time?

A No, I haven't.

Q Have you ever seen Cynthia?

A No.

Q Have you ever seen Carol?

A No.

Q Tell the jury, if you would, what you remember happening after the explosion.

A Right after the explosion, I called my sister.

Q What did you say?

A I said -- I called about three times -- I said, "Addie, Addie, Addie."

Q Did Addie answer you?

A No, she didn't.

Q What happened after that, if you recall?

A Then I heard somebody calling out. They said that somebody had bombed the church.

MR. HANES, JR.: Your Honor, we are going to object to what somebody said.

CIRCUIT-169

-95-

It's hearsay, and we move to exclude the answer.

THE COURT: Overrule.

Q What did you hear?

A I heard a voice.

MR. HANES, JR.: Your Honor, we are going to object to the voice she heard. It's hearsay.

THE COURT: How long was this after you heard the explosion?

A Right after.

THE COURT: Overrule.

Q You may answer.

A Right after.

THE COURT: All right, you may answer.

Q What did you hear?

A I heard somebody say that they had -- somebody had bombed the church.

Q What happened after that point, if you recall?

A Well, then someone come in and brought me outside.

Q Were you taken to the hospital?

A Yes.

Q Could you see at that time?

A No.

Q Could you see any?

A No.

Q How long was it after that before you were able

CIRCUIT-160

-96-

to see anything, if you remember?

A It was about a month.

Q About a month later?

A Yes.

Q Could you see out of both eyes after about a month had passed?

MR. HANES, JR.: Your Honor, we are going to object to the specificity of the injuries herein.

This young lady is not on trial.

Furthermore, Mr. Yung is leading the witness.

THE COURT: Overrule. You may answer.

Q I will ask you whether or not, after a month, you were able to see out of both eyes.

A No.

Q Could you see out of one eye?

A Just one.

Q Which one?

A My left.

Q What about your right eye?

A No.

Q Do you still have your right eye?

A No.

Q What, if anything, was done to it as a result of that explosion?

CIRCUIT-169

-97-

A I can't see.

MR. HANES, JR.: Same objection.

THE COURT: Overrule. You may answer.

A They had to take it out.

Q Take it out?

A Yes.

Q You have a glass eye now, on the right side?

A Yes.

Q As a result of that explosion?

A Yes.

Q I will ask you whether or not the glasses you are wearing are prescription glasses that the doctor gave you?

A Yes, they are prescribed.

MR. YUNG: I think that's all, Your Honor.

MR. HANES, JR.: We have no questions.

THE COURT: No questions?

MR. HANES, JR.: No, sir.

THE COURT: All right, you may go back out to the witness room.

(WITNESS EXCUSED)

THE COURT: Who will you have?

MR. YUNG: State calls Captain W. E. Berry.

WILLIAM E. BERRY

The witness called on behalf of the State,

CIRCUIT-169

-98-

*Sarah Collins Rudolph Testimony at Blanton Trial in 2001 in the state of Alabama. (Courtesy of Sarah Collins Rudolph)

Sunday morning before she left for Sunday school and church?
A On her way before she left? Yes.
Q And after she left or you left, did you ever see your daughter alive again?
A No.
MR. JONES: That's all we have, Your Honor.
MR. ROBBINS: I don't have any. No questions, Your Honor.
THE COURT: All right. You may step down, sir.
MR. MCNAIR: Thank you.
(Witness excused.)
THE COURT: Next witness.
MR. JONES: Sarah Collins Rudolph.

SARAH COLLINS RUDOLPH,

having been duly sworn, was examined and testified as follows:

DIRECT EXAMINATION

BY MR. JONES:

Q Would you state your full name, please, ma'am?
A Sarah Rudolph.
Q And what is your maiden name, Ms. Rudolph?
A Sarah Collins.
Q You live in Birmingham, Alabama?
A Yes.
Q And have you lived in Birmingham, Alabama all your life?
A Yes.

Julie W. Carter
505 Criminal Justice Center
Birmingham, Alabama 35263
(205) 325-5277

2

Q Were you living in Birmingham in September of 1963?
A Yes.
Q Where did you live?
A On 6th Court West.
Q Did you live there with your mom and dad?
A Yes.
Q And did you have any sisters?
A Yes, I had some sisters.
Q Who were your sisters?
A Juni, Janie, Flora, Addie and I had another sister named Addie Bea.
Q You had an Addie Mae that was a sister and an Addie Bea. that was a sister?
A Yes.
Q Were you a member of a church in September of 1963?
A Yes.
Q Which church was that?
A 16th Street Baptist Church.
Q Do you remember Sunday morning, September 15th, 1963?
A Yes, I do.
Q Did you and your sisters go to church that day?
A Yes, we did.
Q Who did you go with?
A Addie and Janie.
Q All right. And did you walk or ride?

A We walked to church.
Q When you say Addie, Addie Mae?
A Yes.
Q And how old were you at the time?
A I was twelve.
Q All right. And Addie Mae was just a little bit older than you?
A Yes, she was.
Q And when you got to the 16th Street Baptist Church, what did you do?
A When we got to church that morning Janie, she went to her class and me and Addie went down to our class downstairs. Janie's class was upstairs.
Q And did you go down into the basement of the church?
A Yes.
Q Who all was down there?
A When we got down to the basement wasn't nobody down there but Addie and I.
Q Did anyone else come down?
A Yes.
Q Who else came down?
A Carol Robertson, Denise McNair and Cynthia Wesley.
Q All right. Did you know them?
A Yes.
Q While you were in that downstairs area, did anything

happen?
A Yes.
Q What happened?
A There was a loud explosion.
Q Debris come crashing in?
A Yes, it did.
Q And were you injured in that explosion?
A Yes, I was.
Q And what injuries did you sustain?
A I had glass that cut my face. And I had glass to get in both of my eyes and I was blind in both eyes at that time.
Q Okay. Did you have to go to the hospital?
A Yes, I did.
Q Ms. Ruldolph, let me show you a picture of State's Exhibit 52. Is that a picture of you?
A Yes.
Q In the hospital?
A Yes.
Q Do you know how long you were in the hospital?
A Yes, sir. I was in the hospital about two months.
Q And you have patches over your eyes there. Was that as a result of injuries sustained in that explosion?
A Yes.
Q That morning just prior to the explosion, what were you doing?

Julie W. Carter
505 Criminal Justice Center
Birmingham, Alabama 35263
(205) 325-5277

A That morning we were downstairs and I was over -- first I was looking out the door, and then I went over to the sink.
Q Did you see any of other girls, what they were doing?
A Yes. When they came to the lounge that morning, they came straight through the lounge and went on the other side to the restroom.
Q And did you see them doing anything over there?
A Well, after they came out the restroom they passed my sister. She was standing there by the couch. The girls over by the window. So when the girls passed my sister, Denise asked my sister to tie her sash.
Q Did you see her tying the sash?
A Yes. I looked toward that way when she started tying her sash.
Q And then did you look away toward the sink?
A Yes. When I looked toward them and all of a sudden I heard this loud explosion.
Q And that's when the debris came crashing down?
A Yes.
Q That's when you were injured?
A Yes.
Q Did you call out for your sister?
A Yes, I did.
Q Could you see anything at that time?
A No.

Q What did you say?
A I called out to my sister. I said Addie, Addie, Addie.
Q Did she answer you?
A No, she didn't.
Q Did you ever see your sister alive again?
A No. I didn't see her again.

MR. JONES: No further questions, Your Honor.

MR. ROBBINS: We don't have anything, Your Honor.

THE COURT: All right. You may step down.

(Witness excused.)

The Cincinnati HERALD®

AWARD-WINNING NEWSPAPER A SESH COMMUNICATIONS PUBLICATION

Oct.12, 2013 - Oct. 18, 2013 75 ¢

www.TheCincinnatiHerald.com · Follow us on Twitter @CinciHerald · Like us on Facebook at The Cincinnati Herald

Former mayors head Cranley campaign

John Cranley's mayoral campaign announced that former Mayor Dwight Tillery has joined former Mayor Charlie Luken as campaign co-chair. Tillery and Luken will provide strategic advice and appear at events on behalf of the campaign when needed. Tillery said: "I support John Cranley because he has a fresh vision for our city."

Cranley said: "I am honored to have two former mayors serving as co-chairs of my campaign. This reflects the manner in which I intend to unite the city."

John Cranley

City trash changes now in effect

Citywide changes went into effect Oct.7, for both residential and commercial waste collection.

Residents are now required to place all household trash in the City provided trash cart for collection. No additional bags or trashcans will be collected.

These changes will allow for a semi-automated operation, which means City workers won't manually lift and dump trash anymore. Instead, they will roll the carts to the truck. They will hook the cart's lift bar onto the trucks mechanical arm, which does the heavy lifting. This method will protect worker's health, improve the cleanliness of neighborhoods, and save taxpayer money by reducing worker injuries.

Commercial waste

The City will no longer collect trash from commercial buildings, mixed-use buildings or buildings with five or more residential units. Owners of these properties are responsible for contracting with a registered commercial waste hauler for their trash collection.

If they have not already done so, commercial property owners can visit www.cincinnati-oh.gov/trash to find a registered commercial waste hauler.

Residential cart delivery

While most of the carts have been delivered, the final aspect of the deployment includes correcting any missed deliveries and delivering smaller or larger carts for residents who have made requests. The City will continue working with these residents on an individual basis until the remaining carts have been delivered. Residents who have not yet received their cart are being encouraged to use their old cans until their new one arrives, and then begin using their new cart as soon as it is delivered.

Residents who have already received a cart should use the cart correctly using the new requirements. Residential changes include the following requirements to:

- Put all household trash in the City provided cart
- Fully close the lid of the cart
- Place trash at the curb by 6 a.m. on the scheduled collection day

Trash amnesty days for residential collections

On residential collection amnesty days, residents will be permitted to set out additional trash in sealed plastic trash bags next to their approved City provided container. Amnesty weeks are centered around holidays when households typically generate more trash than normal. Upcoming amnesty days include:

- Thanksgiving Nov. 30, 2013 to Dec. 6, 2013
- Winter Holidays Dec. 26, 2013 to Jan. 3, 2014
- Memorial Day May 27, 2014 to May 31, 2014
- Independence Day July 5, 2014 to July 11, 2014
- Labor Day Sept. 2, 2014 to Sept. 6, 2014

Recycling

With the new trash changes, residents can save space in their trash cart and help the community by recycling! Many of the items tossed in trash carts can be recycled which can significantly reduce the amount of trash thrown away each week. Residents should continue to fill their recycling carts with acceptable items on their recycling collection week and can have more than one recycling cart.

A recycling pickup schedule

See City trash on page A6

Two Cincinnatins enter Ohio Civil Rights Hall of Fame

Cincinnati human rights activist Robert Lee Harris receives a plaque from Leonard Hubert, chair of the Ohio Civil Rights Commission, signifying her induction into the 2013 Ohio Civil Rights Hall of Fame during a ceremony at the Ohio Statehouse in Columbus on Oct. 3.

Former publisher of The Cincinnati Herald Marjorie Parham receives a plaque from Leonard Hubert, chair of the Ohio Civil Rights Commission, signifying her induction into the 2013 Ohio Civil Rights Hall of Fame during a ceremony at the Ohio Statehouse in Columbus on Oct. 3.

See Ohio Civil Rights Hall of Fame on page A5

Cincinnati embraces 1963 church bombing survivor

The fifth little girl

Sarah Collins recovers from injuries sustained from the bombing at her church in 1963. Photo provided

By Dan Yount
The Cincinnati Herald

Sarah Collins Rudolph, the survivor of the 1963 bombing at the16th Street Baptist Church in Birmingham, Ala., stands in front of a painting titled "Four Little Girls" by Cincinnati artist Trelan Jones. The painting, now on exhibit at the Cincinnati YWCA Art Gallery Downtown, was inspired by the incident, which killed four girls, Jones said. At left is Charlene Ventura, president and CEO of the local YWCA. At right is Scott Kadish, Esq., who with law firm associate and Cincinnati Councilwoman Yvette Simpson, has established a Website - www.sarahcollinsproject.com - to raise funds to assist Mrs. Rudolph with continuing medical bills and to help her retire. Mrs. Rudolph was guest of honor at a YWCA Civil Rights Movement art exhibit opening. Photos by Dan Yount

Five young girls were in the basement of the 16th Street Baptist Church in Birmingham, Ala., when a bomb planted by the Ku Klux Klan exploded on Sunday, Sept. 15, 1963.

The world remembered the four little innocent girls - Addie Mae Collins, Cynthia Wesley, Denise McNair, and Carole Robertson - who were murdered in the basement women's lounge of that Church 50 years ago in the racially charged city of Birmingham.

The explosion marked a turning point in the Civil Right Movement of the 1960s and contributed to the support and passage of the Civil Rights Act of 1964.

The title of the sermon to be preached on that terrible Sunday morning was "A Love that Forgives." It was not "A Love that Forgets," and yet that is what the city of Birmingham did for 50 years in regard to a fifth girl in that church lounge that morning who survived the dynamite blast, although she was terribly injured and disfigured by its effects. Her name is Sarah Collins; she was 12 years old and youngest in a family of eight children at the time. Even 50 years later, she is rarely mentioned along with the four little girls who died, one of whom was her own sister, Addie Mae. Sarah in time recovered from her injuries, went back to school without counseling or acknowledgment, and was scrubbed from the

See The fifth little girl on page A5

"The Fifth Little Girl": Birmingham Church Bombing Survivor Still Seeks Compensation 50 Years On. SEPTEMBER 17, 2013
STORY
GUEST: *Sarah C. Rudolph survived the bombing of the Baptist Church in Birmingham, Alabama, on September 15, 1963, which killed four young girls. She was 12 years old. She was hit with shards of glass, lost an eye and was hospitalized for months. Her older sister Addie Mae Collins, 14, died in the blast.*
ADAM GOLDMAN
Pulitzer Prize-winning journalist at the Associated Press. He covered the trial of Thomas Blanton, the last surviving Klansman convicted in the church bombing.

Fifty years ago this week, four young girls — Denise McNair, Carole Robertson, Cynthia Wesley and Addie Mae Collins — were killed when the Ku Klux Klan bombed the 16th Street Baptist Church in Birmingham, Alabama. The bombing came less than a month after the landmark March on Washington for Jobs and Freedom. Hundreds gathered in the nation's capital last week to honor their memory when lawmakers posthumously awarded the girls the Congressional Gold Medal. We're joined by Addie Mae's sister, Sarah Collins Rudolph, who is often referred to as the bombing's "fifth victim." Just 12 years old when the church was attacked, Collins Rudolph was hit with shards of glass, lost an eye and was hospitalized for months. Today, she continues to live in Birmingham, suffering from the physical, mental and emotional effects of the bombing….

TRANSCRIPT

AMY GOODMAN: "Birmingham Sunday," sung by Joan Baez. You can go to our website to see Monday's segment featuring Angela Davis speaking about the Birmingham church bombing. She grew up near Birmingham and knew two of the little girls who were killed. We also have an in-depth page that features all of our recent interviews about the civil rights movement in the pivotal year of 1963.This is *Democracy Now!*, democracynow.org, *The War and Peace Report*. I'm Amy Goodman, with Aaron Maté.

AARON MATÉ: Well, Denise McNair, Carole Robertson, Cynthia Wesley and Addie Mae Collins, those are the names of the four young girls who were killed 50 years ago this week, September 15th, 1963, when the Ku Klux Klan bombed the 16th Street Baptist Church in

Birmingham, Alabama. The bombing came less than a month after the March on Washington. Denise was 11 years old. Carole, Cynthia and Addie Mae were all 14. Hundreds gathered in the nation's capital last week to honor their memory, when lawmakers awarded the girls the Congressional Gold Medal.

AMY GOODMAN: Well, today our guest is a woman who is often referred to as the fifth victim of the bombing. Sarah Collins Rudolph was 12 years old when the church was attacked. She was standing next to her sister, Addie Mae Collins. Sarah Collins Rudolph was hit with shards of glass, lost an eye, was hospitalized for months. Today she continues to live in Birmingham, Alabama, where she joins us now.

It's such an honor to have you with us today, Sarah Collins Rudolph. Can you talk about that day 50 years ago, where you were when the dynamite exploded?

SARAH COLLINS RUDOLPH: Yes. I was in the ladies' lounge when the bomb went off. You know, I remember Cynthia, Denise and Carole walking inside the lounge area and went in where the stalls was. So when they came out, Denise passed by Addie and asked my sister to tie the sash on her dress. And I was across from them at the sink. And when Denise asked her to tie the sash, and I was looking at her when she began to tie it, and then all of a sudden, boom! I never did see her finish it, finish tying it. So, all I could do was say, call out, "Jesus!" because I didn't know what that loud sound was. And then I called my sister, "Addie! Addie! Addie!" And she didn't answer me. So, I thought that they had—the girls had ran on the other side of the church where the Sunday school area was.

But all of a sudden I heard a voice outside saying, "Somebody bombed the 16th Street church!" And it was so clear to me, as though that this person was right there, but they was outside where the crater was, a bomb in the church—where it bombed the hole there. And all the debris came rushing in, and I was hit in my face with glass and also in my—both eyes. Well, when the man came in—his name's Samuel Rutledge—he came in and picked me up and carried me out of the crater, and the ambulance was out there waiting. And they rushed me to Hillman Hospital, which they changed the name. It's now UAB Hospital.

And while I was there, my sister came in, Janie. She came in, and I asked her where was Addie. And she said that Addie had hurt her back, but she would be here tomorrow to see me. So they rushed me on up to the operating room, and they operated on both of my eyes and took the glass from out of my face. And I had glass in my chest and stomach. So they operated on me. And when I went back to the room—and I stayed there in the hospital for about two-and-a-half months. But at that time, when they took the bandages off my eyes, the doctor asked me what do I see out of my right eye. I told him I couldn't see anything out of my right eye. And when he took it off my left eye, all I could see was just a little light.

AMY GOODMAN: I'm so glad that you were able to join us today. We wanted you over the past few days, but you work as a maid in Birmingham, and this is your day off. Can we talk about compensation? Did you ever receive compensation for what happened to you?

SARAH COLLINS RUDOLPH: No, I haven't received anything yet. I don't know why, but I have been seeking for compensation for years, and—but I never did get anything. And looked like the people just looked over me. They didn't realize that being in a bomb at the age of 12, I lost a lot of things, you know, concerning my health, you know. And also I wanted to be a nurse, but by having post-traumatic stress syndrome, that never did happen, because that bomb just really changed my whole life. And I had to work as being a maid simply because I wasn't as smart as I were, because at first, before the bomb, I was an A student, but after the bomb, I just couldn't think like that anymore.

AMY GOODMAN: And, of course, you lost your sister, as well, Addie Mae Collins, your older sister. You were 12. She was 14. Did you feel you could not find a safe place? I mean, after all, you were bombed in a church, the place you went for sanctuary.

SARAH COLLINS RUDOLPH: Yes, you would think that going to church is really a safe place, but it wasn't. You know, somebody that would put a bomb in a church and kill four innocent girls, you know, that's just the work of the devil, because that shouldn't never have happened. These girls was young, and we was waiting that day for a youth service. But by the bomb going off, we didn't get a chance to attend youth service.

AARON MATÉ: And, Ms. Rudolph, how does it feel when you hear that people say that this bombing helped set off the civil rights movement?

SARAH COLLINS RUDOLPH: You know, I've—yes, I've been hearing that for a long time, but for people to just get peace from four girls getting killed, that should never be. You know, we should always just love each other anyway, because we're all human being, and God made us all. And by them getting killed, that was just something awful. You know, I think about it all the time, that we should have peace. We should love one another, because we shouldn't be prejudiced and violent like that to place a bomb in a church simply because of people's race.

AMY GOODMAN: Sarah Collins Rudolph, we're also joined by Adam Goldman. We were just talking to him about the New York Police Department. But, Adam, before you were at AP, you were at *Birmingham News*. We only have a minute. Talk about who did this and your correspondence with the killer.

ADAM GOLDMAN: Right, so when I was a reporter there for the *Birmingham News*, I covered the trial of Thomas Blanton Jr. He was one of three people who were convicted of carrying out this horrific bombing. Thomas Blanton is the only surviving bomber. The other two guys, Bobby Cherry and an individual named Chambliss, they're dead. And Blanton was put away in prison. He got a life sentence. And I've been corresponding with him, trading letters with Blanton. And he's unrepentant and 'til to this day says he didn't have anything to do with this bombing.

AMY GOODMAN: Sarah Collins Rudolph, you almost refused the Congressional Gold Medal. Why?

SARAH COLLINS RUDOLPH: You know, during that time, I really didn't even know they had offered me a gold medal, until last week. Somebody was telling me about—it was in the *USA*. And I said, "No." I said, "I never did see that article about they was going to present me with a bomb—I mean, with a medal." I thought that just my sister and the other girls were going to get the medal. Well, why I said—the reason why I said—

AMY GOODMAN: Well, I have to leave it there, but we'll continue this conversation after the show. I want to thank you so much for being with us, Sarah Collins Rudolph.

"A Stain on the Legacy of Birmingham": 1963 Church Bombing Survivor Struggles to Pay Medical Bills

"A Stain on the Legacy of Birmingham": 1963 Church Bombing Survivor Struggles to Pay Medical Bills

SEPTEMBER 17, 2013

GUESTS

SARAH COLLINS RUDOLPH

survived the bombing of the 16th Street Baptist Church in Birmingham, Alabama, on September 15, 1963, which killed four young girls.

ADAM GOLDMAN

Pulitzer Prize-winning journalist at the Associated Press. He covered the trial of Thomas Blanton, the last surviving Klansman convicted in the church bombing.

Part two of our conversation with Sarah Collins Rudolph, who is often referred to as the "fifth victim" of the Sept. 15, 1963, bombing of the 16th Street Baptist Church in Birmingham, Alabama. Rudolph's sister, Addie Mae Collins, was killed along with three other young girls. Collins Rudolph was hit with shards of glass, lost an eye and was hospitalized for months. She is struggling to pay her medical bills. We also speak with Adam Goldman of the Associated Press who covered the trial of Thomas Blanton, the last surviving Klansman convicted in the church bombing. Click here to watch Part 1 of this interview.

AMY GOODMAN: This is *Democracy Now!* democracynow.org, *The War and Peace Report.* I'm Amy Goodman, with Aaron Maté. Denise McNair, Carole Robertson, Cynthia Wesley and Addie Mae Collins, those were the names of the four little girls who were killed 50 years ago this week, September 15th, 1963, when the Ku Klux Klan bombed the 16th Street Baptist Church in Birmingham, Alabama. The bombing came less than a month after the 1963 March on Washington for Jobs and Freedom. Denise was 11 years old; Carole, Cynthia and Addie Mae, 14. Hundreds gathered in the nation's capital last week to honor their memory when lawmakers posthumously awarded the girls the Congressional Gold Medal.

Well, today our guest is a woman who is often referred to as the "fifth victim" of the bombing, Sarah Collins Rudolph. She was 12 when the church was attacked, standing next to her older sister, who was 14, Addie Mae Collins. Sarah Collins Rudolph was hit with shards of glass, lost and eye, was hospitalized for months. Today she continues to live in Birmingham, Alabama, where she joins us now.

We're also joined by Adam Goldman. He's the Associated Press Pulitzer Prize-winning reporter, whose new book is just out, called

Enemies Within: Inside the NYPD's Secret Spying Unit and Bin Laden's Final Plot Against America. But that's not why he's here. He's here because before he was at AP, he worked for the *Birmingham News*, and to this day he continues to correspond with one of those who were convicted of the Klan bombing of the 16th Street Baptist Church. As we go from talking about terrorism and 9/11, we're talking about another kind of terrorism, 50 years ago: innocent people killed by a bomb that was planted in a church on a Sunday morning.

Adam Goldman, if you could start by explaining what actually is understood about what happened on that morning, September 15, 1963?

ADAM GOLDMAN: Well, there are a group of Klansmen who plotted this bombing in Birmingham. At the time, in 1963, Birmingham was going through a wave of bombings. In fact, its nickname was "Bombingham." And these individuals got together, and they built this bomb. And at about—authorities suspect that at about 2:00 a.m., they put the bomb at the side of the church. And Thomas Blanton, one of the bombers who was convicted, his car was seen at the church and—driving the car, and he drove away, and the bomb went off. There is some speculation that the bomb was supposed to go off while the church was empty, and it wasn't, in fact, meant to go off while it was filled with people. But regardless, it did go off, and people were killed, and they were held responsible for that.

The case went unsolved for many, many years until this individual named Chambliss was eventually convicted in state court, and he was put away for life, and he died. And then, later, I believe in 1996, 1997, the FBI reopened this investigation. In fact, right at the time as Spike Lee was beginning this documentary, the FBI reopened this investigation. I know that because I got the FBI's investigative files; I FOIAed them. And they worked to solve this—they worked to solve this horrific crime and eventually zeroed in on the two surviving bombers: this guy named Bobby Cherry and Thomas Blanton. And they initially were going to squeeze Cherry to rat out Blanton, but these two old Klansmen weren't going to tell anybody. It had been so long, they weren't going to spill the beans about what happened.

And eventually the FBI found recordings sitting on a shelf in the Birmingham's field office, recordings of an informant they put in a car with Thomas Blanton talking about the bombing. And they managed to get the recordings digitally enhanced, and they used that, along with the testimony of the informant, to convict Blanton. And eventually Cherry was convicted, too. Cherry—they both were sentenced to life in prison, and then Cherry later died.

So, for years and years, I've been writing Blanton letters. He only recently responded to me. And I've been learning a little bit more about his life and who he was and—

AMY GOODMAN: Where is he imprisoned?

ADAM GOLDMAN: He is in St. Clair County, Alabama, in a place called Springville, in a little town called Springville. And in these letters, he expresses some—some regret that four little girls had died, that there was a loss of life. But he is insistent that he didn't carry this out and in fact he's innocent. So—

AMY GOODMAN: And yet, you say he is unrepentant.

ADAM GOLDMAN: Yeah, he is unrepentant.

AMY GOODMAN: What does that mean?

ADAM GOLDMAN: Well, despite all the evidence, despite all the indications that he did this—and this was actually ferreted out in court, and he was convicted—that he refuses to acknowledge his role in this. And, you know, I thought about why—why would you—why wouldn't you just come clean? Why wouldn't you just tell the story? Because what's fascinating about the 16th Street bombing is we still don't know really what happened. We have an idea of what happened. You know, we think some guys, some Klansmen, built a bomb, they put it in a car, and they put it next to the church, right? And the bomb went off. But nobody who participated in that event has ever told the true story of what happened. And Blanton is the last individual alive who can tell us why they did it, how they did it, when they did it, and did, in fact, that they mean to kill—did, in fact—was their intention to blow up that church.

AMY GOODMAN: Sarah Collins Rudolph, you're with us from Birmingham, Alabama. You are a survivor of that church bombing, when you were 12 years old. Your sister, Addie Mae Collins, died at the age of 14. You were with her. You lost your eye. Can you describe your other injuries? What else happened to you? And also what Birmingham was like? As Adam was saying, people described it as "Bombingham."

SARAH COLLINS RUDOLPH: Yes, I had had injury in my left eye. I have had glaucoma for years, where I have to take pills—I mean, pills and also drops in my eyes every day. But last June, they operated on it and put an incision in my eye to drain the fluid, because my pressure had been up for a long time.

And also, yes, Birmingham was—it was a way of life back then. We would hear bombs going off, and we would see the police beating blacks with billy sticks and water hose. And it was just a terrorist place, really, to live in. But we stayed. We wanted to leave, but we just didn't have the money to do it, to go. So, things are a little better now. So, we're still here in Birmingham.

AARON MATÉ: You went to the Birmingham City Council last year for help. Your husband asked for help in covering your medical bills. What was their response?

SARAH COLLINS RUDOLPH: At first they said, "Go to the county." See, we stay in the county part of Birmingham. "Go to the county, because they don't do things like that here in the city." But anyway, the City Council people said, "Well, we can help her." They do it all over in other cities. They get funds to help people that's been in a terrorist attack. He said, "We can do it here." But when they offered me something, it wasn't what I had expected, because it was very little, because, you know, during these 50 years I've suffered a lot. And I just wanted to let them know that it was time for restitution, because the city was involved in all this—the fire department, the police department. They was involved in all the terrorist act that was going on in Birmingham, because during that time, we couldn't—we couldn't call the city police and ask for help, because we weren't going to get any help, since they was involved.

AMY GOODMAN: I wanted to ask Adam Goldman—you have just written a book after the September 11th attacks and how the police in New York deal with investigating terrorism, and you're very critical. But I want to go this issue of terrorism. What is defined as terrorism, and what isn't, as a person, yourself, who investigated after September 11th and investigated the 16th Street church bombing in Birmingham 50 years ago?

ADAM GOLDMAN: I mean, this was—what the Ku Klux Klan was doing in Birmingham, this was terrorism. They had a political agenda. They didn't want to see the Jim Crow laws essentially rolled back. They wanted to make sure that blacks remained segregated. And, you know, we forget this, but this was—for the people living in Birmingham, especially for the black community, this was a reign of terror, literally. I mean, there were—I remember in one year, I think it was 1963, I mean, dozens of pipe bombs were set off across the city. I mean, it was a campaign of intimidation. And the blacks living in Birmingham, they couldn't trust the police. They couldn't trust the police. I mean, the police were infiltrating their organizations, the same way that they were doing now in some respects. Then, it was because they were black and because they wanted certain rights. But, you know, the level—there are certain level—there are certain similarities to what we see today in Birmingham then with the Birmingham Police Department and the NYPD today. There is a level of mistrust in the community today, just as there was among minority communities in Birmingham. They couldn't trust the people who were sworn to protect them.

AMY GOODMAN: And then the issue of compensation. I mean, here you have Sarah Collins Rudolph, who lost her sister, who lost her own eye, was deeply injured. The Congress, a delegation goes down and honors the community, the families, with the Congressional Medal of Honor, but in terms of help, for example, for this survivor, Sarah Collins Rudolph, she has not seen it.

ADAM GOLDMAN: No, and that's extraordinary itself, because after the Boston bombing, right, after the Boston bombing that we just went through, the community rallied. I mean, people came together, and they gave these bombing victims—you could go online, and you could pledge. And I was watching it. It was just extraordinary. One couple, you know, within days, they had raised a million dollars. A million dollars, you know? And that's—that's a stain on the legacy of Birmingham, and they know this, that the community didn't come together, everybody didn't come together after this bombing and make sure that, you know, the people who were injured or that were—were taken care of.

AARON MATÉ: Ms. Rudolph, you have been denied compensation. Initially, the Congressional Gold Medal wasn't going to—it didn't include you. Do you feel as if history has forgotten what happened to you?

SARAH COLLINS RUDOLPH: Yes, I feel like they have forgotten, and they wasn't really concerned about what happened to me, because I'm still suffering. I have a piece of glass still in my good eye, and also I have cataracts. And I have a piece of glass still in my stomach, and I suffer from post-traumatic stress disorder, and I've been going through a lot. And just getting up in the morning, I had to go and clean houses just to make money. Like yesterday, I should have been resting, getting some rest from what I went through on the weekend, but I had to go get up at 6:00 and still go to work, when if there was money that was—that had been given to me, I wouldn't have to do this. So, I feel like I have been forgotten, because all of—I know the four girls should get all the praise, because they died, they was killed. But I'm still here suffering. I'm still suffering from that bomb. And post-traumatic stress disorder is something that I've suffered with, and I look like I just can't get over it. And right now, my husband, he would pay for my medical bill because he had insurance at the place that he worked, but he's retired, and I don't have any insurance now. So, I just don't know when my—when my next check-up is going to be in November, I don't know how we're going to pay for it. But I just thank God, though, that I'm alive, because if it had not been for God, I would have, you know, been killed, myself. So I just want to let the people know that I give him all the praise. And I believe one day, one day, it going to come, and God going to do it. The money will come.

AMY GOODMAN: Sarah Collins Rudolph, what is your message to the people who carried out this attack that took your sister from you, that killed four little girls, that wounded you and others, that changed Birmingham, Alabama?

SARAH COLLINS RUDOLPH: My message to the people is that we can all love one another. We don't have to hate one another because of race. We can just get together and have peace in this world, because God [inaudible]—you know, he gave us peace, and we should have peace with one another. It don't hurt, you know. Violence, it hurts, and it leaves you like the bomb left me. I'm not the same anymore. So they just got to realize we can love each other, we can love people all over the world, because we all the human race.

AMY GOODMAN: Has anyone reached out to you from the Birmingham government, or even when the congressional delegation came down—I believe it was the House speaker, John Boehner, who awarded the Congressional Medal—to talk to you about compensation—something we have seen over and over again when these terrorist attacks happen, from the Boston Marathon bombing to 9/11?

SARAH COLLINS RUDOLPH: No, I haven't had anyone to talk to me about any compensation yet, but I'm just hoping, soon, that they will, because it's really overdue. You know, it's 50 years now, and I've suffered. And yet, like I say, people are not concerned. They're not concerned like they ought to, because when they offered me the little money that they did offer, they wanted me to speak four times for it. But I—like I said, I was in a bombing, and why should they set up something to speak four times, when they have known all along that I was injured? And I was badly injured. This wasn't something that—a scratch. I had to have my eyes removed—my right eye removed because of this attack. And it don't—it really don't feel good at all, you being looked over, like they're saying, "Well, you didn't die, so don't expect anything." But I expect something—

AMY GOODMAN: What do you mean you were expected to talk? What do you mean you were expected to talk?

SARAH COLLINS RUDOLPH: They wanted me to speak four times about the bombing, four times, and I was going to get what you call—have somebody to coach me, and I didn't need to be coached. When you go through something like that, it rings in my ears and in my mind all the time. You know, what's next? What's next? 'Cause it was a scary thing, and I still jump when I hear loud sounds. So I'm suffering every day. I had the scars on my face. And also, I try to live, but, you know, living like I live, where I shouldn't have to really just suffer for anything. And people—like the man was saying, people around the world, over there in the marathon bomb, they get—they get moneys for their injury, but I haven't yet had anything, and I suffer every day.

And also, my sister, we can't even find her remains. I don't know where her remains—we wanted to move my sister to a new—another cemetery. But when they exhumed her body, it wasn't there—her there inside the casket. It was somebody with false teeth. And we don't know where Addie's remains today. It seem like people wasn't even concerned about that. So I'm just wondering—I look at Birmingham, and they say they changed, but Birmingham, they got a long way to go.

AMY GOODMAN: Sarah Collins Rudolph, I want to thank you for being with us. Sarah Collins Rudolph did survive the bombing of the 16th Street Baptist Church in Birmingham, Alabama, September 15, 1963, 50 years ago, that killed her older sister, Addie Mae, who was 14 years old, and three other little girls. Sarah Collins Rudolph has been referred to as the fifth little girl. She was hit with shards of glass, lost an eye, was hospitalized for months. This is *Democracy Now.*

Conversations from Penn State
Episode 709: Sarah Collins Rudolph
(See excerpt from Transcript)

>> Satalia: On September 15, 1963, a bomb exploded at the 16th Street Baptist church in Birmingham, Alabama. Five girls were preparing for worship in the basement of the building. Four were killed by the blast, but the fifth girl survived .... We'll talk with her about living in the shadows of that historic tragedy, about delayed justice, and about today's most pressing civil rights struggles. Here's our conversation with Sarah Collins Rudolph. Sarah Collins Rudolph, welcome to the program.

>> Rudolph: Thank you.

>> Satalia: I just watch the critically acclaimed movie "Selma," and I have to say that the scene, which is a little different from what happened in real life, of the girls walking down the steps. Of course, you were actually one of them. When that explosion happened, I literally jumped out of my seat, and so did so many of the people—

>> Rudolph: I did.

>> Satalia: -- sitting around me. I can't imagine what being there must have been like. You saw the movie too.

>> Yes.

>> Rudolph: Well, for one thing, the girls weren't walking down steps. That was one. And when the bomb went off, my husband was with me, and we both almost jumped out of our seats, because I wasn't expecting that on that scene. But it just really scared us, and it took me back to that moment, that sound. And it just really scared both of us.

>> Satalia: This incident, on September 15, 1963, is referred to as a turning point. As having energized the Civil Rights Movement. As having created a consciousness among White Americans that nothing else prior to that could have. And I'm wondering how you feel about that...

>> Rudolph: Well, I know those girls did things to change, but it was just a shame that those young girls had to die like that, because only thing we was trying to get was our rights. And it had to take death to get it?

>> Satalia: And they [the mass meetings] were held in the very church where the bomb exploded?

>> Rudolph: Yes. And we would stay home be ourselves. She [my Mother] would go to the meeting. She was very interested in marching, and she wanted our rights. Birmingham wasn't right. When you're in Birmingham at that time, if we needed a policeman, call the policeman, we couldn't even get a policeman, because they were against us.

>> Satalia: One-third were known to be Klansmen.

>> Rudolph: Yes. And the people in the fire department, they put the water hose on the people.

>> Satalia: If you were to pinpoint what you see as the most pressing civil rights issue of today, what would you say it is?

>> Rudolph: I still see some of the maybe some of the police might be strict. But I really haven't noticed it because they haven't stopped me driving or anything…. Maybe things like that. When we go to our mayor, we try to let him know what happened. People they're not really concerned…. But other than that, Birmingham has...changed.

>> Satalia: The three men who were ultimately convicted of this crime, only one is still living. And he, like the other two, continues, despite overwhelming evidence, continues to deny that he was involved in this…. Has anyone reached out to you? And would there be more closure if someone apologized for this?

>> Rudolph: Oh, yes. My husband reached out to Blanton, Thomas Blanton. He's the only one--

>> Satalia: Who's still living--

>> Rudolph: Yeah.

>> Satalia: --and in jail, in prison.

>> Rudolph: So when he wrote the letter, the first thing he said, that he didn't do it. He said it was the man that killed Viola Liuzzo. It was that person. And I haven't had anybody to apologize. I went to court with all of them. Robert Chambliss, Thomas Blanton, and Cherry. But they never said, they haven't said they'd apologize.

>> Satalia: What has it meant to you to finally share your story?

>> Rudolph: Well, it meant a lot. Because I was there…

>> Satalia: It was just another day, another Sunday, that forever changed all of your lives…. Finally, what did all of this do to your faith in God?

>> Rudolph: I believe it made my faith stronger because, when the bomb went off, I called on the Lord. And I really believe that since I had the opportunity to call on Him, He came and He save me, simply for that purpose...….

>> Satalia: Sarah Collins Rudolph, thank you so much for talking with us.

>> Rudolph: Thank you for having me.

>> Satalia: I hope that you enjoyed our conversation with Sarah Collins Rudolph. I'm Patty Satalia. We hope that you'll join us for our next conversation from Penn State. (END OF INTERVIEW)

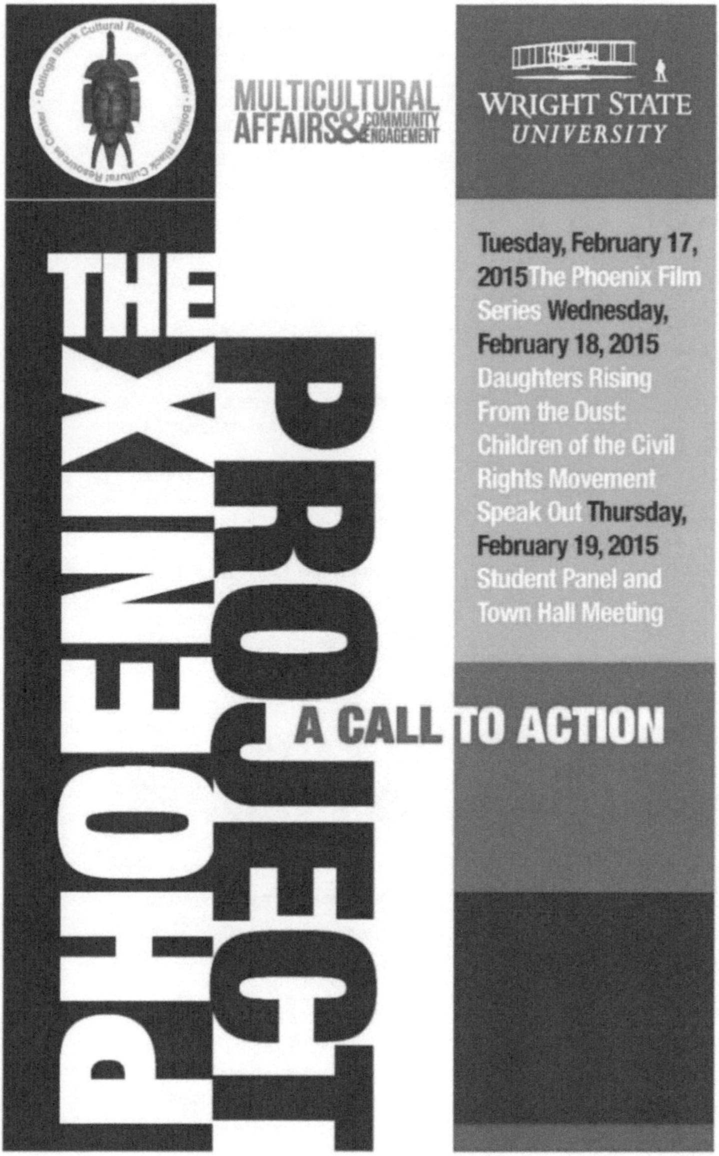
Bolinga Black Cultural Resources Center
MULTICULTURAL AFFAIRS & COMMUNITY ENGAGEMENT
WRIGHT STATE UNIVERSITY
THE PHOENIX PROJECT
A CALL TO ACTION
Tuesday, February 17, 2015
The Phoenix Film Series
Wednesday, February 18, 2015
Daughters Rising From the Dust: Children of the Civil Rights Movement Speak Out
Thursday, February 19, 2015
Student Panel and Town Hall Meeting

Tuesday, February 17,2015 **The Phoenix Film Series**

Fruitvale Station Malcom X 4 Little Girls

Fruitvale Station	
Welcome and Introduction	Joann Mawasha, Interim Director, Bolinga Black Cultural Resources Center
Introduction of Film/Speaker	Hazel Rountree, University Ombudsperson
Featured Speaker	Cephus Johnson ("Uncle Bobby")
Moderator for Q&A	Hazel Rountree
Malcolm X	
Welcome	Nycia Bolds, Assistant Director, Bolinga Black Cultural Resources Center
Introduction of Speaker	Shakur Ahmad, former Wright State athlete
Featured Speaker	Sharif Liwaru, Executive Director, Malcolm X Foundation
Moderator/Q&A	Steve Bognar, Lecturer, Filmmaker in Residence and Film Community Outreach Liason
4 Little Girls	
Welcome	Kristin Sobolik, Dean and Professor, College of Liberal Arts
Introduction of Speaker	Rev. Vanessa Oliver Ward, Co-Pastor, Omega Baptist Church
Featured Speaker	Junie Collins Williams, Civil Rights Public Speaker
Moderator/Q&A	Christa Agiro, Associate Professor and Co-Director, Language Arts Program, College of Education and Human Services

Ilyassah Al-Shabazz

Joanne Bland

Reena Evers-Everette

Angela Lewis

Mary Liuzzo Lilleboe

Sarah Collins Rudolph

Wednesday, February 18, 2015 **Daughters Rising From the Dust**

Opening Remarks	Kimberly Barrett, Vice President, Division of Multicultural Affairs and Community Engagement
Welcome	David R. Hopkins, President, Wright State University
Musical Selection	Conductor: Jeremy Scott Winston, Assistant Director of Music and Chorus Director, Central State University Chorus

Introduction of Distinguished Panelists:

- Ilyassah Al-Shabazz: Author, daughter of Malcom X and Betty Shabazz
- Joanne Bland: Civil and human rights worker, marched in Selma's "Bloody Sunday" and "Turn Around Tuesday"
- Reena Evers-Everette: Communications representative, daughter of Medgar Evers and Myrlie Evers-Williams
- Angela Lewis: Nurse, theology student, daughter of James Chaney, one of three civil rights activists killed on June 21, 1964
- Mary Liuzzo Lilleboe: Daughter of Viola Liuzzo, killed by Ku Klux Klan members on March 25, 1965
- Sarah Collins Rudolph: The "Fifth Little Girl," survivor of the 16th Street Baptist Church bombing September 15, 1963

Moderator/Q&A	Kimberly Barrett

Thursday, February 19, 2015 **Student Panel**

"Faces of the Protest: From Protest to Change"

Co-moderators	Simone Polk, Assistant Vice President for Student Services, Student Affairs, and John Feldmeier, Professor, Political Science
Members of Student Panel	Shayla Cothran, Malaya Davis (Alternate), Prentiss Haney, Darsheel Kaur, Carl Foster, Jason Stelzer, Kayelin Tiggs

---

Thursday, February 19, 2015 **Town Hall Meeting**

"Toward 'A More Perfect Union': The Intersection of Civil Rights, Policing, Voting Rights and Civil Liberties: From Ferguson to Dearborn to Beavercreek"

Welcome and Introduction	Charlotte Harris, Dean and Associate Professor, College of Education and Human Services
Moderator	Nicole Austin-HIllery, Director and Counsel, Washington Office of the Brennan Center for Justice at the New York University School of Law

Panelists

- Richard Biehl, Chief of Police, City of Dayton
- Lecia Brooks, Outreach Director, Southern Poverty Law Center, Montgomery, Alabama
- Reverend Damon Lynch III, Pastor, New Prospect Baptist Church, Cincinnati, Ohio
- Amy Hunter, Racial Justice Director, YWCA of Metro St. Louis
- Paul Leonard, Instructor of Political Science, Former Ohio Lieutenant Governor and Mayor of Dayton
- Amaha Selassie, Docotoral Student, University of Cincinnati; Member, Ohio Student Association
- Michael Wright, Attorney, Wright & Schulte LLC

Ties That Bind Two Holy Cities

Program Schedule

6:00 Emanuel AME Church Praise Dancers and Claire K. Washington Choir

6:30: Opening Comments and Introduction

+ Mr. Maurice Cannon, Principal of Burke High School
+ Lilyn Hester, Southeast Public Affairs Manager – Google
+ Dr. Bernard Powers, Historian, College of Charleston
+ Emanuel AME Church Representative

Minute of Silence for Victims and Survivors

Panel Discussion with Survivors

– Dr. Tracy Snipe (moderator)
+ Mrs. Sarah Collins Rudolph
+ Mrs. Janie Collins Simpkins
+ Junie Collins Williams

Question and Answer with Panelists and Audience

Proclamation from the City of Charleston

Thank you to the sponsors and supporters of this event:

Burke High School, Emanuel AME Church, Google, International African American Museum, Sophia Institute, SunTrust, Wright State University. The College of Charleston: Libraries, Avery Research Center for African American

The Ties that Bind Two Holy Cites: Reflections by Survivors of the 1963 Birmingham Church Bombing

16th Street Baptist Church, Birmingham, AL

Emanuel AME Church, Charleston, SC

A Mass Meeting and Conversation of Healing with Survivors of Racial Violence

Press Release: To Distribute **Updated 9/7/15**

Announcing a College of Charleston event series to address racial violence targeting African American churches, September 14-15, 2015

Google-funded grant award to support community conversations around social injustice and racism

Community Forum: "Ties That Bind Two Holy Cities: Reflections in Charleston by Survivors of the 1963 Birmingham Church Bombing"

Tuesday, September 15, 2015
Burke High School Auditorium
244 President Street, Charleston SC
6:30pm, doors open at 6:00pm
Free and open to the public

Film Screening: *4 Little Girls*, directed by Spike Lee
Monday, September 14, 2015
College of Charleston Addlestone Library
205 Calhoun St., Charleston, SC
Room 227
6:00pm
Free and open to the public

"Ties That Bind Two Holy Cities" is the first series of the College of Charleston's new Race and Social Justice Initiative, funded by Google and led by the Avery Research Center for African American History, African American Studies, and Addlestone Library. Additional supporters include SunTrust Banks and the International African American Museum (IAAM). Over the next eighteen months, the College will host various events to promote dialogue about race and social justice in Charleston, South Carolina, and beyond.

In response to the tragic shootings at the Emanuel AME Church on June 17, 2015, the College of Charleston and community partners will host events on September 14th and 15th to examine the history of racial violence targeting African American churches. These programs will particularly reflect on the historic connections between the 1963 bombing at the 16th Street Baptist Church in Birmingham, AL, and the 2015 shootings at the Emanuel AME Church in Charleston, SC. The goal of these events is to create awareness about past racial violence, and to facilitate dialogue and community healing in the aftermath of ongoing racial violence today.

The featured event is an open community forum held on Tuesday, September 15th at the Burke High School Auditorium at 6:30pm, with doors opening at 6:00pm. Speakers will include Sarah Collins Rudolph, Junie Collins Williams, and Janie Collins Simpkins. Their sister, Addie Mae Collins, was one of the four victims of the church bombing that took place in Birmingham on September 15, 1963. A representative of the Emanuel AME Church will also speak. The Mother Emanuel Claire K. Washington Choir will perform musical selections beginning at 6:00pm to honor the victims and survivors of these tragedies.

Prior to this forum, on Monday, September 14th, the College of Charleston will host a screening of Spike Lee's Academy Award-nominated documentary, *4 Little Girls* (1997), at Addlestone Library in Room 227 at 6:00pm. The documentary traces the events and aftermath of the bombing at the 16th Street Baptist Church in Birmingham, and features family members of the victims. Dr. Jon Hale from the College of Charleston and Dr. Tracy Snipe from Wright State University will moderate the discussion after the film screening.

"It is important that we remember that the brutal attack on Mother Emanuel happened within a larger context," College of Charleston's Dean of Libraries John White said about the upcoming events. "White terrorism aimed at African American churches has a long history. Nowhere is that more apparent than in Birmingham, Alabama, which faced a similar, unspeakable tragedy in 1963. We hope that an honest discussion about this history of racial violence can help us make certain that we never have to confront another tragedy like this in Birmingham, Charleston, or elsewhere."

Dr. Tracy Snipe stated, "Í was struck by the disturbing similarities yet distant parallels between the tragedies at the 16th Street Baptist Church and Mother Emanuel despite the nearly fifty-two-year interval. The stories of the victims, as well as the message of survival shared by individuals like the Collins sisters, must be told not only in a community forum but globally to promote healing and justice."

For more information about these events, contact Jon Hale (halejn@cofc.edu), Tracy Snipe (tracy.snipe@wright.edu) or College of Charleston Libraries (843-953-8002).

These events are free and open to the public. Come join the conversation.

Congress of Racial Equality

817 Broadway • 3rd Floor • New York, NY 10003
(212) 598-4000 • Fax: (212) 598-4141/982-0184

November 5, 2002

Mrs. Sarah Collins Rudolph
[redacted]

Dear Mrs. Rudolph:

Greetings and I hope that this letter finds you well.

I wish to thank you personally for all your help in participating with the Congress of Racial Equality (CORE), Civil Rights Legal Seminar this past summer. Thanks to your generosity, this event was a success.

Not so long ago, I completed a shortened video version of the seminar for the private use of CORE's friends and supporters. Please find your copy enclosed for your personal review and use.

Allow me to close by saying that it was an honor to have met you, and to share in the recount of the tragedy and triumph of your experiences.

If there is anything that I can further assist you with, please feel free to contact me through my assistant [redacted]

Thank you and God bless.

Sincerely,

Kimathi R. Innis
Media Director

Voices of Civil Rights
AARP
601 E St. NW
Washington, DC 20049

Dear Sarah J. Rudolph,

Thank you for sharing your story with the Voices of Civil Rights project. This certificate recognizes your invaluable contribution to the successful effort to build the world's largest archive of firsthand accounts of the American Civil Rights Movement. Your personal story—along with thousands of others from people across the country—will now be transferred to the Library of Congress in Washington, D.C. The permanent collection will inform and educate future generations and inspire the civil rights leaders of tomorrow. You may take great pride in your contribution. Thank you for making a difference, and please display your certificate proudly.

Sincerely,

Rick Bowers
Director
Voices of Civil Rights

P.S. The History Channel will air a special documentary on the project on February 12, 2005 (check local listings). I encourage you and your family and friends to watch this important program.

www.voicesofcivilrights.org

THOMAS BLANTON
AIS # 216691 E-30-1A
[redacted]
JUNE 9, 2014 MONDAY

GOD BLESS YOU SARAH, YOU HAVE A NAME FROM
THE BIBLE, SARAH WAS THE NAME OF
ABRAHAMS WIFE, AND GOD BLESS YOUR SISTE[R]
ADDIE MAE COLLINS, I HAD ABSOLUTELY NO
INVOLVEMENT IN THAT CRIME, SO HELP ME GOD.
I DONT HOLD HATE IN MY HEART EITHER FOR
THOSE WHO FRAMED ME. HOWEVER I DO WANT
THE TRUTH TO COME OUT SO I CAN CLEAR MY
NAME. IN JULY OF 1978 THE NEW YORK TIMES
PUBLISHED A SERIES OF ARTICLES ABOUT GARY
THOMAS ROWE JR. COMMITTING VIOLENT
CRIMES WHILE WORKING AS AN FBI INFORMANT
INSIDE THE KU KLUX KLAN. THE NEWSPAPER
STORIES WERE FOLLOWED BY AN ABC 20/20
TWO PART PROGRAM CONCERNING THE INVOLVE-
MENT OF GARY THOMAS ROWE IN THE MURDER OF
CIVIL RIGHTS WORKER VIOLA LIUZZO, ROWE WAS
INDICTED BY THE STATE OF ALABAMA AFTER THE
ABC STORY RAN FOR THE LIUZZO MURDER.
HOWEVER THE FEDERAL COURTS BLOCKED HIS
TRIAL CLAIMING HE HAD IMMUNITY FROM
PROSECUTION FOR THE MURDER. CONCERNING THE
CHURCH BOMBING AN ARTICLE IN THE BIRMINGH.
NEWS OF SUNDAY MAY 20, 2001, PAGE 12 TITLED
"BUREAUS BLUNDERS" BY DIANE MCWHORTER

1. (OVER)

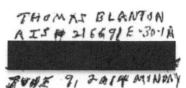

STATES IN PART "FBI AGENTS DID NOT SHOW ROWES PICTURE TO POTENTIAL WITNESSES AND ORDERED HIM TO STAY AWAY FROM THE CRIME SCENE." THE FBI COVERED FOR ROWE AS LONG AS HE LIVED (HE DIED IN 1998). I BELIEVE THE FBI KNEW OR STRONG SUSPECTED THAT ROWE BOMBED THE CHURCH BUT THEY WERE TIED SO CLOSE TO ROWE THAT IF ROWE WAS FOUND GUILTY IT WOULD MAKE THE FBI GUILTY ALSO. THEREFORE I BELIEVE THE FBI COVERED FOR ROWE TO PROTECT THE FBI. I BELIEVE THEY DID THIS BY CREATING A DIVERSION TO TAKE THE SPOTLIGHT AWAY FROM ROWE. THE DIVERSION WAS TO INVESTIGATE OTHER PEOPLE LIKE MYSELF. THEN I BELIEVE THE FBI WOULD LEAK INFORMATION ABOUT THE PEOPLE THEY WERE INVESTIGATING TO THE MEDIA, TO HELP THE FBI BUILD PUBLIC SUPPORT FOR THEIR DIVERSION

JOURNALIST MARK RATLEDGE GAVE ME YOUR ADDRESS IN HIS MAY 21, 2014 LETTER TO ME.

★ LOS ANGELES TIMES SUNDAY FEB. 1, 2004
"EVEN PROSECUTORS SOUGHT PELLICANO FOR HIS EXPERTI
HOME EDITION, MAIN NEWS, PAGE A-1, METRO 2,786 WORDS
BY SCOTT GLOVER AND MATT LAIT TIMES STAFF
WWW.LATIMES.COM. 202 WEST 1ST STREET L.A. 90012
→ ANTHONY PELLICANO FABRICATED A TAPE IN MY CASE.

2.

LOS ANGELES TIMES FRIDAY MAY 16, 2008
"PRIVATE EYE TO THE STARS IS GUILTY"
MAIN NEWS, PART A, PAGE 1, 1548 WORDS
BY CARLA HALL AND TAMI ABDOLLAH
(PELLICANO CONVICTED OF 76 FEDERAL CRIMES)
PELLICANO IS NOW SERVING TIME ON THESE
76 FEDERAL CONVICTIONS.

WIKIPEDIA ENCYCLOPEDIA ON ANTHONY PELLICANO
http://en.wikipedia.org/wiki/anthony_pellicano

"VENGEANCE IS MINE, I WILL REPAY, SAITH
THE LORD." ROMANS 12:19

SINCERELY
Tom Blanton

7

*Letter to Sarah C. Rudolph from Thomas E. Blanton, Jr., dated June 9, 2014

JUNE 23, 2014
MONDAY

GOD BLESS YOU SARAH, THANK YOU FOR YOU JUNE 19TH LETTER. SARAH I DON'T HAVE ANY ACTUAL KNOWLEDGE OF WHO WAS RESPONCIBLE FOR THAT CRIME. ALL THE INFORMATION I HAVE CAME FROM THE MEDIA OVER THE YEARS WHICH I GAVE YOU IN MY JUNE 7TH LETTER. IF THE MEDIA REPORTS ARE TRUE ABOUT GARY THOMAS ROWE JR. COMMITTING VIOLEN CRIMES WHILE WORKING AS AN FBI INFORMAN INSIDE THE KU KLUX KLAN THEN YOU WOULD NOT BE ABLE TO TELL ROWE THAT YOU FORGIVE HIM BECAUSE HE DIED IN 1998. PLEASE LOOK AT MY JUNE 7TH LETTER CONCERNING THE CHURCH BOMBING AND AN ARTICLE IN THE BIRMINGHAM NEWS OF SUNDAY MAY 20, 2001 PAGE 1C TITLED "BUREAUS BLUNDERS" BY DIANE MCWHORTER THAT STATES IN PART "FBI AGENT DID NOT SHOW ROWE'S PICTURE TO POTENTIAL WITNESSES AND ORDERED HIM TO STAY AWAY FROM THE CRIME SCENE." I BELIEVE THE FBI KNEW OR STRONGLY SUSPECTED THAT ROWE BOMBED THE CHURCH BUT THEY WERE TIED SO CLOSE TO ROWE THAT IF ROWE WAS FOUND GUILTY IT WOULD MAKE THE FBI GUILTY ALSO. THEREFORE I BELIEVE THE FBI COVERED FOR ROWE TO PROTECT THE FBI.

(OVER)

GARY THOMAS ROWE JR. FAILED THREE (3)
POLYGRAPH TEST CONCERNING THE CHURCH
BOMBING, TWO (2) IN SAN DIEGO CALIFORNIA
PAID FOR BY THE ALABAMA ATTORNEY
GENERAL IN 1977 AND ONE (1) TEST GIVEN
BY ABC 20/20 BY A MAN FROM NEW YORK
CITY IN 1978.
THE FBI GAVE ME A POLYGRAPH TEST
IN 1963 WHICH SHOWED THAT I WAS NOT GUILTY
OF THE CRIME.

GOD BLESS YOUR SISTER ADDIE MAE
COLLINS.

YOUR FRIEND
Tom Blanton

2.

Letter to Sarah Collins Rudolph from Thomas E. Blanton, Jr., dated June 23, 2014

Miles College

Fairfield, Alabama

In recognition of the signal ability in fraternalism and human welfare

And distinguished sacrifice of

Addie Mae Collins

The Board of Trustees of Miles College does hereby confer upon her posthumously

the Honorary Degree of

Doctor of Humane Letters

In witness whereof we have affixed our signatures and seal of this Institution.

Given at Birmingham, in the State of Alabama,

this third day of May, two thousand and fourteen

President of the College

Chairman, Board of Trustees

Founded 1898

Dean of Academic Affairs

Secretary, Board of Trustees

MAY THE LOVE AND PEACE OF THE LORD
FLOOD YOUR SOUL

As We Give Thanks To God For

"TRIUMPHS IN TRAGEDIES"
The A.H.Parker High School
Class of 1969
Invite you to SEE and HEAR the
FIFTH/FORGOTTEN VICTIM
(Of The 16th Street Baptist Church Bombing)
MRS. SARAH COLLINS RUDOLPH
(A Fellow 1969 Graduate)

And Share As We
Pay Tribute to our Deceased Classmates

SATURDAY,AUGUST 4,2012
3:00 p.m. until 7:00 p.m.

SOUTH ELYTON BAPTIST CHURCH
100 FIRST STREET SOUTH 35205
REGINALD BROWN, PASTOR

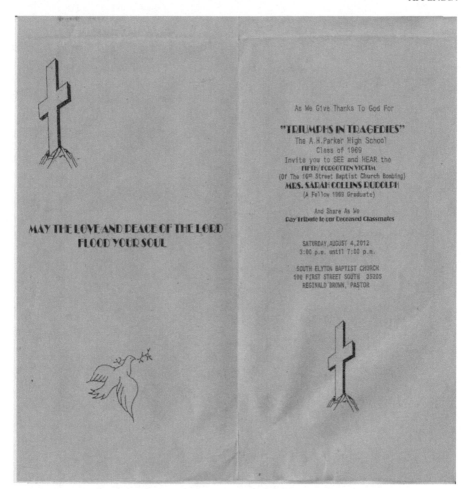

TRIUMPHS in TRAGEDIES

But thanks be to God, who always leads us in triumphal procession in Christ and through us spreads everywhere the fragrance of the knowledge of Him. 2nd Cor.2:14 NIV

PROGRAMME

MASTER of CEREMONIES............James Ray, Jr.

INVOCATION.. Sadie P. Bridges

SONG.. Shirley Abrams

GREETINGS & OCCASION.................................. Abdullah Salaam

SONG.. Shirley Abrams

INTRODUCTION of SPEAKER.............................. George Rudolph

SPEAKER.. SARAH COLLINS RUDOLPH

RESOLUTION(S).. Jeanetta M. Scott

MEMORIAL TRIBUTE.. Willie M.L. Wedgeworth

SPECIAL GUEST RECOGNITION............................ Regina Long

REMARKS & ACKNOWLEDGEMENTS

BLESSING of FOOD & BENEDICTION

MEET and GREET MRS RUDOLPH in the FELLOWSHIP HALL

Selected Bibliography

Anderson, Carol. *White Rage: The Unspoken Truth of Our Racial Divide*. Columbia, MO: Bloomsbury, USA, 2016.

Angelou, Maya. *Maya Angelou: The Complete Poetry*. New York: Random House, 2015.

Alexander, Michelle. *The New Jim Crow: Mass Incarceration in the Age of Colorblindness*. New York and London: The New Press, 2010.

Arsenault, Raymond. *Freedom Riders: 1961 and the Struggle for Racial Injustice*. London: Oxford University Press, 2006.

Baham, Nicholas, Louis III. *The Coltrane Church: Apostles of Sound, Agents of Social Justice*. Jefferson, North Carolina: McFarland & Company, Inc. Publishers, 2016.

Baldwin, James. *Blues for Mister Charlie*. New York, Dell Publishing Company, 1964

Baldwin, James. *The Evidence of Things Unseen*. New York, Simon & Schuester, 1981.

Baraka, Amiri. *Somebody Blew Up America & Other Poems*. Philipsburg, St. Martin (Caribbean): House of Nehesi Publishers.

Bass, Jack and Jack Nelson. *The Orangeburg Massacre*. (With a new introduction by Will D. Campbell). Macon, Georgia: Mercer University Press, 2002.

Boyd, Herb and Ilyasah Al-Shabazz, eds. *The Diary of Malcolm X*. Chicago: Third World Press, 2013.

Branch, Taylor. *At Canann's Edge: America in the King Years 1965-1968*. New York: Simon & Schuester, 2006).

Branch, Taylor. *The King Years: Historic Moments in the Civil Rights Movement*. New York: Simon & Shuster, 2013.

Branch, Taylor. *Parting the Waters: America in the King Years: 1954-1963.* New York: Simon & Schuster, 1988.

Breitman, George, ed. *Malcolm X Speaks: Selected Speeches and Statements.* New York: Grove Press, Inc., 1966.

Brimner, Larry Dane. *Birmingham Sunday.* Honesdale, Pennsylvania: Calkins Creek, 2010.

Caraway, Guy and Candied Caraway, eds. *Sing for Freedom: The Story of the Civil Rights Movement through Its Songs.* (Foreword by Julian Bond.) Montgomery, Alabama: New South Books, 2007.

Carson, Clayborne and Kris Shepard, eds. *A Call to Conscience: The Landmark Speeches of Dr. Martin Luther King, Jr.* New York: Warner Books, 2001.

Carter, Dan T. *The Politics of Rage: George Wallace, the Origins of the New Conservatism, and the Transformation of American Politics.* New York: Simon & Shuster, 1995.

Cobbs, Elizabeth H./Smith, Petric J. *Long Time Coming: An Insider's Story of the Birmingham Church Bombing that Rocked the World.* Birmingham, Alabama: Crane Hill, 1994.

Collier-Thomas, Bettye and V.P. Franklin. *Sisters in the Struggle: African-American Women in the Civil Rights-Black Power Movement.* New York and London: The New York University Press, 2001.

Davis, Angela. *Angela Davis: An Autobiography.* New York: International Publishers, 1988.

Davis, Miles (with Quincy Troupe). *Miles: Davis: The Autobiography.* New York: Simon & Schuster, Inc., 1990.

DeFrantz, Thomas S. *Dancing Revelations.* Oxford and New York: Oxford University Press, 2004.

Douglass, J.D. and Merrill C. Tenney, eds. *Zondervan Bible Dictionary.* Grand Rapids Michigan: Zondervan, 2008.

Dove, Rita. *Collected Poems, 1974-2004.* New York: W.W. Norton & Company, 2016.

Dunbar, Paul Laurence. *The Complete Poems of Paul Laurence Dunbar.* New York: Dodd, Mead & Company, 1958.

Ellis, Catherine and Stephen Drury Smith, eds. *Say it Plain: A Century of Great African American Speeches.* New York: The New Press, 2005.

Etheridge, Eric. *Breach of Peace: Portraits of the 1961 Mississippi Freedom Riders.* (Preface by Roger Wilkins. Foreword by Diane McWhorter.) New York: Atlas & Co, 2009.

Eskew, Glenn T. *But for Birmingham: The Local and National Movement in the Civil Rights Struggle*. Chapel Hill and London: University of North Carolina Press, 1997.

Evers, Myrlie (with William Peter). *For us the Living*. Jackson: University of Mississippi Press, 2007.

Frazier, Herb and Bernard Powers Jr., and Marjory Wentworth. *We Are Charleston: Tragedy and Triumph at Mother Emanuel*. Nashville, Tennessee: W. Publishing Group, an Imprison of Thomas Nelson, 2016.

Fraim, John. *Spirit Catcher: The Life and Art of John Coltrane*. West Liberty, Ohio: GreatHouse Company, 1996.

Frazier, Herbert, ed. *Ninety Seconds Changed a Church, Community and the World*. Contributors Norvel Goff, Sr., Maxine Smith, Willie Glee, Elizabeth (Liz) Alston and Hon. William Dudley Gregorie. Charleston, South Carolina: Emanuel African Methodist Episcopal Church, 2016.

Frazier, Herb, Bernard Edward Powers Jr., and Marjory Wentworth. *We Are Charleston: Tragedy and Triumph at Mother Emanuel*. Nashville, Tennesse: W. Publishing Group, 2016.

Fullen, Marilyn K. *Great Black Writers: Biographies*. Greensboro, N.C.: Open Hand Publishing, LLC., 2003.

Gamboa, Isaias. (Edited by JoAnne F. Henry and Audrey Owen.) *We Shall Overcome: Sacred Song on the Devil's Tongue*. Beverly Hills, California: Amapola, 2011, 2012.

Garrow, David J. *Bearing the Cross: Martin Luther King, Jr. and the Southern Christian Leadership Conference*. New York: Vintage Books, 1996.

Glisson, Susan M., ed. *The Human Condition in the Civil Rights Movement*. New York: Rowman & Littlefield, 2006.

Guy, Jasmine. *Afeni Shakur: Evolution of a Revolutionary*. New York: Atria Books, 1994.

Griffin, Farah Jasmine and Salim Washington. *Clawing at the Limits of Cool: Miles Davis, John Coltrane, and the Greatest Jazz Collaboration Ever*. New York: St. Martin's Press, 2008.

Gregory, Dick. *Nigger*. New York: Pocket Book, 1973.

Hamlin, Christopher M. *Behind the Stained Glass: A History of the Sixteenth Street Baptist Church*. Birmingham, AL.: Crane Hill, 1988.

Holsaert, Faith S., Martha Prescod Norman Noonan, Judy Richardson, Betty Garman Robinson, Jean Smith and Dorothy M. Zellner, eds. *Hands on the Freedom Plow*. Urbana, Chicago and Springfield: University of Illinois Press, 2010.

Hoose, Phillip. *Claudette Colvin: Twice Toward Justice*. New York: Farrar Straus Giroux, 2009.

Huntley, Horace and John W. KcKerley, eds. *Soldiers for Democracy: The Men, Women, and Children of the Birmingham Civil Rights Movement*. (Introductions by Robin D. G. Kelley and John W. McKerley.) Urbana and Chicago: University of Illinois Press, 2009.

Jones, Doug (with Greg Truman). Foreword by Rick Bragg. *Bending Toward Justice: The Birmingham Church Bombing that Changed the Course of Civil Rights*. New York: At Points Book (an imprint of St. Martin's Press), 2019.

Joseph, Charles H. *Stravinsky & Balanchine: A Journey of Invention*. New Haven, Ct.: Yale University Press, 2002.

Kahn, Ashley. *A Love Supreme: The Story of John Coltrane's Signature Album*. New York: The Penguin Group, 2002

King, Joyce. *Hate Crime: The Story of a Dragging in Jasper, Texas*. New York: Pantheon Books, 2002.

King, Martin Luther, Jr.. *A Time to Break the Silence: The Essential Works of Martin Luther King, Jr., for Students*. (Introduction by Walter Dean Myers). Boston: Beacon Press, 1994.

Lasswell, Harold Dwight. *Politics: Who Gets What, When, How*. New York: Meridian Books, 1972.

Levingston, Steven. *Kennedy and King: The President, the Pastor and the Battle Over Civil Rights*. New York: Hachette Books, 2017.

Lewis, John. (with Michael D'Orso). *Walking with the Wind: A Memoir*. New York: Simon & Shuster Paperbacks, 1998.

Lowery, Wesley. *They Can't Kill Us All: Ferguson, Baltimore and a New Era in America's Racial Justice Movement*. New York: Little, Brown and Company, 2016.

Mannis, Andrew M. *A Fire You Can't Put Out*. Tuscaloosa and London: The University of Alabama Press, 199.

McWhorter, Diane. *Carry Me Home: Birmingham, Alabama: The Climatic Battle of the Civil Rights Revolution*. New York: Simon & Schuster Paperbacks, 2001.

Morris, D. Aldon. *The Origins of the Civil Rights Movement: Black Communities Organizing for Change*. New York: The Free Press, 1984.

Morrison, Toni. *Song of Solomon.* New York: First Vintage International Edition, 2004.

Nagle, Angela. "The Lost Boys: The Young Men of the Alt-Right Could Define American Politics for a Generation." *The Atlantic*, October 2017. Volume 320: No. 3:74-87.

Obama, Barack H. *The Audacity of Hope: Thoughts on Reclaiming the American Dream.* New York: Crown Publishers, 2006.

Parks, Rosa (with Jim Haskins). *Rosa Parks: My Story.* New York: Puffin Books, 1992.

Porter, Lewis. *John Coltrane: His Life and Music.* Ann Arbor: The University of Michigan Press, 1998.

Raines, Howell. *My Soul is Rested: Movement Days in the Deep South Remembered.* New York: G.P. Putnam's Sons, 1977.

Rampersand, Arnold, ed. and David Russell, associate ed. *The Collected Poems of Langston Hughes.* New York: Vintage Classic Edition, 1995.

Rice, Condoleezza. *Extraordinary, Ordinary People.* New York: Crown Archetype, 2010.

Risher, Sharon. (With Sherri Wood Emmons). *For Such a Time as This: Hope and Forgiveness after the Charleston Massacre.* (2019)

Rohler, Lloyd. *George Wallace: Conservative Populist.* Westport, Connecticut: Praeger, 2004.

Scott, John H. (with Cleo Scott Brown). *Witness to the Truth: My Struggle for Human Rights in Louisiana.* Columbia, South Carolina: University of South Carolina Press, 2003.

Shabazz, Ilyasah (with Kekla Magoon). *X: A Novel.* Somerville, Massachusetts: Candlewick Press, 2015.

Shores, Helen Lee and Barbara S. Shores (with Denise George). *The Gentle Giant of Dynamite Hill: The Untold Story of Arthur Shores and His Family's Fight for Civil Rights.* Grand Rapids, Michigan: Zondervan, 2012.

Sikora, Frank. *Until Justice Rolls Down: The Birmingham Church Bombing Case.* Tuscaloosa, Alabama: University of Alabama Press, 1991.

Singleton, Chris. *Different: A Story About Loving Your Neighbor.* (2020)

Theoharis, Jeanne. *The Rebellious Life of Mrs. Rosa Parks.* New York: Beacon Press, 2015.

Thorne, T.K. *Last Chance for Justice: How Relentless Investigators Uncovered New Evidence Convicting the Birmingham Church Bombers.* Birmingham, Alabama: Lawrence Books, 2013.

Till-Mobley, Mamie and Christopher Benson. *Death of Innocence: The Story of the Hate Crime that Changed America.* New York: Random House, 1991.

Tyson, Timothy. *The Blood of Emmett Till.* New York: Simon & Shuster, 2017.

Washington, Harriet A. *Medical Apartheid: The Dark History of Medical Experimentation on Black Americans from Colonial Times to the Present.* New York: Double Day, 2006.

Washington, James M., ed. *A Testament of Hope: The Essential Writings and Speeches of Martin Luther King, Jr.* New York: Harper One, 1986.

Watson, Bruce. *Freedom Summer.* New York: Penguin Books, 2010.

Williams, Michael Vinson. *Medgar Evers: Mississippi Martyr.* Fayetteville: The University of Arkansas Press, 2011.

Wilson, Bobby M. *America's Johannesburg: Industrialization and Racial Transformation in Birmingham.* Lanham, Maryland: Rowman & Littlefield Publishers, Inc., 2000.

Woods, Whyton, Tony. *Beyond a Love Supreme: John Coltrane and the Legacy of an Album.* Oxford: Oxford University Press, 2013.

Woods, Donald. *Biko.* New York & London: Paddington Press, LTD, 1978.

Whyton, Tony. *Beyond a Love Supreme: John Coltrane and the Legacy of an Album.* Oxford: Oxford University Press, 2013.

Index

B

C

D

E

F

G

H

I

J

K

L

M

N

O

P

Q

R

S

T

U

V

W

Y

Z